Library

Talking
MUSIC

ML
390
.D79
1999

Talking Music

CONVERSATIONS WITH JOHN CAGE, PHILIP GLASS, LAURIE ANDERSON, AND FIVE GENERATIONS OF AMERICAN EXPERIMENTAL COMPOSERS

William Duckworth

DA CAPO PRESS

ocm 40076559

Santiago Canyon College
Library

Excerpts from John Cage's *Freeman Etudes* Courtesy of C. F. Peters Corporation

Library of Congress Cataloging-in-Publication Data

Duckworth, William.
  Talking music: conversations with John Cage, Philip Glass, Laurie Anderson, and five generations of American experimental composers / William Duckworth.—1st Da Capo Press ed.
    p.   cm.
  Originally published: New York: Schirmer Books, 1995.
  Interviews with John Cage, Conlon Nancarrow, Milton Babbitt, Lou Harrison, Ben Johnston, Pauline Oliveros, Christian Wolff, La Monte Young, Marian Zazeela, Terry Riley, Steve Reich, Philip Glass, Meredith Monk, Laurie Anderson, "Blue" Gene Tyranny, Glenn Branca, and John Zorn.
  Includes index.
  ISBN 0-306-80893-5 (alk. paper)
  1. Composers—United States—Interviews. 2. Music—United States—20th century—History and criticism. 3. Avant-garde (Music) I. Title.
ML390.D79 1999
780'.92'273—dc21
[B]   98-43425
                                                                          CIP
                                                                           MN

First Da Capo Press edition 1999

This Da Capo Press paperback edition of *Talking Music* is an unabridged republication of the edition first published in New York in 1995. It is reprinted by arrangement with Macmillan Reference, a division of Simon & Schuster, Inc.

Copyright © 1995 by Schirmer Books, an imprint of Simon & Schuster Macmillan

Published by Da Capo Press
A Member of the Perseus Books Group
http://www.dacapopress.com

All Rights Reserved

Manufactured in the United States of America

for Nora
Summer 1994

CONTENTS

ACKNOWLEDGMENTS

This project could not have been completed without the support and encouragement of a number of institutions and individuals. In particular, I would like to thank the National Endowment for the Humanities, which awarded me fellowships in 1981 and 1988; Bucknell University, which provided me with summer research funds, as well as continued technical assistance; Don Gillespie of C. F. Peters and Kyle Gann of the *Village Voice*, both of whom gave me advice and council; and Mindy Weinreb, who, more than anyone else, supported and encouraged this work through some of its slowest times. But most of all, I want to thank the composers themselves, all of whom I hope understand the depth of my feelings for them; it was one hell of an education.

INTRODUCTION

This isn't the book I originally intended to write. The one I was going to write was about music notation in the 1960s, that time when everybody invented their own. It's a topic I've been interested in since graduate school, a fact that probably convinced the National Endowment for the Humanities to fund my idea in the first place. The plan was to look at enough music, and interview enough composers, to be able to develop a general understanding, not so much of *what* happened in the sixties, which had already been documented, but of *how* and *why*.

As the first interviews began, however, an odd thing kept occurring. We would start out talking about notation, but always end up talking more personally about music and life. Perhaps it was because I also was a composer (and could speak on those terms), or maybe that I was already friends with many of them (and didn't have to "break the ice"); but whatever the reason, I knew from the beginning that people were talking to me in ways that I was not accustomed to seeing in the interview books I had read. And because even the earliest interviews drew for me such vivid and articulate musical portraits, not to mention the fact that I was enjoying doing them, I decided immediately to expand the project. My new plan, begun in the mid-eighties, was a freewheeling exploration of twentieth-century American experimental music—five generations' worth—as described to me by the composers themselves. Surprisingly, I actually managed to accomplish most of this goal through a wide-ranging series of interviews (almost fifty before it was over), fueled by the support of several more grants, and taking over a decade to complete.

Although I significantly altered the first project, I decided not to change my original method of working. From the beginning, I prepared for each interview by familiarizing myself with as many of each person's published scores and articles as I could locate, and listening to any of their music that was available on record or CD, a task that sometimes took months. With this information, plus additional material that many of them sent me, I developed worksheets of four or five pages, outlining each person's career, and suggesting not only specific questions, but the general direction each interview should take, as well. These *facts* were then memorized, my intention being to work without notes, thus obscuring the preparation, and allowing each session to be conducted as much like a conversation as possible. Toward the end, I even began hiding the tape recorder.

Most conversations took place in New York: in the composer's home, if he or she lived in the city; or in hotel rooms and coffee shops, if the person was just visiting or passing through. Generally, each lasted for two or three hours, although some went on as long as six. All were recorded on cassettes, and later transcribed and edited. During the mid- to late eighties, I regularly interviewed, or prepared to interview, composers; some years only a few, other years, more. A second NEH fellowship, in 1988, allowed me to spend the following year completing the majority of the interviews. This book of sixteen conversations is the first volume of material to result from those efforts.

Although I have classified each of the sixteen composers included here as either an experimentalist, avant-gardist, minimalist, performance artist, or post-modern, these labels are primarily a convenience, locating each person, as it were, in time and space. John Cage and Milton Babbitt, for example, are both experimentalists, but no one considers their music to be similar, either in sound or in intent. The same can be said of "Blue" Gene Tyranny and John Zorn, both post-moderns according to me. Labels, it seems, never do experimental composers, or their work, justice.

The problem is that experimental composers in America, from the time of Charles Ives, if not Anthony Philip Heinrich (the Beethoven of Kentucky), are all individualists. They work alone. What groups them is a spirit, a compelling personal goal, and a loner's sense of adventure. Considered as a group, they appear to have something of the pioneer spirit preserved in them. Always a part of their time (though seldom in fashion), they simultaneously transcend it, inventing new philosophies, new scales, new instruments, and new ways of doing, uniquely their own. They never fit easily into categories. To truly understand them, they must be approached as individuals, each with his or her own distinct claim on the musical landscape. The German composer and journalist Walter Zimmermann, who interviewed American experimental composers in the early seventies, called them "desert plants." Perhaps that's another dimension of the pioneer spirit. And if it's true that that's what they are in twentieth-century America, then twenty-first-century American experimental music begins well prepared. Desert plants, after all, can be beautiful, majestic, and tenacious survivors; *sui generis*.

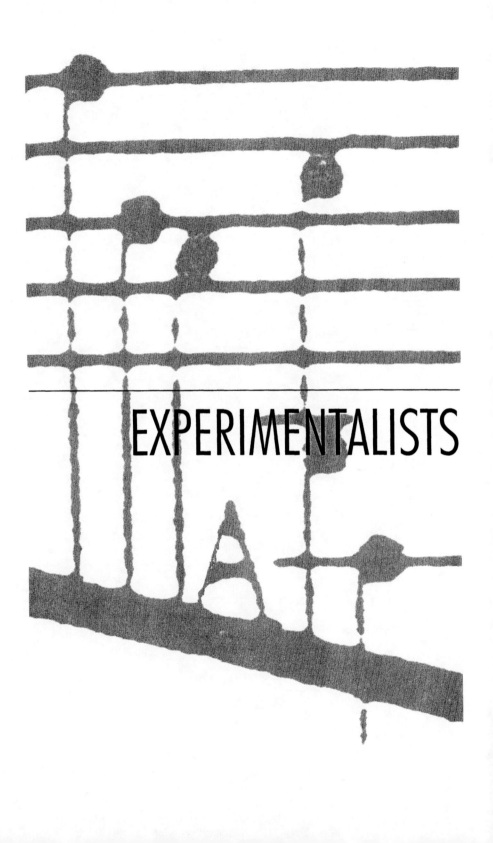

EXPERIMENTALISTS

JOHN CAGE

Born Los Angeles, 1912
Died New York, 1992

W H E N   P E O P L E   O N L Y   know one name in contemporary music, that name is usually John Cage. Until the time of his death, Cage was still regarded in some circles as the *enfant terrible* of modern music. And the year of his death—1992—may well become the "text-book" date for the end of the avant-garde, a style he both fathered and epitomized. Although not without his detractors, Cage came to be recognized worldwide as the perfect embodiment of the experimental attitude so essential to avant-garde music. The key to understanding why this was so, and why Cage played this role so well, is to remember that his father was a successful inventor, and that Cage grew up with the image of his father, at home every day, inventing. When he was older, Cage often said that he knew early on that the only thing he had to offer music was in the area of invention. But at this he was, as his former teacher Arnold Schoenberg once suggested, "an inventor of genius."

By the late 1930s, Cage was experimenting with unusual sounds, and creating music with instruments previously considered nonmusical. At first, he focused on percussion music, building orchestras out of everything from tin cans and radios to automobile brake drums and kitchen containers. But in 1938, attempting to create a percussion orchestra under the control of a single person, he invented the prepared piano. The prepared piano is a regular grand piano into which various objects of wood, metal, rubber, and felt are placed. These objects, or preparations as they are called, are put between various strings of the piano and individually alter the sound of each note, often eliminating or obscuring pitch, coloring the timbre, and emphasizing the percussive qualities of the sound. For the next decade, Cage wrote primarily for this instrument, his work culminating, between 1946 and 1948, in the piece many people still consider his most traditionally

3

beautiful: the twenty *Sonatas and Interludes,* for which he won both a Guggenheim fellowship and an award from the National Institute of Arts and Letters.

But by the mid-forties, Cage, who was now living in New York, had become interested in Eastern philosophy. This was to have a profound effect on the direction his music would take. Studying first Indian philosophy, through the writings and lectures of Ananda K. Coomaraswamy and privately with Gita Sarabhai (a student of Coomaraswamy with whom Cage studied for six months), and later Zen Buddhism, by attending Daisetz T. Suzuki's lectures at Columbia University, Cage came to believe that Western music during the Renaissance had taken a wrong turn, becoming too egocentric and making itself ineffective in the process. By the early 1950s, he had accepted a more traditionally Eastern view of art, namely, that the purpose of music was to sober and quiet the mind, thus rendering it susceptible to divine influences. Along with this went a belief that music should imitate nature in her manner of operation.

This view, of course, altered his music considerably. Turning to chance as a means of removing his own ego from the compositional process, Cage experimented with magic squares and tossing coins, before settling on the sixty-four hexagrams of the ancient Chinese book of oracles, the *I Ching,* as a way to compose music free of his ego. Working closely with fellow musicians Morton Feldman, Christian Wolff, and David Tudor, who met almost daily at Cage's loft on Monroe Street, Cage, in essence, invented a new philosophy of music—one in which individual sounds, chosen by chance, are valued in themselves rather than for their connections to other sounds, and where silence is considered musical, as is noise.

Cage's first effort composing by means of the *I Ching* produced, in 1951, the *Music of Changes,* a four-volume work for solo piano, in which every sound was chosen and placed by chance operations. The result was what Cage called nonintentional music, meaning that though it was produced by chance, it was fixed as a piece of music thereafter. The following year he wrote his infamous silent piece *4'33",* in which no intentional sounds are made for that length of time, and also created the first "happening" while teaching that summer at Black Mountain College in North Carolina.

By the mid-1950s, Cage was writing what he called indeterminate music, meaning that both the composition and the performance of the work have elements of chance in them and that no two performances of the same piece will ever be exactly alike. He also began to allow cer-

John Cage, 1958. Photo Credit: Bob Cato

tain of his works to be played in combination with each other. Pieces in this category include *Winter Music*, for one to twenty pianists, written in 1957; the 1961 orchestral work *Atlas Eclipticalis*, for eighty-six instrumental parts to be played "in whole or part, any duration, in any ensemble, chamber or orchestral, with or without *Winter Music*"; and, from 1970, *Song Books*, consisting of ninety-two solos for voice, some of which may be used with *Atlas Eclipticalis*.

In the late 1980s, Cage undertook two large-scale projects that are, in some ways, the culmination of his mature work. The first was a large series of number pieces, with titles like *Five*, for five voices or instruments; *Two*, for flute and piano; *Four²*, for soprano-alto-tenor-bass voices; and *101*, for 101 orchestral players. In these pieces, Cage gives the performers time brackets into which they must fit certain prescribed sounds and actions. The result, in the case of *101*, is an eerie stillness surrounded by constantly shifting colors. The other project was the five *Europeras*, written between 1987 and 1991. *Europera I/II*, for full opera company plus orchestra, combines the arias, orchestral parts, and scenery of traditional European opera in chance-determined ways that preserve the integrity of the original while, at the same time, creating a completely new operatic experience. The other three, all chamber operas, use smaller forces to create a similar experience.

For the final fourteen years of his life, John Cage lived on the top floor of the old B. Altman department store building on the corner of Sixth Avenue and 18th Street in New York. It was large and airy, with windows completely covering two walls. At one time it contained more than four hundred plants. We held our conversation at a small table against a wall at the edge of the kitchen. Although I had visited a number of times before, this was our first talk "for the record," and I confessed to John that I was a little nervous about it. He said not to worry; he'd think of something to say.

DUCKWORTH: It occurs to me that I don't have a very good understanding of what your early musical training was like. Is that because you've been intentionally vague about it?

CAGE: No. I've told everything I can think of. I've told, for instance, about studying piano with my Aunt Phoebe and my love of music "the whole world loves to play." And loving the music of Grieg, and being kept away from the music of Bach and Beethoven, and so forth.

DUCKWORTH: I guess what I don't understand is: Were you a good pianist?

CAGE: I was never interested in the scales. I had what was called a beautiful touch, which means that you have a sense of continuity. I hated scales and anything like that, and I still do. I'm not interested in virtuosity, per se. I was always, and still am, interested in the variety and nature of musical activity outside my own tastes and inclinations. So I did a great deal of sightreading—first of the nineteenth century, later of earlier music, and later of modern music.

DUCKWORTH: Was this before you went to Europe, before you started composing?

CAGE: The interest in nineteenth century was. It was in Europe that the teacher I took one lesson with, Lazare Lévy at the Conservatoire, sent me to a Bach festival because he learned that I knew nothing of Bach. I had found out about Beethoven, but not about Bach or Mozart. I went to a whole festival of Bach's music, and found it very interesting. At the same time, I heard John Kirkpatrick play Scriabin and Stravinsky. I went to visit him, and through him I became aware of that collection called *Das Neue Klavierbuch* of other modern composers. And I began writing music in response to all that music.

DUCKWORTH: What was your first music like?

CAGE: It was mathematical. I tried to find a new way of putting sounds together. Unfortunately, I don't have either the sketches or any clearer idea about the music than that. The results were so unmusical, from my then point of view, that I threw them away. Later, when I got to California, I began an entirely different way of composing, which was through improvisation, and improvisation in relation to texts: Greek; experimental prose from *transition* magazine; Gertrude Stein; and Aeschylus. Then, becoming through Richard Buhlig and others aware of my disconnection with musical technique or theory, I began studying the books of Ebenezer Prout. I went through them just as though I had a teacher, and did all the exercises—in harmony, primarily. I don't think I did counterpoint. It was later, with Schoenberg, that I studied that.

DUCKWORTH: If you studied primarily Romantic music with your aunt and you had gone through those harmony books, why do you suppose you had such a lack of feeling for harmony that Schoenberg talked about?

CAGE: I don't have an ear for music, and I don't hear music in my mind before I write it. And I never have. I can't remember a melody. A few have been drummed into me, like "My Country 'Tis of Thee," but there will come a point in even those songs when I'm not sure of how the next note goes. I just don't have any of those things that are connected with solfège and with memory and with what you might call imagination. I don't have any of those things. I have other qualities which are, I would say, more radical than those. But all those things which most musicians have, I don't have.

DUCKWORTH: Well, most of the people I know who would admit that would have never gone into music.

CAGE: I know that. Demosthenes wouldn't have gone into oratory if he'd told you his experience beforehand. He was the stutterer who overcame stuttering by speaking with stones in his mouth. But I didn't have the desire to overcome those absences in my faculties. I rather used them to the advantage of invention.

DUCKWORTH: Early, though, in your training, did you see them as problems?

CAGE: Oh, yes.

DUCKWORTH: Real problems?

CAGE: No. I saw them always as perfectly good for what I could offer to the musical world—namely, invention. I knew that from my father, because I had the example every day of a person in the house inventing. And I knew that that was the only thing I would be able to do in the field of music.

DUCKWORTH: How do you think about your early pieces now—*A Metamorphosis* and the *Sonata for Clarinet*?

CAGE: I don't think *A Metamorphosis* is an interesting piece. It's the least interesting of them all. But I think the others are very interesting.

DUCKWORTH: In those early works, were you beginning to envision that being a composer was something beyond what you were doing at the moment, or were you still being influenced by your teachers, and writing in the style of your teachers?

CAGE: None of those pieces are written in the style of my teachers.

DUCKWORTH: No, but they show influences of them.

CAGE: No, they don't, really. What? How do they?

DUCKWORTH: Well, if you think about the *Sonata for Clarinet*, there's a lot of twelve-tone work there.

CAGE: No, it's not twelve-tone.

DUCKWORTH: I know what you're saying; you're saying that it's not the traditional way of dealing with twelve-tone.

CAGE: And I hadn't yet studied with Schoenberg when I wrote it.

DUCKWORTH: That's true, but before you composed *A Metamorphosis* you had. But again, that's a totally different way of dealing with twelve-tone.

CAGE: Um hum. So it doesn't show his influence.

DUCKWORTH: Is there any influence of Schoenberg on your work?

CAGE: I would say not, in that sense. I would say in a radical sense there is. Because of his insistence upon the importance of structure, harmony, and tonality as a structural means in music, I devised the macro-micro-cosmic rhythmic structure for a music which wouldn't have its basis in pitches and frequences, but rather in time.

DUCKWORTH: Do you have a favorite piece from among your early works?

CAGE: Every time anyone has asked me what is my favorite piece from the past, I've consistently said I don't have any favorites. Anytime you say that something is your favorite, you're negating all the things that are not.

DUCKWORTH: What's the difference, then, between saying that you don't have any favorite pieces and saying that *A Metamorphosis* is not a good piece?

CAGE: I think not having any favorites is seeing each thing as unique and being at its own center. Then, when you look at the *Metamorphosis* and see the nature of its center, you see that for certain reasons it was not interesting, and really would have been better not written. It had no life in it. It had something else in it, but not a real life. If something has life in it and is at its center, it's very hard and useless to say that you prefer it to something else which also has life and is at its own center. But if something doesn't have any life in it, and is nothing but a set of relationships that are so forceful that the things that are being related cannot be heard apart from the relationship, then what you have is an intellectual situation that has no, I will say, physicality. And the thing about that piece is that it has no physicality. It's not a piece of music worth listening to. We could think about it, and we could teach people how to write another one like it, but we wouldn't want to listen to it.

DUCKWORTH: How about the transition, then, to percussion music?

CAGE: It wasn't a transition, Bill; it went on at the same time.

DUCKWORTH: Simultaneously?

CAGE: Yes. I thought that when I was writing for instruments the music should be chromatic rather than diatonic. And when I was writing for noises that the music should have a rhythmic structure. Those were my thoughts. And those were going on simultaneously. Instead of a transition, there was a dialogue between those two attitudes that brought about a number of changes. It brought about the invention of the prepared piano, on the one hand, and then the application of rhythmic structural ideas to instrumental works, that is to say, nonpercussion instrumental works. So that all those ideas that were, at first, in two different parts of my work came together.

DUCKWORTH: How did it come about that writing for noises was musical in your mind?

CAGE: I was introduced by Galka Scheyer to Oskar Fischinger, the filmmaker, and he was making films—abstract films—to the *Hungarian Dances* of Brahms. Galka thought, I think rightly, that his work would be more interesting if he used modern music. And she thought that my music could get more interesting through some connection with his work. He, in fact, made a remark to me which dropped me into the world of noise. He said: "Everything in the world has a spirit, and this spirit becomes audible by its being set into vibration." He started me on a path of exploration of the world around me which has never stopped—of hitting and scratching and scraping and rubbing everything, with anything I can get my hands on. I don't seem to be doing it as much as formerly; but when I was first doing it, I was doing it constantly.

DUCKWORTH: When you were developing the percussion orchestra, did you know Varèse's work in percussion music?

CAGE: Yes. I heard Nicolas Slonimsky conduct the *Ionization* at the Hollywood Bowl, and that experience, together with Fischinger's remark, confirmed my decision to work with percussion instruments.

DUCKWORTH: For a number of years you used rhythmic structure based on duration. Then, all of a sudden, you seemed to stop and you went in another direction.

CAGE: It wasn't all of a sudden. The gradual renunciation of those things is recounted in the essay in *Silence* called "Composition as Process." Rhythmic structure was characteristic of composition as object. And what I'm talking about in those three lectures is composition as process. That's why the notion of rhythmic structure was gradually dropped. It didn't happen all of a sudden. The *Music of Changes*, and even the time-length pieces for percussion and voice and stringed instruments, are all written in rhythmic structures, but structures that have become so flexible through the admission of accelerandos and ritards that the time is no longer fixed. At that point, then, where you introduce accelerando and ritard into a structural principal based on time (in other words, when it becomes flexible), it's on its way to no longer being necessary and it's moving into process. Had it remained fixed, without accelerandos and ritards, there would have been no reason to drop it. When David Tudor worked on the *Music of Changes*, he learned a kind of mathematics to translate the notation of accelerandos and ritards into clock time—stopwatch time. His copy of the *Music of Changes* has all the exact time lengths for the appearance of each event.

DUCKWORTH: Your early comments about the *Bacchanale* and the reason you invented the prepared piano all center on the fact that you didn't have space for percussion, and that the piano, in essence, gave you a percussion orchestra. When did you become aware that the prepared piano was more than a percussion orchestra?

CAGE: It was through the social problems here in New York City. You can't get a group of people to work together in New York for any length of time, because they're all too busy making money. So that when I had to give a concert of percussion music at the Museum of Modern Art, I found that I couldn't get a full rehearsal—ever. Even for just a short time. So I threw my energy and everything into the prepared piano. I had already written *Amores* and some other pieces, *Bacchanale* and some dance pieces, but then I began to write *A Book of Music* for two pianos, the dances, then the *Sonatas and Interludes*, and, finally, the *Concerto for Prepared Piano and Chamber Orchestra*.

DUCKWORTH: When you were writing *Sonatas and Interludes* did you understand the full possibilities of that piece as you were writing it, or is it only as it developed that it became such a major piece in your life?

CAGE: It's not in my life; it's in *its* life. Many people have been attracted to playing it. And I think anyone will have to remark eventually on the fact that all of the performances are different, because my table of preparations is not precise, and only suited the piano that I was actually working on. So that the result is that everyone's performance of the *Sonatas and Interludes* is a fresh experience. And this is a feather in the hat of indeterminacy, I think. Or it could be a black eye on indeterminacy, according to how you look at it. I think David Tudor feels that the *Sonatas and Interludes* only existed when I played them on the piano for which they were composed. I think he thinks that the work has disappeared in the various transformations that have taken place.

DUCKWORTH: But I would think that you'd like the idea that they change every time they're played. Is that not true?

CAGE: I didn't like it when I first wrote it. I was persuaded to like it through what I call practicality and circumstances. And it was one of the things that committed me to indeterminacy and chance operations.

DUCKWORTH: Was your interest in Indian and Oriental philosophy simultaneous with this move toward indeterminate music, or did one lead to the other?

CAGE: No, they were coexisting.

DUCKWORTH: Are they two sides of the same coin?

CAGE: No. I think it has more than two sides. I think it's different aspects of a life experience or mind experience, different aspects of a changing mind, which I was trying to describe in a variety of ways in that essay in *Silence*, "Changes."

DUCKWORTH: How do you feel now compared to the way that you felt then? For instance, is self-expressive art, art since the Renaissance, still radical?

CAGE: I would say so, yes. Some of it is very beautiful, but I think it's ineffective. I mean to say that the self is not really expressed when it expresses itself. It takes the mind of the person who's doing the work off his proper work.

DUCKWORTH: Which is what?

CAGE: Either the imitation of nature in her manner of operation, or the sobering and quieting of the mind making it susceptible to divine influences. Those are the two reasons for making music that are traditional.

John Cage (r.) and David Tudor, Japan, 1962

DUCKWORTH: If you're doing one, aren't you doing the other, at least
   to some extent?

CAGE: I think probably.

DUCKWORTH: Let me ask you a few questions about *4'33"*. Is it true
   that it was actually conceived of in the late forties and just not presented until the fifties?

CAGE: Yes. I knew about it, and had spoken about the possibility of
   doing it, for about four years before I did it.

DUCKWORTH: Why were you hesitant?

CAGE: I knew that it would be taken as a joke and a renunciation of
   work, whereas I also knew that if it was done it would be the highest form of work. Or this form of work: an art without work. I
   doubt whether many people understand it yet.

DUCKWORTH: Well, the traditional understanding is that it opens you up to the sounds that exist around you and . . .

CAGE: . . . to the acceptance of anything, even when you have something as the basis. And that's how it's misunderstood.

DUCKWORTH: What's a better understanding of it?

CAGE: It opens you up to any possibility *only* when nothing is taken as the basis. But most people don't understand that, as far as I can tell.

DUCKWORTH: Is it possible that instead of being taken as too foolish, it's now taken too seriously?

CAGE: No. I don't think it can be taken too seriously.

DUCKWORTH: What I mean is that it's approached too intellectually. My own feeling is that it's not a piece to approach intellectually— maybe not even a piece to approach, in the traditional sense.

CAGE: Well, I use it constantly in my life experience. No day goes by without my making use of that piece in my life and in my work. I listen to it every day. Yes I do.

DUCKWORTH: Can you give me an example?

CAGE: I don't sit down to do it; I turn my attention toward it. I realize that it's going on continuously. So, more and more, my attention, as now, is on it. More than anything else, it's the source of my enjoyment of life.

DUCKWORTH: But it seems to me that when you focus on that piece it becomes art silence rather than real silence. And that the understanding of real silence is what that piece is about. But that the only way you can get to real silence is through artistic silence. Is that accurate?

CAGE: Thoreau came to this same attitude of mind and use of his faculties without my being anywhere around.

DUCKWORTH: Yes, but you'd be hard-pressed to name another one who came to that attitude, wouldn't you?

CAGE: Well, I would think quite a lot of people in India feel that music is continuous, it is only we who turn away. This is a cliché in Indian thinking and, surely, in Indian experience. My affirmation of this is within the context of twentieth-century art music. But the important thing, surely, about having done it, finally, is that it leads out of the world of art into the whole of life. When I write a piece, I try to write it in such a way that it won't interrupt this other piece which is already going on. And that's how I mean it affects my work. But I don't mean by the silent piece, or any other, that I accept all the intentional self-expressive actions and works of people as suitable interruptions of this other activity. I don't believe that a bad, thoughtless, undevoted performance of one of my works is a performance of it.

DUCKWORTH: So that even in indeterminate, nonintentional music value judgments still play a part?

CAGE: Oh, certainly.

DUCKWORTH: How do you distinguish between appropriate and inappropriate value judgments?

CAGE: This is our problem, and one that we can't set down in any strict way. You'll have to study the situation thoroughly to find out what needs to be done at the time.

DUCKWORTH: So it's different for every situation?

CAGE: Yes, I think so. That's where the critics don't understand. I mean just because my name comes up doesn't make a failure a success.

DUCKWORTH: No, that's true. But you've suffered from performances like that forever.

CAGE: Oh, yes.

DUCKWORTH: How . . .?

CAGE: How do I manage?

DUCKWORTH: And overcome it?

CAGE: Well, I take as primary to the whole thing the purpose of music, which is to sober and quiet the mind, thus making one susceptible to divine influence. So that when I find myself being taken away from that purpose, I veer back toward it. It is more important for me to be at home with the silent piece than it is for me to get irritated by what some critic says, for instance, or how badly somebody plays something.

DUCKWORTH: From all I've read, it appears that those early meetings on Monroe Street with [Morton] Feldman, [Christian] Wolff, and

[David] Tudor were very significant meetings. The image that comes out is one of daily activity and daily changes of attitude. Is that true?

CAGE: Yes.

DUCKWORTH: How long did that last?

CAGE: It lasted at least a year, maybe two years. Then I went to Colorado and met Earle and Carolyn Brown, and they became so interested in the work that they decided to leave Colorado and come to New York and live here. I, meanwhile, had started a tape music project with Louis and Bebe Barron and David Tudor. And Earle went into this. Well, the appearance of Earle Brown on the scene infuriated Morton Feldman, so that the closeness that I had had with Morty, David, and Christian was disrupted by the advent of Earle Brown. Later, that whole problem was resolved by our raising the money to present a concert of the music of Brown and Feldman at Town Hall. Then both Earle and Morty became friends, and had a truce.

DUCKWORTH: Did the intensity of that group of people extend outside of the group?

CAGE: Oh, yes. There were other people who wanted to enter the group and enjoy the exchange of ideas and so forth, but Morty refused to let that happen. He insisted upon its being a closed group. It was through my acceptance of Earle Brown that Morty then left. The group then dissolved. Morty was literally furious that anyone else was allowed into the group. Another one who might have been in it but wasn't was Philip Corner. And I don't know, but I imagine Malcolm Goldstein and James Tenney. However, the fact that they weren't brought into it inspired them to form their own group, which was called Tone Roads. And they did beautiful work.

DUCKWORTH: Do you think everything works out for the best?

CAGE: Maybe not the best, but everything works out to something.

DUCKWORTH: What is your current relationship with the members of the group?

CAGE: The closeness that I had with Morty, even though it was always revived when I saw him again, didn't go from day to day. It only bloomed again briefly when we were together. We loved one another very much, but each life had gone in its own direction. And that's true of Christian too.

DUCKWORTH: Is that less true of David Tudor?

CAGE: No, I don't know David Tudor really anymore either in that close way that I knew him to begin with, though we're more frequently together than the others. But we're together through the circumstances of being musicians for the Cunningham Dance Company. If we weren't that, I would never see David anymore. Not because I don't enjoy seeing him, but because circumstances just don't bring us together. He's doing such beautiful work in electronic music that I have no desire to do any in that field. And that's because I'm an inventor. He's doing all the inventing that's necessary in that field. Where invention is required now, it seems to me, is in the field of piano, the violin, and possibly the flute, which I intend to work on.

DUCKWORTH: Even after all of the flute pieces from the sixties? Every composer in the world had to write an obligatory flute piece in the 1960s. Does it still need invention?

CAGE: I think so.

DUCKWORTH: What direction is it?

CAGE: I'll have to find it out.

DUCKWORTH: Have your ideas about the function of notation changed recently?

CAGE: I use notation in a variety of ways, all the way from the explicitness of the *Freeman Etudes* to the indeterminacy of the *Variations*. I'm not concerned with one particular kind of notation, but with many. I've done also a number of things in which there isn't any notation except verbal directions. Those things have been done by other people, but I continue to work in all those ways rather than in one of them exclusively. When I write, for instance, for orchestra, I'm writing for strangers and so I tend to write very conventionally. I'm careful to make something that can be understood without spending too much time.

DUCKWORTH: But that hasn't always been true, has it? I'm thinking about something like the *Concert for Piano and Orchestra*.

CAGE: No, that was always true. I developed that notation with the players themselves, so the notation was not strange to them, but arose out of our conversations.

DUCKWORTH: But you worked with people who were in some way interested in and dedicated to new music. When that piece is hand-ed to orchestra musicians, who are more dedicated to music of the past, it becomes very confusing for them.

CAGE: The people I wrote it for were the first ones. The subsequent ones are a result of circumstances over which I have no control. But when I made the notation, it was made with people who knew its meaning. Since then, the ambiguity that you speak of is certainly present, and sometimes it works and sometimes it doesn't. But that's true of any notation. The classical notation sometimes works, and sometimes it doesn't. I've heard Beethoven played very badly, and Mozart, too.

DUCKWORTH: Well, I was thinking also about that seven- or eight-minute performance of *Atlas Eclipticalis* with the New York Philharmonic in the sixties.

CAGE: So what relation does the notation have to that? The rehearsal was seven minutes long. You can scarcely say that they could tell you what the notation was.

DUCKWORTH: So intent and commitment transcend notational problems?

CAGE: I wouldn't say intent and commitment; I would say spending time with something. It's that simple. I mean, even a desultory spending of time over a thirty-hour period would result in something different than paying no attention during a seven-minute period.

DUCKWORTH: Are your experiences with orchestras getting better now that you've become more well known?

CAGE: Yes. I'm now more demanding of what happens in the way of rehearsal. And I've refused to work with them unless they will give time. That, of course, is not always in my control. It's only in my control at the time of the first performance, in the case of a com-missioned work. I can't, for instance, demand of an orchestra with which I have no connection, who gets the music from Peters, I can't demand anything of them. I don't even come into the picture.

DUCKWORTH: Does that worry you?

CAGE: It doesn't worry me at all.

DUCKWORTH: Your piece has a life of its own at that point?

CAGE: It has to have a life of its own, because I don't wish to be a policeman in the society. I have too many things to do to add to them the police function, which I'm not interested in, in any case.

DUCKWORTH: But it must be worrisome, if not painful, to know about bad performances.

CAGE: I don't have time to be worried, and I have little occasion to be pained, because the people who are not caring about something are not apt even to invite me to the performance. And worrying accomplishes nothing. So I try, in my life and in relation to my work, to do the things that are useful (and I frequently use that word) rather than to spend my energy and time in a way that results in nothing. You might say that worry could result in a change of attitude, but I'm too old to do that.

DUCKWORTH: And you never worried about it? There was never concern?

CAGE: I do my work as well as I can, and as practically as I can. And I've always done that. I've always advised certain people who ask me for advice to keep their feet on the ground. I don't like it when people write large works for orchestra when they have no commission from an orchestra. The reason I don't like that is because my early teacher, Adolph Weiss, had a stack of music that was never played, and he became embittered in the society. And so he was an example to me of how not to behave. I don't think I have any pieces that haven't been performed.

DUCKWORTH: Of course you're in the situation now where any piece you write is going to be performed.

CAGE: That was always the case. And the reason it was the case was because I had the example of Adolph Weiss, for whom it wasn't the case. He was such a bitter, ugly-tempered man as a result that I knew I didn't want to become that way.

DUCKWORTH: Was Schoenberg bitter?

CAGE: No, never. Everything he wrote was performed. He organized the society in Vienna which played all the music that he was interested in, including his own, without the audience knowing what was being played.

DUCKWORTH: But his work was questioned and ridiculed at times.

CAGE: That didn't bother him. But everything was played. He was a fighter from the word go.

DUCKWORTH: Did you pick that up from him?

CAGE: No, I think I picked all of these qualities up from my father.

DUCKWORTH: Wasn't there a point, say in the late fifties, where the actual look of the music that you were writing made performances difficult?

CAGE: No. Are you thinking of the *Concert for Piano and Orchestra*?

DUCKWORTH: I was thinking of the pieces around that, yes, and then beyond. The *Variations*.

CAGE: No. Those were all written for David Tudor.

DUCKWORTH: And you had very little concern beyond David Tudor? I mean, I'm sure you were aware of the controversy.

CAGE: If you knew David Tudor, and worked with him as I did over a long period of time (I would say we worked closely together for between fifteen and twenty years), he's one of the greatest musical . . . I was going to say minds. I would say that of Schoenberg. But David Tudor is not so much a musical mind as he is a musical . . . . At that time, he was, as [Sylvano] Busotti said, "a musical instrument." And when Busotti wrote a piece for him, he didn't say for piano, he said for David Tudor, meaning him as an instrument. David still has that aspect in the society. I noticed him recently in California after a concert with the Cunningham Dance Company, and the young composers of the Bay area flocking around him because of his technical knowledge and technical experience in the field of live electronics. And formerly, it was in the field of piano. And before that, it was in the field of the organ. But he was such an extraordinary musician that if you were near him, and even now if you're near him, you don't need anything else. The world is immense through him, has no limits, has only inviting horizons.

DUCKWORTH: Why do you suppose David never played any Ives?

CAGE: I asked him why he didn't play Ives, because that's the remarkable thing that is missing in his history. He said: "It's too difficult." And I didn't know what that meant. This is why he's so fascinating. At first, I didn't know what that meant, because it was not too difficult from the point of view of his hands. He played the

Boulez Second Sonata, which is more difficult. Either he told me or I then realized that he would have had to change his mind over into that of a transcendentalist, which he didn't wish to do. When he played the Boulez sonata, he read all the poetry that Boulez was reading at the time—René Char. He learned the French language in order to read that poetry; he didn't know it until then. He became, insofar as he could, the composer. And he said it would be too difficult to do that in the case of Ives. Had he done it, we would have had performances of Ives that we haven't yet had. This sounds very elitist, and I think I am actually an elitist. I always have been. I didn't study music with just anybody; I studied with Schoenberg. I didn't study Zen with just anybody; I studied with Suzuki. I've always gone, insofar as I could, to the president of the company.

DUCKWORTH: Yes, but now you're the president of the company.

CAGE: I have tried to indicate that there is no company. And I don't teach. So it makes it difficult. It obliges people to do what I think is finally important, and that is to work from their own centers. This is what I keep writing about.

DUCKWORTH: But unless you're dealing with extraordinary people, their own centers aren't well enough defined to understand how to work from them.

CAGE: But Bill, I think they are. I don't believe in education. I don't believe in things being explained or understood. I believe in things that are inexplicable.

DUCKWORTH: That statement might be misunderstood if we leave it at that.

CAGE: And the elitist business. All of those things can easily be misunderstood, because people don't think clearly. I think, for the most part, people don't think. I don't know how they do what they do, but I guess it's that they're on the lookout for some advantage and that when one thing gives them an advantage they go in that direction rather than in the one where they don't get an advantage.

DUCKWORTH: Yes, but I think you do believe in education. You've been educating yourself all of your life.

CAGE: That's different.

DUCKWORTH: What's different about it?

CAGE: Well, the difference is that when I was in school I learned very little. When I was thirty-five years old, I began to learn what school had not taught me, and I did it through my own efforts and through my own studying.

DUCKWORTH: Could you have done it without school?

CAGE: Yes. In fact, I'm a dropout you know. The question arises: Why didn't I drop out sooner?

DUCKWORTH: Is there an answer?

CAGE: I think there may be one. I've never tried to find it. But there was something about the things that I did in high school that seemed to me to be challenging. They filled up my life, and I was able to expend my energy on them with interest. In high school, I studied Greek and geometry (I didn't get as far as calculus) and literature and botany. In addition to which I won a cup for the school in oratory—giving speeches. After hours in high school, I conducted the Boy Scout radio program which I arranged each week. I had some speaker from the Protestant, Catholic, or Jewish community give an inspiring ten-minute talk, and then the rest of it was jokes and stories and music. It went on for an hour over KNX for two years. Those were my two years in high school.

DUCKWORTH: You were valedictorian; you must have believed in education at that point.

CAGE: No, that was through my interest in oratory that I did that. It wasn't education. My valedictorian speech was on international patriotism, the devotion to the whole world, which I was not taught in school. I was taught only the patriotism part—swear allegiance to the American flag—and I was saying we must swear allegiance to the whole world, which no one taught me in school.

DUCKWORTH: Are you positive now or negative about the state of the world?

CAGE: I'm positive. I think the world is only part of creation, and that creation is going to continue willy-nilly. If we destroy this earth, which we may very likely do, it would be like destroying one leaf on a tree. So why should I feel pessimistic about that?

DUCKWORTH: So where in high school you were talking about the family of the world . . .

John Cage (r.) and Merce Cunningham, circa 1980. Photo Credit: Henry Grossman

CAGE: International patriotism, the universal creation, I would think.
We all cling to what we have done, and others have done, on this
planet. But we surely know, as well as any Buddhist or any Jewish
mind, the futility of placing faith in anything of this earth. Doesn't
the prophet say: "Vanity of vanities, all is vanity"? We're well aware
that at any moment we may go out of existence. We already know

as individuals that death can take us at any moment, that each one
of us is the central character in a mystery that's going to end with
death. And we don't know who killed us. But the one thing we're
certain of is our death.

DUCKWORTH: Where do you put your faith then?

CAGE: You don't put it outside of yourself; you put it inside of yourself
and in your energy. And you put that as close to zero as you can.

DUCKWORTH: Do you pay much attention to current events?

CAGE: I think more and more people, like Thoreau, just don't read
the newspapers. I don't even bother looking at the television anymore. I don't even listen to the radio. You could say, perhaps, that
I'm not a proper member of the twentieth-century society. On the
other hand, I'm aware that we are very close to destroying ourselves. And I think when that news arrives, one way or the other, I'll
be aware of it.

DUCKWORTH: Most people seem only to read the headlines.

CAGE: Recently, I found myself, because of airplane travel and so
forth, reading more than usual. And I must say the best newspaper
I picked up in the course of the last month was the *Christian
Science Monitor*. It was so amusing to see that even *they* were not
able to make sense out of current events. They actually had an article that said that it was important for there to be a balance between
the United States and Russia, and that we had to keep up the
defense. I mean they actually said that. Whereas if one of the countries would be willing to approach zero and open itself to attack,
the other would immediately . . . we know from Thoreau, from
Martin Luther King, from Gandhi, and everything, that defenseless-
ness is the best protection against attack. Daniel in the lion's den.
Throw us in there where the Russians can *really* get us! The other
thing that the newspapers have headlines about is unemployment,
because it's going up very high. Instead of being seen as the nature
of the future, unemployment is seen as some horror. None of the
jobs that anyone is offered are of any interest. No one wants a job.
What everyone needs in order to do his best work is, as you know
very well now, self-employment. Here we are almost halfway
towards self-employment, and all we do is complain about the fact
that we have this big unemployment problem. It's stupid. It's as
stupid as believing in God.

DUCKWORTH: That statement's going to be misunderstood too.

CAGE: Almost anything I would say is going to be misunderstood. And if we say that, then maybe somebody will understand.

DUCKWORTH: How do you handle your critics, and I don't mean professional critics, but people who profess a love for music, who have trouble with what they consider the feeling that anything goes in your music?

CAGE: They don't understand it. And mostly they don't understand anything. So I don't handle them, and I stay as far away from them as I possibly can. I don't even object to their idiotic statements.

DUCKWORTH: Did you ever pay attention to the professional critics, and worry about what they said?

CAGE: I worried about their liking my work.

DUCKWORTH: What is your current feeling about critics?

CAGE: I've just returned from a month in Europe, and I met one of the most brilliant music critics who's living now. His name is Heinz Klaus Metzger. He was a pupil of [Theodor] Adorno; so he comes, as I came, from the president of the company. He said to me, when we were in Frankfurt together recently, speaking of my *Etudes Australes*, that it was not composed by me but by God. And the reason he said God was because he's witty, and because the piece used star maps. That, theoretically, God's heaven is somewhere close to the stars, I think is what he meant. Also, the *New York Times* critic recently said that if the *Etudes Australes* lasts beyond my life that it will be not because of me but because of the stars from which it was derived. Now, neither Heinz Klaus Metzger nor the *New York Times* know what they're talking about when they make such statements. We know, for one thing, that God doesn't exist; therefore he didn't write the music. I know perfectly well that I wrote it. God had no more to do with writing that music than you did . . . or than Heinz Klaus Metzger did.

I am working in a way in the field of music that does not correspond to the way critics are working in the field of music criticism. They don't know what I'm doing, so that they make such stupid remarks as that. The brightest critic I know of says that God wrote my music. I really think that a form of music criticism has not yet been practiced which is suitable for chance-determined or indeterminate music—or even process music, you can put it that way. I don't think any critic has come up with a valid way of approaching that work, including Heinz Klaus Metzger.

DUCKWORTH: How would they go about coming up with something like that though? What's the process?

CAGE: They would have to place themselves where the composer placed himself: at a point which was indifferent to the end result. If I use chance operations, it's evident that I don't care whether this sound, this, this, this, this, or this comes up, that I will welcome any one of them. Or as they put it in the program of the Bremen festival: "I welcome whatever happens next." The critic has to put himself at that point, rather than at the point of attacking what happened as being earthshaking. He has to change his mind from seeing what he's actually hearing (as being what he's writing about) to finding out the source of that as what he's writing about. I don't know whether you understood what I just said. How would you say it?

DUCKWORTH: Oh, you're putting me on the spot. I'll come at it from a different direction: that certain basic things have changed in the way a composer looks at the process of writing a composition and, in fact, what that composition is. And that critics continue to bring . . .

CAGE: No, the composition, you see, becomes sounds, and so appears to the critic that it's a piece of music like any other piece of music.

DUCKWORTH: Right. But it's not.

CAGE: It's not.

DUCKWORTH: And the critic comes to it like he comes to other pieces of music . . .

CAGE: . . . and attacks it from the old-fashioned point of view, and finally comes to the conclusion that God created it, which is stupid.

DUCKWORTH: For a long time you've talked about the fact that we've got to put memory and values and all of that in its proper place. How do people go about doing that though? How do you weaken taste and memory?

CAGE: The Zen method is by sitting cross-legged.

DUCKWORTH: But the majority of Western civilization doesn't feel it can do that.

CAGE: No. The way I have chosen to do that is to compose by means of asking questions rather than making choices, and to use chance operations to determine the answers.

DUCKWORTH: And how should the listeners do that?

CAGE: The listeners and the critics have a problem. And I would like to find out how to solve that or how to indicate where that is. I know that I may be able to answer it, because instead of hearing music in my head before I write it, I write in such a way as to hear something that I have not yet heard. Therefore, I'm in the position that the listener is in, and the critic is in with respect to my music. How do I approach it? How do I hear it, is the answer. Not because I know anything that they don't know, but because I haven't heard it anymore than they've heard it.

DUCKWORTH: Do you think resistance to change is the problem?

CAGE: No, because people love new automobiles and new refrigerators. They have no resistance to change.

DUCKWORTH: What is it then?

CAGE: They have preconceptions and likes and dislikes, and memories from which they are not free.

DUCKWORTH: Are there any underlying concepts that continue throughout all of your music?

CAGE: I recently made a text. It's mesostics on what seem to me to be the most important things in my work. The way I found out those things was by giving ten lectures, improvised lectures, at the University of Surrey in Guildford for a group of professional composers. What I did was I took all of my work and divided it into twelve areas. Then I said I would sit down and attempt to write mesostics on the subject of the improvised lecture. So I tried to find the most important word or idea in my work in order to write the mesostics on that word. So there were ten lectures, and the first was on the subject of METHOD; the second was on the subject of STRUCTURE; the third was INTENTION; then DISCIPLINE fourth, fifth, and sixth; then NOTATION, then INDETERMINACY, then INTERPENETRATION, and then IMITATION, DEVOTION, and finally CIRCUMSTANCES. Those seem to me to be the most important things, and they omit, curiously enough, the word invention, and the word nonintention, or even such things as chance and so on, which mostly come in under the word discipline.

DUCKWORTH: What's your current feeling about what seems to be necessary?

CAGE: Well, what I'm searching for is what the next step is in any field. What next step is implied. My father said he always got his best ideas while he was sound asleep. Other people say that ideas come to them from out of the air. That's what I'm trying to say— that we must be open if we're interested, as I am and still am, in what is called the avant-garde. We must then remain open to what seems to be necessary not to us as persons but to us as members of the musical society.

DUCKWORTH: Do you like recordings of your music?

CAGE: I don't use them.

DUCKWORTH: Would you just as soon they didn't exist?

CAGE: Yes. I don't listen to any of them. I really don't believe that that's where music is. And yet, for many people that's all that music is . . . even some people I love. And I myself, more and more, have to concern myself with records. I made a recording of all of *Empty Words*. I think it's fourteen sides.

DUCKWORTH: But you're not enthusiastic about that?

CAGE: I'm not enthusiastic about it. On the other hand, I made it. I know that many people want it, so I not only don't stand in its way but I further it.

DUCKWORTH: Isn't that contradictory?

CAGE: Yes.

DUCKWORTH: You're not bothered by that?

CAGE: No. I'm not bothered by contradictions. Inconsistency, we know from Emerson, is not a bad thing.

This interview first appeared in a slightly different form as "Anything I Say Will Be Misunderstood" in *Bucknell Review: John Cage at 75*, vol. 33, no. 2 (1988). Parts of this interview have also appeared in *Conversing With Cage* by Richard Kostelanetz, New York: Limelight Editions, 1988.

CONLON NANCARROW

Born Texarkana, Arkansas, 1912

I REMEMBER CLEARLY the first time I heard Conlon Nancarrow's music. It was the late 1960s and Columbia Records had just released twelve of his *Studies for Player Piano*. They sounded so odd, beautiful, and unique that I immediately wanted to hear all of them; he had written thirty-two by that time. But hearing more was almost impossible. In the 1960s, Conlon Nancarrow was all but unknown, having spent the past twenty years in self-imposed exile in Mexico. Had it not been for John Cage, who arranged six of Nancarrow's player-piano studies for a dance by Merce Cunningham, thus bringing him to the attention of a wider public, Nancarrow may have remained obscure far longer.

Born in Texarkana, Arkansas, in 1912, Nancarrow studied briefly at the Cincinnati Conservatory before moving to Boston in 1933. In Boston he studied counterpoint with Roger Sessions, became acquainted with Walter Piston, and had his music championed by Nicolas Slonimsky. A self-described "fiery radical" by the time he arrived in Boston, Nancarrow joined the Communist Party and, as one of the few musician members, soon found himself organizing the musical program for a Lenin memorial in Boston's Symphony Hall.

A trumpet player who began playing jazz and popular music as a teenager, Nancarrow worked his way to Europe in 1936 playing in a dance band on board a ship. The following year he returned, this time to enlist in the Spanish Civil War, where he fought for two years as a foot soldier in the Abraham Lincoln International Brigade. Upon returning to America, his request for a new passport was denied, and Nancarrow, partly in retaliation, moved to Mexico where he has lived since 1940, becoming a Mexican citizen in 1956.

One of the few books Nancarrow took with him to Mexico was Henry Cowell's *New Musical Resources*. Having long known he was more interested in rhythm than in pitch, Nancarrow was intrigued by

Cowell's suggestion that complex rhythms, such as five against seven, could be performed easily on player piano. Partly because of isolation, but mostly because of his rhythmic interests, Nancarrow used a small inheritance from his father to return to New York and purchase a player piano plus the punching machine necessary to create the holes in the piano rolls. He later bought a second player piano in Mexico, altering the hammers of both with metal and leather to create a sharper, more focused, percussive sound. Eventually, he redesigned his punching machine, enabling him not only to compose directly on the paper roll, but to achieve more complex and precise rhythms and temporal relationships as well.

From 1940 until the early eighties, Nancarrow worked in relative obscurity in Mexico, producing more than forty *Studies for Player Piano*. These studies explore rhythmic relationships far beyond the capabilities of human performers, and often sound as if several pianists are playing at once, all in different tempos. In the early eighties, he returned to writing works for live instruments and began allowing his studies to be transcribed for live ensembles. Although well known by reputation at this point, few musicians had ever had the opportunity to speak with him directly.

But all of that changed rather suddenly in 1982. That was the year Nancarrow was honored at the twentieth annual Cabrillo Festival in Aptos, California. A month earlier he was one of two composers in the first group of recipients of the prestigious MacArthur Award, a five-year grant that temporarily eased his financial worries. Later that same year he toured several European cities, including stops at the West German Radio in Cologne and IRCAM in Paris. Though less now, Nancarrow continues to travel, his most recent trip being to New York in May 1994 to be included on the New York Philharmonic's week-long celebration of American music. Although prevented by his health from participating in the preconcert panel, he was able to attend part of the chamber music concert at Merkin Hall and hear the pianist Ursula Oppens play his *Two Canons for Ursula*. The standing ovation he received was long and enthusiastic.

Several years before, on his first trip back to New York in forty years, I spoke with Nancarrow. He was in New York for a concert of his music at Lincoln Center, and the activity around him was enormous. It had taken at least ten phone calls to arrange the meeting, and I had yet to speak directly to Conlon. The morning I arrived at his hotel, it didn't look any too promising. There were several people in the suite, including his wife and son, and the telephone was constantly ringing. But

Conlon Nancarrow, New York, 1989. Photo Credit: Sabine Matthes

eventually everything subsided, all the people left, and we sat down with a cup of tea at a small kitchen table in the dining area. It was the first time we had met, and I wasn't sure what to expect. Everybody I knew, who knew him, had warned me that he was a man who didn't like to be asked too many questions.

DUCKWORTH: You have the reputation of being an extremely difficult man to talk to. Is that reputation deserved, or is it unfair?

NANCARROW: It's exaggerated, but there's probably some basis for it.

DUCKWORTH: Is that because you want to be left alone, or because you don't see any value in talking about your work?

NANCARROW: I really don't know. Maybe a little of both.

DUCKWORTH: Well, now that you're more well known, it must be a lot more difficult to protect your privacy.

NANCARROW: Of course it is, except for one thing. Fortunately, I haven't encouraged any publicity in Mexico. I'm almost totally unknown there. And I like that peace and quiet. Then I go out somewhere and there's a big fuss. Okay, that's temporary . . . for a short time. Then I go back to my peace and quiet.

DUCKWORTH: Do you think of yourself as a Mexican composer, or are you an American composer living in Mexico?

NANCARROW: Well, I'm a Mexican now. Of course, I was raised in the United States and my culture is American. Certainly my music doesn't reflect any Mexican influence. There's possibly a slight Spanish influence, but not a Mexican influence in my music.

DUCKWORTH: Do you have any contact with Mexican musicians and Mexican composers?

NANCARROW: Very little. I've met most of the composers there, but I just know them to say "hello" and that's about it. One good friend of mine from way back is Rodolfo Halffter. He was a Spanish refugee, one of the few that I've been friendly with for many years. Actually, I haven't seen him for a long time now; he lives in a whole different area.

DUCKWORTH: Has the isolation been good for you artistically?

NANCARROW: No, not necessarily. I don't think it's been either good or bad; it just happened that way.

DUCKWORTH: If you had had a choice, would it have happened differently?

NANCARROW: Oh, I don't think so. I have no regrets about any of these things.

DUCKWORTH: I heard recently that you might want to return to the United States to live. Is there any possibility of that?

NANCARROW: No . . . but it is a big problem. My doctors told me I should get out of Mexico City because of the altitude. (I have a lung thing that's not too serious, and that altitude's bad for it.) For me, moving to another country is a tremendous thing. And further-more, the problems I would have . . . You know I'm an undesirable alien. In fact, I thought I wasn't going to get the last visa I got. They kept me waiting three weeks for it while they did their investiga-tions, then finally gave it to me. I don't want to go through the trau-ma of moving everything and getting set up so that the govern-ment can say "Out!" No, I don't want to take a chance on that.

DUCKWORTH: Why do you suppose you're still an undesirable alien?

NANCARROW: My whole political record, obviously. They never forget. In fact, it goes back to fifty years ago when I was in the Communist Party. As things are now, there are several crimes. There's that; I fought in the Spanish War; and I became a Mexican citizen. All three of those things are sort of unforgivable sins.

DUCKWORTH: Can we talk a little about your childhood? I know you grew up in Arkansas, but I understand your parents came from the North.

NANCARROW: Only one. My mother was born in that area; my father came from the North. He was born somewhere in New York State, I forget where, but he was working in Philadelphia when he went south. Some oil company sent him down there to set up a factory for making barrels. That was the reason he went there. He stayed there full time.

DUCKWORTH: When did you start playing the trumpet?

NANCARROW: Oh, very young. All families want their children to get culture. The piano teacher was some horrible old spinster. I never learned any piano, I was so irritated with the whole thing. Finally, to get away from that, they let me take up trumpet, which was a relief. The trumpet teacher was a nice old drunk who was very pleasant and there was no problem.

DUCKWORTH: Were you in the school band, or were you taking pri-vate lessons?

NANCARROW: Private lessons. Then later, of course, I played in the town band and different things there.

DUCKWORTH: Do you remember how you got attracted to jazz? Who did you listen to?

NANCARROW: I don't remember when, but at some point I found Louis Armstrong, Bessie Smith, and Earl Hines (he was one of my favorites).

DUCKWORTH: Did you have access to a lot of records?

NANCARROW: Not there in the town. Later I did; I finally had a tremendous collection.

DUCKWORTH: How did you hear those people then? Did they travel through?

NANCARROW: No, no. I'm saying I don't think I'd heard these people at that time. It was later. Early, there was nothing.

DUCKWORTH: What trumpet style did you play?

NANCARROW: People have made a lot about this thing with the trumpet. I played all kinds of things. In Cincinnati I played in a symphony, German beer halls, jazz groups, whatever. And I was no outstanding trumpeter in any of these fields. I was just a competent trumpeter, that's all.

DUCKWORTH: But your interest in jazz certainly shows up in the music that you write.

NANCARROW: Yes, that's true. From way back I've had that interest.

DUCKWORTH: When you were in high school, did you know that you wanted to be a musician?

NANCARROW: Yes, but at that time I wasn't really thinking of becoming a composer. It was only later that that developed.

DUCKWORTH: Did you want to be a performer?

NANCARROW: Not any virtuoso or anything like that. Just playing trumpet. I liked trumpet and I enjoyed playing, and that was it.

DUCKWORTH: Could you support yourself playing trumpet?

NANCARROW: Yes, later.

DUCKWORTH: When you got out of high school, you went to the Cincinnati Conservatory. You've talked about the revelation of hearing the *Rite of Spring* there. What else did you hear that impressed you?

NANCARROW: The things that were being played at that time were certainly not ultramodern. The Stravinsky *Rite of Spring* was from twenty-five years before. I did hear some Bartók then for the first time. They also played Strauss, Debussy, and a few others that weren't quite as dramatic for me. Mainly Stravinsky and Bartók were the ones who impressed me most.

DUCKWORTH: Where did your interest in Bach come from? Did it come from the Cincinnati period, or before that?

NANCARROW: That's from way back. That was one thing I had heard in the town. Also, as I got more and more interested in writing music, Bach seemed to be the beginning of it all.

DUCKWORTH: Did you study composition at the Conservatory?

NANCARROW: No. Look, all these stories that I went there for several years . . . '29 to '32 . . . it wasn't like that. I think I spent one semester there and decided that that wasn't for me.

DUCKWORTH: Well, what did you do between 1929 and 1932?

NANCARROW: Nothing special. I was there playing. Sort of studying on my own. I'm an autodidact, basically, in everything. I didn't get anything out of my education in school, for example. I got most of my education from the *Little Blue Books*.

DUCKWORTH: Before you left Cincinnati, had you decided to be a composer?

NANCARROW: Oh, yes. I'd already done a few little pieces.

DUCKWORTH: Had you studied with anyone?

NANCARROW: At that time no one.

DUCKWORTH: But you went to Boston thinking that you wanted to be a composer and that you wanted to study composition?

NANCARROW: Yes.

DUCKWORTH: Am I correct in assuming that you only worked for a short time with [Nicolas] Slonimsky, [Walter] Piston, or [Roger] Sessions?

NANCARROW: Sessions was the only one I worked with for quite a while. Very rigid studies in counterpoint. In fact, that's the only academic discipline that I've ever had. He, of course, was a real taskmaster. At that time I was writing music so I would take him a piece that I'd done and say, "What do you think of this?" He'd say: "I think it's fine; now where's your counterpoint exercise?" So I stopped taking him pieces. It wasn't very encouraging. I guess he figured I wasn't ready to be writing pieces.

DUCKWORTH: He never looked at one of them?

NANCARROW: He just sort of glanced at them. He wasn't interested. The thing was, I should do my counterpoint.

DUCKWORTH: And he didn't want to encourage you at all to compose?

NANCARROW: I guess. I don't know.

DUCKWORTH: Did either Slonimsky or Piston look at your music?

NANCARROW: Oh, yes. Slonimsky sent my pieces to *New Music* when I was in the Spanish War. I didn't even know about it. I guess I'd left some pieces with him and he sent them to be published. Piston also looked at the music. Both of them were sort of vague as far as teaching went. Actually, I became very friendly with Slonimsky. I used to go to his house and have dinner with him.

DUCKWORTH: Did he encourage you to be a composer?

NANCARROW: Oh, yes, definitely. In California recently there was some reception for me and he was there. So he gave a talk and said: "I discovered him."

DUCKWORTH: When you went to Boston, did you have contact with other composers?

NANCARROW: A few . . . not many . . . no, I didn't.

DUCKWORTH: So there wasn't a group of people that you were involved with?

NANCARROW: No. I suppose there were groups there, but I wasn't in them.

DUCKWORTH: When did you begin to be motivated politically?

NANCARROW: That's another thing that came from childhood. I started to tell you about those *Little Blue Books*. It was a collection of books that this old Wobbly, Haldeman Julius, started publishing. They were the first pocket books. Five cents each. They had everything: the classics of literature, art, science, and, of course, political things. He was sort of an anarchist, so there were all kinds of books on politics . . . and sexual things . . . everything. There were thousands of titles in that series. I think I mainly got my education from those books. There were a lot of political things and I became quite interested very young. By the time I got to Boston I was already a fiery radical. And I joined the Communist Party in Boston. I still today believe in a form of democratic socialism which practically doesn't exist anywhere. As you know, the Communist Party was certainly not democratic socialism.

DUCKWORTH: Were the *Little Blue Books* readily available? Could you buy them everywhere?

NANCARROW: No, they were all mail order. Maybe they had them on sale in other bookstores, but not in that town. There were ads in the newspapers for them. I would get these ads and would order them on my little allowance . . . and also watch for them coming, because my parents would be shocked at the titles. (I had to stash them away and hide them.) In fact, many years afterwards my brother told me once that they were remodeling the house and in the attic my mother came across them, and going through the titles looking at them she was sort of shocked. Well, she was resigned to all kinds of things. So she said, "Now I understand what happened to him."

DUCKWORTH: How old were you when you started reading them?

NANCARROW: I must have been ten or eleven.

DUCKWORTH: And you continued through high school?

NANCARROW: As I say, that was my education. The school there was at that time the backwoods of Arkansas. I've never been very enthusiastic about schools anyhow.

DUCKWORTH: So your parents weren't political at all?

NANCARROW: No. It's strange. After my father died I was looking through some of the books that he had read. I found one by some sort of Marxist writer. He had read this book and there were comments in the margin of it. That surprised me, because he was quite a conservative person.

DUCKWORTH: When you were reading the *Little Blue Books*, did you discuss them with anybody?

NANCARROW: Who would I discuss them with in Texarkana?

DUCKWORTH: Did you join the Communist Party as soon as you got to Boston, or did it take awhile?

NANCARROW: Not very long. I don't remember exactly, but it was fairly soon. I don't know how I came into contact with the few people who were in that area. They weren't musicians. In fact, they did a Lenin memorial meeting in Symphony Hall in Boston. (Boston is the center of everything conservative; I don't know how they got that hall.) Since I was the only musician in the party, I was designated to arrange the musical program. I arranged quite a good program, good enough so that nonpolitical critics came. Piston played his *Sonata for Oboe and Piano*; he appeared himself. Incidentally, he was teaching at Harvard and was told that if he ever did that again he'd be fired. And he never did it again, naturally. He wasn't political at all; he just liked to have an independent point of view and to do what he felt like. Well, they told him he couldn't do what he felt like.

DUCKWORTH: Was being in the Party fashionable at that time?

NANCARROW: Not so much in Boston, but apparently in New York everyone at one time or another was in it. When the McCarthy period started, everyone was there. I don't know how some of these people got off the hook at the time. Some of them just simply named names. Some went to jail. I'm curious as to how Copland got off the hook, because he was involved too. He had done music for movies and he had gone, as far as they were concerned, too far left. He was never in the Communist Party but he had been associated with leftist things.

DUCKWORTH: Would you describe yourself as an active member? Did you go to meetings regularly, or were you on the fringe?

NANCARROW: I was active, but I wasn't a leader or anything like that.

DUCKWORTH: So you were in Boston studying privately, going to Party meetings, and playing jazz?

NANCARROW: No, by then I'd stopped playing trumpet. Stopped playing entirely. That's when I dropped it. Because then I was thinking I wanted to be a composer. I got onto the WPA, first as a conductor of one of the orchestras that they organized in this period. Although I knew the whole technique—and musically I guess that was enough—I found out right away that I didn't have the personality for being a conductor. So I got transferred from that to the theater project, which consisted of writing incidental music for plays and things, which I did the whole time there until I went to Spain.

DUCKWORTH: Did you go to Europe to enlist in the Spanish War, or did you go for something else and then enlist after you got there?

NANCARROW: I worked my way to Europe in 1936 on a boat. I was playing in a jazz group for a dance thing on a tour. It was a thing to go there, spend two months, and then come back with the same tour. So I had two months in Europe and the trip. After that I went back to Spain.

DUCKWORTH: Specifically to enlist?

NANCARROW: Yes, yes. I went for that.

DUCKWORTH: Well, you must have begun playing trumpet again. When you went to Europe on that two-month tour didn't you go as a performer?

NANCARROW: Oh, I forgot about that. You see, I'd stopped and then someone I knew got in touch with me and said: "Look, they want a group to play on this tour." It sounded wonderful to me—a trip to Europe and everything else—so I frantically started brushing up on my trumpet to get in shape. It wasn't too much shape, but it was enough to get by. It was after that tour that I finally dropped it.

DUCKWORTH: Did you see a lot of action in the Spanish Civil War?

NANCARROW: Two years of it.

DUCKWORTH: I mean, were you in the thick of things, so to speak?

NANCARROW: Of course.

DUCKWORTH: Being fired at and all that?

NANCARROW: Well, naturally! That's what wars are about.

DUCKWORTH: You never know these days. There are people who served in Vietnam who never fired a rifle and were never fired on.

NANCARROW: In modern warfare there are all kinds of bureaucratic jobs and then there are foot soldiers. I was a foot soldier. Most of the International Brigade was that. That was, in a sense, a more primitive war compared to later ones. Also, the international brigades were used all over the place when there was trouble. So we were at it full time.

DUCKWORTH: Did they train you before you went out?

NANCARROW: They taught us how to load and fire a rifle. Most of the so-called training is training to march in step and so forth. That's useless when you're in a trench.

DUCKWORTH: Were you surprised when you came back and started having trouble with the government?

NANCARROW: It wasn't trouble; they simply refused a passport.

DUCKWORTH: Where were you going to go that you needed a passport?

NANCARROW: Nowhere. I just wanted to have a passport in my hand. As a matter of fact, I think I suspected trouble because some other people I knew had already applied and been refused. I think I did it to see if I could get a passport. Well, I couldn't.

DUCKWORTH: Was it immediately after that that you thought about moving to Mexico?

NANCARROW: I began thinking of it fairly soon, yes.

DUCKWORTH: When you first arrived in Mexico, how did you support yourself?

NANCARROW: Odds and ends. At first I had some help from my family at home. And when I got there I did some teaching of English. I lived very, very frugally. My father had left a trust fund for all of us at a certain age, but I couldn't get it at first. Later, when I did get it, I decided to go to New York to get the [player] piano, the punching thing [for cutting rolls], and everything to do it. This money kept me going for quite awhile.

DUCKWORTH: Can you remember the kind of music or music books you took with you to Mexico?

NANCARROW: I had a few scores and other things; not too many. What I did have, which was a very important thing to me, especially at the beginning, was the [Henry] Cowell book *New Musical Resources*. That had a very strong influence on me. He talks in there about certain rhythmical problems. He says, "Of course, it can be done on player piano." But he never did it! Well, I did it.

DUCKWORTH: Until you read Cowell's book, had you realized that your major interests were rhythmic rather than melodic?

NANCARROW: Oh, yes. I was aware of that from way back, more or less on a primitive level. I was always interested in rhythm. My interests got more complicated and sophisticated, you might say.

DUCKWORTH: Do you think that's a carryover from jazz?

NANCARROW: I think that probably had a lot to do with it. And (this was also later) in Boston I went to the Uday Shankar Ballet with Indian music. It was a little westernized, but for me it was another shock. So from then on I started collecting and looking for records of Indian music. There's one fantastic record called *Tabla Terran*.

What it is is twelve tuned tablas, played like a harpsichord. It just bowled me over. It's really fantastic.

DUCKWORTH: As I understand it, when you got to Mexico you kept in touch musically through buying recordings and subscribing to a number of periodicals. Which periodicals were you most interested in? Which ones gave you the most information?

NANCARROW: I subscribed to *Perspectives of New Music* and *Musical Quarterly*. I have a huge collection of *Musical Quarterly*. And various things that came out. What was that fancy one that lasted a few years?

DUCKWORTH: *Source?*

NANCARROW: Yes, I have all of those.

DUCKWORTH: Do you have the feeling that you kept in touch with what was going on?

NANCARROW: More or less. Of course, I didn't hear the music, but I'd get some idea of what people were doing. As far as I'm concerned, you can more or less just read about minimalism and know what they're doing. You don't really have to hear it, I think.

DUCKWORTH: Did you buy records by mail order, or did you have a good store in Mexico?

NANCARROW: No, there's no store for that in Mexico. In fact, the Indian music was quite a problem. I sent away for catalogs from record companies in India. The catalogs were in English, but with lists of people I'd never heard of. I had no idea of anything, so what I would do was to pick at random. A lot of things I'd just throw away, but then I'd find some person that was good and I'd order more of that person. And little by little I built up quite a large collection.

DUCKWORTH: What countries interested you most?

NANCARROW: India, Africa, Indonesia. But India and Africa were the main ones.

DUCKWORTH: Do you still do a lot of listening?

NANCARROW: Many years ago I used to listen a lot, but the last few years I haven't. For one reason or another, especially when I'm working on music, I don't have much time to listen.

DUCKWORTH: The two reasons I've heard given for your decision to write for player piano were that you were isolated and out of touch with musicians, or that you were growing increasingly interested in rhythmic complexity and needed an instrument like the player piano to realize your work. Which of these is really true?

NANCARROW: The second one is the main reason. The first one wasn't so important. I mean, I knew musicians.

DUCKWORTH: Through correspondence?

NANCARROW: No, no; musicians in Mexico. One thing that happened there, for example, was Rodolfo Halffter, who was a friend of mine, asked me to write a piece for the Monday Evening Concerts in Mexico City. So I wrote a trio for clarinet, bassoon, and piano. I went to the first rehearsal. They just read through it very clumsily and I noticed they were very vague about when they were going to get together to rehearse it. There was nothing definite, and then they left. The pianist I knew fairly well—well enough for him to tell me that they were not going to play that and have the audience think they were playing wrong notes. Actually, the program was already printed with that piece on it, but naturally it was never played.

DUCKWORTH: Do you see any connection between your interest in rhythm and Schoenberg's interest in manipulating the twelve tones?

NANCARROW: Well, maybe, though they're totally unrelated in a sense. For example, Schoenberg wasn't interested at all in rhythms. His rhythms are quite four-square. It was all the pitch thing, which I'm not interested in. I mean, they're two different worlds.

DUCKWORTH: What was your feeling, though, about the music that preceded yours? Did you think that the harmonic system was breaking down, as Schoenberg did?

NANCARROW: I don't have much sensitivity to pitch relations. In fact, different tunings don't mean much to me; I don't hear them. I'm a little deaf on that end.

DUCKWORTH: But you hear your rhythmic things.

NANCARROW: Oh, that . . . yes. And I hope other people do.

DUCKWORTH: Some of those sliding values, though, are very difficult. I hear the result, but I don't know if I hear 17 against 18 against 19 against 20. I don't know what I'm supposed to be hearing when I listen for that.

NANCARROW: A later piece was a canon with a tempo ratio of 60 to 61. No one could conceivably hear 60 against 61. That's a relation of speed. One starts out at a certain speed and the other one starts out at a very close speed. They are not supposed to be heard as a close rhythm. The one you're talking about, Number 36, with the 17, 18, 19, 20 ratio is on the borderline. There are a few places in that piece, which I did deliberately, when all four voices are together. There's actually one point where you can hear that temporal relation specifically. Otherwise, again, it's just the speed of one part against the whole.

DUCKWORTH: Do you hear the relationships before you write them?

NANCARROW: Yes.

DUCKWORTH: I understand from John Cage that you have developed a set of patterns that deal with time relationships. Is that true?

NANCARROW: When I write a piece with a certain tempo relationship, I make strips. So when I draw it out, I've already worked out the relationships of, let's say, two things. So I have a strip for this and a strip for that. I keep all of these things even though I very seldom go back to the same relationship. But I have a whole stack of things that I have used. And I have a whole stack of different acceleration ratios that I also keep. Occasionally I use parts of some of those things for other things. But yes, there's a big collection of them.

DUCKWORTH: But for the most part, you don't return to them?

NANCARROW: For the most part, no. They're there. Occasionally I use some of them again, but not too often.

DUCKWORTH: Do you think if your player percussion orchestra had worked successfully that you would ever have gone to the player piano?

NANCARROW: I was already doing player piano things when I started that percussion thing. I wanted to add that to the player piano, with all of it played by rolls. That was the whole point. But it just didn't work. That was a mistake of someone—taking a picture of the drums and publishing it everywhere. In fact, it's had the effect of some nonmusicians hearing a record of my player piano music and commenting on how interesting that percussion music is.

DUCKWORTH: Did you ever actually hear sounds out of the player percussion instrument?

NANCARROW: No, I never got to the point of it functioning. It was a very primitive concept anyhow.

DUCKWORTH: How did you settle on the Ampico pianos as the ones you wanted to use?

NANCARROW: When I started on the whole player piano thing, I didn't know anything about it. I started from scratch. I think some-one told me that Ampico was a good player piano. It's called a reproducing piano. The advantage of a reproducing piano is that you have wide dynamic control, all kinds of things. You control pedals. You can even do different kinds of crescendos on it, slow or fast. I don't use those ever. When I want a crescendo I do it in steps, which you can do with the dynamics. Actually, they're very efficient machines.

DUCKWORTH: Had you tried several before this?

NANCARROW: No, no.

DUCKWORTH: You went straight to the Ampico?

NANCARROW: Yes. Well, I was told that. And after that I heard others which were similar. Each has a different system. You can't play a roll from one system on another system. Each has its own codes for marking those things, so they're not interchangeable.

DUCKWORTH: You grew up with a player piano in your home, didn't you?

NANCARROW: Right. I loved it, just going around playing all kinds of things.

DUCKWORTH: What kind of music did you have for it?

NANCARROW: Well, that's the thing. It was my father's taste. There was a little Chopin. I forget all that was there.

DUCKWORTH: Was it mostly popular music though?

NANCARROW: No, it was so-called serious music. I think some of it was MacDowell-type romantic pieces. Light classical, I guess is the word.

DUCKWORTH: When you decided to begin working with the player piano did you know anything about it mechanically?

NANCARROW: Oh no, I had to start from scratch. As a child I didn't know anything; I just looked at those rolls going through.

DUCKWORTH: So when you got the inheritance, you went to New York and bought a piano?

NANCARROW: And had a machine made for punching, all at the same time. I spent two or three months in New York when I went for that. I didn't know at that time that I could have gone to people in Mexico, which I did later. I have two pianos; I got the other one there. I could have gotten even more. You know there's been a movement in the United States of player piano reviving, and there are many people who make a business of rebuilding those old player pianos and putting them in good condition. Those older ones were very well made. Of course, they eventually wear out. But they're sort of like Rolls Royces; they keep going.

DUCKWORTH: Are you at the point now where you can make almost any repair you need to make?

NANCARROW: Oh, no! That's another thing. People think that if I write for player piano I must have much mechanical ability. In fact, the one man in Mexico who was really good and kept my pianos in shape died not too long ago. So I don't know what I'm going to do. Since he died there have been only a few minor things, which I could do. But a serious repair, I can't do it. The mechanisms are as complicated as a Rolls Royce engine, or more maybe.

DUCKWORTH: Did you decide almost immediately to change the hammers on your pianos?

NANCARROW: Yes. From the very beginning I wanted that. Before I settled on what I have now, I made several experiments. There used to be a thing that they had in player pianos called the mandolin attachment. First I tried that. It was very nice sound that I liked. The only trouble was these little leather strips kept getting tangled among the strings. It was just impractical, so I dropped that. Then I tried soaking the hammers in shellac. Well, that didn't work.

DUCKWORTH: Is it true, as some people have suggested, that you were looking for a harpsichord sound?

NANCARROW: Yes. I like the harpsichord sound and the clarity of the lines that come out. The only trouble is that there are no player harpsichords. It's a very impractical instrument for one thing. I don't know the harpsichord—I've never used one—but I understand that they go out of tune in a few hours. It was just a thought that I would like that harpsichord sound with my pianos.

DUCKWORTH: Which hammers did you finally settle on?

NANCARROW: There are two. One has the regular hammer on the
piano covered with a leather strip that has a little metallic thing at
the striking point. It's not a thumbtack exactly. It still has the cush-
ion of the regular hammer plus the metallic thing. It's not a harpsichord, but it's vaguely in that area.

DUCKWORTH: It puts an edge on it?

NANCARROW: Yes, it sharpens it. The other one is very, very aggressive and hard. It has wooden hammers, pure wood, covered with a
steel strip. That's the one that's much harder.

DUCKWORTH: Which one do you use the most these days?

NANCARROW: I don't know why, but for some time I've been using
what I call the thumbtack piano more than the other. I guess
because the things I've been writing are less aggressive than before.
I still use the other one some, but not as much.

DUCKWORTH: During the period from the 1940s to the 1960s, when
your ideas about rhythmic procedures and polyphonic textures
were developing, what were the models for those?

NANCARROW: There were no models. I started out more or less feeling my way. The first fifteen or twenty studies were just feeling my
way. Also, another thing I had to do was feel my way while learning
what those player pianos could do: how fast they could repeat a
note and how many notes they could hold down at one time. A
hundred different things, which took some time to get used to,
also. Originally I started out thinking just of polyrhythms with a
more or less fixed tempo within that. It was much later that the
idea of polytempo started to develop. One thing led to another.

DUCKWORTH: Why do you suppose that there's that five-year gap in
your writing from 1960 to 1965? Do you have a clear idea why you
quit writing for five years?

NANCARROW: How did you know I did? I don't remember ever men-
tioning it. What happened was I went through a sort of a depression. It wasn't very serious, but enough so that I didn't feel like
writing. I took that time catching up on making legible scores.

DUCKWORTH: Have you always worked directly on the roll?

NANCARROW: No, at the beginning I wrote a piece on regular music
paper. At that time there was no problem; the pieces were mea-

sured and so forth. With the later things, I would get an idea of a tempo relationship—a piece in general outline without details. So I'd take a roll and draw out just the tempo relationships with the smallest value that I would be likely to use. Of course, later, if it was an even smaller one, I'd go back and put it in. Basically that. Already from the beginning I knew how long it would be and the other factors. So I made this roll. Then I would mark off the roll the width of my music paper. I would transfer these temporal things onto this music paper and then just sit down and write the piece. If I had a piece that had to be in 4/4, it was both on the roll and on the paper. Then I would punch it with a score that was pretty much illegible for anyone else, which I called my "punching score." After the piece existed on the roll and punched, I would make the legible score so that people could see it.

DUCKWORTH: With something like the *Boogie-Woogie Suite*, would you have written that out totally and then punched it in?

NANCARROW: Yes, I was writing standard notation.

DUCKWORTH: Did you ever sit down at the piano and try things out as you were writing?

NANCARROW: I don't play.

DUCKWORTH: You don't play piano at all?

NANCARROW: None.

DUCKWORTH: Well, you do have a pitch imagination then, because that piece has some very interesting pitch relationships.

NANCARROW: I can hear the difference between, say, C and D, if that's what you mean!

DUCKWORTH: So you don't see not playing the piano as a problem?

NANCARROW: No, it's not a problem.

DUCKWORTH: A moment ago you were talking about you early works, and you said that in the first fifteen or twenty studies you were just feeling your way. For a long time, one of my favorite pieces of yours was *Study No. 21, Canon X.* Was that a transitional piece in any way?

NANCARROW: In many ways it was. On my original punching machine everything was in notches. That's the way standard pianos make things—by the notches, sixteenths or whatever. There's nothing between notches. *Study No. 21* was the final piece where this just wouldn't work, and I had the punch modified so that I could move the thing that punches to any point. In other words, I'd draw it on the roll and just line it up on a wire. With *No. 21*, that's when I just had to have it. But I didn't have it, so what I did . . . oh, that was an awful amount of work . . . holding the machine halfway through a notch and then a quarter of the way through a notch for the next note. Later, after I got this other thing, I thought of going back and redoing *No. 21* because it's not as smooth as it could be. But I thought, "That's just too much work; I'll let it go that way." It functions, but it could have been better.

DUCKWORTH: So you had a new machine built then?

NANCARROW: No, no. I just had a modification made on the same machine so that I could move it anywhere without having to put it in a notch every time I punched.

DUCKWORTH: Which gave you moving tempos?

NANCARROW: Totally. A note exists somewhere in time, and with this I could put it anywhere in time I wanted to. Of course, I'd draw it on the roll where I wanted to punch it.

DUCKWORTH: *Study No. 25* is usually talked about as the most spectacular of those early pieces.

NANCARROW: Well, it is sort of dramatic. But there's nothing special; it's just a lot of flurry.

DUCKWORTH: I've heard that you don't like the Columbia record that was put out in the early 1960s with twelve of your *Studies* on it.

NANCARROW: No.

DUCKWORTH: Do you think that it misrepresents your music?

NANCARROW: Oh, no. They're accurately recorded, except that the man who recorded it was an amateur electronics fiddler-around, you might say, and he modified the sounds. I don't know whether it's noticeable or not, but it certainly is if you compare that with the Arch recordings.

DUCKWORTH: What about the New World Records recording?

NANCARROW: That recording is just a terrible sound. The pieces they used of mine were done from what Roger Reynolds once recorded with his little portable tape recorder. There's a Cage, a Cowell, and a Johnston on that record, and the sound on all of them is terrible; it's not just mine.

DUCKWORTH: Between the early 1940s and 1960, when you were writing most of your *Studies*, was anyone hearing your music besides you?

NANCARROW: No.

DUCKWORTH: Were you just playing them for yourself?

NANCARROW: Occasionally someone would hear it, but very occasionally. Oh, but there was one thing that happened, also again with this same composer, Rodolfo Halffter. I told you about that concert; that was before the player piano. And then after the player piano, he heard them and he suggested that I give a concert there in the concert hall of the fine arts building. I was very reluctant, but finally he persuaded me. So I took the two pianos down there. Just the trip from where we lived to downtown, and putting the pianos in shape (they are touchy things, those pianos), and going to give a concert for twenty or thirty people, most of whom had already heard it in my studio anyhow, seemed pointless. I never thought of doing that again.

DUCKWORTH: In all that time, though, with so few people hearing your music, did you see any problem with being a composer whose music was never heard?

NANCARROW: What do you mean by problem?

DUCKWORTH: Did it bother you personally?

NANCARROW: Not really. I suppose . . . Actually, I don't know why I kept doing it without some sort of encouragement. I guess deep down I felt, "Well, this is worthwhile doing." Naturally, at times I wondered, "Maybe I'm crazy?" because there are plenty of people who do just that. And they think that it's something but they're doing nothing. Sometimes I thought of that: "Well, maybe this is too."

DUCKWORTH: Did the money from the trust fund allow you to live comfortably during this time?

NANCARROW: Oh, yes . . . for some time. Then I got married and had a child and had to build more living quarters and so forth. Really, the last few years before this MacArthur grant came I was living pretty much on my wife's salary. Now you couldn't buy beans with my wife's salary there. The MacArthur has run out, so I don't know what we're going to do.

DUCKWORTH: Well, you're famous now.

NANCARROW: Famous is not money exactly.

DUCKWORTH: It can be translated into money, though, but at a terrible inconvenience.

NANCARROW: Inconvenience and all kinds of compromises, which I'm not too happy about. Well, we'll see.

DUCKWORTH: Has winning the MacArthur changed your life any way other than making it financially easier?

NANCARROW: Only that.

DUCKWORTH: It hasn't changed you as a composer?

NANCARROW: No, not at all. I think they felt that giving all of that money would have a lot of people going off to a desert island and lying in a hammock doing nothing. It's a possibility; some people react in different ways. At one point, the MacArthur people wrote and asked what effect it had had. I wrote them that it's no more stimulus to work than to be relaxing about where the money's coming from. Some people apparently work better when there's the tension of uncertainty, but I don't think that's the normal way. The normal thing would be you don't have to worry then about these other problems.

DUCKWORTH: How would you describe your working pattern? Do you work every day?

NANCARROW: In the period of my doing all of those things before, yes, I worked every day. And quite a bit every day. But since I have a family it's changed. Sometimes it's this, sometimes that. A recent commission was such a pressure that I was working all the time to get it done. I wasn't used to that kind of pressure. For some years now, I've been turning out less music because of being busier with other things.

DUCKWORTH: Do you work well under pressure?

NANCARROW: No, I don't at all.

DUCKWORTH: Do you ever put yourself under self-imposed pressure when you do your own work?

NANCARROW: No. That's why I think it turns out better. That's the way I prefer working. When I was working a lot, I solved the problem of getting stuck in a piece by working on several pieces at the same time. I would shift to another piece until that cleared up.

DUCKWORTH: You've recently begun to write for traditional instruments again. After not writing for instruments for a long period of time, are you encountering any unexpected problems?

NANCARROW: Not unexpected. They're expected in the sense that I knew I had forgotten about the different things that instruments can do. When I write for player piano I don't worry about those things: Will a finger go there? Will it do this? Will it do all of these other things? With a live pianist you have to be constantly aware of that; with player piano, you don't. If you want a note there, you put that note there.

DUCKWORTH: What about writing for string instruments and wind instruments?

NANCARROW: Since I'm out of touch, I have to look up the range of the oboe and that sort of thing.

DUCKWORTH: Are you able to anticipate the timbres and how things are going to fit together?

NANCARROW: I think so. Maybe not very well.

DUCKWORTH: How do you want history to remember you?

NANCARROW: I don't know. Whatever history thinks of me. And furthermore, I have nothing to say about it anyhow.

DUCKWORTH: Are there any things that you expected me to ask you that I didn't ask, but perhaps should have?

NANCARROW: No, to the contrary. You asked more than I expected you to.

DUCKWORTH: And I think that for somebody with the reputation of having nothing to say that you've said a lot.

NANCARROW: Well, you've provoked me. I can answer questions.

MILTON BABBITT

Born Philadelphia, 1916

THE MORE ONE learns about Milton Babbitt, the more contradictory he seems. The party line on him is that he is a technologically oriented, mathematically inclined, twelve-tone, academic composer. John Rockwell, in his 1983 book, *All American Music*, refers to him as "perhaps the most complex composer ever." And Babbitt would probably agree with much of that, except maybe the "most complex" part. He offers both Brian Ferneyhough and Kaikhosru Shapurji Sorabji as examples of composers who write far more complicated and difficult music than he has ever written.

But there are other sides that complicate the picture. For example, Babbitt once wrote a musical comedy based on Homer's *Odyssey*, calling it *Fabulous Voyage*. He also wrote a film score for Pathescope. And he claims to remember the lyrics of more than 4,000 popular songs. Furthermore, there is the question of exactly what type of secret government work he did in Washington during World War II; whatever it was, he doesn't feel free to talk about it even now. And for all the talk about the mathematical fastidiousness of his music, there is the memory of his office at Princeton, which was, without a doubt, the messiest academic office I have ever seen.

Although born in Philadelphia, Milton Babbitt grew up in Jackson, Mississippi. He began studying violin at four, and later took up the clarinet and saxophone. His interests at the time were primarily popular music and jazz, although he did have some exposure to European classical music—primarily Italian opera—through his father, who was foreign born. But when Babbitt was ten, he heard something that changed his musical life forever. On one of his summer visits to his relatives in Philadelphia, an uncle, who had studied piano at Curtis, played a piece by Arnold Schoenberg. And although Babbitt has never been able to determine exactly which piece it was, he still describes the moment as his "great awakening."

Milton Babbitt at the RCA Mark II Synthesizer, New York, 1964

An accelerated student who started school early, Babbitt began college at the University of Pennsylvania in Philadelphia at the age of fifteen. There was no music major, he could not get the courses he wanted, so he completed his final two years at New York University, graduating in 1935. Through Martin Bernstein, one of his teachers at NYU, Babbitt met Arnold Schoenberg, who lived briefly in New York. And through others he became acquainted with Igor Stravinsky and Edgard Varèse.

Instead of going to graduate school, Babbitt, who was nineteen by this point, began studying composition privately with Roger Sessions, who had recently returned to New York after an extended stay in Europe. Babbitt worked with Sessions for three years, becoming a friend as well as a student. Later, when Sessions began teaching at Princeton, he hired Babbitt to be his assistant.

After his work in Washington during the war, Babbitt returned to Princeton. In the late 1950s, he and Vladimir Ussachevsky of Columbia University, with a grant from the Rockefeller Foundation, established the Columbia-Princeton Electronic Music Studio, the centerpiece of which was the RCA Mark II synthesizer, the most powerful electronic instrument available to musicians at that time. Working in this New York studio, Babbitt created some of his most compelling music, including the 1961 *Vision and Prayer*, for soprano and synthesizer, and, in 1964, *Philomel*, written with poet John Hollander for soprano Bethany Beardslee. For Babbitt, the importance of the synthesizer was never the creation of new sounds. Instead, he was always fascinated by the amount of control over events that it offered.

We decided to hold our conversation in his office at Juilliard, where he continues to teach after retiring from Princeton. Appropriately, I was scheduled in between a graduate composition student that morning, and a committee meeting later in the afternoon. But when we sat down to talk, we were comfortable and relaxed. For some reason I don't quite yet understand, I have, since our first meeting, always been friends with Milton. Perhaps it's because we're both from the South.

DUCKWORTH: How old were you when your family moved from Philadelphia to Jackson, Mississippi?

BABBITT: My family never lived in Philadelphia. I'll be happy to get that straight.

DUCKWORTH: Weren't you born there?

BABBITT: Yes. But only because my mother's family lived there. My mother was always going to have me born in Philadelphia. My two later brothers were also born there. It was just an old American tradition: you go back to be with your parents when you're going to have a baby.

DUCKWORTH: So your mother went back to Philadelphia?

BABBITT: My mother went back to Philadelphia; my father was teaching mathematics in Nebraska. He was an academic mathematician who had gone to Penn State University and did his graduate work at Illinois. And just about the time that he was going to continue his work, what happened to him is something that later happened to me. That is, he was grabbed up to teach mathematics for people who would be involved in the war. (People don't realize they did that in World War I.) And he was shipped out to the University of Nebraska.

DUCKWORTH: What kind of mathematics did your father teach?

BABBITT: It was a kind of applied mathematics that had to do with probability, which later led him into actuarial work. So he was wanted for that, and he was directed to go to the University of Minnesota. I think, actually, I was conceived at the University of Minnesota. Then he went to Nebraska. My mother had me in Philadelphia only for a few weeks. Then she rejoined my father and we all went to Jackson as soon as the war was over.

DUCKWORTH: So you're really a good ol' Southern boy.

BABBITT: Oh, completely. My education was totally in the South: primary school, secondary school, and high school. Of course, they were all public schools; you never heard of a private school. No indeed, I was brought up in Jackson. I'm strickly a native Mississippian.

DUCKWORTH: I understand you began playing the violin when you were four.

BABBITT: You know, it was a curious thing. I don't know about your part of the South, but in our South boys did not study the piano. Girls went for piano lessons. Boys started strings and all the things one would play in a band.

DUCKWORTH: Four years old is pretty young though, isn't it?

BABBITT: I started school when I was five.

DUCKWORTH: Did you show a talent for the violin?

BABBITT: I guess it was that. You know, you go to the piano and you pick out things. We didn't have a piano, as a matter of fact. My family was not musical. We had a Victrola; we had records. But there were neighbors next door, and I went there and picked out stuff on their piano.

DUCKWORTH: Do you have perfect pitch?

BABBITT: Yes. And so I went to Maude Hutchenson, my first violin teacher. A dear, routinely competent violinist who played in sort of a Palm Court trio at the Edwards Hotel down on Capitol Street. We used to go there for Sunday dinner.

DUCKWORTH: Were you a good student?

BABBITT: I wasn't really interested in practicing. I soon discovered that I could play by ear, and I could remember things easily. I'd take the violin and play tunes on it . . . play around.

DUCKWORTH: Did you play in any school groups?

BABBITT: I played in the orchestra, but it was terrible; you know, kids playing stringed instruments. But we had what we called the Jackson Boys' Band. It wasn't a high school band, it was a municipal band. And I went to Mr. Pulow, who could hardly speak English (He was an Italian trumpet and flute player who married a Mississippi girl; she brought him back to Mississippi to live in Jackson at a boarding house. And he hated it.) I said "I want to learn trumpet." But he told me, "I think since you're really interested in music you'd enjoy more playing the clarinet, because you'd have a chance to play more interesting things than with the trumpet, which has limited parts." So I started playing the clarinet and it became my instrument.

DUCKWORTH: Did your interests always lean toward music?

BABBITT: Oh, indeed. I played clarinet; I played every reed instrument; I played in every jazz group; I played in the band; and I played in every pit orchestra that came to town. That's how I know all these tunes. One night we'd be playing at a country club trying to imitate Guy Lombardo, the next night we'd be playing for younger people and we'd try to imitate Jean Goldkette, who led one of the early big bands we used to hear on the radio from Detroit. I grew up with pop; I grew up with jazz. I played on Saturday nights when I was ten years old with some musicians who had come up from New Orleans. And there was a kind of music—not that I played, but that I heard— called "pig stand jazz." The pig stands were barbecue, pork barbecue. You'd drive up and you'd be waited curb service, as they used to call it. You'd eat in your car. They would have bands to attract people. Well, those bands couldn't have pianos by the very nature of the installation, so they would have a very strange instrumentation. (They were mixed black and white. When it came to music, of course, nobody paid any attention.) And they would normally play a kind of Dixieland. The one music we never heard was ragtime. That was considered old-fashioned stuff. By the mid-twenties ragtime belonged-to the past. What we were hearing was jazz.

DUCKWORTH: Was your early interest primarily in popular music?

BABBITT: Bill, it was all of it. I can remember playing, for example, in
the pit of Victor Herbert operas. I remember playing in *The Red
Mill*; I remember playing in a road version of *No, No, Nanette*. I
read *Metronome* magazine; I read *Variety*. I played all kinds of
music.

DUCKWORTH: Did you have an interest in classical music at all?

BABBITT: Yes, because of my father. My father was foreign born, and
he knew a lot of Italian opera. We had all those [Victor] Red Seal
records—one-sided Red Seal Records—with Italian opera, a great
deal of French and Russian opera, not much German opera. Quite
typically, he really wasn't interested in Wagner. I didn't hear much
chamber music. But, remember my Philadelphia connections. My
mother would take me to Philadelphia every other summer to stay
with my grandparents. And at the age of ten came, really, the great
awakening. This sounds melodramatic, but it happens to be literally
true. I have a dear old uncle who was a Curtis [Institute of Music]
product, who actually studied with all kinds of people who later
became justly celebrated. He studied piano; he went to Curtis; he
composed. And at the age of ten (I'll never forget), he thought it
would be amusing to play some music at me. What he played at me
we're not sure, because he was playing a lot of contemporary music.
Probably, it was the Schoenberg Opus 11 (I'm not sure it wasn't the
Opus 19 pieces), and the Stravinsky Piano Sonata.

In those days there was a lot of contemporary music being
played around Philadelphia. There was Marc Blitzstein, for example,
who was on his way to study with Schoenberg in Berlin. There was
a man named Isadore Freed, who had been studying in Paris, who
later edited *The Masters of Our Day* series for [Theodore] Presser
[music publishers]. And there was a man named Paul Nordoff, an
extraordinary musician who was one of the great white hopes of
American music in the twenties. He could sit down and play eighty
concerti from memory; most of them were contemporary. He was
in Curtis being supported by Paul Whiteman. Extraordinary man;
we often played together. I remember playing the Reger *Clarinet
Sonata* with him. So there were these people, and my uncle was
very much in the middle of this. And when he played these things
at me, it was one of those unforgettable experiences. That same
year I heard the Philadelphia Orchestra play the Brahms Third
Symphony, and that I haven't forgotten either. I began to try to imitate this music.

DUCKWORTH: As a composer?

BABBITT: As a composer . . . preposterous things. But I never, never
forgot that. And the one name that stuck with me was Schoenberg.
Later, when I went up to Philadelphia and got to know these people more, they would even give me scores. I had an uncle who was
one of the first serious film critics. He went off to Paris, and when
he came back he brought me a miniature score of the Honegger
First Symphony. It must be a collector's item. So I had a very fortunate family relationship there.

DUCKWORTH: In retrospect, why do you suppose the Schoenberg
piece stayed with you the most?

BABBITT: You know, I don't know. I simply remember that I kept
thinking about it. It had a tremendous effect. My uncle just thought
it was sort of amusing; he couldn't make much of it. My uncle was
one of these real Curtis products. He would practice the Schumann
Novelettes all summer.

DUCKWORTH: Is there a lot of musical talent in your family?

BABBITT: Actually, my uncle and his wife are the only ones who had
anything to do with music.

DUCKWORTH: Did that open any doors for you?

BABBITT: Oh, sure it did. Remember, I entered school when I was
five years old. And they decided I wasn't correct for the first grade,
so they put me up in second grade. Now I tell you this only
because it was one of the most dreadful things that ever happened
to me, and I'm not being coy or modest. The result was I graduated
from high school when I was fifteen, and went off to college. I
wanted to go to Tulane, but they wouldn't accept me because I was
too young. So I went off to the University of Pennsylvania—back to
Philadelphia again—my mother's family's traditional school. The
whole family was there: I had an uncle who was in the law school, I
had a cousin who was in the graduate school.

DUCKWORTH: Had you thought about going to a conservatory?

BABBITT: I remember my father walking me down to the basement
in Jackson and saying, "Shouldn't you go to a music school?" My
father was European; his idea was musicians go to conservatories.
But I had already seen enough of these kids at Curtis. I had seen

them; I had talked with them; I had played a great deal with them during the summer. I was a virtuoso clarinet player. And I played a lot of saxophone, too. So I said to him, "No, I've seen this. I don't want to be an orchestral clarinetist. Even if I can get a job, it's no life. I've been playing all of my life. I'm tired of it. I'm tired of practicing and I'm tired of playing. I'm not interested in going to a conservatory. I just want to go to college." Well, remember, there was practically no place you could go to college and study music at the same time. There were no music departments to speak of. The only music department that was sort of fun, but not for composers, was Harvard. Remember, Elliott Carter went to Harvard and majored in English.

DUCKWORTH: Did you major in mathematics?

BABBITT: You know, Bill, that's another one of the things I hope we'll finally clear up. My undergraduate major was music; my graduate degree is in music. I never took a degree in mathematics. Do you think if I were in mathematics I'd waste my time in this ridiculous profession?

DUCKWORTH: What kinds of things did you study?

BABBITT: I was interested in math. I was never going to major, but I wanted to learn some stuff. But I got so sick of, what can you call it, cookbook mathematics—differential equations, engineering mathematics—uninteresting stuff. I then took a course in logic. It was sort of Bertrand Russell logic, very much the *Principia*. It was a freshman logic course, but symbolic logic, very close to mathematical logic. There were also things that I wasn't interested in. I wasn't interested in languages, for example. But I took a lot of philosophy of science, mainly in the philosophy department. I thought I would major in philosophy . . . until I discovered I would have to take an aesthetics course. Well, I took an aesthetics course, and an ethics course, and I found it such unadulterated bullshit, I really couldn't take it. That's when I decided I really had to get out of Penn.

DUCKWORTH: Were you involved in a lot of musical activities at Penn?

BABBITT: I played in the marching band; it got me out of ROTC. And I shared first-chair clarinet with a man named David Raksin, who later wrote "Laura." David was a real Philadelphia kid, he knew the ropes. We were playing gigs everywhere. We played in every studio band, we played at every dance. We both played clarinets and saxes. David was older than I, I think by a couple of years. In any case, we became very, very close friends. Then, he went off to New York and became an arranger. He worked for what is now Chappell [music publishers]; it was then called Harms. Soon after, he was out in Hollywood where he was writing Charlie Chaplin's music for him. And he was one of those Hollywood arrangers who went to study with Schoenberg and Stravinsky. He then wrote some very famous scores; "Laura" is the most celebrated because of the tune. He's still alive and well. I see him all the time out in Hollywood. He had a tremendous effect on me, because during those two years we were together—my freshman and sophomore years at Penn—we heard a great deal of music. We heard the Philadelphia Orchestra, and we talked about a lot of music together. He had tremendous curiosity. And that was really a very important aspect of my life at that time, much more important than anything I did in the classroom.

DUCKWORTH: Were you writing popular music at that point?

BABBITT: I wrote a lot of pop tunes for school productions; I made lots of arrangements. But every once in a while into those arrangements I'd sneak in things that I thought I had learned from looking into more serious scores. God knows what it all sounded like because we had enough trouble playing. There were some very, very adept musicians among my friends, and some who weren't so adept. I'd write out lead sheets for pop tunes. In those days you didn't write chords, you didn't need to do any of that. We sometimes wrote ukelele indications; we all played ukelele.

DUCKWORTH: Did you ever consider a career in popular music?

BABBITT: I came to New York and talked to Max Dreyfus, who was the great man who ran Harms Music in those days, who had discovered and nurtured Gershwin, Rodgers and Hart, and Cole Porter. The reason I got to him was because the Dreyfus family was a very big family in Jackson; they gave me a letter of introduction. I didn't really work there, but I did hang around there a great deal, played around at the piano, and taught people songs. On the one hand, I did think maybe I would be in the popular song business, which is rather ironic considering what I got caught up in later. But I really wanted no part of show business. I couldn't stand the people; I couldn't stand the milieu. I was fifteen, and I simply went to college.

DUCKWORTH: What kind of aesthetic distinction were you making at that point between popular and serious music?

BABBITT: Bill, I never thought in terms, I must confess to you (even less than I do now), of aesthetics. When I began thinking about so-called serious music there was a kind of confusion in my mind. Not between popular and serious, but between the music I read about in [Ebenezer] Prout and [Percy] Goetschius, and the Schoenberg, which I'd already heard, the little Webern violin and piano pieces, which I had heard at Curtis, and a great deal of contemporary music, which I heard played by my uncle and his friends. By the time I went to Penn, when I was fifteen, I had heard a lot of ill-assorted pieces of all kinds. I certainly knew I wanted to study music; the question was how to do it.

DUCKWORTH: What was your earliest serious music like? Do you remember it?

BABBITT: Unfortunately, I do. It seems so anecdotal it's preposterous. When I was studying the violin (I couldn't have been more than five or six), my dear teacher said, "Look, here's the sort of piece you want to learn to play someday," and she gave me the violin part of the Mendelssohn Violin Concerto. Well, I thought this was the piece; and in those manuscript pages you always got in the back of your exercise book, I began writing a violin concerto. Don't ask me what it was like; it was for unaccompanied violin, which was, after all, pretty cute. It was totally, totally imitative.

DUCKWORTH: What did your family say about your decision to leave Penn?

BABBITT: I had, as I told you, an uncle in law school and a cousin in the graduate school. These were sophisticated people, cultivated people. They said, "Look, you spend all your time in music. You're either hanging around the piano, or you're out playing one kind of gig or another, or you're going to listen to music. You have to be in music. It's ridiculous. Leave this place."

DUCKWORTH: Where did you go?

BABBITT: I decided maybe I was a southern boy misplaced, and I looked around for a music department in a university. It was a question of either Vanderbilt or Chapel Hill, and I chose Chapel Hill, because Vanderbilt had no music department. It was the Depression;

it was 1933. American tobacco B was in very bad shape. My room-
mate never turned up, for example; nobody could afford to go to
school. I couldn't take it, so at Thanksgiving I went home. I've
never wanted to talk about this because it really had to do with the
whole state of the South. It was such a dreadful time. My father
understood. I went home at Thanksgiving.

DUCKWORTH: How did you get from there to New York University?

BABBITT: I read this book by Marion Bauer called *Twentieth Century
Music*. That was one of the great turning points. Here was a book
about twentieth-century music in which there were musical examples that I could sit down and play, or at least look at. And she knew
about Schoenberg; she had examples from, I think, *Erwartung*.
And she had Stravinsky, Roy Harris, and Richard Donovan. And I
thought, "This is where I have to be," so I went to Washington
Square College/NYU and had the happiest days of my life. I spent
my last two years of college there. I graduated in '35.

DUCKWORTH: What was Marion Bauer like?

BABBITT: Marion Bauer was one of the dearest, most wonderful creatures in the world. The only thing was that her basic orientation
was [Nadia] Boulanger. She had studied with Boulanger. She was
very French oriented, very much in the Boulanger tradition, except
she wasn't that kind of personality. She was a dear lady from Walla
Walla; she wasn't a stern lady from France. And she was very much
a . . . let's simply say unmarried. But she was an absolute dear. I
didn't really learn much from her. She had nothing much to say
except what was in her book. And if you've ever looked at the book
you know it's a collection of quotations from everybody. But look,
it was the only one in English.

DUCKWORTH: What made NYU so exciting for you? Why was it the
best time of your life?

BABBITT: I went to study with Marion Bauer, but as I say, it turned out
that she was just a dear lady. But I encountered Martin Bernstein.
Now Martin had very little to do with contemporary music, but he
was a terrific teacher; he was an extraordinary man with broad, broad
interests. And as soon as I ran into Martin and he discovered I'd had
so much experience playing, we became very good friends within a
matter of a couple of months. And he said, "You know, of course,
that Arnold Schoenberg is in town." Schoenberg had decided he

couldn't take the Boston climate and had moved into the Ansonia Hotel. And I'll never forget saying to Martin, "Should I go? I understand he's giving courses." He said, "No, they're not real courses. He's making some money. These are just amateurs, he's talking in the most general terms." Then he said, "He's going to teach here next year." Every school thought that Schoenberg was going to teach there next year—NYU, Juilliard. They all wanted him to teach. Martin asked Schoenberg to write the *Suite for String Orchestra* for the NYU student orchestra and he agreed. But Schoenberg's brother-in-law, Felix Grassler, who had a job at [the music publisher] Schirmer's, said to him, "Look, you don't want a student orchestra to have a first performance of a new piece by Schoenberg." And Schoenberg said, "Well, this is not really an important piece. It's not a twelve-tone piece, it's just a little tonal . . . ." He says, "Klemperer is out in Los Angeles; he'd love to have it." So, the piece was sent to Klemperer and Martin Bernstein never forgave Schoenberg; it was supposed to have been our piece. At that point, of course, Schoenberg decided he couldn't take the New York climate anymore than he could the Boston climate and off he went to California. And that was the end of that. But Martin Bernstein became a dear friend.

DUCKWORTH: Had you talked to Schoenberg by that point?

BABBITT: Oh, sure. But let's have one thing clear, Bill. (I want to do this to protect myself since I've become so close with the whole Schoenberg clan.) I didn't see much of him, really. It's become very unclear to me what times I did have a chance to talk with Schoenberg. I met him mainly through Martin Bernstein.

DUCKWORTH: Does the story about you suggesting the term *set* to Schoenberg have any truth to it?

BABBITT: That was that business about twelve-tone set, twelve-tone series, twelve-tone row. Schoenberg heard people calling these things *rows* and he didn't like that term. He was learning English assiduously. It was bad, but he was learning it. And he didn't like the idea of a row. He said, "This makes people think it's like a theme. I don't want that. I want another word." I said *series*, which is the logical word. I mean, that's the word from other fields in which some way there's an ordering. It doesn't imply in music anything about a theme or a motive; that's what he wanted to avoid. He wanted to get this underlying notion of an ordering. And he talked to some of his German friends, who obviously knew more than I did because they were German, and they said, "Oh no, no. Series is no good. Series always implies a trigonometric series, or an arithmetic series." Which is nonsense, of course. It's a serial relationship; it's a series in the most traditional, relational sense. So finally, one day, I came up with *set*. I said, "Look, it has no meaning in music, therefore, it doesn't have any connotations. And it doesn't mean an ordering in any other field; it just means a collection. Perhaps if you apply it to a twelve-tone, twelve-note, twelve-pitch-classes, it should be *set*. Then it might imply that it's ordered." He loved *set*; it was something new to him. Then he went out to California where he was corrupted in that way like others, so he called it *basic set*, which of course is misleading, because how do you know it's basic? The whole idea of contextual determination and what is the central reference was lost. Schoenberg, I'm not sure—I must be honest about it, Bill—I don't know how much he understood me when I talked to him. I talked too fast. His English was poor. I tried hard, and I didn't dare ask him to speak to me in German, which I probably could have handled (I already knew some German). But that would have been insulting because he wanted to learn English. And though he talked German with other Germans, for an American boy to say, "Please talk German," would have been patronizing.

DUCKWORTH: It's beginning to sound like you had a number of conversations with him.

BABBITT: No, because I saw him when he came East, later on, when he came back to conduct the first *Pierrot Lunaire*. That was at Town Hall, and I can tell you about that. By that time I already knew [Rudolf] Kolisch and [Edward] Steuermann quite well, and I knew, I guess, the other people playing. And I was sitting with my little *Pierrot* score, getting as close as I dared, and at one point Kolisch stopped Schoenberg and said, "Schoenberg, you've notated a harmonic here in a certain way. I don't really think that I have to play it that way; it makes for a very difficult transition. Why don't I give you the same result but I'll finger the harmonic differently from the way you have it. See if you don't think it's alright." Schoenberg said, "No, do it the way I wrote it." Kolisch said, "Well, let me play it both ways to you and show you why it's easier for me to make a better continuity and phrase it better if I use my fingering." Schoenberg said, "No, no, no. Do it the way I did it. That's it." Later on, I said to

Steuermann, "You know, Kolisch is his brother-in-law and he calls him Schoenberg. Does anybody call him by his first name?" Steuermann said, "Well, sometimes his wife does, but he doesn't like it." Another thing: Schoenberg would not go near a piano. He wouldn't so much as touch a key on a piano.

DUCKWORTH: Why not?

BABBITT: Because he was embarrassed that he wasn't a piano virtuoso. He didn't want to make a fool of himself. Even in harmony classes he would always have a Leonard Stein, or a Gerald Strang, and he'd say, "Mr. Stein, play a C major triad." He just wouldn't do it. He had these wonderful ears, and he'd write on the board very quickly and could hear everything he was doing with the greatest of ease, obviously.

DUCKWORTH: Did you ever actually study with Schoenberg?

BABBITT: Oh no, absolutely not. I never saw him for that length of time.

DUCKWORTH: By that point, were you more interested in him than in any other contemporary composer?

BABBITT: Oh, absolutely. No doubt about it.

DUCKWORTH: Wasn't there a period of time when you were also interested in Stravinsky's work?

BABBITT: Oh, I was always interested in Stravinsky. I met Stravinsky for the first time, I think, when he conducted *Jeu de cartes* at the Metropolitan Opera House's first performance. I think Arthur Berger introduced us. And we talked a little bit. He remembered that. Out in Santa Fe, he asked me, "How did you really feel about my music?" But by "me" he meant all of us who were obviously more oriented toward Schoenberg, or even toward certain American composers. He had a strange feeling that there was a real dichotomy, and that all music was divided into three camps: Schoenberg; Stravinsky; and those who didn't like either. We had a very hard time. And I say "we," because I was not the only one of whom he asked this.

DUCKWORTH: What attracted you to *Jeu de cartes*?

BABBITT: I went to hear *Jeu de cartes* because I wanted to hear *Jeu de cartes*. And, of course, we all studied Stravinsky. But you know, we did have a tendency to take two composers much more for granted than we did Schoenberg: Stravinsky and Hindemith. We all found Hindemith much easier to imitate. And though his music never, never attracted me that much, it was very much more imitable. By this time there was a party line going on—I don't mean among other composers so much as teachers and performing musicians—that ran: "Poor Stravinsky, he's finished. He wrote those wonderful early works, and then he wrote these dreadful, thin, bad, Baroque imitations, this really sterile music such as the *Symphony of Psalms* or the *Octet*. All this awful stuff now; the poor man is obviously finished." But the fact was that I knew the *Octet* better than practically any other piece; I made a piano arrangement of the *Octet* for myself to study it.

DUCKWORTH: What other composers did you have an interest in?

BABBITT: Well, down the street on Sullivan Street, two blocks from NYU, was Edgard Varèse. And Marion Bauer said, "Why don't you go talk to Varèse?" And when I did, the main thing about the discussion with him that surprised me was that he felt very close to Schoenberg. He said, "We exchange scores." He said he hated Stravinsky. He denounced Stravinsky; loved Schoenberg; talked to me about Schoenberg; and I told him what I was interested in. And there was some question of my going to study with him, but then we both decided that that was not for me . . . not yet, at least.

DUCKWORTH: What made you decide that Roger Sessions was the person you should study with?

BABBITT: What happened was, when I was at NYU I had a tremendous time; I had a marvelous time. New York in the thirties, my boy, it was the most eloquent, beautiful, quiet, safe, remarkable city, with bookstores lining the streets between Astor Place and 14th Street on Fourth Avenue . . . at least twenty bookstores, just a block from NYU. It was absolute heaven. So when I got out of there I knew I was going to stay in New York, and I went to Marion Bauer and I said, "Now I really have to get down to serious work as a composer." I was nineteen. And she told me that Roger Sessions was back from Europe and I would probably find him interesting.

DUCKWORTH: Were you familiar with Sessions's music?

BABBITT: When I went to study with Roger, the only pieces of his that I really knew were *The Black Maskers* and his First Piano Sonata.

DUCKWORTH: Did you know him personally?

BABBITT: No, never met him. He'd just come back from Europe. He came back from Hitler's Germany in terrible shape. He was living on the top of a dreadful brownstone on 61st or 62nd Street over something called the Grandbury Piano School. They gave him an attic in which there were a couple of old grand pianos. Well, he was living like a pig. I'll tell you very honestly, my father kept him alive for the next couple of years. We were very well off and my father simply paid for my lessons well in advance so that he could have money to get a divorce. So I went there with my scores. And by that time I'd done my student work; I had a string quartet.

DUCKWORTH: Was your father understanding about private study, or did you have to convince him?

BABBITT: My father was simply wonderful to me. He said, "Sure, go ahead. You don't want to go to graduate school." There was really no place to go. People were trying to convince me I should go into ethnomusicology; that was the future. Do you realize they were saying that in 1935? I wasn't interested in ethnomusicology. But there was no place to go as a composer. The only possibility was Harvard; Walter Piston was there. I didn't want to go to Boston. I had met Walter a couple of times and liked him very much, but who wanted to be in Boston? I liked New York and I wanted to stay here. So I went to study with Roger privately.

DUCKWORTH: How long did you study with him?

BABBITT: Three years. The first lesson I took was on a Saturday afternoon, and the person who took the lesson either before me or after me was David Diamond. I'll never forget, we walked downtown together and we went to Associated Music Publishers, who had an office in a building in the forties where they had all the European scores. And we bought miniature scores of the Bartók *Music for Strings, Percussion, and Celesta*, which we had never heard but we'd been reading about in *Modern Music* magazine. That's the way the world was.

DUCKWORTH: What kind of music did you show to Sessions at that first lesson?

BABBITT: When I went to Roger I brought him several scores. One was a huge orchestral piece which I had just started called *Generatrix* . . . strictly Varèse derived. And he said, "Well, this is an orchestration exercise." Then he looked at the quartet, which was . . . oh, you name it . . . Hindemith, Ernst Toch . . . obviously imitations.

DUCKWORTH: So even though you were interested in Schoenberg, he hadn't played any real part in what your early music sounded like?

BABBITT: No. As a matter of fact, Webern played more of a part. There were some little imitation Webern pieces in the collection. And I didn't know what the hell I was doing, and I knew it, and I said so. I was just sort of imitating by ear.

DUCKWORTH: Did you get many performances of your serious music in college?

BABBITT: No, nobody did.

DUCKWORTH: So as a student, you wrote music that you didn't hear except in your mind?

BABBITT: Bill, you can't imagine what life was like. There was simply no contemporary music played. I heard Roger Sessions's *Black Maskers* at a WPA concert out at the Brooklyn Museum conducted by a conductor, Chalmers Clifton, who happened to come from Jackson, Mississippi. That's how I knew about the concert. I heard his First Piano Sonata in a class; Marion Bauer had John Kirkpatrick come and play it. She had another pianist named Harrison Kerr come and play for us the Griffes Piano Sonata, which nobody knew. Kerr lived up the street, and my wife-to-be, who was in school with me at that time, studied piano with him. There was no music to be had. You know, when I left NYU in 1935, Marion Bauer asked me if I would do reviews for *The Musical Leader*, a sheet like *Musical Courier* and *Musical America*, except it was centered in Chicago. Well, I was sent to *all* the contemporary music concerts, which meant about one a month. The only contemporary music concerts of any significance were a series of chamber music concerts at the New School for Social Research, each devoted to a composer. There was one for Roger Sessions, Virgil Thomson, Aaron Copland, Walter Piston, and Bernard Wagenaar, who cut a large figure in those days. He was a Dutchman who taught at Juilliard—very good, solid, sort of international music. Then Ashley Pettis founded the Composers Forum in the late thirties. Two composers would be presented in each concert with questions from the audience after-wards. That was down in a little basement on Park Avenue. And that was it. There was no other contemporary music, except an

Milton Babbitt, 1983

occasional League of Composers concert, of which there couldn't have been more than three or four a year.

DUCKWORTH: Were the orchestras not playing any contemporary music?

BABBITT: No, of course not. Yes, there would be an occasional American composer who would come along. For example, Robert McBride: I think Artur Rodzinski, who was conducting the Philharmonic at that time, played a work of his called *Prelude to a Tragedy*. There were a few people like that who were performed, and there were the small concerts, but there was very little activity. For a student in school . . . out of the question!

DUCKWORTH: Were there many young composers in New York at that time?

BABBITT: Well, when the preliminary meetings for what became the ACA were being held, Roy Harris, Roger Sessions, Aaron Copland, and some other people of that generation were in charge, and they were all asked to bring any of their students who might be interested in becoming future members of ACA. The main qualification was that they were dedicated to becoming composers professionally. Well, there were about twelve of us. That was it.

DUCKWORTH: Had you given up playing the clarinet by that point?

BABBITT: More or less. Does the name Philip James mean anything to you?

DUCKWORTH: I know you studied with him at NYU.

BABBITT: Well, he had been a band conductor in World War I. He was such an accomplished conductor of a certain kind that he had one of the most strategic jobs in New York: he was the conductor at radio station WOR. Remember, every radio station had its own symphony orchestra.. And he gave a different concert every night. Philip would send people to me who wanted to learn enough on the clarinet so they could write for it, or who had wind arrangements they were working on. My performance dropped to that—a certain amount of teaching.

DUCKWORTH: Were you still playing jazz and pop music?

BABBITT: Not anymore. By that time it was all over.

DUCKWORTH: Had your interest in it waned, or were you just too busy?

BABBITT: Oh, my interest in popular music began to wane. I heard it on the radio, purely passively.

DUCKWORTH: A few moments ago you said that a critical aspect of your work with Sessions had been the fact that he knew a lot of people from Europe. What did you mean by that?

BABBITT: Roger was important to me, not only because he was Roger, but because he had come from Europe. And every European refugee who came here was a friend of Roger's. The day [Ernst] Kreneck got off the boat I had Christmas dinner with him at Roger's house in Princeton. (Roger by that time was teaching at Princeton.) I met Kreneck the day he arrived here. I even got my only piano lesson that way. Roger took me over to see [Karl] Schnabel one afternoon. We were just going over to say hello and talk. You know, Schnabel's favorite composer in all the world was Schoenberg. And once somebody said to him, "Schnabel, why don't you play Schoenberg if you love the music so?" He said, "It's very simple. Schoenberg is not problematical to me; I play only problematical music." Well, one day I walked in there with Roger and Schnabel said to me, "Babbitt" (we were on last name terms, naturally), "you know popular music, don't you?" I said, "I used to know a lot; I don't keep up much with it now." He said, "Do you know something called 'The Music Goes Round and Round?'" He'd been reading a magazine, I think it was *The Nation*, in which there was some offhand remark about the kind of junk that's dominating the world. He said, "Do you know how it goes?" So I went over to the piano and played a little bit of it. He said, "You're twisting your wrists. That's no way to play." I said, "Look, I'm not a pianist. And I've never really had any piano instruction." He said, "Well, look, you've got to bring your hands over like this. You can't twist them." I don't know what I was doing, but I'm a student of Schnabel's in piano!

DUCKWORTH: How often did you meet with Sessions for a lesson?

BABBITT: I met him for a lesson once a week, but I saw him much more than that. By that time, Sylvia and I were rather deeply involved and he was deeply devoted to her. We would bring him cologne; he loved colognes. He couldn't afford anything. He was involved with a librarian who became his second wife. He wanted to get a divorce from his first wife, who was in New England by then. He didn't have the money to go out to Reno. He had an old car. And that's when my father gave advance money for lessons for the next eleven years so that he could go there. That's a slight exaggeration, but only slight. We became very, very close. So much so that we didn't talk about certain things.

DUCKWORTH: What was Sessions position on the Schoenberg/ Stravinsky question?

BABBITT: Roger, at that time, was still very anti—I don't want to say anti–Schoenberg, but that would be fair, too—but sort of anti– Central European. He had just come from Germany. He'd seen Hitler come to power. He regarded all of this as being one and the same. On the other hand, he was very upset at being called a Stravinskyian, because he had grave reservations about Stravinsky's music. But one of the first pieces we looked at together was Stra- vinsky's Piano Concerto. And something your generation doesn't realize, none of those were available in score. All of that stuff was published by Boosey and Hawkes after World War II. He only had a two-piano arrangement. He had learned *Le sacre du printemps* from a four-hand arrangement, though by that time we had a score of that. And he was very much interested in what Stravinsky was thinking about. He had met Stravinsky, had known him from Europe as he had most people. And he knew my Schoenbergian tastes, so he said, "Look, you go ahead and write your music."

See, I didn't finish that story about when I met him the first time. He looked at my music—the fake Varèse, and the fake what have you—and he said, "Tell me, how long do you want to study with me?" I said, "Three years." He said, "What do you want to do?" I said, "I want to start from the beginning; I want to start from scratch." See, he had written about Schenker in *Modern Music* magazine. We were all talking about Schenker; Schenker was filling the air, and Roger obviously knew it well. So I said, "Look, you know I've been through the academic mill in many sorts of haphaz- ard ways. I'd like to just start from scratch, species counterpoint." He said, "Fine. We'll do that. We'll start from scratch." The first thing we ever did, as a matter of fact, was look at Beethoven's Opus 2, No. 1 together and the *Tonville* analysis of Schenker, and talked about what we agreed with and how we would go about it. He said, "What would you like to accomplish compositionally? What music that you know would you like to be able to compose at the end of the three years?" Now, I knew he was too sophisticated a man for me to name a piece of his; he wouldn't go for that. And I couldn't really give the one honest answer, which would have been the Schoenberg *Orchestral Variations*. I didn't want to irritate him; I knew about his feelings at that moment. But the rest was honest. I said, "The Stravinsky *Octet* and the Copland *Piano Variations*." He said, "Well, you'll be able to write the Stravinsky *Octet*; the Copland *Piano Variations* won't take you three years."

DUCKWORTH: Did that prove true?

BABBITT: Well, no, of course not. But it gives you an idea of how he thought and what the atmosphere was. He said, "Look, you go write your music. We'll look at pieces; we'll do everything from scratch." We did all kinds of species counterpoint. We went on for three years doing basically what were sort of elaborate exercises. What he made all of his students do, and there weren't many of us, was look, for example, at a Mozart quartet movement and decide what we thought were the crucial aspects that made the piece (I hate to use this expression) work: what we liked most about the piece; what attracted us (that's a much more reasonable way to describe it). And then incorporate that kind of a musical concept into music imitating Mozart, or a totally different idiom if you wished. We had to do one of those movements a week. The other thing he made us do was learn—memorize—a movement a day from the standard literature . . . a Brahms quartet or Schumann piano sonata.

DUCKWORTH: Memorize it in what way?

BABBITT: We would walk around with it in the street. And when we came back, we had to know it, so that we would know exactly where we were at any moment when he played it—even just the bass line. He loved games like that.

DUCKWORTH: Did you do that?

BABBITT: Sure we did. It became a game. He imposed this rigor upon us. But by the time Roger came back to Princeton, and by all means by the time he came to teach at Juilliard, he was no longer interested in doing that. He was really interested in teaching at that point. He was interested for himself; he was really teaching himself at that time. Because Roger was not a facile musician. Roger insisted upon playing the piano, but he wasn't much of a pianist. And at that time, he was very sensitive about the accusation that he had written so little. I saw him waste months on one measure of the viola part of his Violin Concerto. Look, Roger was, and I want to say this because one can have such different impressions of this man who spoke so slowly and seemed so very dry and even pompous . . . he was a genius. He was a genuine, honest-to-God genius in many,

many respects. What he could hear musically, I mean, what he could hear in the deepest sense. And his language abilities were incredible. He spoke fluent German, Russian, you name it, and knew these languages better than most natives.

DUCKWORTH: What do you think are the really crucial things you learned from him?

BABBITT: There's simply so much. Remember, he was the first real composer/teacher I had. First of all, you could argue a great deal about all kinds of things, and draw him out on the way he really felt about how details went in a piece. We looked at so much music together, Bill. By the time I had been with him three or four months, we became very close. You asked me how many times I saw him. I can't even tell you. Drop up and have tea at the Childs around the corner together. He'd call me up and say so-and-so was in town, we could meet and have lunch together or something. It was a perfectly ongoing thing.

DUCKWORTH: How did the teaching job at Princeton open up for you?

BABBITT: Roger got offered a job at Princeton because a dear man named Roy Dickinson Welsh had been taken from Smith College to form a department there. Princeton had never had one because it's a good Presbyterian school and Presbyterians didn't really care very much about music. Roy Welsh had known Roger at Smith College, and asked him to commute there for practically no money. When they found that the department began to grow and they needed some young guy to be Roger's assistant and do some of the dirty work of the department, he turned to me because I was the only one of his students with an academic background. But the first year it didn't work. I thought I better tell Roger that I was Jewish. And, of course, Southern Babbitt; who can believe this? Roger was very embarrassed because, you know, his musical god was Ernest Block, who was really Jewish. And he said, "I'm sure that won't have any effect on anything." But I thought I'd better tell him because I'd been to Ivy League schools, I'd been to Penn, and I knew the way the world was. He came back and said, "You know, Roy could care less, but he thinks maybe the first appointment . . . ." Then they hired a good Harvard boy and it didn't work. And the following year I went, and that was the end of that problem.

Look, I owe Roger so much, both practically and otherwise. But the real thing is, we had fundamental disagreements. One day he said, "What are you composing?" I said, "As a matter of fact, I just started a big piano piece." "Let me look at it." I brought it to him; it was very obviously twelve-tone. I can even remember it now, but the piece has long since been discarded. It was quite obvious that he didn't think it was too terrible because he said, "You know, I'd like to show this to Kreneck." Now one could have misunderstood; I could have been flattered, but he was going to show it to Kreneck and say, "Look, any child can do it." Later, when Roger came from Berkeley and wrote his unaccompanied violin sonata, which by any reasonable judgment was a twelve-tone work, he'd had a fundamental transformation. There was no question that he was very remorseful. One time he took a piece of mine at a seminar in Princeton. Remember, I didn't study with Roger at Princeton, I was his assistant. But, of course, as anyone would, I sat in on the seminars. Most of the students were at least as old as I, some of them older. So once he asked me what I was doing. I brought in a piece for eight instruments, which was already very close to my *Composition for Four Instruments*, and he took it and threw it in the wastebasket. The students were outraged and he was very embarrassed; it was a totally spontaneous gesture, the piece had made him angry.

DUCKWORTH: Did you pick that quality up from him? Is there any music that makes you angry?

BABBITT: No, not really. Angry would be incorrect. Honestly. There's music which doesn't interest me. But I'm not given to that; I don't lose tempers either.

DUCKWORTH: Do you never feel that way?

BABBITT: Oh no, no. Roger, by the way, stopped. Roger changed enormously. Look, Roger (we're still talking up to about 1940) was almost desperate. First of all, his domestic situation was desperate; his monetary situation was desperate (he had a wife plus alimony on only a trivial academic salary); and his career was desperate. I mean, Roger was not a played composer. Roger was very well known without being performed. He's a little bit like Schoenberg; not as much, but just reduce Schoenberg's image. Schoenberg was a famous composer whose music you couldn't hear. We couldn't hear any Schoenberg in the thirties except for *Verklarte Nacht* and the recording of *Gurrelieder* [Leopold] Stokowski had made. The first performance of *Pierrot* was his which he brought here and conducted with his Viennese friends. As for the late stuff, the

Woodwind Quintet, never; the *Orchestral Variations*, forget it, it got its first performance with [Dimitri] Mitropoulos in the fifties. So Roger was in that even more. He didn't have that much music. His Violin Concerto had been a great scandal; it was never done by Boston, where it had been commissioned by Albert Spalding. His big pieces hadn't been done. His First Symphony had been done in 1928, but wasn't done again in New York I don't think.

DUCKWORTH: In addition to being Roger's assistant at Princeton, didn't you also get a degree there?

BABBITT: Well, that's one of those funny things. As I said, I had my undergraduate degree in music from NYU, and nobody ever got graduate degrees in music in those days. When I went down there, there was no graduate department at Princeton. We were teaching undergraduates and we had a few majors. The first majors were the class of 1939—two majors. The following year there were eight. The department was growing very quickly. They decided to have a graduate department. In composition, there were three of us. Two of us were already teaching in the department; Ed Cone (who had been an undergraduate there, had gone to Columbia for graduate work, had come back and joined the department) and me. By that time, there were a lot of young instructors; we were all over the place. So Ed and I were asked if we wouldn't like to go ahead and try for the first graduate degrees. So we were teaching and getting our degrees at the same time. We got our degrees in '42. Both Ed and I got the first MFAs; there was no Ph.D. offered until much later.

DUCKWORTH: Was your *Composition for Orchestra* written as part of your degree requirement?

BABBITT: It could have been; I was writing it at that time. But actually, the degree was much more a French Prix de Rome degree. We had to write a piece over the weekend; I wrote a piece for clarinet and piano. We had to do an analysis in a day or two. We had to do a history in a day or two. We had to do an essay in a day or two. That died with the war and never returned, that old Prix de Rome business. The reason they did it, I think, was because they knew that Ed and I could do that kind of thing. Why not do it and set a precedent? A precedent, of course, that disappeared. We were the last people to get it because the war came.

DUCKWORTH: Is the *Composition for Orchestra* the piece where you really made a commitment as a composer to twelve-tone music?

BABBITT: Oh, I had made a commitment before that, but that was one where I tried to do it in a big, big piece. No, before this I had written some little piano pieces which a pianist named Robert Turner played. We had concerts at this point, it was played publicly. And then I wrote a string trio. The string trio was probably started around 1940.

DUCKWORTH: How did you feel about committing yourself to twelve-tone music? Was that an easy or a difficult choice?

BABBITT: I got so excited about Schoenberg's music. By that time I had a full score of the *Orchestral Variations*, I was studying the score of the Third Quartet, and I heard the first New York performance of the Fourth Quartet. By the time I went to teach at Princeton this was my primary interest.

DUCKWORTH: When the war came, what kind of work did you do? I know you moved to Washington.

BABBITT: I don't know how much one can say. I got involved in the war before we were involved. I was asked to do intelligence work as early as 1939, as soon as there was war in Europe.

DUCKWORTH: What were you doing? Can you talk about it?

BABBITT: No. I can't.

DUCKWORTH: Even this late?

BABBITT: You know, it sounds so damn secret. But I'll tell you this much: I don't even know what I dare say. I really don't know, Bill. What happened was that we signed a secrecy agreement by Act of Congress, by war act, whereby we're not even allowed to use certain words, such as "intelligence," in public. It was one of these unbelievable secrecy agreements. Now, you know, the people in Britain decided that they could talk after thirty years, and they began to. We've never found out here. Nobody has ever dared. And after all, I was hardly a big shot; I was a kid in it.

DUCKWORTH: How did it all begin? How did you get into that kind of work?

BABBITT: They came and got three people in Princeton whose backgrounds they had looked into, and asked us if we'd be willing to train for certain secret work. And there would be a messenger coming to my house, back and forth, our little house on Nassau Street. As soon as war was declared, early in 1942, I was asked to teach in the math department. Now that was the second term of that year when I was also getting my graduate degree, as was Ed Cone. We both taught math, and I was doing the intelligence work. By the end of that term I got my degree and that was it; everybody said goodbye. We closed up the music department. I went to Washington.

DUCKWORTH: Did your work in Washington involve math research?

BABBITT: I can't tell you. No, it wasn't that; I can tell you it wasn't math. But we were doing very secret work, there's no question about it. The funny part of it was all the incredible pork barreling in that scene that was Washington during the war. They suddenly decided that nobody under thirty could be billeted in Washington. Well, I was well under thirty; I was twenty-six. So I was in real trouble. We were all running around Washington finding some place else we could go with our work. In fact, at one point the Navy Intelligence wanted to send me to Russia. I found myself spending more time running around than doing the work I was supposed to be doing. Everybody was quite sympathetic to us because they thought it was a ridiculous order. The reason I tell you this is suddenly, one day, an order came to go to Princeton University to teach mathematics under the highest priority. Now this is what's hard for people to understand. They were taking people out of the Battle of the Bulge to come back and teach math, because people had to learn mathematics for radar, sonar, and a lot of new secret stuff. Teachers had to be security cleared, which of course I already was, and they had to have at least some mathematical background in teaching. And I not only had a teaching background, but I had already taught some mathematics at Princeton in that last term. But why I was sent back to Princeton, there were hundreds of schools where these programs were going on. Whether some nice guy in personnel said, "Lets send him back there," or whether it was an accident, I'll never know. And I was under order: go back to Princeton and teach mathematics. I taught six hours a day starting at 7:30 in the morning, teaching all kinds of mathematics to people in uniform. It was an incredible time. I didn't have a place to live; I lived in the attic of the Welchs. My wife stayed in Washington. I didn't know where I'd be from day to day. But for the next two and a half years I commuted between Princeton and Washington. Music was out of the question.

DUCKWORTH: How did you get back into music after the war?

BABBITT: We went down to Jackson, finally, in 1946, and we decided we wanted to have a child; we were going to have our first child. We went to stay with my folks, rest up a little bit. We were both terribly exhausted. My wife worked for a war agency in Washington all through the war. We didn't know what we were going to do. Obviously, I had a right to go back to Princeton, but I wasn't ready to go back to teaching yet. Now you're going to hear about one of the biggest mistakes I ever made in my life. We decided we would come back to New York. And I was sucked into the sucker deal of all time. A dear friend of mine from Princeton, and a friend of his from Yale, met a very famous musical comedy star who wanted us to write a musical comedy. That's when I wrote a musical comedy called *Fabulous Voyage*.

DUCKWORTH: Why was it such a bad experience?

BABBITT: I got involved with show business, deeply involved with agents, with producers, with dreadful wives of famous stars. It taught me one thing, Bill, and I mean this sincerely: I never wanted to go near show biz ever again. And my colleagues felt the same way.

DUCKWORTH: What was the music for the Broadway show like? Did it have any connection at all with your more serious music?

BABBITT: I introduced into my pop tunes all kinds of little constructive things which you would recognize. One was motivic stuff. I got a lot of fun out of that, but staying well within an idiom that I didn't even have to think about, because I knew the words, the lyrics, of 4,000 popular songs. The music came very much out of Kern, who is certainly my favorite of all Broadway composers. But I would never have dared do what Steve Sondheim does; you couldn't do that in those days. These were still pretty well formulized and formalistic little pop tunes. No, that's not fair . . . show biz songs with clever lyrics—extremely intricate lyrics—with a very intricate book. And everybody wanted to make a change, make it a little bit less sophisticated. It was an adaptation of Homer's *Odyssey*. By the time the husband of the great star decided that Calypso should have a calypso song, my boys said, "We're walking out. This is it." And then we all felt, "This is not for us." We really just walked out on it. We just couldn't take it anymore.

DUCKWORTH: Do you sometimes hide popular things in your serious music?

BABBITT: I must confess I don't, no. Except when I wrote *All Set*, of course. There's a little quotation in that.

DUCKWORTH: Didn't you also write a film score about that same time?

BABBITT: Yes. The film was called *Into the Good Ground*. It was one
of those very complex, pretentious movies that they were making
in New York just before television came. They would take stage
stars from New York and make films. This was an outfit called
Pathescope; very successful for a few years. The film had flashbacks, within flashbacks, within flashbacks. And because they had
consulted me about technical stuff in sound reproduction when
they were making some of their other films (and that was when I
was already getting deeply into electronics) they asked me to do
the score. And I learned another lesson: I could never, never do
that kind of thing ever again. I was supposed to have six weeks with
the score, which was little enough; I had six days. I ruined my eyes;
my stomach; I couldn't stand it. The last parts were being brought
in by the copying agency while we were recording the last
sequence. We never got the last sequence done. I had the best
orchestra in the world, but physically I could never do it again. I
was sort of fond of the score. Some of it was a result of my old jazz
training. It wasn't jazz, but old arranger's stuff that I could do. And
some of it was really a little bit, almost, of my own music.

DUCKWORTH: Do you think your vast knowledge of popular music
has had any lasting influence on your serious music?

BABBITT: It had to, Bill; it had to.

DUCKWORTH: What is it?

BABBITT: Well, I don't know. When I get interviewed by people who
are not professional musicians, and above all not composers, they
always ask "What things influenced you?" Well, what things didn't?
All that variegated music that we've all heard; all the things that I
read. I mean, I can't imagine . . . And to be specific about it, one
would almost be, I think, dishonest. So many things have crept in
and determined one's thinking. I don't have to tell you, a composer. You know, as a piece germinates, the forms that it takes. If you
had to go back and retrace that, it would not only be superficial . . .
you've forgotten it.

DUCKWORTH: Do you compose every day?

BABBITT: I try to. I do compose every day unless something terrible
happens.

DUCKWORTH: Do you have a set time that you work? Are you methodical about working?

BABBITT: No, I'm very nonmethodical. I'm not trying now to disabuse everyone of the notion that I'm a mathematical formalist. I'm very sloppy. Both my wife and I are kind of sloppy; we lead sloppy lives.

DUCKWORTH: Well, I remember the first time I visited your office at Princeton. You must have had 200 unopened letters and packages lying around.

BABBITT: That's right. And you don't have any idea what my study at home is like. It's even worse. I just walk over things on the floor. We can't keep things straight. I'm very sloppy, and methodical only in the sense that I'm most likely to compose late at night and into the early morning. I can work all day long. When I had my hepatitis, for example, and couldn't leave the house, I could start working at 9 o'clock in the morning and work to 1 o'clock the next morning. That I can do, and I love it actually . . . not to break the concentration. But under normal living conditions, I'm likely to work through an afternoon and into the night. Never in the morning. I never get up early; I can't get going. I do trivial things in the morning— answer letters, try to write recommendations, things of this kind. The solid work can begin as late as 9 o'clock at night and go until 2 or 3 in the morning.

DUCKWORTH: Do you work primarily at a desk?

BABBITT: Yes, I work at a desk. But I can work in a car; I can really work anywhere. It doesn't bother me. Maybe the war had something to do with it.

DUCKWORTH: How do your ideas come to you?

BABBITT: Well, it's a very interesting question, but the answer, I hate to say, is I don't know. I'm simply incapable of knowing when I think, "Hey, this is right."

DUCKWORTH: When you begin a piece, do you know where it's going?

BABBITT: I never start writing a piece unless I have a conception of the piece.

DUCKWORTH: All the way through?

BABBITT: A huge conception of the piece. Otherwise, you'll write down that wonderful first page with every dynamic, everything set, and realize you don't know where the piece is going. And it completely inhibits you from continuing. And that's certainly the way I feel about influences. I can't possibly imagine what goes into when I finally make a decision. If I really wrote music mathematically, I wouldn't have that problem.

DUCKWORTH: Does this initial sense of the piece in total always happen?

BABBITT: Yes, that's right. Well, let me put it this way: if it doesn't, I feel I don't have the piece.

DUCKWORTH: Do you work mostly on commission at this point?

BABBITT: Yes. Well, nonpaid commissions, mainly. I long since have decided the hell with it. The trivial amount of money that one gets would hardly pay for the parts. So the hell with it. I'm going to write for the people who played my music in the past, who care about it.

DUCKWORTH: Once you begin a piece, do you get maniacal with it? Do you work all the time?

BABBITT: Absolutely, you've hit it right on the head. Maniacal might be a perfectly reasonable description. I become impossibly consumed with it, let everything go by, let the letters pile up, and get very irritable. I'll discuss this with you because you're a fellow composer, but I hate to say these things because then it sounds like the creative genius posture. But it's a very simple fact of life. As I've often said, if I really knew how to write music mathematically, I'd be delighted to. It would make my life much easier. And this kind of misunderstanding about what one does with numbers . . . What did Bach do with numbers? You know, there are §s written under his chords. People don't realize that those numbers are *exactly* the same as the numbers you see in a twelve-tone series. They mean exactly the same thing. They were interval classes; they didn't tell you exactly how many 6s above. And when there was a 4, it simply indicated, again, the degree of assumption with regard to what he was going to have in that particular vertical structure. So numbers today signify exactly the same thing as they did in a figured bass with Bach. But getting back to the more crucial issue, when I think about a piece, of course I think in twelve-tone terms. I don't think about the fact that it's not fashionable. It really never was. I find that always very funny about Schoenberg. His music was never fashionable, and now it's considered old-fashioned. Honestly, I don't want to seem to be heroic about this, but it never occurs to me whether this is fashionable or not. This is my language. This is what interests me more. This is where I still find things that I've never thought of before. And so it's going to be.

I have no wish to make an issue of twelve-tone or not twelve-tone, serial or nonserial. I'm very much more interested in people who *don't* write that kind of music. Now I am definitely sounding heroic, but I have to say that the notion, somehow, that if I'm on a jury I'm going to choose the twelve-tone piece . . . On the contrary, you usually have much stronger ideas about how you feel about the music that's close to your own, and how you'd like to see it go, rather than something you've never seen before which you become interested in because you can't figure out what you're hearing when you hear the piece.

DUCKWORTH: You've referred to being labeled a couple of times now. How do you think you've been mislabeled?

BABBITT: It's when people talk about mathematical composition. I resent that only because, as I say, I wish it were true. Mathematics has little or nothing to do with the way I write music. If [Iannis] Xenakis says he gets a mathematical formula and realizes it musically, fine. I don't. For me, those numbers that people associate with me are numbers indicating intervals—the musical relation, a rather remarkable musical relation, pitch classes. These are traditional musical relationships, and, therefore, to say they're mathematical is exactly like saying that Bach is mathematical because he's got $\frac{6}{4}$ or $\frac{5}{3}$ under a chord, or because one talks about the second oboe, or one talks about $\frac{3}{4}$ Those are mathematical terms too.

DUCKWORTH: Aren't you being a little too easy on yourself though? I'm thinking about John Rockwell's statement in *All American Music* where he called you the most complex composer ever. Do you think it's a fair statement?

BABBITT: Oh, I don't know whether it's fair or not. But how can you compare my music, quantitatively, with the music of [Kaikhosru Shapurji] Sorabji, for example? Or, for that matter, with Xenakis. Or let's look at Brian Ferneyhough.

DUCKWORTH: Do you see anything you would call complicated or complex in your music?

BABBITT: When San Francisco had a series of contemporary music
    concerts, they got Lucky [Stephen] Mosko to do Elliott Carter's
    Double Concerto and my *Aria da Capo*. And I was with Lucky, and
    we were working, and things went fine. There were no problems.
    We got a good performance. So Lucky said, "God, it's amazing that
    we brought this thing off, considering the complexity of the piece."
    I said, "Lucky, is the piece really that complex? I'm genuinely puz-
    zled by that. After all, you did Elliott's *Double Concerto*, and it's
    much thicker, there's much more going on." He said, "No, but it's
    much more difficult to realize your piece as you've written it, to get
    the ensemble things that you want." Now in that sense, fine; I'm
    flattered if that's the sense of complexity. But I never think of any
    kind of quantative complexity. I really don't. For example, the prob-
    lem I had with the Philadelphia Orchestra. Well, that turned out to
    be artificially complex. There was a strike in the orchestra, and a
    resentment of the conductor, whom they've since gotten rid of,
    which had nothing to do with my piece. But I was surprised. And I
    saw how other people were surprised, too. The advisor to the
    orchestra and the program-note writer didn't even come to the first
    rehearsal. They said they looked at my score and decided it was so
    transparent and would be so easy for the orchestra that they saw
    no reason to be there. (They usually went to the first rehearsal of
    contemporary pieces to soothe feelings and ease the way.) Then, of
    course, I had a blowup, and the piece had a forty-five-minute
    rehearsal and was canceled. But I was surprised and so was Mr.
    Muti. When Mr. Muti finally came back and looked at the score, he
    said, "I don't know what all the fuss was about. I've seen much
    more difficult music than this." It has to do with dynamics, which
    they're not accustomed to playing. It has to do with balances.

DUCKWORTH: Why do you suppose there's so much reluctance, not
    only to do your music, but to do any of the music in that genre? Is
    it just the level of difficulty?

BABBITT: I think one has to be simply rational about it without
    appearing to be accusatory, which I have no desire to be because it
    doesn't serve any purpose. It takes more rehearsal time. Look, we
    don't have to go through the arithmetic of two and a half hours for
    a twenty-minute piece. That is the first thing. Furthermore, you
    take a young American conductor. What is the sense of playing diffi-
    cult music? The musicians resent it; the critics resent it; the audi-
    ence resents it. He has to work twice as hard. What is in it for him?

(It's not like my dear friend Lenny Bernstein, who said, "Milton, I'm so sorry we have to postpone your piece; I spent all day Saturday studying the score.") I saw the harpist of the Philharmonic take the harp part of the Webern Symphony, come down and throw it at Mitropoulos's feet, and say, "I will not play this shit," and walk out. And Mitropoulos turned to the people at the rehearsal and said, "What can I do?" This is bound to create resentment. There will always be a few men in the orchestra who will be on the composer's side, but the conductor can't count on that. Why should he do it? What's in it for him? Nothing, except usually resentful reviews and a resentful audience.

DUCKWORTH: Well, if you're going to say that, then I think you have to address the question of why you write difficult music. What's in it for you?

BABBITT: I write it because this is what I want most to write. It interests me most. You can call it self-indulgence; I can answer there's nobody whom I would rather indulge. It's the music I want to hear. I'm terribly anxious to hear it. When I turned to electronics, it certainly wasn't because I was dissatisfied with the sound of the orchestra. I'd love to hear orchestras play my music with the care that some of my chamber groups in New York do. I mean, I have a recording on CRI with a performance of my *Elizabethan Sextet* with six girls singing. It's just absolutely wonderful. This is the way I wrote the piece. If I could only get an orchestra to play any of my orchestral music that way. I still keep hoping. I don't think I'll probably ever write any more orchestral music. I was lucky to get a piano concerto recorded. Well, it's not bad, but my God, it's not a great performance. How could it be? These poor kids in the orchestra had two and a half hours in carrels where they couldn't hear each other, and where the pianist was rehearsing with a piano with no pedal. Then they had a half-hour on stage at Carnegie Hall, mainly to move around the chairs, and suddenly they heard different things and they got their cues wrong. Then they played it once and recorded it the next day.

DUCKWORTH: Who do you see as the audience for your music?

BABBITT: Of course, it's a small audience, but you see, what I have said (and what has been misunderstood too, like that ridiculous title "Who Cares If You Listen") is that this is something one learns to share. I have my colleagues in philosophy who have their colleagues and a few interested people. I'm perfectly willing to settle for that. And if people say, "That's not what music should be," I'd like to know from where those imperatives derive. See, I could be very nasty about this. I could say, "Where do you expect me to get an audience from, from the people who eat MacDonald's hamburgers and drink Budweiser and listen to *Dallas*, or read *Playboy*?" However, if they mean where's your *big* audience, why don't you rate the masses, there are many answers. Forgetting musical issues for the moment, how can you ask me to reach out to the masses, who don't even know I exist, when I can't even reach out to my colleagues, who do? I can't see the scores of friends of mine on the West Coast. What do I do, ask them to send me a score, which may not be highly legible anyhow, which will cost them a hundred dollars to reproduce? No, it's impossible. And by the way, I can't tell you how many conductors have said to me, "Look, how can we do yours or your colleagues' music in manuscript? The music itself is difficult enough. Why should we work when we get these beautifully published European scores which make life so much easier for us." And I have a pretty good manuscript; it's not great. You know, not a single note of my orchestral music has ever been published, not one note. And I will not pay for it to be published. Beyond the fact that it requires more money than I have, the idea of being a vanity composer . . . One hoped in our early days that if not by virtue of eminence, at least by virtue of advanced age, that we'd have our music handled. We'd finish a piece and turn it over to a publisher and start our next piece. Well, of course, I'm sitting there seeing my scores . . . .

DUCKWORTH: You're living in the wrong century.

BABBITT: Or in the wrong country, I regret to say.

DUCKWORTH: I'd like to get back to the question of the audience. Do you see any basic problems with the audience for new music?

BABBITT: Yes. And that is, where are the educated people in other fields? I confront my dear friends from other departments at Princeton with the fact that they never ever come to concerts. I'm not talking about my music now, but about a wonderful performance of the Schoenberg *Serenade*, for example. The best performance I've ever heard. There were fifty people in the audience, and nobody from any department other than music, as far as I could see. And they all say, "Oh, well, you know, we don't get anything out of it." "Why don't you get anything out of it?" Well, it turns out that most of them, when they go to any concert, go to casual social events. When I said this out at Bowling Green somebody said, "Well, that may just be Princeton, because they're all so consumed with their own work and their own importance." Certainly they're consumed with their own work; so are we. And they're too busy, but that's not the answer. They go to other things. They go to movies. Most of them can go out much more than we can because they've finished their professional work during the day; their nights are free. We finish our work at night. Our own work is not our professional work, in many respects.

DUCKWORTH: Do you think that as composers we've alienated the audience, or has the quality of the audience degenerated?

BABBITT: What audience? And I don't want to avoid the question. I don't think we've alienated the audience; I think they've been misinformed. I think we've been misrepresented by journalism. I think journalists should keep out of music unless they're willing to do what they should do, which is try to find out what we're up to and represent us honestly. Then let people judge. Not simply begin with evaluations of our music with normatives without any description. Can you figure out what a piece is about from reading a journalistic description? Of course not. You don't know what the musical content is. You know that the guy says, for one reason or another, that he didn't find the piece expressive, which means he didn't like it.

DUCKWORTH: Are you concerned when audiences react negatively to your music?

BABBITT: The notion that I'm not interested in audiences is absolutely preposterous. Wouldn't it be wonderfully stimulating to have people who disliked your music for reasons that would indicate that they've heard something in the music that they didn't like? The people who have serious objections to my music, I'm perfectly willing to countenance, and sometimes I understand perfectly well that we disagree. I lived in mathematics perforce because of the war. Do you know what an algebraist thinks of a highly sophisticated problem for a statistical mathematician? He calls that "truck-driver mathematics." I would never, never dismiss another composer in the way that many of the mathematicians used to dismiss other people doing mathematics . . . with a kind of contemptuousness.

Not at all. Who was one of my closest friends in music? Morty Feldman. Quite literally, I think we could say we loved each other. We've been together on many occasions. I've known him since he was a small boy. I talked to him the day before he died. Morty and I couldn't come from more different backgrounds in every conceivable point of view. And we've had tremendously serious talks about music. Morty was sitting up in the balcony with me at the first performance of my *Composition for Four Instruments*. Would you like to guess who the composer was who wrote the first review of a published score of mine, my *Composition for Four Instruments*? John Cage in *Musical America*, whom I've also known for at least forty years. You know, I'm sorry, Bill, if I suddenly begin to sound, in my old age, as if I'm not only going soft, but hypocritical.

DUCKWORTH: Well, you don't have a reputation for being soft. It might be interesting to explore that.

BABBITT: Well, what I mean is I love this variety of musics that's going on. What I resent is people who become parochial, in the sense which I never wanted to be. This tremendous variety of music is something that didn't exist when I began. Well, it did exist; I wasn't aware of it. It was happening in Paris. In America, there was a contention between the Eastman group and the League of Composers group, and there was a left-wing thing with the workers' stuff. But there was not any sense of this really incredible spectrum and range of music going on. In Boston, where I spent the term recently, different concerts had almost discrete groups of concertgoers. I went to a computer music festival, and there was absolutely nobody there from any of the other concerts. I was the only one there who represented the legitimate, academic wing of music from ol' Harvard. (Of course, there are members of the Harvard Department who don't talk to each other.) I find this extremely stimulating. And I'm not going to say for a minute that I sit there and I'm interested in every piece that gets played. Of course not. But I try to be, damn it. I don't see any reason to go to listen to a piece of music unless you try to make the most of it.

Look, I'm not going to pretend to be the utmost in tolerance. Because tolerance is not what I feel is involved here. There's something patronizing about saying one tolerates this. I'm genuinely interested, and I mean this very sincerely. I'm interested in what any composer has to say about music. I always feel that if a composer has thought about creating a piece, even though ultimately what he says just doesn't happen to hit me, I'll be interested in what he says.

DUCKWORTH: Are you surprised that twelve-tone music in general hasn't developed more of a following? And are you surprised at the direction in which music has gone in the last ten to fifteen years? I'm thinking first of the minimalists and then of the downtown school.

BABBITT: Oh no, I'm not surprised. I'm not at all surprised by that. There were never that many people deeply involved and really committed to writing twelve-tone music. That's one of those great myths. Some were affected by it one way or the other. Do you think of Irving Fine as really being a twelve-tone composer, though he was very much influenced by it? There weren't that many people, ever at any time, who were that deeply involved. We thought it would have its influence, and it has. How can one say that one wasn't influenced by serial thought? But reactions were always going on. Don't forget Norman Dello Joio and Bill Bergsma. They continued to write their music; they simply were not being played. I'd ask them how they felt about all of this. What's happened to their music? I would think that they would feel, perhaps, a little more left out than we. Look, you might think there was a certain sense of martyrdom in our attitudes toward what we were doing; that wasn't true. It's very simply that this interested us more than anything else. And we were damn lucky to have academic positions.

DUCKWORTH: Do you think having an academic position hurt you artistically in any way?

BABBITT: Not me. I'll assert again that I'm proudly academic, because I'm happiest in an academic atmosphere. Nobody has to tell me about the politics, the hypocrisy, the nonsense. I know it full well. But when the chips are down, for me the term "academic" simply suggests the most imaginative disciplined, the most responsibly problematical, the most informedly advanced activity. It is in so many other fields, and that's what I take it to be in music, too. I'm not going to say I'm not an academic composer. I'm an academic composer in the sense that the academy makes it possible for me to write the music I want to. It has never imposed on me in the slightest.

DUCKWORTH: Can we talk a little about your work with the RCA synthesizer? How did that get started?

BABBITT: It actually started back in the thirties, when I began teaching at Princeton. I had been reading about the handwritten sound
track for films in Germany. And the people at RCA, who had just
opened the David Sarnoff Laboratory nearby at Princeton, were
very happy to be cooperative. And we began to work on a handwritten sound track. We never really got it going; we did make
some sounds. But we did do enough so that I realized that this was
what interested me. Then came the war, and it was forgotten.
When I went back in the fifties and got together with Vladimir
Ussachevsky and Otto Luening, I had no interest in tape. It just
wasn't for me as a composer. I wanted to be able to start from
scratch, and not have to work with tape dissection. But I was with
them all the time, and knew what was going on technically.

The way it all got started was that when they made that silly
record down at RCA, that voice of the RCA synthesizer, I went over
and saw Olsen. I went over and talked to this old-fashioned Iowa
engineer who couldn't imagine what I was interested in. He'd
never heard of me, but when he discovered that composers were
interested in something which had been built as just a little birthday gift for David Sarnoff, very secretly they went back and got
another man in on it and built a second synthesizer, which had
enormous advantages over the first. Then, we were invited—I say
by we, Vladimir and I and Roger Sessions if he had been willing—to
go over to RCA. The original agreement was to find out whether we
thought it was worthwhile enough to suggest to one of our universities, or to a combination of the two, that they should have such a
machine built for them. So we went down—Vladimir and I—under
the tightest security. We were searched every time we left the place.
We went down in that terrible little room down there and I realized
that this was for me. This was where I could talk to the machine.

DUCKWORTH: How did you actually get the machine into the
university?

BABBITT: When we got our little Rockefeller grant (and it was a puny
grant, we couldn't have even begun to build a synthesizer), they
said, "You people seem to want to do something with it. We don't
know what to do with it. Take it; it's yours." And that's how it all
began, and how it got moved up to Columbia. And it's still sitting
up there. I'd be working with it right now were it not for what's
happened to the neighborhood and to the studio. I mean, it's just
impossible to work there for any length of time and go out in the

street and not be murdered. So I've just had to give up. I've got an unfinished violin concerto, but I don't know how I'll ever get it done. In a couple of months we could put the thing back into good working order, but I don't see how I can work there. You know, of course, the studio was badly ripped off; we had a very bad robbery up there. They didn't take any of our tapes, but they messed up a lot of the equipment. They weren't interested in the synthesizer. They wanted the new amplifiers, the new speakers—stuff they could sell. But they ripped out so many wires that rewiring the studio took months.

DUCKWORTH: Do you still see it as a viable musical instrument?

BABBITT: I'd still be working with it because it still has advantages for me. Look, it's clumsy compared with what you can do with the computer. But it still has that wonderful advantage of being there where I can try what I want immediately. I don't have to put in a great deal of information. I punch out a couple of things, try them, if it's not what I want I change it immediately, put it on to tape. Now there are lots of things, of course, that though in theory can be done with this machine, I would never want to try to do, that could be done easily with a computer. There's no question about the computer's abilities. But I simply do not feel at home with the computer . . . having to put all that information in before I can hear what I've asked for. With this one, you know, I go punch, I listen, if it's not what I want I change it immediately. I can hear it at any speed; do what I want to. It still has a man/machine relationship that is much more comfortable for me.

DUCKWORTH: Was your interest in the synthesizer more with the sounds themselves, or with the control of events?

BABBITT: The second, absolutely. I wasn't dissatisfied with the sound of the symphony orchestra. It's a wonderful, marvelous sound if you can get it. For me, there was one particular emphasis, and that was the temporal, rhythmic aspect—the control of rhythm, of ensemble rhythm, of individual linear rhythms, as we simply couldn't get it with performers. When we tried to get it we encountered difficulties with just the notation. As I don't have to tell you, much of the problem of having unusual, intricate rhythms performed has nothing to do with the incapacity of the performer or the incapacity of the ear. It's the damn notation. We have a binary notation in which we have to write down 7 in the time of 4. What kind of nonsense is this? If one begins from a rhythmic unit, as you can with a synthesizer, there are no discriminations against 7s or 11s. It's just a preposterous notational problem. I'm not interested in what can't be heard. We could always produce things electronically that couldn't be heard. Big deal, you know. What kind of an achievement is that?

What interested me was the control of events, particularly temporal events. Of course, when you're controlling temporal events, you're controlling everything. You're controlling the pitch events (which are assigned temporal values), timbral events, dynamic events, time rate-of-change of timbre, time rate-of-change of everything. That is exactly why I turned to it. And also, the satisfaction of being able to be the performer in every sense of the word, as one never was before. I mean that the acts of performance and composition can be so compounded into a single act that you could walk into that studio with a piece in your hand, and walk out with your performance on the tape under your arm. Now I don't want to say that you always got exactly what you wanted, that would be a misrepresentation. But I was perfectly willing, there in the loveliness of that studio, the wonderful solitude of that studio, to sit there for a week trying to get one second that I wanted. And some days I'd get twenty seconds. It took a long time, of course it did. But that wonderful satisfaction of doing everything yourself. I don't know, maybe that's the way Rachmaninov felt when he played the piano. But I think this is even more so.

DUCKWORTH: In your mind, where is the balance between musical instincts and musical intelligence? Where does that fit in your music?

BABBITT: Here is where I can agree with a lot of people from other fields. I never feel any kind of discrepancy there. I refuse to maintain that old-fashioned dichotomy between heart and mind, the emotional and the intellectual, the cognitive and the sentient. One reacts to what one understands. Just try holding a gun to some primitive who doesn't understand what a gun can do; he won't react the way you would. So I can't make that distinction. I don't even think in terms of a dichotomy of that kind. The two are constantly interacting all the time. Haven't you reacted very differently to a piece when you've suddenly seen something, heard something, in the piece you never heard before? I know perfectly well that I hear things in pieces that I couldn't have imagined I heard

when I was a student. Things in the most familiar pieces in the
world . . . the Mozart *G-minor Symphony* . . . I suddenly heard
things I didn't realize were there, and which struck me as being terribly important. Were they terribly important to me when I didn't
realize they were there? I don't know.

DUCKWORTH: Are you comfortable being labeled as an experimental
composer?

BABBITT: Oh, I'm perfectly comfortable. It's not that you're going in
and playing around with dangerous material, although that's alright
too. But you have certain ideas and you want to see what kind of a
piece you get if you do this. I must say that one of the most interesting aspects of being a composer is that transformation from the
role of composer to the role of listener. I mean, we don't compose
in real time. We have to *imagine* real time. Then we sit back and
have the piece presented to us in real time. That's a totally different
position into which to be put. This is what Stravinsky called the
"hypothetical other." Well, the *other* isn't even hypothetical; it's me.
And I sit there listening to this piece of mine and I'm seeing how
this experiment . . . seeing what has happened. And very often I
think to myself, "You know, I should have done this." But I don't go
back and revise pieces. I just can't bring myself to do it. The piece
was done. And to revise something you'd need to write a whole
new piece. So I write a whole new piece.

LOU HARRISON

Born Portland, Oregon, 1917

L OU HARRISON, who was a touring child actor until he was three, likes to say that he has never stopped being the child himself. A self-described sensualist, he claims that he wandered into music because of his avaricious interests and appetites, without ever once actually making a decision to be a musician. But however it happened, once there, he continued to wander. And his love affair with the music of the whole world, coupled with his lifelong sensitivity to the nuances of melody and intonation, have combined to produce a composer of uncommon sensibility. Drawing freely on all the musical resources he has ever encountered, Harrison has created his own world of sound, with a uniquely personal brand of East/West synthesis, often colored by specific tunings.

Harrison likes to credit the San Francisco Public Library with part of his education. He claims to have gone through almost all the music they had, a vast amount, paying particular attention to the complete operas of Rameau and Lully; all of the nineteenth-century French organ works; and all of Schoenberg—not to mention all of the standard literature. But he is also quick to credit Henry Cowell, Arnold Schoenberg, Virgil Thomson, and Charles Ives as the people in his life who influenced and helped him the most.

In 1934, Harrison, whose family had moved to San Francisco when he was nine, began studying with Henry Cowell at a branch of the University of California. He had read *New Musical Resources*, and recently heard Cowell speak at a concert. His first class with Cowell was the famous Music of the Peoples of the World course, a topic that would sustain his interest throughout his life. Harrison also studied counterpoint and composition with Cowell, and, through a developing friendship between the two, met Edgard Varèse and Arnold Schoenberg in the Cowell home. Cowell also brought Harrison together with John Cage, and the two of them organized a series of percussion

Lou Harrison (r.) and Richard Dee accompanying a Lorle Kranzler dance class, Palo Alto, CA, circa 1960. Photo Credit: Hank Kranzler

concerts during the early forties, performing some of the major percussion music of the time. In 1942, Harrison moved to Los Angeles where he worked in the dance department at UCLA, and studied for about a year with Arnold Schoenberg, who was, at that point, teaching there.

Because of a job accompanying the Lester Horton dancers, Harrison moved to New York in 1943. Cage, who was already there, introduced him to a number of musicians including the composer and critic Virgil Thomson, with whom he developed a close friendship. Through Thomson, Harrison was hired to write music reviews, taking Paul Bowles's place on the *Herald Tribune* when Bowles left. Long intrigued by Charles Ives, Harrison had maintained a correspondence with him since his days in San Francisco. In 1946, Harrison conducted the first performance of Ives's Third Symphony at Carnegie Hall. He also, while in New York, copied and reconstructed several of Ives's manuscripts for publication. Although he lived in New York for almost a decade, Harrison never really adjusted to life in the city. In 1948 he left, going briefly to Portland to teach, before returning east to teach at Black Mountain College. While in North Carolina, Harrison, on a second Guggenheim fellowship, wrote his serial opera *Rapunzel*, a section of which was premiered in Rome, sung by Leontyne Price. The performance, at a composers' competition, won Harrison the "Twentieth Century Masterpiece" award, which was presented to him by Stravinsky.

One of Harrison's lifelong passions has been just intonation, a system of tuning in which the intervals are kept mathematically pure rather than altered slightly as they are in a tempered system. Harrison first became interested in just intonation in 1948 when Virgil Thomson gave him Harry Partch's recently published book *Genesis of a Music*. He was helped later in California by musicologist Peter Yates, who introduced him to various Renaissance and Baroque tuning systems. Saying he prefers just intonation because it makes the music sound better, Harrison, over the years, has written a number of works in a variety of tuning systems. Today, he keeps the piano in his home tuned in Kirnberger's Number 2 temperament, an early eighteenth-century system, and threatens regularly to stop writing music in equal temperament.

Harrison has also continued to pursue his other passion, world music, first introduced to him by Henry Cowell. Beginning in the early sixties, he has made a number of trips to Asia, studying, among others, Korean Court Music, Chinese classical music, and Javanese gamelans. Additionally, he and his longtime companion, Bill Colvig, have built several Javanese-style gamelans, a largely metallic percussion orchestra requiring a number of players. Today, Harrison still maintains an interest in and composes for gamelan. And occasionally he will refer to European orchestral instruments as the instruments of northwest Asia, and say that he is not going to write for them anymore. But most musicians hope that's a promise he won't be able to keep.

Since 1967 Harrison has lived in California, teaching primarily at San Jose State University and, beginning in 1978, at Mills College, where he was appointed to the Darius Milhaud Chair in 1980. He retired from teaching in 1985. Today, his threat to stop composing having never materialized, he maintains a home in Aptos, California, but continues an active schedule traveling and writing.

We decided to hold our conversation in Philadelphia the week Lou was there for several performances of his Third Symphony by the Philadelphia Orchestra. His mornings were usually free, and we met on one of them in his hotel room overlooking some of Philadelphia's most interesting architecture. The conversation went straight to music, and Lou, who is never at a loss for words, freely offered his opinions and recollections. There were times, when he really got going, that I hated to interrupt him with another question.

DUCKWORTH: I've heard you describe yourself as being in the research-and-development end of music. Would you explain that for me?

HARRISON: There's been a regular tradition; it started in the last century, you know. But the labels for this kind of activity change all the time. During Henry Cowell's tenure in the new-music world, we were all called "ultra-modernists." After the second World War, we became "avant-garde." So it dawned on me after awhile that there's this long tradition, whatever you name it, that always functions almost the same way. And then I thought: "What is that to the larger field of music, including the commerce of it?" Well, it's the research and development department. So I regard the so-called avant-garde as a research and development section of a bigger enterprise, which is the whole world of music.

DUCKWORTH: Do you think the idea of avant-garde research and development is unique to the twentieth century?

HARRISON: Oh no, this has been going on for centuries. The only time it doesn't go on is when you have religion very strongly intruding. For example, at the end of the Greco-Roman Age (this is broad-scale, but is pertinent), when Justinian closed the academies in Athens and Egypt somewhere around the fourth century, the enormous richness of intonation studies by scientists and musicians was simply canceled. What happened then, as a direct result of dogma, was that intonation simply disappeared, and Europe, in its Dark Ages, reverted to ditone tuning.

DUCKWORTH: Why did it revert?

HARRISON: Because it's instinctive; you can do that without having to know anything, actually. Then, of course, in the Renaissance they said, "Oh my gosh, look what they were doing back there." They got all this stuff back through Islamic civilization, which had preserved it and added its own. And they said, "Oh boy, look at that." So then we have thirty-one-tone harpsichords, nineteen-tone clavichords . . . all this sort of thing began. And you have this ferment again because by this time, of course, Christianity was a dead duck, let's face it. So the Renaissance is a reblooming in Europe of musical intelligence, and R&D starts "BOOM" like that again, and really hasn't stopped.

DUCKWORTH: What was the effect of this reblooming on intonation and tuning?

HARRISON: All the time, tuning studies were going on, and they went on until the middle of the last century. The invention of the iron pianos is when it stops. Because, in the Western world, the keyboard instruments, somehow, typify compositional use and have for ages. It is forgotten now, for example, that the string orchestra does not play twelve-tone equal temperament, and would have a hard time doing it, in fact. Trombones don't either, and singers can't. So the pretense goes on. But it's the keyboard that's the problem. Chopin didn't choose equal temperament, you know. Well temperaments were one of the solutions. But this problem has been going on for a long time now. We've had a period, in the West at any rate, of this awful twelve-tone equal temperament, which is dull, industrial grey. Every interval . . . my God! Who would want it? That's exactly what Bach said. He's on record in letters of disapproving of equal temperament. That's why he wrote those forty-eight preludes and fugues in well temperament, which is a much better kind of tuning. So it's back now. And of course the avant-garde or the R&D section started with Harry Partch, Julian Carrillo, Alois Hába . . . There are lots of people who do not take twelve-tone equal temperament for an answer. And I firmly believe, now that Western music has become another branch of ethnomusicology, that you don't know a composer's music unless you've heard him on his instruments, or duplicates of them, and in the intonation he asked for. So it means you wouldn't play Couperin, for example, in Rameau's intonation for the simple reason that Couperin said he didn't like it. And you shouldn't play Mozart in twelve-tone equal temperament either. Nor should you play him on an iron piano; the iron piano is a different instrument from the wooden piano, or the fortepiano. So we're discovering these things.

DUCKWORTH: Is the fact that we have an R&D section a sign that we're in a flowering period?

HARRISON: Yes it is. Well, that it's continuing, let's say.

DUCKWORTH: I'd like to back up just a little bit. Were you interested in jazz when you were young?

HARRISON: Oh yes, yes. I used to play it in Oakland, this must have been the early thirties. Later, I was working at Mills College when Pauline Benton came by with the Red Gate Shadow Players, a Chinese shadow show. At that time her musician, who played Chinese instruments and arranged all the music for her, was William Russell. I became acquainted with him then. He stayed in San Francisco because they were also playing there, and we got sufficiently acquainted that he brought stacks of records up to my apartment and sat down very seriously and gave me my first education in jazz, beyond the jazz piano I'd had. This was a general, how shall I say it, Class A appreciation course of the then state of things.

DUCKWORTH: Who influenced you when you were growing up? Who did you listen to?

HARRISON: I don't know; I don't even know who they were. Jazz was a product that everybody shared. There were no personalities except in the movies . . . Jon Hall singing "Island Paradise" . . . this kind of thing. It was a very popular education that I had. I should add that there was another class of music at the same time. Nowadays people tend, I think rather badly, to think of pop music as a kind of homogenous tyranny. But when you crossed San Francisco bay on a ferryboat, or when you went into a cafeteria or a restaurant in San Francisco during the twenties and thirties, those ferryboats and cafeterias had, at least, a string trio playing the fifty standard classics. Everybody knew them. And in school we had already learned to sing "To the Evening Star." And we learned Wagner and Verdi as well. All of this has totally disappeared in the name of educationism and commerce. Somebody discovered that you could write a book for say the fourth to fifth grades with new examples to learn. In the course of this, just in a few years, the common culture that we all shared was wiped out. And now music itself doesn't exist in most of the schools. So there was this other heritage which was wiped out by commercial enterprises and by educationism. It's very difficult to retrieve a common culture; we don't have it anymore. There is an effort on the part of the pop people to impose it. And I don't think that that should be done, myself.

DUCKWORTH: How old were you when your family left Portland?

HARRISON: We left Portland when I was nine.

DUCKWORTH: Where did you go?

HARRISON: We went to California.

DUCKWORTH: Did you go straight to San Francisco?

HARRISON: No, we went to all the small towns. Before I graduated from high school, I was in eighteen different schools. I've never regretted it because, of course, you learn survival techniques.

DUCKWORTH: What did your father do that required so much moving around?

HARRISON: Oh, everything. The money in the family was Mother's and she put him into different businesses. Finally he decided he wanted to be with his brothers, who were in California and were big automobile dealers; one of them was many times a millionaire. We moved to California to do that. And we moved around and around in California. So I had a good taste of all the school systems. To give you some idea, the minute I got to my first school in California I was jumped one grade, and then the next year jumped another grade. And this was because of the training I had had in Oregon, you see, which was a very good system.

DUCKWORTH: When did you decide that you were going to be a musician?

HARRISON: I never did. I wandered into it, because of the training that was given me, and just sort of got elected. I always wanted to be a painter, you know. But I was so crushed by the comments of a high school art teacher in San Francisco about a volunteer painting I'd brought in that I just never went on with it. Part of my plan for retirement is to do art.

DUCKWORTH: I know you've been interested in dance for a long time. Did you ever consider being a dancer?

HARRISON: Well, I always liked that, and remember that was part of my training. . . . I started working with dancers in San Francisco, and really haven't stopped. I like to work with dancers, though increasingly my interest is puppetry.

DUCKWORTH: Did you ever consider going into architecture, or was that just a passion?

HARRISON: No, I didn't, though of course as a child I always wanted to build mother a dream house. But it has gotten to be more and more of a passion over two or three decades.

DUCKWORTH: I know by 1934 you were studying with Henry Cowell in San Francisco. You must have made some kind of a decision toward music by that point?

HARRISON: No, I've never made a decision. The word "decision" I've always thought of as implying those people who can think. I can't think. I just go where the attraction is. I eat my way through life, as you can see by my shape.

DUCKWORTH: What do you substitute for thinking? How do you maneuver in the world?

HARRISON: Actually by affections, and by personal relationships and enthusiasms, that's what it amounts to. I'm a sensualist, so anything that appeals to me sensually will get investigated. That's too dull a term . . . will get grabbed. I'm greedy.

DUCKWORTH: What was studying with Cowell like?

HARRISON: Well, it was quite marvelous, and I don't think it ever stopped, you know. In the first instance I went to him to take his course in world music, which was called Music of the Peoples of the World, at the University of California, San Francisco. And I was delighted by it and we got acquainted. He made me his monitor in class, and then I showed him pieces, and I began to study with him. Well, it was catch as catch can; we would meet here and there and yon. I invited him to the house finally and Mother made dinner. And Dad and Mother were just awfully nervous . . . a composer coming. You know, they just didn't know what they would talk about, so they were completely out of water. And Henry sat down and in, I suppose, an exchange of three or four sentences had the whole family entranced. He somehow quickly found out that Dad was interested in automobiles and knew something about them, so he described a complete transcontinental trip that he had made in a converted diesel-engine car, which at that time was far out. Dad was absolutely awestruck. It was Henry; he could deal with anything. Then I attended the Cowell house and became a friend of Olive Cowell. She ran a salon in the old style. Olive was very instrumental in introducing me to everybody. In her house, for example, I met and played for Varèse, and I met Schoenberg, and just oodles and oodles of people, because everyone was invited to the Cowell house.

DUCKWORTH: What did you play for Varèse?

HARRISON: It was a ricercare on the name of Bach, in disonant counterpoint.

DUCKWORTH: That you had written?

HARRISON: Yes. And he liked it very much, right off the bat. He was a very good friend to me. In New York, he sponsored a concert in which I was sort of featured. He was very impressive to me, and also, since he was very friendly, it made quite an image. I visited him every so often.

DUCKWORTH: Was it Cowell's suggestion that you study with Schoenberg, or did you make a decision to change teachers?

HARRISON: Oh, no. What happened was that I decided to move to Los Angeles. I had a friend who wanted to dance, so I decided to move with my friend. I had worked with Lester Horton many times before and I knew that I could work with Lester there. And I also asked the people in the dance department at UCLA whom I already knew if they had a post that I could take, and they said, "sure." By this time I had learned how to do dance notation, Labanotation, so I taught that; I taught musical form for dancers; and I accompanied classes. And then I felt, well, Schoenberg is here and he has a symposium. So I went up and asked his assistant, Harold Halma, if I could join in. He said, "Let's go ask Schoenberg." So he knocked on the door of Schoenberg's study, and then without further ado he opened it. And Schoenberg was apparently in high concentration because he looked up and started twitching all over. And I thought, "Oh, my God." But then he got control of himself, and said, yes it would be okay if I came. So I did. And I don't know how long that was, whether it was one or two semesters, something like that. There were just a few of us. But I thought it was wonderful.

DUCKWORTH: How did the symposium work? What was the format?

HARRISON: If we had a piece we would show it to Schoenberg and he would comment. The first thing I did was to be a naughty boy and take him a neoclassic piece. And he didn't bat an eye. He wasn't interested in the style at all. He was interested in the musicality, whether the piece worked, et cetera. Boy, my admiration for him went up like that. There were obviously no clamps in that man's mind. And he was very sweet and very humorous, and at one point (I guess it was a piece of mine; I'd written a quite light one) he said, "I wish I could write light music. Everything I touch turns to lead." And of course we sort of had to help him when airplanes went over; he had a tendency to want to crawl under the piano . . . Berlin, you know. And then occasionally we would listen to birds. If there wasn't anything, we'd ask him to do something, like we asked him to analyze one of his string quartets and he said, "Oh yes, I'll show you. It's very easy to write." So he brought it in and he showed us how he did it and anybody could have written it. It was perfectly clear. It was very easy, once you learned the tricks by which he did it, you see.

DUCKWORTH: I was under the impression he never told anybody how he did it.

HARRISON: Oh no, he was perfectly friendly about it. He had a grand time showing us how to do it. Also, if nobody could think of anything to ask him, he would ask us to analyze a part of a Beethoven symphony or something.

DUCKWORTH: Did having Schoenberg explain his music make you want to write twelve-tone music?

HARRISON: No. It wasn't a twelve-tone piece; it was the pre–twelve-tone period. And as a matter of fact, I already knew how to write twelve-tone music. I got myself into trouble with a twelve-tone piece and took that to him. Halma had told me he wouldn't look at it, but I took it. I was stuck. I'd just written myself into a corner. It was a piano suite. I played for him what I had done in the third movement, and I said, "I'm having trouble; I don't know what to do." And he said, "Is this twelve-tone?" And I said—trembling—"Yes, it is." He said, "It is good. Go on. Go on." And then he just plunged in. "Nothing but the essentials," he said, "Only the salient things, don't complicate it. Go where the line goes." And, boy, was I relieved because it sort of threw all this garbage off me and it meant take the salient line where the music goes. So that was a real help all the way down the line; I've never forgotten it. Also, when it was clear I was going to New York (again with Lester's group—he was going to New York and my dancer friend was going) . . . so I was leaving and I told him that and he said, "Why are you going?" And I said, "Well, I don't really know." And he said, "I know. You're going for fame and fortune. And good luck." And then he added, "Don't study with anybody; you don't need to study with anybody. Study only Mozart." So I quickly went out and got the piano sonatas and studied Mozart. And then later I thought, "Well, on his own desk he had on one side Mozart and the other Bach." Apparently I had gone as far as I needed in Bach. Apparently I could write polyphony, that was my conclusion.

DUCKWORTH: What did you learn from Mozart?

HARRISON: Balance, proportion, and the salient, exactly what he had told me about my own piece, in fact . . . that light clarity.

DUCKWORTH: Was it in his class that you first met John Cage?

HARRISON: Oh no, John had studied with him ten years before. No, I met John Cage because . . . when I was in San Francisco, Henry Cowell had mentioned that there was somebody in Los Angeles at that time with whom I had things in common and he thought we would get along. I sort of forgot about it, and then one day at my door there was a knock and there stood John, and he said, "I'm John Cage and Henry Cowell has sent me." So I said, "Please come in." And within a couple hours we were very good friends. He showed me a piece and we exchanged ideas and pieces and so on. And we've been friends ever since.

DUCKWORTH: How did the idea of the percussion concerts the two of you organized come about?

HARRISON: Many years before, when I was just getting acquainted
with Henry, he did a piece . . . actually, it was a theater piece and he
did music for it. The Palo Alto Community Theater was just opening and this was one of their earliest productions. What Henry did,
of course, from his vast background in world music, was to make a
box on the stage just like the Kabuki has it. But you didn't know
this until later, it was part of the set. Inside it was a tiny little piano,
and percussion everywhere—both melodic and nonmelodic percussion. And every scene was accompanied by a percussion ostinato. As I recall, there may have been one or two songs, but I'm not
quite sure of that. At any rate, it was accompanied; the whole
drama had this musical background, and only at the end was the
curtain drawn aside and you saw that this was what it was. And I
became fascinated with that idea. Not too much later, Henry introduced me to [Varèse's] *Ionization*, and [Amadeo] Roldán and
[Alejandro Garcia] Caturla, and such percussion music as existed.
So I started writing for it right away. And then John Cage and I organized concerts. We used Mills College when the Bauhaus was there
and they helped us stage it. We did the big masterpieces on one of
those concerts. We did the Varèse, the Caturla, and the Roldan
Ritmicas, which is for a large ensemble too. It was fun. We continued to give concerts. I had introduced John by this time to Bonnie
Bird and that took, and he went up to the Cornish School and
worked. So we were in communication between San Francisco and
Seattle. In the meantime, I was busy working with dancers at Mills
College. So we did keep in touch, and we had a summer session at
Mills and we invited William Russell, too. Then at some time John
moved back to San Francisco and we gave a fairly famous concert,
the California Hall concert, in which we alternated our pieces. And
at his suggestion we wrote *Double Music* together, which is still
holding the boards. All of this, plus the work of Gerald Strang, Ray
Green, and a number of others, produced what is now thought of
as a classic age of percussion orchestra on the West Coast that
spread everywhere after the second World War.

DUCKWORTH: How were those early concerts of percussion music
received?

HARRISON: The last one I gave in San Francisco at the Fairmont
Hotel, for example, the man who sold tickets sold them twice over.
People were hanging on chandeliers and clinging to windows . . . all

sorts of things. And we always got critical attention, both before and after. I mean really serious critical attention.

DUCKWORTH: Did you have the feeling that you were doing something new and important?

HARRISON: No, we didn't care, we were having fun. This question didn't enter. We were just doing things. Then, we sort of threw away the manuscripts; now, people search for them.

DUCKWORTH: Did you go to New York without a real plan of what you were going to do there?

HARRISON: I just knew that I had a job accompanying dancers, that was all. Of course, John was already there. He'd gone to Chicago, and then to New York. In the meantime, in L.A., I'd read Virgil Thomson's first book, *State of Music*, and enjoyed it enormously. So I asked John to introduce me, and we got acquainted. Very quickly, through Henry and John and Virgil, I got acquainted pretty well.

DUCKWORTH: And you started writing music reviews too, didn't you?

HARRISON: Yes.

DUCKWORTH: Did Virgil Thomson get you involved with that?

HARRISON: Yes. I took Paul Bowles's place on the *Herald Tribune* when Paul left. I'd been doing a little writing before that; Minna Lederman was my editor on *Modern Music Quarterly*. She was the first to ask me to review. That was within a month or so of my arrival, in fact. And of course, working with and for Virgil, too, is great help. I learned an awful lot about writing from Virgil, who writes very well.

DUCKWORTH: Were you influenced by him musically?

HARRISON: Yes, of course. Because it dawned on me at once that just as serial music is a watertight system, so is the extreme simplicity of Virgil. And they represent the polar balances—in the middle is sort of lush romanticism. But the polar balance is this clear, sharp wit of Virgil's music and the closed, perfectly functioning system of Schoenberg. It was wonderful to find the polar balance. Virgil understood right away, and we got along very well. As he once said, "We're both round, pink-faced intellectuals." And we've always loved one another.

DUCKWORTH: How did your interest in Ives's music develop?

HARRISON: That happened before I left San Francisco. I had already encountered in the *New Music Edition*, which I subscribed to, such printings of Ives as had been done up to that point. And I also had read Henry Cowell's marvelous essay on Ives in *American Composers on American Music*. I was fascinated. So I asked Henry, "How do I get better acquainted with Ives's music? How can I contact all this?" And he said, "Why don't you write to Mr. Ives?" So he gave me the address of the brownstone in New York, and I used Henry's name, and within about a month, I think, arrived a big crate. It contained eleven volumes of chamber music, which Mr. Ives asked me eventually to give to the New Music Society, and which I did when I moved to New York; it had a torn-up and reconstructed version of the "Emerson" sonata, plus a section that I don't know if it's now incorporated or not; it had four violin sonatas; it had the two string quartets; it had just about the bloody works . . . everything. When I got to New York, I already knew Mr. Ives through letters, you see. Though he didn't write at that time, his wife did. One of my letters, the first one, turns out to be from Edith,* a daughter, I think. All the rest are Harmony's transcriptions from Mr. Ives's sketches.

DUCKWORTH: Have you published those letters?

HARRISON: No, I gave them all to Yale. John Kirkpatrick came out and spent a week helping me get them together. Then I just gave them all . . . and I got a letter: "Thanks for this princely gift." I'm a little naïve; I wasn't aware of the commercial value. But in any case, I don't think it would have bothered me. I just gave them where they should go, which is Yale.

DUCKWORTH: When I think of your music I don't think of Ives and Ruggles. What attracted you to them?

HARRISON: R&D. You know I wrote a little booklet on Ruggles. I liked that kind of counterpoint, secundal counterpoint, which I'd also studied with Henry. I liked that kind of sound. Also, I spent hours at the piano with both the Ruggles and the Ives scores . . . hours and hours and hours struggling to get through, and to hear, and to study, and so on. They're a real part of me. And also

---

*Heidi von Gunden says that that was from Chester Ives, and she quotes it in her book.

Wallingford Riegger. That whole . . . what I have called the New Music Group: [John J.] Becker, Riegger, Ives, Ruggles, Cowell. Yes, those were the ones that interested me.

DUCKWORTH: What did you feel about the American composers of the French School that came from Nadia Boulanger? Did they seem to be doing interesting things?

HARRISON: When I was growing up in San Francisco, I was able to hear recordings of Roy Harris, which I liked. I also got the score of the piano sonata and learned that; I found that fascinating. Aaron Copland, I liked the *Variations*. Those had been recorded, I think by Aaron himself. Actually, when I was in Los Angeles, he was making a movie right across the street. I lived across the street from Metro-Goldwyn-Mayer Studio. He was right there, so I made an appointment with him and went to his studio. He was just marvelous. Right off the bat, he was friendly as all get out. He said he wanted to become an authority on my music. Well, this goes very well with a young composer. And he showed me around the set, too. So I have known Aaron from that time on. This was while I was working with Schoenberg, too. And Peter Yates was important in my life in Los Angeles. He was actually my first contact with early-music intonation through Wesley Kuhnley, who is a very good friend of his and and who built harpsichords and virginals, and tuned them in mean tone and other such things. He, very early, was doing Baroque and Renaissance tunings, so I heard them right away. Peter Yates was into this and did a lot of his own playing on that. His book *An Amateur at the Keyboard* comes out of that experience as well. He had also, as you know, founded the Monday Evenings on the Roof, which were literally on the top floor of his home there, and I visited there many times. We were good friends during my period in Los Angeles.

DUCKWORTH: Were the introduction to world music through Henry Cowell and the introduction to intonation through Peter Yates the two major early influences on you?

HARRISON: Yes, along with one other: the San Francisco Public Library. I haunted it. I took out every book I could. And the music department was well equipped. By the time I was a midadolescent, I had gone through all of the Rameau and Lully operas; I'd gone through all the Pedrell collection from Spain; I'd gone through all the organ works of France in the nineteenth century; I'd gone through all the standard literature; and every work of Schoenberg, which they collected. This is just to begin with, not speaking of theory and so on. By the time I had finished my two years at San Francisco State, I was an expert madrigal singer and had gone through the entire Tudor collection of madrigals and church music, as well. So I have a background in European music that precedes all the rest. Also, remember this: San Francisco's Chinatown was where you went and sat in opera all evening, too, every night of the year.

DUCKWORTH: Did such divergent interests always influence your music, or did you reach a point where you consciously brought them into it?

HARRISON: I've never consciously done anything. I wish I could. I would probably live a better life if I had a mind.

DUCKWORTH: How did they get in there then?

HARRISON: Well, just because I loved them: "me, too," that's the idea. If I like something, I want to do that too. It's greed; that's the basis of it.

DUCKWORTH: When you moved to New York, did it feel like a more exciting place to be than California?

HARRISON: I don't know what to answer there. It was confusing. It was hard to get adjusted. I never did, you know; I finally broke down. I had a big breakdown at the end of my stay in New York. I've often referred to it, since returning to my native area, as having done ten years in New York. It was exciting, but it was very unproductive in some ways. But there was a lot germinating, of course. Remember that I already knew and had done things about Ives, was already friends with Henry Cowell and John Cage, and already an admirer of all the composers that I was to meet in New York— Wallingford Riegger especially, who was very good friends with Henry. It wasn't a big blast of revelation, if that's what you're suggesting. It was during the war, too, remember. New York was very different then than it was after the war. I just worked as I worked in all the other places, as a matter of fact. There was a lot more going on, but I just . . . as you grow older, things get more complicated and you do more. This doesn't seem to stop.

DUCKWORTH: Do you miss New York in any sense?

HARRISON: Oh no. I couldn't live there for the world. When John Cage recommended me and I went to Black Mountain College, I had my conversion to country living. About three days in a big city and I'm starting another breakdown. I just can't stand it; I'm a country boy. I have to have quiet. I don't want my ears ringing from motors all day long. I still have my hearing you know, it's very acute . . . at least for music. And I don't want to lose it . . . until I retire, and then I don't care. I would miss the loss of sight more than the loss of hearing.

DUCKWORTH: Did you go to Black Mountain to teach?

HARRISON: Yes.

DUCKWORTH: How long were you there?

HARRISON: Well, I was there about a year. Then I went back again because I got my first Guggenheim Fellowship and wrote an opera while I was there. That's my *Rapunzel*. Black Mountain was fun. There were a lot of people there, too—painters, poets, Charles Olsen was there, Paul Goodman came, Rauschenberg, Twombly, and Ben Shahn.

DUCKWORTH: Was Black Mountain the artistic nirvana that all the recent books portray it as being?

HARRISON: Well, it wasn't nirvana. It was, as all artistic milieus are, turbulent, and exciting, interesting, and troublesome. After all, it snows there. And the harvest had to be got in, because it was a farm. It was also beautiful, and there was much exchange of ideas and lots of humor and fun. And the student/faculty ratio was very low.

DUCKWORTH: I understand Leontyne Price once sang in *Rapunzel*. How did that come about?

HARRISON: She sang when I went to Rome in 1954 for a conference. Pieces were done, and that was the one I submitted. It was actually a contest for young composers, so to speak. I submitted the third act in an arrangement for a small chamber orchestra. Leontyne Price sang it there and it won a prize. Ben Weber and I got up in the morning and I gaily said, "Oh, let's go down and collect our prizes." We had to go down for the ceremony. And you could have knocked me over with a piano when they called me. I was very much surprised. It was a shared prize with [Maurice] Martenon.

DUCKWORTH: Didn't Stravinsky present the prize to you?

HARRISON: Yes, he handed it to me, and I had a conversation with him. That was when he was like a tennis player, bouncing all the time. And he was a regular chamber of commerce for the United States, too. Amazing. I loved Rome and Italy at that time. Now, I just don't want to have any more to do with Italy.

DUCKWORTH: Why is that?

HARRISON: Oh my God. Within two hours of landing in Rome a few years ago, Bill Colvig was tumbled on the street by three motorcycles and was quite ill from it . . . injured. We got sick from smog in Pompeii. I physically fought off a robber in a park in a public street on a Sunday afternoon. It was just one damn thing after the other. And I concluded that I don't like Italians; I don't like Italy. What I like is the Roman Empire.

DUCKWORTH: They're not there anymore.

HARRISON: They sure aren't! Or it wouldn't be an anarchy conducted as a pandemonium, which is what it is now. No thank you, I don't like it. Unless you're a devout Christian there's nothing to see, because all the antiquities are wrapped in green plastic, trying to save them from the motor car. There's not going to be anything left but Christian churches. And if you're not a devout Christian, who wants to go? It's awful.

DUCKWORTH: If you were going to send a young composer to Europe these days, where would you tell him or her to go?

HARRISON: Oh, Germany. Germany and England. Or also Holland. Those three. It's northern Europe. France is absolutely . . . I don't think they even have blinders, they're simply blind. And deaf. There's nothing there. And Italy is too dangerous; it's not a civilized community anymore. No, I'd send them to the North.

DUCKWORTH: Can we talk a little bit about how you work? How do you compose?

HARRISON: Fundamentally, I'm a melode; I write everything from the melody. Everything. No matter how big a symphonic thing it is, say, or gamelan, or whatever, it's a melody and all the rest is subsidiary to that. The melody may appear or, if I have a multi-movement work, a little measure or so will say "write me," and it will appear. I hear it. Also, I don't read subvocally; I hum. So whistling or humming the tunes is important, number one to get the intervals right, and also to be specific about the rhythm. Again, I suppose, following up from two things—Schoenberg's pointing out about the salient, and also a breakdown which relieved me of a lot. I threw off a lot. Then I took that even more seriously, so there was a time when I would not write down any note that I couldn't hear, that I wasn't actually hearing in my head. That meant accompaniments, too. Everything. Everything I had to hear or be able to hum quickly, before I would put it down.

DUCKWORTH: What was your rationale for that?

HARRISON: That was the only integrated stuff; that was the salient, the real thing. That was what counted in the long run. And I do believe—fundamentally, cross my heart—that your take-home pay from a piece of music is a melody . . . the tune. And that's it. How do we recollect almost anything we know? It's the tune. So I write them. It's the melodic basis which counts. And that's both vocal and kinetic. If it doesn't have the kinetic underpinning, the kinetic pleasure as it goes, then it isn't working. So that's the basis. I'm a melode.

DUCKWORTH: Do you hear music all the time in your head, or can you go in and out of it?

HARRISON: I still am victim, as we all are all our lives, of some damn tune that won't shut up. Sometimes it's my own; sometimes it's another one; sometimes it's a brand new one—which I suppose to be new, I don't know where they come from.

DUCKWORTH: So sometimes you pay attention to it and sometimes you don't?

HARRISON: Yes. And sometimes I just complain to my companion, "How am I going to stop it? Do something, please."

DUCKWORTH: I often have a situation where I'm in some meeting but inside my head I'm off in another world writing or hearing a piece.

HARRISON: Yes, yes. It's a place we all go to. That's why we're composers.

DUCKWORTH: Do you feel like your life has always been integrated with your music, or is music the "job"?

HARRISON: No. When I see a deadline approaching I have to just say, "Sorry, I can't go to your party," or, "Sorry, I can't attend your performance." I just have to do it, so I do it . . . which we all do. As I get older, I'm very careful with anyone who wants a piece. I'm very, very careful to be sure.

DUCKWORTH: How much will you work each day when you are confronted with a deadline?

HARRISON: I'm manic. If it starts, it's almost impossible to stop. I have to drug myself out, or ask Bill to hit me with a two-by-four to get any sleep. Once it has started, it's a disease. It's terrible. I get up all night long; it won't stop. And all day long until I'm just totally exhausted. I go as far as I can.

DUCKWORTH: Is that technical and mechnical work you're doing, or do you mean you're hearing things continuously?

HARRISON: It's composing. I'm hearing, yes. It becomes a fever, a bodily fever.

DUCKWORTH: So you just tune into it instead of ignoring it?

HARRISON: Tune in? I can't help it. I wouldn't tune into it for anything. Because once I allow it to start—just two or three notes—there it goes. I'm helpless. Put a quarter in me and I'm like a jukebox. It's not at all pleasant from that point of view. Aren't you the same?

DUCKWORTH: Yes, I can get crazy with it, but I'm one of the people who can work a little bit each day.

HARRISON: Oh, lucky you.

DUCKWORTH: Some people have told me they can go six months without doing a lick of work, but when they do start it's the way you've described.

HARRISON: Oh, I'm not that way. I work. But there are little jogs. I can't be that methodical, though I do remember advice that Virgil gave me a long time ago, which is to make an appointment with the muse and keep the regular appointment. If she doesn't come, at least you're there.

DUCKWORTH: Well, do you keep your appointment?

HARRISON: When I'm actually working I see to it, yes. It's all done at home; I have no other place to go. And the home is also a studio of the college, and it's connected, apparently, on a sort of planetary basis by phone. It's really one huge office. Now I have a trailer that I go out to. There's no phone, so I can get away to my trailer and work there. I have a little electronic keyboard that helps me if I need that, though I prefer working on my big piano that Henry and Sydney Cowell gave me; it's an 1871 nine-foot Steinway. And it's in Kirnberger's Number 2 temperament. And of course it's so much more beautiful than equal temperament.

DUCKWORTH: Do you tune it yourself?

HARRISON: No. I used to, but I'm so damn busy I don't have time to tune the piano anymore, or even the harpsichord.

DUCKWORTH: Is the computer useful to you in your work with tunings and temperaments?

HARRISON: No. Electronics, generally, I regard as phonography. They're very useful for finding out what is going on in the highlands of Mongolia, or somewhere else. But I don't use them. Of course, I'm not young; I'm not raised for it. Also, I don't like the sound of loudspeakers.

DUCKWORTH: Do you have a standard answer for why you prefer just intonation over equal temperament? Why does it appeal to you?

HARRISON: No, I don't. There are lots of answers. Number one, the music sounds better, it just does . . . because I'm a sensualist. Also, the hearing of those just intervals pulls me, whereas in equal temperament I feel as though I'm on ice skates. I get vertigo in equal temperament whereas I don't in just intonation. And I find it more deeply affecting; it really pulls at you. Because that's the way we're built, too. It's the same inside and outside then. It's not a fabrication of the mind.

DUCKWORTH: Do you think one reason that's so might be that with equal temperament most of the intervals are high-ratio intervals, while with just intonation you have a wider variety of low ratios?

HARRISON: Oh right, yes. It's the surds that are difficult. They turn up in mean tone, as well. Rameau was the first to observe in northwest Asia that nature never puts two of the same thing together. There are no examples of it. But in all the equal-division affairs you have two of the same thing. And the result is neither one is right. I'd rather have some of them right, or as many as you can. Mean tone also, you see, has the "mean" tone, and it's an exact split of

(L. to r.) Aaron Copland, Virgil Thomson, and Lou Harrison, Alice Tully Hall, New York, 1976

the 5/4, which means that it is neither a 9/8 or a 10/9, or anything. It's a surd. By the way, in mathematics the word "surd" means deaf. And there's another point about just intonation; it's not from deafness. The intervals of just intonation are rational; they're ratios, in short. They correspond to the way we're built. Ever since I took up studying just intonation, which was when Virgil gave me Harry Partch's book and when I went out and bought a tuning hammer, I've been training myself in interval recognition. Basically, I know all the useful ones and know my way around in a continuum of structural relations, let's put it that way. I've always had, also, an architectural interest; I've always had a certain gift at structural visualization anyway. And to that I've added now the precision techniques of music. And this is after a long time, from 1948 to today, that's quite a lot of years. So there are not too many intervals that I don't instantly recognize. I don't even name them mentally anymore; I just know what they are. Which also makes living fun, because you know what the ratios of the bells are, and you listen to the noon whistles and you say, "Oh yes, there is a 9/4," if you want to. It makes the objective world a little more fun to know the exact ratios.

DUCKWORTH: When you listen to an orchestra concert—Wagner, Elgar, your own music—does music written in that intonation seem grayer to you, or more bland?

HARRISON: It depends. The orchestra, as you're perfectly well aware, Bill, is a mixed bag. The strings, if left to their own devices and if they're really playing well, are playing in a form of just intonation. So are the trombones. And woodwinds, if it's slow enough, will bend, as they say, to get it into some sort of intonation. Conductors spend hours sometimes just balancing, as they call it, woodwinds. What they mean is, get that to a five to four ratio, not a tempered third. And you'll hear them doing that. If you listen very carefully you'll hear the winds, even the valved brass, doing things like this. All the way through, the Western orchestra is that way with the exception, of course, of the pretuned instruments, which are in equal temperament. That's why I use them for drones for the most part. Because I want the rest of the orchestra to sound as much in tune as they can. And the assumption is they will. For example, if you actually write a 7/6, you can get it if you have enough rehearsal time to explain it. That will do it. I have tuned full orchestras, and it works. You can retune an orchestra. Of course, you have to know what you're doing.

DUCKWORTH: Do you have any worries, given the current influence and control exerted by Western European instruments of the nine-teenth century, that people like yourself are in some ways beating their heads against a wall?

HARRISON: I would first remind you, Bill, that over 85 percent, nearly 90 percent, of the music that I experience during a week is not such music. It is not current practice. It's Javanese gamelan tuned in just intonation. That's what I spend twenty hours a week teach-ing, and I hear a whole orchestra of it in my house all the time. And the other gamelan (that's plural) that I'm associated with are all in just intonation, too. For example, the *pelog* of both *Si Betty* and the Mills gamelan, *Si Madelene*, are overtones 12, 13, 14, 17, 18, 19, and 21. That's regarded as high stuff. But it was, in fact, actually chosen by a Javanese out of things I was doing who, when he said it's a good *pelog*, also said, "It'll be very good with voices." So immediately I knew that there were gamelan that were harder to sing with than others. Well, if you had told me fifteen years ago that voices could easily sing overtones 12, 13, 14, 17, 18, 19, and 21, I'd have said, "No way." The minute we tried voices it was like falling off a log. So there you go.

DUCKWORTH: But you're in an unusual situation. Most of us don't hear a gamelan once a year, much less daily.

HARRISON: Well, I'm talking from where I am, see. I find I don't listen much to normal northwest Asian music. I used to get up and put on Handel's *Water Music* or something like that. Now it's rare that I put on a record of anything. I have to go to concerts of course, and listen to people's music, and performers, and so on. Some of it I enjoy; some of it I don't. But as I said in desperation last year (and this is prelude to giving up writing for northwest Asian instruments), "If you don't like the pitches, why write for them?" How can you, finally, write for them? It is a torture to me. I've arrived at this compromise and everybody knows that I'm doing it: I've tuned my piano into Kirnberger Number 2, which is superior, and I write for northwest Asian instruments in that. And then I don't really care whether I hear it in their production; that's what it amounts to. Because I will know whether the piece is any good through that. That's the way I want to hear it. But I don't want to trouble people, is the point. And so they will make do. That's the way I deal with that. I can't stand to work in equal temperament anymore!

DUCKWORTH: Do you think of yourself as an experimental composer?

HARRISON: No! I'm always identified as one of America's experimentalists, you see, and here I couldn't be more conservative. I write melodies. I see that they are in just intonation. Everything has to be right. I even put costumes proper on my gamelan players. I'm a rank conservative.

DUCKWORTH: Well, how can you be both in R&D and conservative at the same time?

HARRISON: In order to get these things right, you have to do research and development.

DUCKWORTH: But then you're an experimentalist.

HARRISON: Well . . . any way you want it. I have fun at it, anyway.

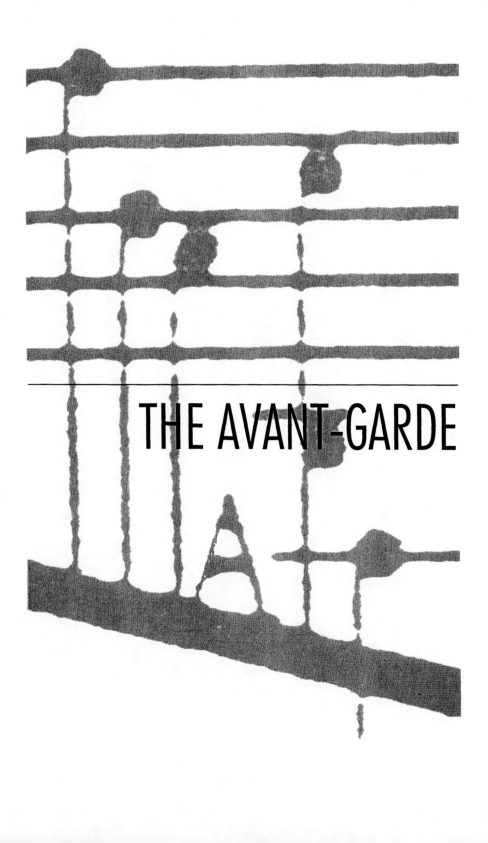

THE AVANT-GARDE

CHAPTER **5**

BEN JOHNSTON

Born Macon, Georgia, 1926

WHAT INTERESTS Ben Johnston the most is getting his music precisely in tune. To do this, he writes in a form of extended just intonation that, more often than not, uses more than fifty-three pitches per octave. The reason he does this is because he believes not only that it "sounds" better, but that irrationally dissonant music, that is, the tempered music we hear every day, is physically and psychologically unhealthy for us.

Johnston has been composing with microtones almost exclusively since 1960, and now has a significant body of works, the heart of which is a group of nine string quartets. Although fiendishly difficult, and including a unique set of special accidentals to indicate varying degrees of sharpness and flatness, these quartets exhibit enormous variety. *Number Two*, for example, applies a strict twelve-tone technique to the fifty-three-note scale, while *Number Four* is a set of variations on the well-known hymn-tune "Amazing Grace." As a group, these quartets are widely taken to be masterpieces, and Johnston is universally regarded as one of America's foremost composers of microtonal music. Johnston, himself, however, likes to say that he doesn't deal in microtones; they are just a by-product. He prefers to be known as a composer who works with the nuances of pitch and intonation.

Ben Johnston was born in Macon, Georgia, in 1926, the son of a newspaperman. He attended the College of William and Mary in Virginia, and from there went to the Cincinnati Conservatory for graduate work. While studying in Cincinnati, a musicologist on the faculty gave him Harry Partch's book *Genesis of a Music*. Although the teacher thought Partch's ideas about tuning were worthless, Johnston was fascinated, and immediately wrote to Partch, telling him of his own interests. Partch wrote back, and within the year Johnston, along with his new bride, moved to California to live and work with Partch. Johnston did this based solely on his enchantment with Partch's ideas; he had never actually heard any of his music.

Although refusing to play the role of teacher, Partch willingly answered any of Johnston's questions, of which there were many. Unfortunately, within six months of arrival, Partch's health deteriorated to the point where any further work was impossible. He did, however, arrange for Johnston to begin studying with Darius Milhaud, who was teaching at Mills College. Johnston worked with Milhaud for two years, completing a second master's degree in 1953.

In the early fifties, Johnston began teaching at the University of Illinois in Urbana, first as a composer in the dance department, later as a member of the composition faculty in the school of music. His first year at Illinois, John Cage arrived, and gave a talk about composing by chance that, according to Johnston, "created an absolute scandal." Most of the audience shouted, booed, and walked out. Afterwards, only three people stayed to speak with Cage, two of them being Johnston and his wife, Betty. Inviting Cage over to their apartment, they spent the remainder of the evening in discussion. That next summer, at Cage's invitation, Johnston went to New York, where he helped splice tape for Cage's electronic work *William's Mix*.

In 1959, at the age of thirty-three, Johnston returned to New York on a Guggenheim fellowship. His purpose was to use the RCA Mark II synthesizer at the Columbia/Princeton Electronic Music Studio to facilitate his work with microtonal music. But when that didn't work as planned, he turned to Cage for advice. The solution was that he studied with Cage, and Johnston began driving to Stony Point, New York, once a month for lessons. At the end of the fellowship year, Johnston returned to Illinois and began composing with microtones.

I spoke with Ben at his home in Rocky Mount, North Carolina, where he and Betty had moved, shortly after his retirement from Illinois in 1983. In some ways, this was the easiest of the interviews. Ben had been my teacher in the late sixties when I was a student at Illinois. And, as with many of Ben's students, our relationship had grown into a friendship. So we had a lot to talk about. Too much, in fact. It was one of the most difficult interviews to edit.

DUCKWORTH: What's the basic problem with being a microtonal composer?

JOHNSTON: Well, obviously, it's that performers are not always prepared to undertake altering their performance practice to the

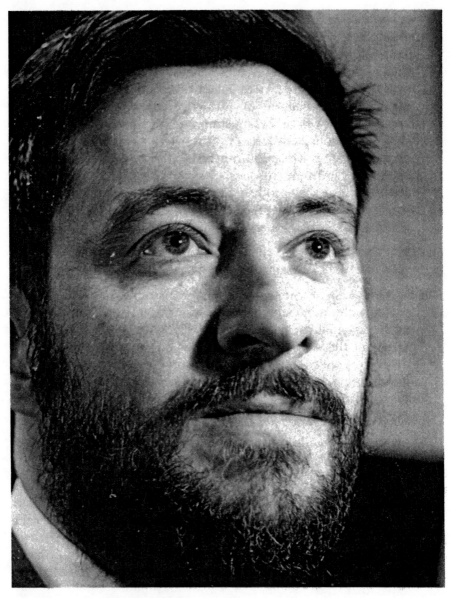

Ben Johnston, Urbana, IL, circa 1966

extent necessary. So you have to make sure that either you get very dedicated people, or you have to make the music a lot easier than, perhaps, you would make it if you had your druthers. Another problem is that with experienced players of contemporary music you can take for granted that they know the kind of sound that works well with an atonal piece. And they know how to play tonal music, too. They may even know how to play a variety of modal musics. But they haven't got the foggiest notion about blend and balance when it comes to these microtonal relationships. They don't know where their note fits into the general sound, and they can't react with that sort of instinctive adjustment because they don't know yet what that adjustment ought to be. So it has to be largely conscious, and that means there's a kind of learning process going on while you rehearse. The other thing is, I'm not just dealing with microtones. Microtones are the least of it. Microtones are a by-product of what I've asked for. I'm dealing with getting music very precisely in tune. And this means that the level of accuracy has got to be higher than usual.

DUCKWORTH: So you see the basic problem as the people involved, rather than the nineteenth-century instruments that they play on?

JOHNSTON: Well, of course, it's both. The instruments were designed for the twelve-tone tempered scale. But that still represents the best average that you could come to. If you're not going to have an instrument that has hundreds of holes bored in it—that will give you every conceivable nuance—you're going to have to make adjustments. So I don't really know how you could design instruments that would be a great deal better without their also being a great deal more difficult, as well as a great deal more expensive.

DUCKWORTH: What do you say to people in the orchestra who might say to you, "I don't hear these fine distinctions you're asking for and I don't see why they're so important."

JOHNSTON: They don't say that; I've never had anybody say that to me. The approach I use, you see, is that I don't tell them I want these fine distinctions. I say, "In order to get this in tune you're going to need to play this note a quarter-tone sharp or a quarter-tone flat. And it will sound smoother if you do that. That's what I'm after: that smooth sound. So go for maximum smooth. My indications with the accidentals are simply to help you discover which way you move your finger in order to get that." So if the player is willing to do that, and has got enough knowledge of the possibilities of his instrument to do that, then you're in good shape. Everything depends on willingness and on sharpness.

DUCKWORTH: What if they say they can't hear it?

JOHNSTON: If it comes to that, I just show them that they can. I say, "Well, can you just play this note a little sharper?" And they do. And then I say, "Now, listen to that. You can hear that blends." And they can hear that it blends; they don't have to hear that it's higher.

DUCKWORTH: Is that what you're hearing, the blend?

JOHNSTON: Sure. It's a harmonic matter. I hardly ever write music where you have melodic patterns unsupported. Since they're supported, you go by the harmonic blend to find where the notes are. And if you're doing it right, you'll get the notes right.

DUCKWORTH: What's the basic difference between, say, quarter-tone and eighth-tone music, and the extended just intonation you're working with?

JOHNSTON: Just intonation is a harmonic series with harmonic logic to it. The other is an arbitrary series in which any harmonic logic that you get comes not from the way the scale is put together, but from totally outside.

DUCKWORTH: Do quarter tones and eighth tones just compound the tuning problem inherent in equal temperament?

JOHNSTON: Well, they refine the grid, you might say, so that you can get closer to what you want. Alois Hába, in writing all those quarter tones and eighth tones, was really trying to get the sound that he heard in Balkan folk music. Balkan folk music is very rich because it was influenced by the Ottoman Empire all those years when the Turks dominated that part of the world. And from proximity to Asia . . . from ancient roots. So the sounds that Hábaiv was after were often scales that are not in the European tradition at all. In trying to get those, he simply made the grid of notes that he had finer and finer until he could get pretty close to what he was hearing.

DUCKWORTH: So quarter-tone music and extended just intonation are not an either/or situation?

JOHNSTON: Not really. I'll give you another example; American, this time. Ezra Sims is writing music with pretty much the same intentions as mine. And Ezra uses what he calls quarter tones because he realizes he can get close enough to the notes that he wants performers to hear. Then they tune it by ear. After they get the notes he'll say, "Well, just fine-tune it. Adjust it yourself." Essentially, that's not any different from what I do myself. The difference is that I'm telling the player *exactly* what it ought to be and saying, "Make your own adjustment as close as you can," which is just a nuance of difference.

DUCKWORTH: Do you think the people who write microtonal music are a subspecies of composer with superior hearing?

JOHNSTON: No. Definitely not. And neither did Harry Partch think that.

DUCKWORTH: Why, then, is there such a discrepancy between this relatively small subsegment of composers who write microtonal music and the vast majority of composers who seem perfectly satisfied in equal temperament?

JOHNSTON: Well, I don't think they *are* perfectly satisfied in equal temperament—even though they say they are if you ask them— because the history of music shows they're not. Pitch relationships in music have suffered a great decline in the twentieth century. Now, why did they do that? Well, because the old pitch relationships seemed tired and overworked and tedious. Well now, looking at the situation intellectually, a person—say Schoenberg, because he is a person who looked seriously at that problem—could say, "Well, we have a finite number of relationships that are possible and we've been overworking this small subset that we call tonality. Let's go for the others that have not been overworked, so as to get away from this rather tired situation." Well now, I think that, in fact, is a misjudgment as to why things were in a state of doldrums, I guess you could say. But it's plausible. So he made the solution to go for the unfamiliar relationships. And he was getting chords built out of the same notes Beethoven was using, but he used C-F-B, whereas Beethoven wouldn't have used that chord. The nearest Beethoven would come to even combining C and B would be C-E-G-B.

DUCKWORTH: What do you think the real reason for the problem was?

JOHNSTON: The clarity that had been the ideal in the eighteenth century was watered down. It was in that change from classical to Romantic [music] that the twelve-tone, equal-tempered scale was first adopted. There had been a period of two or three centuries before that when experimentation was going on about forms of temperament, but they were all unequal temperament. What you had in those earlier forms of temperament were a bunch of notes that were pretty well in tune, and a bunch outside that were screamingly out of tune. So you just didn't modulate any further away from home than a short distance, so as to avoid getting one of those so-called wolf tones that howled. That is a situation in which the difference between blended sound and distorted sound was sharply understood. Now, when you get to equal temperament, everything is slightly distorted, but nothing violently so. To get back to that sharp distinction between blending and not blending, heavy amounts of dissonance were added to the music, and that's the difference between early nineteenth-century music and late eighteenth-century music. Between late Beethoven and early Beethoven is the altered treatment of dissonance. It's not the only difference, but it's a very important difference.

DUCKWORTH: Which continued through Schoenberg.

JOHNSTON: It continued on. In fact, you could say it never has passed. Schoenberg's life strides that divide between sonata music and post–Romantic music of all types. And the post–Romantic music was aiming to get away from what had become clichés. Well, what was Romantic music aiming at? It was aiming at a richness which they somehow missed. And they were getting that by complication, by adding notes, by piling up notes.

DUCKWORTH: Are you suggesting that nobody understood that it was an acoustical problem?

JOHNSTON: I don't think anyone did. I won't say no one, because the Impressionists, I think, really had an insight into that. That's why I have frequently referred to an acoustics lecture I went to as a young person. I think I was about eleven. What this guy was talking about was the influence of Herman von Helmholtz's *On the Sensations of Tone* on late nineteenth-century composers and performers. It was the Impressionists who took that on, and it was one of the reasons they were called Impressionists, because the great concern of the Impressionist painter was with the purity of color. They wanted to get away from these muddied-down and blended colors of the nineteenth century—everything having black and white in it.

DUCKWORTH: I thought they wanted to explore the immediacy of the moment.

JOHNSTON: Well, it's partly that. But, you see, the way to get the immediacy of the moment—the way to get the instantaneous effect of light—was to blend pure colors together. Look at pointillism. Dots and dots and dots of pure color which, when you look at them from a distance, blend together in your mind, but which, in fact, are brilliant points of color. Now, that view of color is quite analogous to an acoustical view of tone. And the Impressionists were after a brilliant color in the sounds of music. In Russia, it was Scriabin. In France, more than Ravel (who was something of a neoclassicist in his thinking), it was Debussy. In America, it was Ives. The last works that Ives dealt with before he stopped writing were the quarter-tone impressions for piano. And all his sketches for his *Universe Symphony* show that he was thinking in terms of acoustical pitch relations. Well, this man giving this lecture was pointing out that the reason for Debussy's chords—the logic behind these chords—was that they approximated the higher reaches of the overtone series. Furthermore, you get an actual formulation of that in America by Henry Cowell. Apparently Marion Bauer, who wrote a book on American music, said that Cowell, among others, was dealing with the higher reaches of the overtone series and that you could even view the history of harmony into the twentieth century as a gradual inclusion of the higher overtones and their harmonic meaning.

DUCKWORTH: Well, Cowell had a background of world music to draw from.

JOHNSTON: Of course he did, and that, in fact, is the other aspect of it. It's the ethnomusicological aspect, you might say. Bartók. And Carrillo in Mexico, attempting to get the sounds of Indian music into his music by using all these quarter tones, eighth tones, and even sixteenth tones, in his case. So all these efforts were somehow based on the fact that these people were listening to and attempting to bring into European concert tradition other traditions that had nothing to do with the roots of European music. They didn't go back to the Middle Ages of Christian Europe. They didn't go back to ancient Greece. They went back to something else. To the Incas. To the Aztecs. Who knows? Or they went back to Asia.

DUCKWORTH: I've heard you describe equal temperament as based on an acoustical lie. What does that mean?

JOHNSTON: It means that a triad is not in tune when played in equal temperament and anybody can hear that. The third is way off and the fifth is even a little bit off. The fact that the fifth is off only 2 cents (which is 2/100 of a tone) is not very much if you look at it in a linear sense, but every violinist tuning his strings resents having to tune them according to the piano, and resists it. Well, that's only a 2-cent difference, but it's very audible to most people.

DUCKWORTH: Why, then, do most people claim that they can't hear it?

JOHNSTON: Because they've become acclimatized to it. If you constantly look at an out-of-focus movie you don't necessarily realize it's out of focus. But let somebody focus it and you know. You can get along without glasses, even when you need them, if you have to. But let somebody put glasses on you, that correct your visual problems, and you really see the world; it's quite a bit clearer looking than you were aware that it was. Or look at a poor color reproduction of a painting and you can accept those colors. They don't make you say, "Oh, no. Something's wrong with that." They make you say, "I don't see what's so great about that." But you then see the painting as it should be, as it really is, and you say, "Oh, well, yes, that's different." So I think it's that kind of reaction you really get from people. If they hear a triad that really is in tune, and can contrast it with one that isn't, nobody is in any doubt as to which one is in tune.

DUCKWORTH: How did you settle on a fifty-three-note scale as the one you felt was the most useful?

JOHNSTON: Well, there's a logic to it having to do with the derivation of the scales. I wanted to really go into this question of how scales are derived from acoustical materials because I think both Hindemith and Schoenberg, in their separate ways, made such a botch of it. I developed the scale using a computer, in fact. It's like Chinese boxes . . . how they fit into each other. You start with a triad, let's say, in a so-called five-limit system where you're not using any prime number larger than five, and you begin adding notes to it. You thicken the scale. Then you get your seven-tone major scale. Then you combine that with the parallel minor and you've got all but two notes. And you go on. You get a fifteen-note scale beyond the twelve-note scale, which is not very useful. Then you get a nineteen-note scale, which is quite useful. Then you get a thirty-one-note scale. You can compare that with Adriaan Fokker and the Netherlands composers. That's why they chose thirty-one-note equal temperament . . . so as to approximate that scale. Then you get a fifty-three-tone scale.

DUCKWORTH: Is what you're getting in each instance a closer approximation of pure intervals?

JOHNSTON: It isn't even that. It's that you get more different pure intervals.

DUCKWORTH: What do you mean by "more different"?

JOHNSTON: Well, for example, with the nineteen-note scale, what you've got is both versions of the black notes—the sharps and the flats both.

DUCKWORTH: What happens when you go to thirty-one?

JOHNSTON: With thirty-one, you've got every version of all seven notes as well as the five. What you're getting into, you see, is enharmonics. You're dealing with C double-sharp, D double-flat, notes like that. And with the fifty-three, you're dealing with the syntonic comma, and you've got all the comma inflections. And sixty-five is simply a greater refinement of that.

DUCKWORTH: Do you ever deal with a scale so complicated you can't hear it?

JOHNSTON: Oh sure. In the Seventh Quartet I deal with a scale that has over 100 notes in it, and I'm sure I can't hear that. But the point is that what you hear is this chain of relationships that the scale will produce. At the end of the chain you have moved a certain pitch difference. And that chain of relationships is easy enough to hear; the quartet deals with that chain of relationships, rather than with the scale.

DUCKWORTH: I'd like to back up a little bit and talk about how you got into all this. Wasn't it while you were studying at the Cincinnati Conservatory that you first encountered Harry Partch's book *Genesis of a Music*?

JOHNSTON: Yes. There was a musicologist there who had a copy of it and he gave it to me. I, in effect, said, "Do you recommend this?" He said, "I think it's terrible, but you'll like it." That was because he knew that I was interested in an acoustic approach to music.

DUCKWORTH: How soon after you read the book did you write to Partch?

JOHNSTON: Right away.

DUCKWORTH: Did he respond immediately?

JOHNSTON: Yes. And he told me all what I should do, like buy an old organ and start tuning it. Well, I didn't have the money to buy an organ, or any knowledge about organs. The harmonium was just something I'd heard of, so to speak. And I didn't have a place; I would have had no place to put it. Besides, I knew that I wasn't good at that kind of thing. So it was like a momentary dash of cold water to realize that was what he was saying I ought to do. So I wrote and told him I didn't have the money or any place to do it in, and that, evidently, met with real sympathy because he had such a hard time in his whole career. And I told him I would very much like to come and work with him. That was just a pipe dream, but he set things in motion to try to see if he could work that out.

DUCKWORTH: Didn't you get married just before going to California to work with Partch?

JOHNSTON: Yes. And I wrote Harry and said, "I'm going to be married when I come out there," and got back this letter about biological traps . . . a nasty letter. That letter got lost. I'm real sorry. That was a classic. Anyhow, he was very upset. He thought this was idiotic. And not only idiotic, but unfair to her, to me, and to the history of music. I think he wanted me to come out there and be his paramour. I really do. But that was not going to happen. When I showed up with Betty he adjusted, but he deliberately gardened in the nude to embarrass her. And he brought boyfriends up to the ranch to embarrass both of us. That was, maybe, a week or two. After that, everything just dropped away and he stopped showing off and everything was adjusted, so to speak, on mutual terms. So that was one of those shoals that one rode over, finally. That was an interesting and difficult situation.

DUCKWORTH: How were you planning to support yourself while you worked with Partch?

JOHNSTON: Well, you see, what Harry arranged was to get me into Berkeley. And I had the G.I. Bill, which paid me $50 a month. So we lived on $50 a month plus whatever our mothers would send us. They were fairly generous, but we didn't have a lot of money. We were really living on nothing. Still, we had more than Partch did.

DUCKWORTH: What was your first impression when you met Partch?

JOHNSTON: He was unlike anything I had ever thought of or could have expected. But I rather quickly adjusted because I thought,

"Now what kind of a guy would do all these things?" He looked like his pictures in the book, as far as physically. But the way he dressed! He dressed like somebody who lives out in the middle of the woods and gathers firewood. He liked purple shirts . . . really special, Partch-type, bad taste. And he had this incredible house he'd made himself out of an old blacksmithy. He was a wonderful carpenter, aside from being an instrument builder. And all these marvelous instruments . . . I thought I was dreaming. . . . This was unbelievable.

DUCKWORTH: Did you and Betty live with Partch?

JOHNSTON: For the time being we stayed in a guest house he'd made—a little Japanese-style guest house with no furniture in it, just mats on the floor. Then, we had to adapt a cottage for our use, and that meant rebuilding the place. So under his supervision that's what we did. We climbed up on the roof and replaced all the shingles. I was very clumsy and not at all good with tools. I had to be trained, like some idiot, because no one had ever shown me how to do those things. My upbringing just never included any- thing like that. And Harry had grown up with this, you know. He was very scornful—just as harsh as he could be—but he realized we had to learn, so he had to put up with our clumsiness. Betty was no better than I. She had to learn how to cook on a wood stove. She made some impressive food and he liked that. I think he accepted her a little more readily because of that. As far as I was concerned, I wasn't afraid of work. I was willing to do all those things, I just didn't know how and I was clumsy. He could see I wasn't going to be any help to him building his instruments, so he set me to tuning. Every day I had to tune the instruments.

DUCKWORTH: What was a normal day with Partch like?

JOHNSTON: I would practice a part and he would tell me what I was doing wrong. Finally, he would say "That's more like it," and he would begin to get interested himself. "Now try to play it with me." And we would start. We would work up to recordings. And he did the same with Betty, although he would expect her to come down during the morning and work a little while. He would give her some instrument. He would show her. He was very patient with her, but he made her learn how to do these things. She had a pret- ty good ear. She was playing some guitars and a little bit of chromelodeon.

DUCKWORTH: What were the afternoons like?

JOHNSTON: In the afternoons we had to do chores. We had to go
find firewood . . . a great variety of things. Whatever building had to
be done. You see, he liked to use his mornings for creative work,
which made good sense, and then he would go out and do physical
work all afternoon. And he expected me to help him. So we would
get in his old Studebaker and drive where we had to go and do
whatever we had to do. They were building a ridge road up on top
of the coast range and they had bulldozed all of the trees out of the
way so there was a lot of wood lying around. And that's what we
used to do—go up to the road and get manzanita roots and things
like that.

DUCKWORTH: What did you do at night?

JOHNSTON: Well, we had kerosene lamps so we couldn't do a lot of
reading. We would sit and talk . . . go to bed early.

DUCKWORTH: After you got to know him, what impressed you the
most?

JOHNSTON: Total independence. He was irascibly independent. I
learned something about society that I never forgot, and that is, no
matter how few people there are, there are the same problems as
with millions. It's as though there's a certain amount of good stuff
and shit, and they have to go on, even if there are only a few people. That includes war and all the rest of it.

DUCKWORTH: What's the most important musical thing you learned
from him?

JOHNSTON: I learned all this just intonation stuff by ear. He discovered I had a good enough ear to know the stuff. I was beginning to
develop absolute pitch in Harry's system. He would say, "Sing
16/15," and I would do that. And he would say, "Sing 16/11," and I
would sing that.

DUCKWORTH: Did he have absolute pitch in his system?

JOHNSTON: No, no. Relative pitch. Very good relative pitch.

DUCKWORTH: What do you think he heard?

JOHNSTON: I have no idea.

DUCKWORTH: How did he work in his system?

JOHNSTON: I know how he worked, because I watched him do it. He would play one note; he would get the interval; he would get another note. Relative pitch. Theoretically, his mind was so good that everything . . . he had it right at his fingertips. Well, I didn't at that point. But I did better than anybody else he'd ever worked with. He liked me for that and we got along fine on that level. And he assumed I'd studied his book inside out. Well, I hadn't had an opportunity to, so I quickly did as much as I could, but even so, not enough. So I had to fake a little bit and that was unfortunate, because if I hadn't had to I would have learned an awful lot more from him. I had to teach myself later.

DUCKWORTH: Was he willing to teach you anything you wanted to know?

JOHNSTON: Yes.

DUCKWORTH: Did he volunteer anything?

JOHNSTON: No, I had to ask.

DUCKWORTH: Why do you suppose he wouldn't want you to say you studied with him?

JOHNSTON: He's not a teacher. He said, "I don't know how to compose and I don't want anybody claiming to have studied with me because I don't teach." He said, "I need help, and if you give me the help, I'll answer any questions you have." Which is what he did.

DUCKWORTH: Were you satisfied with that?

JOHNSTON: Well, I had to be.

DUCKWORTH: I understand you went out to California without having heard any of his music. What did you think when you finally heard it?

JOHNSTON: I thought *U.S. Highball* was a masterpiece, as I still think. And the *Li-Po Songs* were marvelous. That's all there was to hear, just about. The *Intrusions* that we were working on . . . I thought they were wonderful.

DUCKWORTH: How did you hear *U.S. Highball?*

JOHNSTON: He had put a record out when he was in Wisconsin.

DUCKWORTH: So you could listen to a record? I thought he lived more primitively than that.

JOHNSTON: He had playback equipment. And we had some electricity, but not much. He had a generator and he would run lights and
whatever off the generator. But it was fueled by gasoline and gasoline costs money. There was very little money, so we had to use it
very sparingly. When necessary, he could play records, but he didn't
do it except occasionally.

DUCKWORTH: Did Partch look at your music?

JOHNSTON: Yes, he listened to it. I had made acetates of some things
when I was at Cincinnati, and he listened to it and said, "Well,
you're really a composer." That's all he said.

DUCKWORTH: Did you write any music while you were there?

JOHNSTON: I had a commission from Wilford Leach. Wilford was a
college friend of mine; we did a musical together at William and
Mary. We had a lot of fun, and we won a BMI prize for the musical.
He got a job at the University of Virginia when he graduated. He
was doing a production of one of his plays there, and he wanted
music for the production, and he wanted me to write it. But I
couldn't because I didn't even have a piano, you know. I told him,
"This is hopeless. I can't do this!" But what finally happened was
that he was insistent, and I persuaded Harry, and Harry said, "Let's
do it with the instruments. That's the logical thing. It will get you
acquainted with the instruments." So the first thing we recorded
was music for Wilford Leach's *The Wooden Bird*. Well, Harry wrote
about half of it. He had to because I didn't work fast enough.

DUCKWORTH: How long did you work with Partch before he got sick?

JOHNSTON: Six months. We got all the *Intrusions* recorded, but
Harry's health started to break toward that end when we were
doing *Cloud Chamber Music*. It never got recorded properly
because Harry wasn't up to it and that haunted him. By that time
Donald Pippin was out there. He was accompanying ballet in New
York, didn't like it a bit, and wanted to be doing something else.
The idea of coming to the West Coast appealed to him, so he came
out and we did all the recordings. And Donald was a good keyboard player. He took over the chromelodeon duties and that was
very satisfactory. Harry was pleased.

DUCKWORTH: Didn't you also record *The Letter*?

JOHNSTON: Yes, we recorded all those pieces. We did a recording of his setting of Thomas Wolfe's *Dark Brother*, but it's not a good recording so it's never been released. Well, I have a southern accent, so Harry wanted me to do that and I did. I learned how to intone it and that, I think, impressed him more than anything else that I did. Because I learned it very quickly and very accurately and I didn't need to keep going to the instruments for the notes. I would sing it—and this happened more than once—I would sing it and be right and the instruments would have gone out of tune. I would prove it by going to the instruments and showing him. Things like that happened. That set very well with him.

DUCKWORTH: While you were working with Partch did you have the feeling you were getting information that was going to be useful to you as a composer?

JOHNSTON: I *knew* it. You see, I knew that was what I wanted to do. I knew I wanted to go in that direction.

DUCKWORTH: Did you think it was possible to develop your own personality within Partch's system?

JOHNSTON: Well, I didn't see myself in Partch's terms. Also, he hadn't, himself, gotten involved yet in all these big dramatic productions from later. But I didn't have his fascination with Greek theater, or Oriental theater, or any of the things that really made up the Partch type of thought. So I knew that I wouldn't, in any way, be an imitation of Partch. And I didn't like a lot of that later music, as it happens. I had a very well-developed theatrical sense myself— much better than Partch, if I may say so—and I didn't feel that what he was doing was valid, because he didn't know enough about dance. He didn't know enough about theater. And he wouldn't learn because he wouldn't listen to anybody else. So I felt they were badly flawed productions. But that's all later.

DUCKWORTH: Which pieces are you talking about?

JOHNSTON: Well, the ones we did at Illinois: *The Bewitched, Revelation in the Courthouse Park, Water, Water*.

DUCKWORTH: After he got sick and you left, what kind of contact did you have with him?

JOHNSTON: I would go to see him frequently. And his health was okay. Once he got away from the things that were causing the trouble he was okay. But the doctors were concerned. He was always ailing. He never had good health. I think it was malnutrition, among other things. And there were diseases that he had that he only later discovered. But that's another long story. At any rate, though his doctors were very concerned for his health, they didn't know what was the matter with him exactly. And they knew he was a hypochondriac, which was absolutely true.

DUCKWORTH: Do you worry that you may have been too much under the influence of Harry Partch?

JOHNSTON: I don't know. I'm probably not in a position to say. I think the only piece I've ever done that even sounds like Partch . . . even the piece with the Partch quotation doesn't sound like Partch at all. (There's a Partch quotation from the *Greek Studies* in the Fourth Quartet, but nobody would even spot it.) The only piece that does sound like Partch wasn't one of the ones in which I used any of the intonation procedures. In fact, it's an improvised piece that I was the brains for. The New Verbal Workshop's improvisation that we called *Visions and Spels. That* shows Partch's influence.

DUCKWORTH: What are the ways in which your work goes beyond Partch?

JOHNSTON: Well, it simply doesn't deal with the same things, you know. I can't think of an example, but there must be plenty of examples in music history where you would say, "What's the effect of one composer on another?" Well, the effect is negligible. We're simply dealing with entirely different things and there's almost no connection at all. What's the influence of Schoenberg on Varèse? Zero. There just wasn't any connection. Now you can find similarities, but those similarities didn't come from Varèse examining Schoenberg, I don't think. Certainly not vice versa.

DUCKWORTH: But you did examine Partch.

JOHNSTON: Well sure, but his aims are so different from mine.

DUCKWORTH: In what way?

JOHNSTON: Well, this whole corporeal thing—that no work of music should be deprived of being also a work of theater, also a work of dance, also a work of literature, and maybe a lot more, too. In fact, definitely a lot more: a work of sculpture, in the sense that instruments are sculptural objects. And a work of architecture, even, in that his idea for sets involved the instruments, and built up from there, and everything was unified. That total art-work thing, which is a kind of super-Wagner thing, is foreign to me. I'm just not concerned with it. It's interesting, but that's not what I do. Just as electronic music, which I certainly made an effort towards, is something I'm just not interested in. It's not my way of doing things. Other people can do that. Computers in music; I'm not interested. I know that you could achieve a great deal with microtones that way, but that's for somebody else to do. It's just not what I do. And the same thing goes for much of what Partch was doing. And then there's Partch the world musician. The influences are very much more American Indian, and Japanese, and East Asian (specifically Indonesian), and African. Those influences are much more evident in his music than are European influences. And that's not true of my music.

DUCKWORTH: How was your basic aim different?

JOHNSTON: I wanted to compose music basically in the European tradition, because it's what I'm comfortable with. And the folk roots, such as they are, were certainly Anglo-American, because that's my culture, my background. I don't use African roots, because they aren't mine. There's not a whole lot of jazz in my music, though it's not devoid of it. I played that for some years, but I didn't grow up with it, really . . . didn't play it until my late teens. You know it's an influence, but not as fundamental a one as all those Appalachian folk songs that my grandmother sang to me when I was a child. It's a different background altogether. Harry grew up among the Yaki Indians. I mean, this is quite different. I never saw an Indian until I was at least a teenager.

DUCKWORTH: When you left Harry Partch, how did you come to study with Darius Milhaud?

JOHNSTON: Well, Harry introduced me to Milhaud through Agnes Albert, who was a patroness of his. Agnes was a wealthy socialite in San Francisco, who served on the Mills College advisory board. So she had a dinner party and invited the Milhauds and Harry and us. Agnes made them aware of what I was doing, and Milhaud thought that was interesting. And I had a beard. No one had a beard in those days except the Beat Generation; it was still new. So he was a little impressed by that, I think. He thought I was independent-minded. And the first thing I showed him when I got to Mills to study with him were some songs I had written, one of which was a setting of Baudelaire; it was the setting of "Le Goût de Néant." He liked it and complimented me on my setting of French words. He really took those songs to be an indication of talent. He was unusually complimentary to me, so it was very nice and everything worked quite well. That's how I came to study with Milhaud.

DUCKWORTH: What was it like to go from working with Partch to studying with Milhaud?

JOHNSTON: Well, it was strange. I really felt like some kind of . . . freak is too strong a word, but some kind of curiosity. That's all right. That's good. See, Milhaud understood this type of rebellious artist. He was all for it. His god was Satie. And he was very patient with me. He realized I didn't have very much compositional savvy and I'd have to learn quite a lot.

DUCKWORTH: What do you mean by "compositional savvy"?

JOHNSTON: Well, I didn't know the procedure to sit down and write a piece. Everything was intuitive.

DUCKWORTH: What kind of procedures are you talking about?

JOHNSTON: There are dozens of procedures. You know what I mean. You could plan a structural thing, or you could use the intellectual side to get your imagination going. I knew nothing about those things, so I was helpless. If I wasn't, quote, *inspired*, I couldn't write, you know. So it was a matter of his showing me a great many things that one could, indeed, do. And he was so prolific; he'd never had any trouble writing music. It was the opposite of the way I am. He was very helpful to me in that way. The thing about Milhaud . . . it's very interesting, I would say, how I happened onto types of people who wouldn't teach formally or structurally. I was attracted to people who would never teach you, but who could answer your questions. And that was Milhaud's procedure, unless he could see that you were really weak. Then he would teach you technique. He didn't treat me that way, however, because he didn't think I was weak. And that was, in effect, a kind of signal he would send to people. He would take a score and say, "Now, the way you've done this . . . I would do it a little bit differently. You could do this. And maybe you could move this around. And this sounds a little like Saint-Saëns. You don't want that, do you? Why don't you . . . ," and all this kind of thing. But those were the weak students, you know. With really good ones he would wait until they asked him questions.

DUCKWORTH: Did you have good questions?

JOHNSTON: Yes, I caught onto that very fast. See, I'd been working with Partch. So I would always ask questions. I would say, "I worried about doing this when I wrote it. Was it a sensible concern, or was it one of those silly things?" And he would say, "Ah, that's interesting. Why didn't you do it this way? Why did you do it the way you did?" And he would really bring me around to seeing how my own mind worked. But, you see, he didn't want to interfere with the way people's minds worked. When I was writing, his arch rival, musically, was Hindemith. Well, I thought Hindemith was very good. I was writing some music that sounded like Hindemith. And he said, "Never write a fugue or a sonata or anything else unless you have something to add to the tradition that nobody has added before you." And that was about all he would say about that. But he wouldn't let me go in a direction that would have led to a Hindemithian approach, because Hindemith made little Hindemiths. Well, it's true. And it's a valuable objection. That's one thing I was mercifully spared. If I had had a chance to study with Hindemith I would have jumped at it, but I never had such a chance. So I was just lucky, because I would have swallowed the whole thing hook, line, and sinker, I think. Milhaud refused to show me *how* to compose. I had to find my own way. He would be there to catch me, so to speak. So I really went through a dry period in the middle of the year. He knew that. He waited it out.

DUCKWORTH: Were you taking a lesson every week?

JOHNSTON: Yes. It was a group lesson. We would all bring our music, and he would have somebody play it for him, and he would ask questions or not. Or be asked questions; that was the best. If the person had something good, he would find something to say, but he was really waiting to be asked. I remember, in fact, one time when somebody brought something in to him and he waited. And he waited. And finally he said, "Aren't you going to ask me anything about this music?" And that's the first time I realized consciously that he was quite deliberately doing it that way.

DUCKWORTH: How did you meet John Cage?

JOHNSTON: I was teaching at the University of Illinois, and we had
festivals of contemporary music. During one of the festivals there
was a lecture by John Cage, which turned out to be the first lecture
he did about composing music by chance. It was not the first time
he ever did that lecture, but it may have been one of the first times
he went out into the country doing it. I had heard of John Cage in
connection with the *Sonatas and Interludes* for prepared piano, so
I knew what he was doing. That is, I knew about the prepared
piano, and I knew him as a dance composer by reputation. But I
didn't know much of his music at all and I didn't know very much
about him. Anyway, I went to his lecture and I was fascinated. I was
not convinced, but I was fascinated. And I thought, "This guy is
really something." The lecture created an absolute scandal. People
stood up and shouted at him, and they booed and walked out.
They did everything but throw things at him. And after it was all
over, exactly three people went up on the stage to speak to John—
John Garvey, who was in charge of the festival, Betty, and me. And
we laughed, and John laughed, and he said, "So this is it." And I
said, "Let's have some coffee." John said, "That's an excellent idea."
So we went over to my apartment and sat down and had coffee.

DUCKWORTH: How did your relationship with him develop from that
initial meeting?

JOHNSTON: Well, I was really taken with him. I thought he was the
"Real McCoy"—the first person I had met, other than Harry Partch,
who I thought was a real original. So we talked, and he said, "Look,
why don't you come and study with me next summer. It might be
fun. Come to New York." And I said, "All right. What shall I do to
prepare?" And he said, "Bring what you have. And get the Webern
Symphony and study it, and tell me what you think about it when
you come." Well, I couldn't find a score of the Webern. The library
didn't have it. They wouldn't order it. And I was terribly frightened
and busy with the dance business, and frightened with the school
of music. At that time, Illinois was one of those places where you
could walk down the hall and come out with an ulcer, it was so
churned up. The reason it was so churned up was that the director
had been deposed not two years before in one of those palace rev-
olutions. As a result, I didn't do any of the preparation work that I
said I would do. I got to New York and John said, "What about the

Webern?" And I explained. And he said, "Oh. Well then, you can splice tape." So I spent the whole summer with Earle Brown splicing tapes of *William's Mix*. We cut very carefully according to John's instructions, and we pasted those things up, and made friends. I liked Earle and I think he liked me. We were, so to speak, placed in the same boat.

DUCKWORTH: Did you learn anything from John that summer?

JOHNSTON: Not much. What he did was to let me experience the ambiance.

DUCKWORTH: Was this on Monroe Street?

JOHNSTON: Yes. It was down in the East Village—the Lower East Side, in fact—near the Williamsburg Bridge, I guess.

DUCKWORTH: What was the ambiance?

JOHNSTON: Well, marble slab on the floor. No furniture. Lots of electronic equipment for the time. And tremendous activity . . . artists coming and going. I didn't meet Christian Wolff, but Morton Feldman was assigned to take us out to dinner and did so with great condescension, so we were made to feel embarrassed.

DUCKWORTH: Were you drawn to that environment?

JOHNSTON: No. We stayed in a friend's apartment in the east 60s, which was a nice place to be. So we lived, actually, very well. But it was embarrassing because we weren't really part of this avant-garde, post–Black Mountain ambiance. And we didn't know how to behave. We were being treated nicely, because John insisted, but with great condescension from others. And it really wasn't very nice. The only person I carried away a good memory of was Earle, except for John. And Morty . . . I was impressed with him, but he wasn't very nice.

DUCKWORTH: Did you go back to Illinois thinking that was the end of your contact with John Cage?

JOHNSTON: Yes, I did. I thought he had been very nice to me, but I had failed the test and that was that. So I was embarrassed, and I went back and I thought, "What a gentleman." Because he made nothing of it; he just let it be. But it wasn't over, because John Garvey was not about to let John Cage's visit be the last. He was already dickering with John to bring the Cunningham Company out and do a big concert at the first opportunity. So I heard about that as soon as I got back. John asked me to be on the festival committee, so I knew all about what was going to happen. I had a very active hand in it because I was the liaison with the Dance Department.

DUCKWORTH: How did the performance go? Were they well received?

JOHNSTON: It was a big success. John was there to do the first western hemisphere concert of electronic music. And it was Cunningham's first tour, I think, outside of New York. (I may be wrong about that, but certainly *one* of them.) They did John's *Sixteen Dances*, and a premiere of Christian Wolff's *Suite By Chance*. Then David Tudor played a tremendous piano concert which ten people attended. Suddenly, I had to turn pages for Boulez's *Deuxième Sonate*. That was all I could do; I went by absolute pitch—the only way I could do it. I would wait until I'd hear a certain note and throw the page over, because I could not follow that score . . . at sight, you know. And Earle Brown's, and Morton Feldman's, and John's music, *Music of Changes*, all kinds of stuff. So I was really being thrown in deep water.

DUCKWORTH: Did you reestablish your relationship with John at that point?

JOHNSTON: Yes. He was very nice. He said. "I thought you would write." And I said, "I didn't have anything to say." Anyway, it was on a very friendly level, but he didn't say anything more about studying with him. We kept in touch. And I did write him occasionally.

DUCKWORTH: Didn't you win a Guggenheim fellowship about that time and move to New York?

JOHNSTON: Yes. I asked Cage to recommend me, and he was willing. So I went to Columbia/Princeton, where I discovered that the equipment was in no way capable of doing what I needed with just intonation. It was not at all stable enough. And it was not about to be. The only thing that offered a prayer was the RCA synthesizer. I had actually contacted Milton Babbitt about studying with him while I was there. It didn't work out, because Milton had too many students, but he was interested and thought the project sounded interesting. But he was not about to let me at the synthesizer and, of course, that was the idea. So I was a little hurt, but understood, and thought, "Well, okay, so I can't do what I want to do." So I learned about electronic music. But among other things, I learned

that I didn't like it, I didn't have any aptitude for it, and I didn't particularly like the music people were doing with it. Fortunately, I had
also stepped into the Cage circle when I got there. And John said,
"Well, you really boxed yourself in. If you'd asked my advice I'd
have told you 'Don't have anything to do with Columbia/Princeton.
Go and work with Maxfield at the New School.' But it's too late. If
you were to go down there now, you would make enemies at
Princeton. You can't afford to do that. They would resent you forever. Why don't you come to work with me once a month?" That was
the first time he had said anything like that since I failed my test. So
I did that.

DUCKWORTH: Was he living in Stony Point by then?

JOHNSTON: Yes. So I said to him, "John, I don't feel any affinity for
working the way you do." And he said, "I know that." So I said,
"Why are you interested in working with me at all?" And he said,
"Well, you do interesting things." I said, "You don't mean the
music." And he said, "No, I don't. You do things like work with
Harry Partch."

DUCKWORTH: What were lessons with John Cage like?

JOHNSTON: I was preparing for a Composers' Forum concert which
I'd been offered. So what John did was to criticize the pieces I was
planning for that concert. And he was *the* best critic I ever had.
Much better than Milhaud. He would look at a piece and say, "Oh,
this is what you've done." Like with my *Nine Variations*, he said,
"It's the seasons. It starts and ends in winter. Here's summer in the
middle. But you haven't done summer justice." So we looked at
this middle movement. "There are an uneven number of movements," he said. "This is the centerpiece. It's not an arch form, but
in a way it is. But the keystone's not there. It needs to be longer.
And besides, what is it about summer? It stretches."

DUCKWORTH: Did he mean summer is lazy and doesn't have much
happening?

JOHNSTON: Yes, so you just wait it out. And he said, "Here you've got
an ostinato. It sounds dull because it repeats too much. So make it
repeat much more." Then he said, "Your gestures are all wrong.
They're Mozartian. You can't do that." And I said, "Why can't I do
that?," thinking, you know, "What are you trying to do, say that neo-
classicism never happened or that it wasn't valid?" (I was actually

challenging him a little, I think, when I said that.) And he looked at me and said, "No. That's not what I'm saying. Fashion is the devil, but you must give the devil his due. You cannot ignore it as you are doing. I admire the gesture, but I don't think it will succeed." And I said then, with some asperity, "Well, what do I do to make this fashionable?" He took me quite literally and said, "Take this note and displace it three octaves and jump around like that all through this. You've used a quintolet here for the first time; it's not anywhere else in the work. Let's exploit that. Make this 'five-ness' the characteristic of this movement and it will make it unique. Everywhere you can, superimpose five on the rhythm and that will get away from the tedium of the summer." I'm not quoting him exactly, of course, but this is the gist of what he said. Now that's damn fine teaching, especially when the work was a twelve-tone piece and couldn't have been more distasteful to John from a stylistic point of view.

DUCKWORTH: How old were you at that point?

JOHNSTON: Let's see, that was 1959; I was thirty-three.

DUCKWORTH: How did you synthesize in your mind such a diverse group of teachers as Partch, Milhaud, and Cage?

JOHNSTON: I didn't think that through. I didn't seek them out as a kind of plan, but I was perfectly ready to take advantage of what they had to offer because I could see the value. And to this day I think the American experimental composer is being underestimated. Even that side of Copland which people speak of as though Copland had written some pop tunes is not as bad as people make it. Let's face it, *Appalachian Spring* is a masterpiece. It really is.

DUCKWORTH: Yes, but that still doesn't answer the question. How did Partch, Milhaud, and Cage fit together in your mind?

JOHNSTON: Well, all of this mixture came about because I felt the thing that I absolutely wanted to be *sure* I did was to get the American experimental tradition (and I thought of it as a tradition). When I was a Boy Scout, for God's sake, going for Life Scout—doing a music merit badge—I had to do a schtick on American music, and the only people who interested me were Ives and Ruggles and those people. They were the only ones with any guts . . . with any profile. So when I encountered Partch I recognized this animal. And Cage.

DUCKWORTH: Was it your intention to be that animal?

JOHNSTON: No. My intention was not to leave out that particular guest at the party. I felt I wanted an absolutely full background. I wanted *all* the credentials as a composer. So I spent, what, ten years writing neoclassic music. And then a couple of years, plus a bit at the beginning, writing twelve-tone music. And I never dropped surrealism, even after I was dealing with just intonation, because I considered that an important ingredient.

DUCKWORTH: Do you remember making the initial commitment to just intonation? What brought it about?

JOHNSTON: I thought music was out of tune.

DUCKWORTH: What did you hear that told you that?

JOHNSTON: Things weren't pure. Look at it this way. I wasn't aware of that at all as a child; I just took what I heard and that was that, you know. During high school I was focused on piano and on the nineteenth century. But I had had this lecture, earlier, about acoustics. Intellectually, the seed had been planted. My girlfriend in high school was a violinist who went to Curtis later. I used to accompany her and coach her. One of the pieces she had to play for her Curtis audition was an unaccompanied sonata by Bach. I made her play it in just intonation, not knowing what I was doing. We discovered together that there were hiatuses in the music where the open string wasn't in tune. I didn't know exactly what was happening, but I knew it was because of acoustics. I could hear very early that the piano was out of tune and she was in tune. That made me very aware. So when I got to college I thought, "I really want to develop my ear in that way." It was first an intellectual concern: music was wrong; science was right.

DUCKWORTH: Where did music begin to go wrong?

JOHNSTON: It went wrong when keyboards were allowed, during the Baroque period, to dominate the emerging instrumental music. It's easy to see why the keyboard emerged if people, as they were, were interested in the intonation of music. It was because of the Renaissance revival of classical lore. They realized all these treatises were there, but this whole period of European music had ignored it entirely, and only the Arabs had kept it alive. So this whole business suddenly was focused. Well, if instrumental music was to declare independence of vocal music, then it would need to solve the intonation problem with these instruments, which were notoriously undependable acoustically. They were badly designed, comparatively speaking.

DUCKWORTH: But musicians went in that direction willingly, didn't they?

JOHNSTON: No, there was a ferment. You have to realize how much history has been distorted by musicologists. Talk to a Vincentino scholar. What was Vincentino doing? How *could* he have done that? He wasn't a maverick. He was simply a slightly more pragmatic example of what all the theorists were concerned with. Read the treatises. They're full of ratios . . . and little else.

DUCKWORTH: Well, by the late 1800s, hadn't that problem been solved?

JOHNSTON: Yes, but you're getting way ahead of me. I'm talking about the fifteenth and sixteenth centuries; this is really the Renaissance. So, when Baroque music comes in at the end of the sixteenth century—in Monteverdi's lifetime—what begins to make the difference? It's primarily the introduction of the continuo. Well, what do you do about tuning the keyboard? If you tune in Pythagorean, the thirds are out of tune. But triadic music had already become the norm since the fourteenth century. For two centuries there had been triadic-based music. So to make the thirds sound smooth, Pythagorean tuning, which is tuning in fourths and fifths, is simply not okay. Well then, what *do* you do with the keyboard? Okay, all these experiments: mean-tone temperament, well temperament . . . all these things. All this came up during the seventeenth and, eventually, eighteenth centuries. Well, what they got fascinated with was the coloration that this gave to different keys as you modulated, which is why all this interest in the different meanings of the colors of the keys. I didn't know a lot about all these things, but I knew something was there. And that is exactly what Peter Yates was fascinated by and wanted to know more about. *An Amateur at the Keyboard* is written from that point of view. Well, I only cared to know about that later, from a historical point of view, but I knew perfectly well that music had gone wrong at the Renaissance and I got it from Harry Partch, who pointed it out to me intellectually. But I was predisposed to find that it was because of my interest in acoustics, which is 50 percent of Harry Partch's theoretical stance. No more than 50 percent; the other 50 percent is ethnic. It comes from pre–Christian Western music, Oriental

music, and African music, all of which are not based on temperament. So in a way, intellectually, temperament is the big enemy.
What is it? It's a lie. It's a pretense. It's close enough for jazz, only it
isn't jazz that it's close enough for. It's close enough for classical
music.

DUCKWORTH: Are you optimistic that the coming electronic revolution in music may change all that?

JOHNSTON: No. I don't think so. Because the whole point is that it's
the ear that tells you it's in tune. It's not a question of theory, even
though I say science is right. Why is science right? Because science
is describing the way our perceptual apparatus works. Musicians—
traditional Western musicians—are not. They're imposing something on it. Well, that something is not insignificant. The present
interest goes in directions which are quite different from psychoacoustic ones. The thing is, psychoacoustic thinking is embarrassing
to people because it means mistakes have been made in our tradition. Well, I'm perfectly willing, as was Partch, to say, "All right.
You've been wrong." Look at it from a Platonic or from a Confucian
point of view: music causes psychological results, political results,
and social results. Look at the situation of rock music in the world
today. It's a cause; it's not simply a passive reflection.

DUCKWORTH: Are you saying that theoretically?

JOHNSTON: No. I'm saying it in a very practical, brass tacks kind of
way. It's *causing* social phenomena. I'm inclined toward a view, like
Plato and Confucius, where music has a causative effect on human
relationships, instead of simply being a symptom. I think everybody
would agree that a culture produces music which is representative
of itself. It reflects the way the culture is, in some significant way. Art
is studied as a way to understand a culture for those reasons. But
what Plato and Confucius said is that the nature of the art that you
expose people to molds, changes, and makes them different. And
Confucius was very explicit about it in connection with tuning. They
had tuning guides for the ceremonial music of ancient China called
the Liu. They were like the Bureau of Standards. And Confucius said
if the Liu were put out of tune, it would corrupt the society.

DUCKWORTH: Is our society corrupted?

JOHNSTON: Oh yes, I think so. I think beyond any doubt. And I think
that music can take a great deal of the responsibility.

DUCKWORTH: Which music?

JOHNSTON: A lot of music. And let me say that it isn't a simple or one-sided matter at all. Stravinsky was concerned with one-half of that equation . . . you know, the *Poetics of Music*. That was his Harvard lecture where he put out the Appolonian/Dionysian theory. Well, there's a very interesting essay, dating from earlier than that, by Jean Cocteau about Stravinsky's reactions to the infamous premiere of *The Rite of Spring*. He said Stravinsky separated himself from everybody and walked the streets of Paris most of the night, apparently pondering what had happened. He said it was from that moment Stravinsky disavowed any connections with Dionysian music. He had felt it was a Dionysian event and that it had released, so to speak, demonic forces . . . the dark side of people. And Stravinsky, not long after that—in the very next works—went in the neoclassic direction more and more, until, finally, that was the thrust of his work. And it's summed up later, long after Cocteau wrote that, in the *Poetics of Music*.

   The Dionysian elements in music are those elements that stir up people. Music to excite people; music to get them going. It's what tribal music often is all about: to work people up in a state where they can go to war, or where they will hunt successfully. It has the social purpose of putting people into the right frame of mind to get them to do things they would otherwise not do. Sometimes good things; sometimes not. And Dionysian music is associated, too, with ecstatic states—with getting people out of themselves—with traditions like voodoo, and religions that have to do with spirits, possession, and that sort of thing. Music which deals with that is dangerous in a civilized context. That was Stravinsky's conclusion, quoting Cocteau. Now, that's very interesting, because I think it's true.

DUCKWORTH: Is rock music the worst offender?

JOHNSTON: Well, take a look at rock music and its effects. And I don't think that the tie between rock music—and even jazz—and drugs is a coincidence. And I also don't think it can be explained totally in the fact that these are musics which have often sprung, though not one-hundred percent, from underprivileged people. That is, from people whose lives have been terribly and deeply affected by poverty and deprivation. Because there's also the whole Timothy Leary point of view, which has *nothing* to do with poverty. It's

Faustian. You're willing to sell your soul, as it were, to get something: an ecstasy of some kind . . . get out of yourself . . . transcend your limitations.

DUCKWORTH: Within the experimental music tradition, what's the Faustian element?

JOHNSTON: Well, that's very hard to answer. I would say this, and this is coming at the question from a very different point of view, and with one that has a great deal more to do with me. I think that any music which pretends to be in tune when it's not, which is adulterated, is a bad moral model . . . a very bad moral model. I think that's exactly what music that deals with temperament is doing. I think that the symbolism in music is appreciated and understood by every human being, on some level or other, even down to the vibrations per second. And I think that I don't want to deal, as an artist, with those adulterated symbols, because I think, to some extent, they're poisonous. And I think that one of the things that's wrong with our society is that instead of aiming at the best or at the purest, we're aiming at something a whole lot more pragmatic—what's convenient, what's going to work—and that may, indeed, involve a whole lot of consequences. For example, what works for our needs in the energy domain may also poison the environment and doom the planet to extinction. And we're facing that bit by bit. It was very convenient to release DDT into the plant world to get rid of a lot of pests, but look what happened. And nuclear energy: it's convenient to have the energy, but not at all convenient to have the planet gradually poisoned.

DUCKWORTH: What would you identify as the fundamental acoustical poison in our environment?

JOHNSTON: Well, I think it's carelessness with the pitch relationships. Not just that, but that's the part of it I've singled out and focused my attention on. Carelessness. It wasn't Schoenberg who made that mistake. Schoenberg, in fact, corrected the mistake. Schoenberg took the twelve-tone, equal-tempered scale to be exactly what it is, and used it accordingly. But all those composers during the nineteenth century did not do this. They used it as though it were not tempered.

DUCKWORTH: Who are you thinking about?

JOHNSTON: Everybody. There's nobody you could name to whom that wouldn't apply. It was the keyboards that did it, that made it necessary to temper. And it was the piano which had to be tuned well ahead of time by an expert. It was the Broadwood pianos, specifically, that necessitated the introduction of some form of temperament. And since you couldn't change it once you had it, it had to be the optimum one, which was twelve-tone, equal temperament. It was that late—well into Beethoven's life—before that happened. But all of this produces, I think, a really very unhealthy attitude.

DUCKWORTH: What were the results of this unhealthy attitude?

JOHNSTON: I would say a lot of the traits of nineteenth-century music, such as the escapism of romanticism, and of the famous Russian ballet tradition—that it always deals in little fairy tales and so forth. The larger-than-life aspect of it, the Wagnerian bit, the *superman*, the Nietzschean thing on the one hand, and the sentimental aspects of it, too—treating love as no one ever experienced it. Idealization. All that stuff. Lying, in a sense, is not very helpful to people. Not only is it not helpful, it may be very destructive. Now when you get into the twentieth century, you seem to be dealing with highly abnormal states—Alban Berg's *Wozzeck*, and that kind of work—where you really are dealing with, you could say, insanity. Something, at least, which is not desirable. If you look at it as catharsis, from an Aristotelian point of view, that may be fine: get these things out of ourselves, have a good look at them. Or look at it, even, from the standpoint of description—descriptive of aspects of human nature we haven't clearly looked at until now. But if you look at it as causative . . . well now. So all the dissonant music of the twentieth century may well be very unhealthy for us.

DUCKWORTH: Unhealthy in what way?

JOHNSTON: Not because it's dissonant. Not even because it's complex. But because it's irrationally dissonant.

DUCKWORTH: What should we do?

JOHNSTON: Eliminate the pollution.

DUCKWORTH: That's not possible. That's idealistic.

JOHNSTON: Well, it's a lot more possible than just taking it for granted and ending up with a damaged world.

DUCKWORTH: Do you mean eliminate it personally, or eliminate it as a society?

JOHNSTON: Gradually eliminate it as a society. Work personally for that.

DUCKWORTH: Aren't you talking about censoring music?

JOHNSTON: No. I'm talking about persuading music to deal with us in a way which is conscious of these needs. Just as we're not talking about censoring science in saying let's don't dump things on the environment, things that are going to destroy the planet ultimately. Whether through the greenhouse effect, or fossil fuels, or through nuclear contamination, or—God, you know, there are half a dozen things—chemical poisons in the food chain, or just hundreds of things that our cleverness has brought to bear. But wouldn't it be even cleverer to cooperate with nature instead of trying to fight it?

DUCKWORTH: I can hear a lot of people, even in the classical and experimental worlds, saying, "Boy, Ben Johnston sounds a little paranoid about what's going on in music."

JOHNSTON: Well, I would simply say it's not paranoia; it's true. If Chicken Little comes in and says, "The sky is falling," and the sky really is falling, then Chicken Little is not so simple.

DUCKWORTH: Okay, let's say musicians accept your diagnosis. What's the cure?

JOHNSTON: It's for people to recognize three things. First, it's necessary to recognize that music creates emotional states in people and doesn't just reflect what they already are. Are the emotional states in people that are being reinforced by this imposed common culture of commercialized rock, or commercialized pop, or commercialized country for that matter, really salutary and a good idea? And I have to answer "no," those are bad emotional values. Some of them are okay, most of them are not. And it's reflected in the fact that these same people are involved in the drug culture. And that's not a question of whether or not they ever used marijuana. To turn over your emotional life to random chemical reactions is sick and that's the problem. That's why I bring up Plato and Confucius, and not Aristotle. It is *not* a purgation; it's a training. And that's very different. That's dangerous. So I think that's number one.

DUCKWORTH: What's the second part?

Ben Johnston, Rocky Mount, NC, 1993

JOHNSTON: The second part is simply that people are involved in our culture, inevitably, with tonal music of one kind or another. This, above all, includes pop music. And pop music has never been willing to even flirt with anything else. Neither has jazz, Gunther Schuller notwithstanding. But what I'm saying is this: the preoccupation with tonal music by the rank and file of ordinary musicians is only natural. It's an acoustical response to the way sound behaves and the way our psychology accepts it. Now, much contemporary serious music is a highly artificial construct, no matter how wonderful it is, what a marvelously new idea it may be, and how well you can describe it mathematically. Milton Babbitt is wrong: what is mathematically intelligible is not necessarily musically intelligible. That's a basic mistake to make. What I tried to point out in the "Scalar Order" article, and numerous other pieces, is that even from the point of view of contemporary psychology, to base things on a ratio-based ordering of things is a more sophisticated psychological tool than interval-scale ordering, which serial music is all about. And the result—the mnemonic power of serial music—is not very high. People can't remember it. "If they can't carry the tunes . . . ," to quote Lou Harrison, there aren't any, as far as they're concerned. And so they reject it. They don't reject it, necessarily, negatively; they just aren't interested. It bores them. It isn't even exciting. It doesn't even create a *Rite of Spring* confrontation. It's pedantic. The gut-level response to those things is harder to acquire. But yes, it can be acquired. And therefore, that article, which I know Milton didn't entitle and didn't mean, "Who Cares If You Listen?," is a very instructive article. It does point out it's all right to write music for the very few. But they should then remember they are the very few, and not presume that cultural lag is responsible for its never getting beyond the very few.

DUCKWORTH: What's the third part of the cure?

JOHNSTON: This is a spinoff of the second point, but it's a different point. Music is not simply an intellectual exercise; it's a physical response to sound. And this is something Lou Harrison makes a basic point of, and, for that matter, Harry did, too. If you can't and don't respond honestly on a physical level to the actual nature of the sounds you're dealing with, then you haven't even put the first foot forward, you know. How are you going to walk? Above all, it's a sensory experience. And that entails a lot of other things. It involves the rest of our sensory experiences by association and, therefore, corporealism. Okay, that's basic Harry Partch. Well, music has forgotten about that. But Harry's quite right.

DUCKWORTH: Where does your music fit into all this?

JOHNSTON: I think the great thing about being an American is exactly what Gertrude Stein said: "In America there is no sky. In Europe the sky's very close." "You can almost touch it," as Edna St. Vincent Millay said. Every tradition is mine because I have no tradition. But it's not quite that simple. It is very complex, because what I am is a product of a great many varieties of inbred traditions and outbred traditions and all kinds of stuff. What saves it all is the absolute hybridness of it. Now, that is America. Whether you think of it as a melting pot or something else, it's simply not a unified culture. It's the absolute antithesis of that. And great, as far as I'm concerned. But to discover who you are as an individual in the middle of all this (and we place a premium on that) is very difficult. You really have to look at all these things, and try to separate out strands, and put the thing together. That's what Harry tried to do all of his life.

Well, I don't want to turn away from it. I'm part Freudian, part Jungian; the whole bit, you know. The basic point I'm trying to make is that if we don't, as a culture, find ourselves locked into a tradition, it's because we have too many. We have the world, as it were. I'm an example. So I respond to those things and I try to put all that together.

All right now, in what way does this make sense? Well, in a superior way, to me, than if I were writing twelve-tone music, or minimalism, or anything else. It's because I feel just intonation is a more complete answer, and one that doesn't leave out what I think. And I'm simply not a disciple of anybody. This is one thing that both John and Harry recognized. I'm a follower only insofar as I want something from somebody and they can give it to me. It really is like that, you know. You make it your own, or it isn't yours.

DUCKWORTH: Which do you think are your best pieces?

JOHNSTON: God, I don't know. I like my Fourth Quartet and my Fifth Quartet. I like *Sonnets of Desolation*.

DUCKWORTH: Do those pieces have any elements in common?

JOHNSTON: In fact, I guess they do. What they have in common is religion. That's interesting. I hadn't thought of it, but they do. The *Sonnets of Desolation* are settings of Gerard Manley Hopkins's late sonnets. Hopkins, as you may know, was a priest. And these sonnets are about spiritual crises. And about death, essentially. So it's the heaviest of the heavy, and they're regarded as some of the most difficult poetry in the English language. So when Ward Swingle asked me to do a piece for him, I wanted to do that. I also wanted to push my language, which was by that time extended just intonation, to thirteen-limit and no-holds-barred . . . totally chromatic. So I wrote a piece that I thought would be impossibly hard. But it was not that I wanted it to be hard, it was only that I knew what I was asking, and it was a lot. I got a gorgeous performance.

DUCKWORTH: What's religious about the Fifth Quartet?

JOHNSTON: It's based on "Lonesome Valley," which is a hymn.

DUCKWORTH: And the Fourth Quartet is based on "Amazing Grace." What about musically? Is there anything in common musically?

JOHNSTON: No, they're very different.

DUCKWORTH: Other than extended just intonation.

JOHNSTON: Yes, that connects them. But then, you could say that about everything I was writing from about 1960 on.

DUCKWORTH: You've now written nine string quartets. Are you at the point where you consider the string quartet to be *your* instrument in the way some composers think of the piano as theirs?

JOHNSTON: Well, either Stockhausen said, or somebody said about him, that the *Klavierstucke* were his research pieces. They are, if you view them right. He tried out everything, generally, in those pieces, that he then used in later works. Well, the string quartet is like that for me. It's central, in that sense.

DUCKWORTH: Since you have such a good ear, is there much of a difference for you between hearing music in your head and hearing it in a live performance?

JOHNSTON: Oh, a lot. For one thing, there are no surprises when you hear it in your head. And there need to be.

DUCKWORTH: Are they surprises or mistakes?

JOHNSTON: Hell no. Music is really a collaborative art. It honestly is. A piece is not really a piece until it's performed.

DUCKWORTH: What are the surprises?

JOHNSTON: The nuances. Even the tempos. My tempos are not absolute. I don't know that much about tempo to be absolute about it. It has to do with the feel of playing. So all that type of nuance is to be discovered.

DUCKWORTH: Are you basically happy with recordings of your music? Do you think they're accurate?

JOHNSTON: Yes, pretty much. I've never had one that I was really unhappy with, I'll say that. Some more than others. For example, the Fourth Quartet—I think that the original Fine Arts Quartet recording of that is excellent. Really fine. And I guess, in a way, it's more what I think the work is like than the Kronos Quartet's recording, which is a lot different. But I don't dislike the Kronos version; I think it's perfectly okay to take the work in that direction.

DUCKWORTH: What direction?

JOHNSTON: They make more of a world-music piece out of it. For example, the Harry Partch part happens to use a scale which is an ancient Greek scale, and that scale happens to approximate most closely the commonest of all Japanese scales. So the second violinist, who has the solo at that point, decided to interpret it à la Kabuki, so it becomes a Japanese variation.

DUCKWORTH: Does he alter the scale? Are the pitches true even though he plays with them stylistically?

JOHNSTON: He plays around with them the way the Japanese do. There's a lot of glissando. It isn't clean. So other people have gotten to know the piece from that recording, but have declined to play it that way when they saw the score. But it works, you see, either way. The scale is not as clean when you play it the "Japanese" way, but . . . I don't mind. The scale is the point of departure in that case. It's like a free-jazz performance as opposed to, say, a straight, down-the-line, traditional jazz approach—the difference between Jimi Hendrix and somebody who plays mostly Dixieland. It's a question of interpretation.

DUCKWORTH: Is that kind of flexibility possible in your music?

JOHNSTON: Yes, and I'm very happy that it is.

DUCKWORTH: I guess I've always assumed that most people were working so hard to play the correct pitches that they didn't have time to . . .

JOHNSTON: Well, that's true of a lot of them. And mostly, if I've been dissatisfied with a performance it's for that reason. There've been a few pieces that I'm not awfully happy with.

DUCKWORTH: Are you surprised that you have had so many good performers interested in your music?

JOHNSTON: No. I may be surprised it even got off the ground at all (I do often think that), but if it was going to get off the ground, that's the only way.

DUCKWORTH: Has your career gone where you expected it to?

JOHNSTON: In a way. I think I'm one of the few people who can really say, "I set out to do such and such and I did it."

DUCKWORTH: And are you satisfied with it?

JOHNSTON: No. Because now that I've done that, I can see all those
other things that need to be done. And so I'll never get to the end
of that. But I can really say that all I envisioned at the beginning I
have actually done. Well, not all, because I envisioned the challenge
that I knew I was making to people, which was, potentially, a revolution in performance practice in the music business. And whether
that will take place, I'll never live to see. But maybe it will.

DUCKWORTH: Well, it's closer than when you started.

JOHNSTON: A lot. And I think I had something to do with that. I think
I had a lot to do with that, in fact.

PAULINE OLIVEROS

Born Houston, Texas, 1932

G R O W I N G U P in Houston in the late thirties and early forties, Pauline Oliveros loved to listen to sounds; the more unusual, the better. Even though both her mother and grandmother were piano teachers, and despite the fact that Oliveros went regularly to subscription concerts by the Houston Symphony, she says she actually preferred listening to the insects, or the static on the radio. She also heard a lot of country and western music, Cajun, and swing, as well as the weekly broadcasts from the Metropolitan Opera, the New York Philharmonic, and the NBC Orchestra. But the deciding factor for Oliveros was the moment her mother brought home an accordion. Originally intended for her younger brother, Oliveros fell so in love with it that it became hers, and she grew to feel she was on a mission to play the accordion. At the age of sixteen, she decided to become a composer, saying she was hearing "imaginary music" in her head. The first time she heard it, it was, according to her, like being in a sonic "hypnogogic state," adding, "It was euphoric."

In 1949, Oliveros became a music major at the University of Houston, but left after three years, moving to San Francisco, taking accordion students and freelancing to support herself. She finished college in 1957 at San Francisco State, studying composition with Robert Erickson in a class that included Terry Riley. That same year, Oliveros and Riley, along with fellow student Loren Rush, began experimenting with free improvisations. A few years later, with Morton Subotnick and Ramon Sender, Oliveros began the San Francisco Tape Music Center, housing it at the San Francisco Conservatory, and each contributing various pieces of equipment. Because of favorable reviews of their early concerts by *San Francisco Chronicle* music critic Alfred J. Frankenstein, their efforts were quickly recognized, and by late 1961, they had developed a subscription audience and were giving concerts once a month. Oliveros says she saw tape music as a natural development of her interest in sound, and she "fell in love with it."

An audience beyond San Francisco developed for Oliveros with her 1962 work *Sound Patterns*. Winner of a Gaudeamus prize in the Netherlands, published in Germany, recorded in America, and performed widely, this textless work for chorus brought Oliveros international attention. She, however, moved in the direction of theater, which she first thought of as "something to look at" while the tape music was playing. Fortunately, the tape studio, at that time, was sharing space with dancer Ann Halprin, and there were numerous dancer/performers whose talents could be drawn upon.

In 1966, the Tape Music Center moved to Mills College, and Oliveros became its first director. The following year, she was invited to teach at the University of California at San Diego (UCSD). Although she had some reservations about the academic life, it did provide her with a more secure economic base from which to pursue her own work. In the early seventies, while at UCSD, Oliveros says she began to feel the need for "calming kinds of activities." What began as playing long tones on the accordion in the privacy of her own home, and observing the effects, grew into a series of fifty audience-participative *Sonic Meditations*, which consist of exercises that help people tune, first to themselves, then to each other, and finally to their surroundings. Oliveros says she still continues to practice some of them. Her interest in meditation also led to an interest in ceremonial music, something she describes, in terms of her own work, as putting together different meditations to create a ceremony. She says the ceremonial form provides different entryways into the sonic experience for people who may not be as sound-oriented as she is. She also believes her meditations and ceremonies have a function other than to entertain. Her mission is within herself: the expression of that which comes through her own life force.

In the early 1980s, saying that students had grown too conservative and the bureaucracy too time-consuming, Oliveros quit teaching after fourteen years, moving to New York and taking a loft on Leonard Street, five blocks below Canal. I spoke with Pauline while she was still living there, just before her move upstate to Kingston, where she lives today. The apartment looked like many downtown loft spaces: lots of room, no place to store anything. We sat on pillows on the floor, and from my position I couldn't help noticing the accordion case by the wall.

DUCKWORTH: If your mother and grandmother played piano, how did you wind up playing the accordion?

Pauline Oliveros, San Diego, CA, 1979. Photo Credit: Becky Cohen

OLIVEROS: My mother brought an accordion home very early in the 1940s. She intended it to be for my younger brother, but I fell in love with it and wanted to play it, so eventually I did. I stuck with that until junior high school. I couldn't get in the band because the accordion was an outcast instrument, so I learned to play the tuba and later, in high school, the French horn. But I always wanted to play all the things we played in band on my accordion. I'd make transcriptions and learn to play those things. I had a slightly different kind of musical education than some. It came through the accordion actually.

DUCKWORTH: How do you think that difference affected you?

OLIVEROS: I think I was engaged by a lot of diverse music. Perhaps if I had had a more traditional education, say in piano or an orchestral instrument, then I would have had a different perspective. But as it was, I had my foot in all these other doors. It was the influence of popular culture; Texas is very rich in that—country and western, Cajun, New Orleans jazz, Dixieland, Eastern European polka styles, Tex-Mex. It's a very diverse kind of background.

DUCKWORTH: What can you recall of your earliest experiences with music when you were growing up in Houston?

OLIVEROS: Both my grandmother and my mother were music teachers. They were pianists. So I heard lessons going on all the time. And my mother was interested in popular music; she played by ear as well as by reading. I was taken to a lot of different kinds of musical events, so it was something that I understood as a way of life. The thing that I didn't know was the world of music that was being written at the moment. But by the time I got to college I had come in contact with many different genres, and I was always interested in the unusual sounds. What probably influenced me the most was my own interest in sound, which came out of earliest childhood. Houston, Texas, is lowland: humid, tropical, and filled with insects. I always used to listen to all of that. We lived in the country. I remember that on hot days the sound seemed to float in the air. In this very heavy, humid air you would hear horses neighing, cows mooing, chickens singing all afternoon.

DUCKWORTH: Were those sounds musical to you then?

OLIVEROS: I didn't think of them as music; I just was always listening. I was fascinated by what I heard.

DUCKWORTH: When you listened for pleasure during your childhood what did you listen to?

OLIVEROS: I listened to lots of hillbilly music, country and western, Cajun music. And I listened to swing, Artie Shaw and Stan Kenton. One of my favorite pieces was "Summit Ridge Drive" by Artie Shaw.

DUCKWORTH: Did you go to the University of Houston as a music major?

OLIVEROS: Yes, I did.

DUCKWORTH: What did you plan to be when you graduated?

OLIVEROS: A musician. I never had any other aspiration or thought. I was going to be a concert accordionist and a composer.

DUCKWORTH: Did you have the feeling that the accordion was a mainstream instrument that would support a concert career?

OLIVEROS: No, but I had the feeling that I had a mission to play this instrument. I was going to play the music that I wanted to play. I was very fond of Bach and I played it on my accordion. I don't think Bach would have had any trouble with it.

DUCKWORTH: Before you went to college had you heard much classical music?

OLIVEROS: I went to subscription concerts of the symphony every season in high school, so I had a lot of experience listening to music live. Lots of recitals; lots of radio. I used to listen to the New York Philharmonic on Sunday afternoons, and the NBC Orchestra and the Metropolitan Opera in the evenings. Those broadcasts were very important. I was familiar with the repertoire and with various performers that were playing at the time. And then recordings were very important.

DUCKWORTH: Do you remember when you first became aware that you wanted to be a composer?

OLIVEROS: When I was sixteen. I was hearing music in my head . . . imaginary music. So I announced that I wanted to be a composer. Although I kept trying, I couldn't write down what I was hearing; it was much too complicated.

DUCKWORTH: What were you hearing?

OLIVEROS: Some of it was sounds (which I only realized when I got involved with electronic music much later), and some of it was symphonic. Some of it was very abstract; I don't know how anybody could talk about it. And some of it was sensation that I needed to realize as sound, but I didn't know how to do it.

DUCKWORTH: Did these early sounds intrude on whatever you were doing at the moment, or did you have to be in a certain frame of mind before they would come to you?

OLIVEROS: I was always listening. The first time I heard them, it was like a hypnogogic state except that instead of having vivid visual images, I had vivid sound images. But there it was.

DUCKWORTH: Did it seem like an unusual experience to be having?

OLIVEROS: It seemed euphoric. It was very ecstatic. The only thing that could match it was when I heard my first composition played in class at the university. It was a similar experience: "Wow! I don't want to do anything else but make this music." That's where the strength to stay with it comes from—from that pleasure, ecstasy, and euphoria.

DUCKWORTH: Do you still have similar feelings today?

OLIVEROS: At a different level, yes; they're there.

DUCKWORTH: What level are they now, more intellectual?

OLIVEROS: Sometimes I would say that there's an intellectual euphoria, but basically it's a particular kind of mental state with its own body feelings and mental space. It's an altered state of consciousness.

DUCKWORTH: Is that where most of your pieces come from?

OLIVEROS: Yes, they're attuned to that. It's a source for me. It's like a life force.

DUCKWORTH: Did your study of composition begin at the University of Houston?

OLIVEROS: Yes, and I was disappointed in it, because I had to struggle so hard to try to realize my inner vision. I say vision, but I mean by that my inner sounds—my inner needs of what I was trying to express—in relation to the templates I was given as models. I wasn't interested in models; I was interested in what I was hearing. So I sort of blundered my way through.

DUCKWORTH: Was the University of Houston the place where you first heard contemporary music?

OLIVEROS: Yes. Paul Koepke, who was the composition/theory teacher and composer there at the time, played us some early Schoenberg, which I remember as sounding very strange to me. I was interested immediately, but I'd never heard of him before. Maybe some Ives, but really very little; it was like a tease. Debussy and Ravel were the tops.

DUCKWORTH: So you don't think of Schoenberg, Stravinsky, Debussy, or Ives as the immediate models for your own work?

OLIVEROS: No, I don't. They're part of the landscape, but not what influenced me . . . not until much later.

DUCKWORTH: What caused you to leave the University of Houston and go to San Francisco?

OLIVEROS: I felt the need to have my own private space. I had been living at home until I was twenty years old, and my ambition was to live by myself. I also had heard a lot about the West Coast—a friend of mine had gone there—and I wanted to go connect with some of the music I'd heard about. It was as act of independence for me. It took me a year to get my feet on the ground and begin to work again musically, because I had to earn my keep. I worked as a file clerk for about nine months. Then I began to get a string of accordion students and casual engagements playing around town.

DUCKWORTH: Were you a student then too, or were you just working?

OLIVEROS: I was just working. Then I went back to school at San Francisco State. That's where I met Loren Rush, Terry Riley, and Stuart Dempster. We all were in class together there and were involved with the composers' workshop, which was run by Wendell Otey. They were the first people I could relate to as peers, in terms of composition, who didn't think I was crazy. Loren, Terry, and I began to do free improvisation in '57. We would go into the studio at KPFA, sit down, and play. We'd record what we played and then listen to it and talk about it. We played all kinds of things. I played the horn or a whole battery of stuff. Actually, our first improvisations were done with Terry playing piano, Loren playing bass, and me playing horn.

DUCKWORTH: That sounds like a jazz combo.

OLIVEROS: No, it wasn't jazz. Terry had the French—the Poulenc—kind of style; Loren had been studying koto and was interested in Japanese music; and I was interested in Bartók. So it was a pretty amazing mélange.

DUCKWORTH: Were these improvisations broadcast?

OLIVEROS: No. The first thing we did because Terry had to do a five-minute soundtrack for a film, so we improvised for the soundtrack.

DUCKWORTH: Was there ever an aesthetic conflict in your mind between the music you were composing and the music you were improvising at the radio station?

OLIVEROS: Not at all. I used to sit down and improvise my way
through a piece like the *Variations for Sextet*. I think of composition as a slowed-down improvisation, and improvisation as a speed-
ed-up composition.

DUCKWORTH: But there are so few models for this kind of improvisation in classical music. Why did you think improvising was musical
at that point?

OLIVEROS: Because I'd recorded it, and listened to it, and it sounded
like music.

DUCKWORTH: You didn't have any philosophical problems with the
fact that it wasn't notated on the page and frozen in time?

OLIVEROS: No.

DUCKWORTH: You sound as though the Western European classical
tradition doesn't play a particularly big role in your background.

OLIVEROS: It does in a sense, but it doesn't hold me. I don't feel that
I have to uphold the directions or standards of that world. I have a
more important mission within myself, which is to express that
which comes through my own life force. That's my allegiance. How
it connects with the various influences on the outside is also important, but I have to first plumb my depth in order to get something
that is true to what I want to put out. If I'm hung up in some
model, then I'm not going to get to it, because the values of that
model will be imposing themselves on my self and on the sources
of my material.

DUCKWORTH: So in your music, each piece becomes its own model.
Which explains why your pieces have been so different over a period of time.

OLIVEROS: Right.

DUCKWORTH: How did the San Francisco tape music studio come
about?

OLIVEROS: About 1959 I met Ramon Sender and he was interested in
electronic music. Bob Erickson, who was our composition teacher,
was at the San Francisco Conservatory. Ramon managed to get
them interested in having a studio there. I had a tape recorder at
the time, so we put some stuff together and made the first pieces
of tape music that either Ramon or I had made. Then we did a con-

cert called "Sonics" at the conservatory in 1960. It consisted of pieces by Ramon, myself, Terry Riley, Phil Windsor, and an acoustic group improvisation that we did together. That was the beginning, the nucleus, of it.

DUCKWORTH: So the center came about because the three of you pooled your resources?

OLIVEROS: Yes.

DUCKWORTH: Did you have a physical space in which to work?

OLIVEROS: Yes, up in the attic of the conservatory. When it became apparent that the conservatory was not going to support the tape music center, Morton Subotnick and Ramon joined forces. I was away in Europe when they founded the San Francisco Tape Music Center, but when I came back I gradually became involved in it.

DUCKWORTH: Had your interest in tape music emerged slowly, or had there been some event that created sudden interest?

OLIVEROS: No, it was a natural development. There were tape recorders, and there was the opportunity to work with others who were interested in it.

DUCKWORTH: Did you immediately see the tape studio as a way to realize some of the sounds you had been hearing in your mind?

OLIVEROS: I fell in love with it. I was very, very happy with what I could do with tape. I had a Silvertone tape recorder from Sears Roebuck which I had to hand wind, so I had manual variable speed. I had fun imagining how things would sound if I dropped them an octave or if I speeded them up. Since I didn't have any processing equipment, I used cardboard tubes to make filters. I'd play sounds through the cardboard tubes and get the tube resonance. When I wanted reverberation I'd put the microphone in the bathtub. When I wanted to amplify a sound, I would resonate it against a wooden wall. So I used all sorts of acoustic phenomena and miked it in various ways. I worked with that tape recorder in an improvisatory way.

DUCKWORTH: How many tracks of tape did you normally work with?

OLIVEROS: Two to four. I remember Ramon and I going down the long halls of the conservatory unrolling the tape so that we could get it synchronized. Unroll it down the hall; line it up; start it.

DUCKWORTH: What was your first tape piece like?

OLIVEROS: My first tape piece was called *Time Perspectives*. It was a four-channel piece that was really ambitious, considering what I've just told you. It was full of all kinds of noise. I can't imagine what it would sound like to listen to right now.

DUCKWORTH: What were the responses to the concerts that you were giving at the tape music center?

OLIVEROS: Great! There were people who really enjoyed them and were provoked by them. Alfred Frankenstein, who was a critic for the *San Francisco Chronicle*, was very supportive and interested in all of the things that we did. So we had recognition right away from the music community. And it grew very quickly. I guess the timing was right. We gave concerts at the tape center once a month. We developed a subscription audience, and just did our work there. It was a very important period for me, because I was out of school and this was a peer support system. A place to be, hang out, meet people, put the work on, and grow and develop.

DUCKWORTH: How were you supporting yourself?

OLIVEROS: Sometimes I wonder how I managed to get through that. Odd jobs. Piecing it together. Teaching accordion and French horn lessons . . . playing . . . occasionally some kind of a commission to do music for a film or a play . . . occasionally an orchestration or copying job.

DUCKWORTH: Is this the period of time when you were also writing *Sound Patterns*?

OLIVEROS: Yes, 1961.

DUCKWORTH: What influenced that work? The reason I ask is because that's the piece, because it was recorded, where a lot of people first learned about your music. So I've always thought of it as an important piece of yours.

OLIVEROS: Well, it was. As I just told you, I pieced together my living. And I thought, "Why can't I earn some money as a composer?" There wasn't much in the way of support. I looked around at the contests and a lot of them were for vocal music. So I thought, "Well, I'll write a chorus." I started looking at these various organizations and then I thought, "What am I going to use for a text?" And then I thought, "I don't want to use a text." I liked the sounds that choruses made in between their articulations of words. I liked all of the spin-off sounds.

Pauline Oliveros performing "Dream House Spiel: Deep Listening" at the Whitney Museum at Equitable Center, New York, 1990. Photo Credit: Paula Court

DUCKWORTH: Did the sounds for that piece come to you in your head in one of these visions you've talked about?

OLIVEROS: I worked on making sounds by listening for the sounds that I wanted to hear, making them myself, and then making up the notation for it.

DUCKWORTH: Were you getting many performances of your nonelectronic music at this time?

OLIVEROS: No. Most of my performances I did myself. My *Variations for Sextet* won a prize, so that was performed a couple of times. *Sound Patterns* won the Gaudeamus prize. It was published in Darmstadt, Germany, and was subsequently reprinted and performed a lot. And it did receive a lot of recognition at the time. György Ligeti was the judge for that prize. He was quite taken with *Sound Patterns* and talked about it breaking new ground. He hadn't seen anything like it at the time, but it wasn't long before other people began to work along that line.

DUCKWORTH: How did you get from tape music to theater music?

OLIVEROS: It seemed to come out of a need to have something happen. When you're presenting tapes, there's nothing to look at, so theater suggested itself quite readily in connection with tape. Also, because of the improvisations that we did. We were sharing the space at Di Visadero Street with Ann Halprin and her dancers' workshop, so there were people around who were quite interesting to work with. A collaboration naturally developed.

DUCKWORTH: Am I correct in thinking that *Pieces of Eight* was the first theatrical piece that you wrote?

OLIVEROS: I did a couple of pieces before that. One was the *Theatre Piece for Trombone Player*, which was for Stuart Dempster. That was in collaboration with Elizabeth Harris, as was a duo, but *Pieces of Eight* was the first one that I did on my own.

DUCKWORTH: Did you think of tape music as one thing and more traditional music for instruments as something else, or had everything become theatrical by that point?

OLIVEROS: I didn't think of categorizing things very much. That was just where my attention was. I was focused on tape music for a time, but I was also doing other things, like working with sounds and improvising. I was doing a lot of different things at once. I didn't tend to think categorically about it, although there would be the familiar questions like "What is this?" and "Is it music?" I was used to that because I was an accordion player, and accordion players have to ride in the back of the bus. So I would go ahead and do whatever it was I was doing—sometimes defiantly and sometimes not.

DUCKWORTH: How did the move from San Francisco to a teaching position at the University of California at San Diego come about?

OLIVEROS: I had done all this work with the tape music center, and I was the first director of the tape music center at Mills when it was funded by the Rockefeller Foundation. Then Will Ogdon and Robert Erickson began the department at UC San Diego, and they wanted a person involved with electronics to come and establish some courses there. So I was invited to apply for the job.

DUCKWORTH: What kind of changes in your musical life did moving to San Diego produce?

OLIVEROS: First, I had a long talk with myself about what it meant to join the establishment, because I had been operating outside of it for fifteen years in San Francisco. I had been somewhat wounded by the establishment because of academic notions about categories and about the legitimate pursuits of one's attention. So I wondered if I would be uncomfortable operating inside of such an establishment. In the end, I had to trust that Will and Bob were trying to make a place that was comfortable for composers; that it was a wonderful opportunity; and that I should go there and try it out and resign if it didn't work. So that was the attitude that I took. And I began to have economic support . . . a base that I had not had. But I don't feel that my life changed all that much. I never did get rid of all my apple boxes as furniture. I still have plenty of apple boxes around. Boards and bricks. I always lived fairly simply, although I did have a beautiful house during my time at UC San Diego. And I stayed for fourteen years, which was almost equivalent to my San Francisco time. Toward the end of it, I felt that I needed to change; that I needed to challenge myself again and piece it together.

DUCKWORTH: How did you get involved in meditational music?

OLIVEROS: In San Diego, at the end of the Vietnam War, I felt a need for calming kinds of activities. So I used to play long tones on my accordion and sing, observing the effect on me psychically and physically. Then I began to get other people involved in it. I met Al Huang, studied some tai chi, and began to think about breath and physical coordination. So I started making those *Sonic Meditations.*

DUCKWORTH: Did they start out as solo pieces for you?

OLIVEROS: Yes, things that I did in private at home. Then, when working with groups I would transmit it to them.

DUCKWORTH: Did you do these meditations every day at home? Were they a regular event in your life?

OLIVEROS: It was fairly regular. Consistent, I'd say.

DUCKWORTH: Did the meditations have the same effect when you did them with other people?

OLIVEROS: Yes and no. On different levels. The more I did them—the longer I did them over a long period of time—the easier it was to discern people participating on different levels.

DUCKWORTH: What are the possible levels?

OLIVEROS: More or less awareness of what was happening; more or less commitment; more or less effect. It was possible to see that, to feel that.

DUCKWORTH: Can meditation be successful on all those levels, or is it only with real commitment that it becomes successful?

OLIVEROS: Sometimes things are successful despite commitment, or lack of it.

DUCKWORTH: Do you think of the *Sonic Meditations* as pieces to be performed, or are they pieces to be participated in and experienced without an audience?

OLIVEROS: It can work both ways. Some people will dismiss such pieces as nonmusic, once again. They may be quite right, but in my mind it's a kind of music. At times I think it's just fine to do these pieces without an audience. It's really not necessary to have an audience, so long as people are experiencing it.

DUCKWORTH: Do the meditations still give you the same experience today that they did when you first started doing them?

OLIVEROS: Even more so.

DUCKWORTH: Is there a variety of experiences to be gained from the different meditations, or is it basically variations on the same experience?

OLIVEROS: There can be different results depending on the direction of attention. There are different ways of listening and different ways of responding. For instance, you may want to raise your energy level, you may lower it, you may direct it in another way. Raising or lowering energy levels may be more or less appropriate, depending on the situation.

DUCKWORTH: What made you decide that your music would be useful for doing that?

OLIVEROS: Because I experience it myself. I've felt how it works with me, and then tested it out with others. I took the feedback as the signal of what was working and what wasn't.

DUCKWORTH: What did you say to people who refused to be objective or neutral, and who might participate but be antagonistic?

OLIVEROS: My feeling was that if somebody wanted to participate they were welcome, but if they didn't there was no obligation. And I also came to realize that people, at times, will use anything as a way of releasing their hostilities or feelings of antagonism. I didn't take it personally. But I don't like to do this work with a captive audience. I like it to be a free experience with everyone taking part if they want to. If I feel that the people are captive, I try to give them a way out, a choice.

DUCKWORTH: Do you still practice the meditations yourself?

OLIVEROS: I'm always doing them, yes.

DUCKWORTH: Was it a simple step from meditational music to ceremonial music? I'm thinking about *Crow II* and *Rose Mountain Slow Runner*.

OLIVEROS: I don't know if it was a simple step, but it seemed to present itself quite easily. After a while I could put different kinds of meditations together, and ceremonial aspects could come into play.

DUCKWORTH: Which you liked?

OLIVEROS: Yes.

DUCKWORTH: Why's that, because it heightens the dramatic situation?

OLIVEROS: Yes, I think it does heighten it. And it provides different entryways, a different focus. Some people are not as sound-oriented as I am. Sometimes the ceremonial, visual, or dramatic aspects illustrate the sound aspects; that's what gives you the heightened sense.

DUCKWORTH: But the core of these pieces is still meditational, isn't it?

OLIVEROS: Yes, simply the direction of attention working with a strategy. I probably wouldn't use the word "meditation" today if I were starting at the same place. It's so loaded with different meanings.

DUCKWORTH: In retrospect, do you think it has had a negative impact on how you are perceived?

OLIVEROS: It could have.

DUCKWORTH: You don't experience it personally though?

OLIVEROS: People are not necessarily up front about it. Meditation has religious connotations; there are methods in traditional religious institutions for meditation. That could be read back to me as my meddling around in something that I'm not qualified to do. That might be a negative perspective. Or it might be read as my trying to brainwash someone.

DUCKWORTH: People don't accuse you of that, though, do they?

OLIVEROS: No, not by telling someone that I'm doing these kinds of things, but I might hear about something off in the distance and wonder why that person didn't come to talk to me about it . . . get it off their chest and let me know.

DUCKWORTH: Is there a religious side to your meditations?

OLIVEROS: Religious to me means institution: something that's organized to produce certain effects or results in relationship to a higher force or deity. My meditations are not presented that way; they are presented as ways of listening and ways of responding.

DUCKWORTH: Are they more humanistic, more naturalistic?

OLIVEROS: Yes, those terms could be used. I don't know about more or less, just that that's what it is. When one studies the processes of the mind, then one treads on the territory that is institutionalized by religion. But I'm not interested in establishing a religion! I'm just interested in exploring how this thing works.

DUCKWORTH: Does any of your music have a message to it? Is there ever a political side?

OLIVEROS: I was at a conference recently of arts administrators and officers of funding, and I was asked to do a sonic meditation to open the conference. It was after dinner that I had to do this, so I thought about it and I asked people to do the "Tuning Meditation." I explained the metaphor of tuning: how you tune first to your own imagination and then you tune to somebody else; then you go back and forth by tuning to yourself and tuning to someone else, so that the direction of attention is constantly changing from inside to outside. I felt that was the metaphor as well as the real experience of the moment. Since I had been asked to set the tone, I hoped that that's what would happen in the conference. So you could say that's a political method; it has a function. I've also used the "Tuning Meditation" at times when people need something, like a memorial service, which is not a religious service but is a service for someone who has died. It's a good way for people to communicate and connect with each other without words and without being committed to some message that they might not be comfortable with. It can be done in a nonsectarian way.

DUCKWORTH: But while they may be used politically, your pieces themselves don't have a political message then?

OLIVEROS: No.

DUCKWORTH: Just meditational and ceremonial?

OLIVEROS: Yes.

DUCKWORTH: Does entertainment play any part in them?

OLIVEROS: The whole issue of music as entertainment is something I have trouble with. Although I'm as happy to be entertained as anyone else, I don't think of these things as entertainment. The meditations, and some of the other things that I do, are opportunities to change and to explore who we are, and what we do, and how we do what we do with each other. Tools. They have a different function from just entertaining.

DUCKWORTH: Do you think that you continue to explore and that your music is continuing to evolve, or are you beginning to locate in the meditational/ceremonial side of music?

OLIVEROS: I think it keeps changing, although what I've learned from doing *Sonic Meditations* and from exploring attentional processes goes into the music that I make now.

DUCKWORTH: Are you the kind of composer who works every day, or the kind who works in spells of insight?

OLIVEROS: I work all kinds of ways. One of the things that I can say about my life right now is that I don't have much in the way of routine. When I was younger, it seemed necessary to do something every day, because I needed to feel that I was making progress. Now I don't know that there is any such thing as progress.

DUCKWORTH: So you work when you feel like it?

OLIVEROS: Yes. Or when I have to.

DUCKWORTH: Do you have enough of the Protestant work ethic in you to feel guilty when you don't work?

OLIVEROS: No, because I think that work goes on whether you want it to or not. Most of the stuff that goes on up front in the mind is just like flies buzzing. The *work* is going on on a deep level. The important thing is to get the space, and get rid of the flies, so that the results of the work can surface and be there for you when you need it.

DUCKWORTH: Do you have any interest in going any deeper into meditation and ceremony, or are you where you want to be?

OLIVEROS: I think I'm doing that by just living. I'm not interested in traditional forms. I'm interested, just as I am in composing, in trying to explore my own forms.

DUCKWORTH: Why did you leave San Diego and move to New York City?

OLIVEROS: The conservatism of the students was one thing. I watched them, over fourteen years, go from being wide open to coming down to a very narrow track. And I began to feel like an aging hippie who had all these funny things to do and say to students who didn't want to hear about it. They wanted to learn how to earn a living. They expected me to provide them with skills and tools, and "let's not have any of this nonsense about creativity." So I thought, "I don't belong here any more." And I felt the pressure and the struggle of the university in general: the struggle for funding and resources. An enormous amount of time is spent recruiting new faculty and sitting on committees to govern this bureaucracy. I felt that the academic bureaucracy was beginning to consume too much time. I wanted the energy that I have in this part of my life to go into composing and performing. So I came to New York, because there are more resources here and people are closer together; it's possible to relate to some wonderful performers more quickly.

DUCKWORTH: Do you think contemporary music is in a good place now, or are we in the doldrums?

OLIVEROS: I think it's in an unknown place. Very unknown, in that we're dealing with more numbers of people who are making music than ever before. Things are changing faster than they've ever changed before. So it's hard to know. From my own point of view, there's more opportunity, more interest, more places. Some audiences are small and some of them are large, but a large audience for my work numbers 200 to 300 people in a small theater. That could change. I could see that change to a larger audience in the not-too-distant future.

DUCKWORTH: Do you find New York hospitable?

OLIVEROS: The arts community is very, very wonderful. People are close by; it has a village sense. I find that very comforting and I like it. Plus you can talk to people quickly about all sorts of things. There are a lot of smart people in New York.

DUCKWORTH: Do you feel any relationship at all to the uptown music scene?

OLIVEROS: Well, I'm involved as a board member of the American Music Center and the Composer's Forum, as advisor to Meet the Composer, and on the board of governors for the New York Foundation on the Arts. Those board meetings take me into uptown circles. But by and large, I spend my time with downtown types. I haven't made much effort to go uptown to concerts.

DUCKWORTH: Do you not feel close to that music?

OLIVEROS: I don't. It doesn't interest me very much.

DUCKWORTH: Do you know why not?

OLIVEROS: I really like sound, but I'm not interested in more intellectual or academic styles. I'm not interested in them and I don't get off on them. I'll have to go and check it out someday, but I'm too busy to go to anything except those things that are close by. Recently Phill Niblock has had a very intense series of concerts at his loft. It was really wonderful. Almost every night there's been somebody there doing something. It was very special, somehow. It's an easy walk over to Niblock's loft, and it's very comfortable, and you sit there and get a closeup of someone's work for the evening. Afterwards there's a lot of camaraderie and an easy walk home. That's very nice.

CHRISTIAN WOLFF

Born Nice, France, 1934

C H R I S T I A N   W O L F F thinks he was fortunate to be in just the right place at just the right time. It allowed him to be a founding member of what is now called the New York School: Cage, Feldman, Brown, and Wolff. The time was 1950; the place was Cage's loft on Monroe Street. But Cage was thirty-eight and the others were in their twenties; Christian Wolff was sixteen years old.

Wolff's family came to America in 1941, when he was seven. Both of his parents were publishers, and his home environment was cultured and intellectual. His father, for instance, met Brahms at the funeral of Clara Schumann. At first, Wolff considered being a concert pianist, but by the age of fifteen he was composing. Thinking for a time about studying with a family friend, Edgard Varèse, who lived around the corner in Greenwich Village, Wolff chose, instead, to consult his piano teacher, Grete Sultan, who sent him to her friend John Cage. Living at that time in a building Wolff describes as a five-story tenement, Cage looked at Wolff's music and immediately agreed to teach him free of charge. Chronologically, this all occurred shortly after Cage first met Morton Feldman, and before Earle Brown had arrived from Colorado. Cage, however, had recently won a Guggenheim; Wolff was completing his junior year in high school.

After several months of weekly lessons, Wolff began stopping by more frequently. During the summer, he was there almost every day of the week. Working with Cage, he developed new forms for his music— what he calls "musical scaffoldings"—that remained useful to him for twenty years. He also watched Cage develop his ideas about chance. In fact, Wolff contributed greatly to the process by giving Cage a book his father, the head of Pantheon Books, had just published: the Chinese book of oracles, the *I Ching*. Wolff says he knew Cage would be interested in it.

After high school, and a trip to Europe where, at Cage's insistence, he met Pierre Boulez, Wolff went to Harvard to major in classics. His parents had discouraged him from going to a conservatory, and besides, Wolff knew he would never be able to support himself with the kind of music he wrote. While at Harvard, though, he was able to arrange a concert for Cage and pianist David Tudor; and he wrote a quasi-improvisatory, duo-piano piece for himself and fellow student Frederic Rzewski. From that point, his music opened to performer participation, and he began allowing chance and controlled spontaneity to play a part. At the time, Wolff believed that in order for a piece to "come alive," the performers had to be engaged in a new way, as creative participators.

In 1970, saying the Vietnam War was like a summons that woke him up and made him choose sides, Wolff, espousing a form of democratic socialism, began writing overtly political music. The results include *Wobbly Music*, based on the radical IWW labor movement from the early part of the century, and *Braverman Music*, a set of instrumental variations based on a German concentration camp song. *Changing the System*, a 1973 work, using a text that comes out of the '68–'69 student uprisings in the U.S., is the piece Wolff thinks of as his most successful political work. More recently, Wolff, whose music is not now as political as it once was, has been writing musical tributes. Some are to progressive political figures he admires; others are more personal, written to people like Morton Feldman and Merce Cunningham, both of whom he has known since he was sixteen years old.

Since 1970, Wolff has taught classics at Dartmouth College in New Hampshire, balancing his life as a composer with his teaching and scholarship. Today he is also increasingly in demand for concerts and festivals, particularly in Europe where, in the spring of 1994, he was honored in Germany and Holland with a series of concerts celebrating his sixtieth birthday. A few years earlier, we met in New York in a relative's apartment on the upper East Side, where Christian was staying for several days. His schedule was crowded, but we had the morning and there were no interruptions. I began with the question everybody always asks him.

DUCKWORTH: People who know only one thing about you remember that as a high-school student you were associated with John Cage. How did you first meet him?

The New York School: (l. to r.) Christian Wolff, Earle Brown, John Cage, and Morton Feldman, New York, 1962. Photo Credit: Archives of Earle Brown

WOLFF: I met John through my piano teacher, Grete Sultan. I'd been working with her for a couple of years. She was the first really serious teacher that I had. Early on, I had the crazy notion that I wanted to become a pianist, for which I had no real talent whatever. But I somehow stuck it out. I then began to be interested in writing music, and spent more and more time doing that—without any particular guidance or help, just sort of out of my own head—and practicing less and less. Finally, in order to apologize for being relatively unprepared, I would bring in my pieces to show that I had been doing something. She finally said, "Well listen, you should go to someone else with the compositions." And I said, "Yes, but who?" I had the notion that what I was doing didn't seem like anything else that I knew, and I was interested in going into new directions.

DUCKWORTH: What were your early pieces like?

WOLFF: They were most affected by the Viennese School, sort of Schoenberg and Webern. But the other thing that I got into doing,

which was unlike even that, was very dense, highly dissonant counterpoint—so dense that it would be, in effect, like a moving cluster.
But there wasn't that much of it. There were a couple of pieces like
that, and then there was a song cycle.

DUCKWORTH: How old were you when you first began composing?

WOLFF: I started to write, I think, when I was about fifteen, and I was
about sixteen when we'd reached this point with Grete. But I
couldn't imagine who to go work with. I had the notion that I really
could do it on my own, you know, and the hell with everybody else.
But I also, somehow, felt I needed to talk to somebody; I needed
some kind of exchange and guidance. The one person that I had
thought of, who happened to be a friend of the family in a way, was
Varèse. He lived around the corner from us, down in the Village.
But somewhere in the back of my mind, it didn't seem to me probably the best idea. I didn't know if he would want to do it, and
though I admired his work immensely, I somehow felt that it would
be difficult to get out of the orbit of his work once you were with
him. So I said to Grete, "I don't know what to do." And she said,
"Well, I think I know somebody who might be helpful." And that
turned out to be John Cage. She lived at the time down on 18th
Street in a loft building, and the loft above her belonged to Merce
Cunningham. She first knew Merce as a neighbor, and then,
inevitably, met John and liked him very much.

DUCKWORTH: By the time she sent you to John, had you already
decided to become a musician?

WOLFF: It wasn't that conscious a decision. I think what I felt was
that I couldn't imagine living without doing music. If I couldn't
hear it, it would be like being deprived of food. I learned that much
later when I got drafted, and went for long periods without being
able to hear anything but what you would hear on AM radio. Finally,
I went to a concert for the first time in what must have been almost
a year and heard Mozart, or something like that. It brought tears to
my . . . I suddenly realized . . . I wept tears. I mean, I couldn't
believe what was happening to me. And that was just listening. So I
think early on it was clear that I was going to do something with
music. But I didn't know what.

DUCKWORTH: I'm a little surprised you were that certain, because I
know you went to Harvard and majored in classics. How did that
come about?

WOLFF: Well, I've had a variety of interests, but I was quite clear on this point. My initial thought when I was in high school was that I ought to go to a conservatory. But I was discouraged from that by my parents. They thought that would be far too specialized at that age. And then, thinking realistically, I didn't seem to have any skills, or interest in developing skills, that the conservatory, or that professional musical training, would really help much. So I simply decided that I couldn't make a living with music. I couldn't maintain myself economically by doing the kind of thing that I wanted to be doing with music, let's put it that way.

DUCKWORTH: But you still felt you could be a musician? You didn't question your understanding of music?

WOLFF: Absolutely not, no. It was the one thing I felt I knew. But this feeling was quite drastic, because I knew no harmony, no counterpoint, none of that stuff that you're supposed to have automatically under your belt before you get out there and start writing music. I hadn't had any of that. But I had had a lot by osmosis, because I was immersed in classical music from a very early age, and lived for the stuff.

DUCKWORTH: Were your parents musical?

WOLFF: My father played the cello and came from a musical family. His father was a professor of music and a choral conductor in Bonn, Germany. In fact, there are several funny connections. My father's father was a music professor and choral conductor with some connection to the circle of Brahms and Joachim. My father as a boy met Brahms at the funeral of Clara Schumann, which is sort of my little link with the great tradition. My parents also knew and were good friends, in particular, with the group around Adolf Busch and Rudolf Serkin, so I was taken to concerts from an early age. Some kids might just have really hated it and rebelled, but in my case, I really liked that stuff.

DUCKWORTH: Do you remember your first meeting with John Cage?

WOLFF: Oh, very well. I was given this address down on Monroe Street. I felt myself to be pretty much a native New Yorker, but I'd never been to that part of town. When I first got there, it spooked me. It was at the end of this rather dismal street, and before you got to John's house, there was what had once been some kind of a factory which had burned out. I think it was a huge bakery. There was still a faint smell—actually rather nice—of old bread. And then this dingy lot right next to it which had a shack on it that apparently was supposed to be a pickle factory. I finally found the place, not quite believing that this could be it. It was a tenement house maybe four or five stories high, sort of smelly and so forth. Anyway, I went in, but I didn't know where in this place it was, and almost every floor had at least three or four separate doors. So I worked my way up through the entire thing. If I heard children screaming I knew that couldn't be it, and I just kept going. Of course, he was at the top; it took me about fifteen minutes. I knocked and there was no answer. I knocked some more, and finally this sleepy voice said, "Yes?" John had been celebrating; I think it was the day after he'd learned that he'd gotten some kind of an award, so they'd celebrated the night before and he was just waking up. This was midday, I think. But he was very nice, and much the way one knows him, which was amazing. He sort of remembered Grete had told him I would turn up. He asked to see my work, and looked at it and seemed to like it, especially these very dense, dissonant things. They were canons; that's what they were. All I did was canons, but set up in such ways as to disguise the fact that they were canons, you know. The stuff that's left over at the end of the canon I would just stick back at the beginning so as to fill up all the musical space. And he said, "This is all very well, and it's quite nice, but, you know, you have to do something other than just write canons." Then he agreed right on the spot to take me on, and even without any further inquiries into my background, said that he would do it for free. It was astonishing. Whenever I retell these old stories, I'm amazed at the good fortune I've had over the years. It's really remarkable. I mean, to have met him at that point and to have him be just the person who suited my circumstances.

DUCKWORTH: In retrospect, how much better for you was studying privately with John than being a music major in college would have been?

WOLFF: I don't think it would have made any sense for me to major in music at Harvard, which is where I was going to go, especially given what those places were like in those days. They really had no use for any new music whatsoever. If you did that, you did it entirely on your own, and every effort was probably made to discourage you and to tell you that it was crazy and had no value. And the other thing was, I met him at an extremely interesting point in his career. He'd just come back from Paris where he'd spent a year—I guess it was his Guggenheim—and had gotten to know and be very good friends with Pierre Boulez. And of course he knew the whole American experimental scene. So it was at that one particular moment where one had the sense that everything new was happening, or was going to happen. You could see it, you knew it, you were informed, and you knew the people.

DUCKWORTH: What were your actual lessons like? How often did you go see him?

WOLFF: I think we met once a week, and we had several projects. He had just recently heard the Webern Symphony, Op. 21, which had received its first American performance at the Philharmonic. (That's a famous event, too, because that's where John met Morton Feldman.) It's hard to remember how difficult it was in those days to get materials and information. There was very little. Long-playing records had just come in. Even getting to hear things was difficult; nobody played the stuff. There were very few new-music concerts. So we were desperate for each other's company in that sense, because there was nobody to talk to, and nowhere to get information. John had gone to the library to look at the score of the Webern because you couldn't buy it. And he'd copied out the first movement himself so as to be able to study it, and had begun the analysis of it. So what he did was to just turn it over to me and say, "Now you finish it up, okay." I think he wanted me to go to the library and copy the second movement, but I'm glad to say I never got around to doing that. But I had already been alerted to that music. In fact, that's what really got me started. I had heard the Juilliard Quartet, in Tanglewood of all places, play the Berg Lyric Suite and, I think, the Schoenberg Fourth Quartet and the Webern 5 Pieces for String Quartet. So I was ready for that. On the other hand, this was the first time I had actually been required to get inside a piece like that. And it's a beautiful piece to do that with because it really can be analyzed down to the last note.

DUCKWORTH: Where did you get the skill to do that kind of analysis?

WOLFF: I figured it out. John had started it, and we had the row. And, especially with Webern, you can ferret out the rows pretty fast, and then work out how it works.

DUCKWORTH: What else did John ask you to do?

WOLFF: We did counterpoint exercises. He thought I should do some counterpoint, I think, simply because that's what he'd had to do. When he was with Schoenberg he was put through this sixteenth-century counterpoint course—two years with much of it on the same cantus firmus, apparently. And then, finally, he felt that what I really needed to learn about was form. In other words, how to keep a piece going, because my pieces were just basically these little chunks of stuff. So what he taught me was how to make rhythmic structures. He'd have me write a simple exercise, a short piece, with one voice, and I was to make melodies within the structure using very restricted means, four or five notes, something like that. In the meantime, I would go on making my own pieces. We kept that up for not more than about six or seven weeks, maybe a little longer. I finished the Webern and that was that. We decided it was good enough; we didn't really have to go on and do the next movement. And the counterpoint I turned out to be very bad at. I couldn't, as they say now, get myself motivated for it. And John turned out to be not terribly interested himself, so that kind of died by the wayside. But the rhythmic structures I got the hang of, and started to make these pieces. Partly under the impulse of working with very restricted means, I got into the idea of making music with very small numbers of pitches.

DUCKWORTH: Do any of those early pieces survive today?

WOLFF: Yes. My first official piece, my Opus 1, is a duet for two violins on D, E-flat, and E-natural. It's called *Duo for Violins.*

DUCKWORTH: How long did you continue to go to John's every week?

WOLFF: When the lessons ended I just kept going anyway, for various reasons. Obviously, the main one was that I enjoyed it. And I think he did, too.

DUCKWORTH: Were you still in high school?

WOLFF: Yes. I'm vague about the chronology, but I have a feeling it was in the spring. I had no piano at the time, so John invited me to come anytime to use his. And what that turned out to be was that when school was out I came almost every day during the week. I would usually come about lunchtime, bringing something to eat. He'd been working all morning. He would take a break; we'd have lunch together and talk; and then I would work or mess about at the piano and he would go back to work. It was a tiny place, but with two rooms.

DUCKWORTH: Did you get along well with John's other associates, in particular Earle Brown and Morton Feldman?

WOLFF: I did, yes. In a way it was easy, because I was younger, you see. I was a kid. I think the thing with Morty . . . There was a competitive thing there, which came out when Earle appeared on the scene. But I circumvented that because I was younger and still in school.

DUCKWORTH: Did Earle know that the competition with Morton existed?

WOLFF: I don't know. People don't like to bring it up. Now John occasionally talks about it pretty directly. The relationship with Morty was very close. I mean, Morty was a very intense person. We were all very close. But I lived a different kind of life, that's the other thing. I'm a bourgeois, if you will. I went and had a job and married and had a family and all the rest of it, whereas these guys were devoted artists. Their art was first, and they really laid their lives on the line for it in a way that I never even thought of doing.

DUCKWORTH: Why were you so completely accepted, if you were so different?

WOLFF: Well, I wasn't *that* different, at least musically. I think they liked the work. And I liked theirs. Besides, there weren't that many people to talk to. We really needed each other. And we really were devoted to each other's work. Nothing was more exciting than to go down to Morty's, when Morty moved into that building, and see what he was up to. He had a habit of putting his work up on the wall, so it was like going to a painter's place.

DUCKWORTH: Where was the point when you stopped being a younger student and became an actual member of the group?

WOLFF: You know, I don't think it's ever stopped. But it wasn't really being a student, musically; I was just a younger member living in a different way. It's like your relationship with your parents. To your parents you're always a child. It drives you up the wall at times, but it's very difficult to get out of that relationship.

DUCKWORTH: Do you really still feel that way, even now?

WOLFF: A little bit, yes. I especially felt it with Morty, for some reason. I think I represented for Morty (this is my notion) a period which was very special in retrospect. It was like some kind of Garden of Eden where things were tough, but precisely because they were tough, they were particularly intense and very exciting. I think it was less so for John. John really moves on; I don't see any nostalgia in him. But Morty had this very romantic side, which thought of that period with tremendous affection. And he associated me with it. And I think because John changed, and because they'd had their differences at various times, Morty sort of laid it on me to be the one who represented that period. It's kind of nice, but, of course, then I changed quite drastically, too, over the years, and at times he was baffled by that. I don't know the details of it, but I know Morty was very close to Philip Guston, the painter. But when Guston's work changed drastically that friendship just went to pieces. That's the thing with these guys, their work takes precedence over everything, to the point where someone as passionate about his relationships as Feldman would break with somebody over, essentially, an aesthetic point. Or, to put it another way, the aesthetic point has become completely involved with the total life.

DUCKWORTH: Did you have the opportunity to watch John develop his ideas about chance, or had that begun before you came on the scene?

WOLFF: No, I was there when it was happening. Again, talk about strokes of luck. Initially he didn't speak that much about his own work, but I think what he had just done was the String Quartet and the few pieces that came afterwards. There's a short period where he had that style of writing with what he called "aggregates of sound." He was clearly going through some kind of a crisis, on various levels. I mean professionally, he was just not finding much work, making any money. And then aesthetically, not knowing what to do next. He had already been seriously engaged in the study of Zen, as he had before in Indian philosophy, and all these things were going on at once. The first thing I remember he was working on was the *Concerto for Prepared Piano* and *Sixteen Dances* for Merce, and I think it was in the course of that that he discovered the notion of the magic square. The magic square wasn't entirely random, but it forced you into situations where you had to follow moves that were not quite predictable. And I would try, because I was getting free instructions and we were friends, to make my contribution. My parents were publishers, you see, and they had just produced a very beautiful book, which was an edition of the *I Ching*. It had just come out, and I brought it to John.

DUCKWORTH: Did you know what you were taking to him? Did you anticipate how useful it would become?

WOLFF: I knew he'd be interested, because he was interested in Oriental philosophy and, in particular, things having to do with . . . I won't say randomness as such, but that whole Zen thing of the moment and the intensity of the moment, without regard to past or future. And clearly, the *I Ching* had something to do with that, because the whole point was that the coins that you tossed or the yarrow stalks that you threw at that very moment were what was significant; the moment was significant, and the text was significant for that moment. I think I had some sense of that connection. But mostly, it was something that had just come out that I thought would interest him. And then, when he saw those charts at the back, he suddenly, I think, overlaid that in his mind with the charts that he'd set up for the magic squares, and that was it. Bingo!

DUCKWORTH: Anybody who knows John knows that he's enormously seductive. Do you think that his ideas had too big an influence on your own work? Were you too young and impressionable?

WOLFF: Yes. Well, inevitably, I was impressionable. At sixteen, seventeen, that's an age where's it going to happen. It didn't worry me, I must say. It's true that over the years, when I think about music, it's impossible to think about it without dealing with his ideas. Then I realize how many of my ideas, in fact, either just are his ideas or are very close to them. The effect has been tremendous, there's no question about that. But on the other hand, and this is something that we had to deal with a lot in the early years, all four of us were lumped together as the "Cage School," usually dismissively, but with no sense of difference. Yet right from the very beginning, it seemed to me that our music was notably different. I never had any problem telling a piece by Feldman from Cage, Brown, or mine.

DUCKWORTH: What's your explanation of the difference? How do you tell each other's music apart?

WOLFF: Well, first of all, it's a question of sensibility. Feldman's music, in my view, is unanalyzable. You can't do a normal analytical number on it. Earle's music I have a less concrete sense of; I don't know it as well. John's music is also unanalyzable, except insofar as you can go back and look at the charts.

DUCKWORTH: Earle told me he thought one of the major differences was that he was interested in improvisation and in people working together, whereas John wasn't.

WOLFF: Well, okay. I was trying to get more at the phenomenon. In other words, what is it that makes the sound different in each case, because I have a very strong sense of that. It's really just hearing it, you know. Never mind how the pieces were made, or what the composers were interested in, or any of that stuff. It's just that the actual physical presence of those pieces was very different.

DUCKWORTH: Where did your music fit into that scheme?

WOLFF: From a technical point of view I'm closer to Earle, with the exception of that one area of Morty's early work where he used pitch areas and let people choose any pitches within a high, middle, or low register. My earliest work, the work with only a small number of pitches, was distinctive simply by virtue of that initial choice. Nobody else was writing music with just three or four or five notes in it, so there is no way you can confuse that with anybody else's sound. John's work at the time seemed generous with its material. The earlier prepared piano pieces are sometimes quite minimal, but there's a lot of rhythmic movement. In any case, the sonorities are unique. Then the first chance pieces—I think of *Music of Changes*—though they had plenty of empty space in them, also were very rich in the range of sound possibilities. And Morty's minimalism, if you like, is initially dynamic—low-level dynamics—so that there's a sound, a kind of quietness, which is the initial impression you get from Feldman. While mine, at the time, was just these restricted notes. But within those notes there were varieties of dynamic attack and also structure. I tried to make the rhythmic structures very transparent.

DUCKWORTH: How many years did you work with rhythmic structures?

WOLFF: I used them for the next fifteen or twenty years. It seems to me the one single technical thing that I learned from John that was completely useful in every possible way. It really helped me a lot working with these scaffoldings.

DUCKWORTH: So, basically, you took John's ideas out of his percussion period and carried them on?

WOLFF: Yes, exactly.

DUCKWORTH: Did you add your own ideas to it?

WOLFF: Yes, simply in this way: in John's system, once you set up your rhythmic structure—it's in 2-4-1, let's say—you then repeated it over and over again. It's like a pentameter line in poetry; you have to keep using it. You can vary within it, but essentially that's your given parameter for the rest of the work. You do 2-4-1 twice, you do it four times, you do it once, but you're always doing 2-4-1. And I found that tiresome, so instead of doing 2-4-1 twice, I simply multiplied the whole line by two and got 4-8-2, and so forth.

DUCKWORTH: What did that give you?

WOLFF: It made a very different kind of situation. Where John's use of the rhythmic structure seems more to be focused at a microlevel, the level of the line if we're thinking of poetry, I wanted to be able to include note-to-note composing in large structural spaces, too. What I wanted to do was to get a whole range of structural spaces, where the smallest units might be as little as a half a second, or even smaller, and the largest units could be as much as a minute, so that I would have to think in terms of "What will I do for half a second? What's going to happen for sixty seconds?" And that element I didn't find in John's system. And then I would also superimpose two structures, or rather read the same one in different ways simultaneously. From early on, I was interested in counterpoint, so that I might make the structure, lay it all out, and then have, perhaps, four voices or continuities (I wasn't writing melodically so it certainly didn't come out like regular counterpoint) with one reading in the usual way, another one reading backwards, another might turn the whole thing on its side, and the other one the reverse of that. And then overlay all of those.

DUCKWORTH: What are some representative pieces that work this way?

WOLFF: Well, *For Piano I, For Piano II, Suite*. Lots of keyboard music, because David Tudor had come on the scene.

DUCKWORTH: Is that the style of music you were writing when the Monroe Street group broke up?

WOLFF: Yes. And I had this funny experience. When I graduated from high school, my parents as a graduation thing took me along on a trip to Europe. And when Cage learned I was going to Paris, he said, "Well, you really must look up Boulez." Which I did. I spent almost a week with him. He was really wonderful—exceptionally nice. I showed him these pieces with just these few notes, and he said, "Well, this is very nice, this is all very well, but you know there are a lot more notes out there." He couldn't see it. So as a kind of response to that, the next piano piece I wrote I made a point of using all eighty-eight keys. I sort of blew the whole thing up. If I'd kept going, I could have become a minimalist in my time. I'm sort of the protominimalist with those early pieces. But I decided that I had done it, and I needed to move on, and Boulez gave me a little shove.

DUCKWORTH: What was the piece that moved you on?

WOLFF: It's *For Piano II*. The European music at that time affected us a lot. I think Boulez had a considerable influence on Cage, for instance. The *Music of Changes* owes a lot to the Second Piano Sonata of Boulez, even to the point where the pitch choices that John makes involve using up all twelve tones of the chromatic scale. And the density and complexity, that came from Europe, essentially. We were affected by that. And then there was a certain element of violence in that music. That has some Zen relationship; you knock the student on the head occasionally. And also that aesthetic of Boulez's, a very pure, violent quality in the music.

DUCKWORTH: How did the Monroe Street group break up? Were you in college when that happened?

WOLFF: Yes. It wasn't altogether a breakup. I think we just dispersed. And I'm not sure I could date it. But I left New York pretty soon, because I met John when I was maybe at the end of my junior year in high school, so I had one more year as a senior and then I went off to college. So I wasn't regularly on the scene that much anymore.

DUCKWORTH: What did it feel like working with John Cage one year and studying classics at Harvard the next? Was that a violent shift?

WOLFF: The idea of choosing classics, looking back, is really bizarre. Going from one esoteric thing to one even more so. But in those days that didn't seem so unreasonable. And, in fact, it worked out. I was lucky again. But yes, it was very different. It was a mildly schizophrenic situation. But that was there from the beginning. I was raised in this, I won't say, conventional milieu, but the world that

John moved in and the world that I grew up in were totally different. So I was used to that situation. In fact, I had never thought about this before, but maybe because I came from this Europeanized background, I simply took it for granted that I would be different. That there was some aspect of my life that would not be the same as that of the general environment in which I lived, and therefore I wasn't really taken particularly aback when I found myself in different kinds of environments. Another thing, I was a jock as a kid. I was devoted to sports. I played a lot, and I went to see a lot of baseball games in New York.

DUCKWORTH: What did you play?

WOLFF: Basketball, mostly. I liked baseball a lot, but we had trouble finding places to play. And I'd go from that down to see Cage, and then try to finish up my high school stuff. So the idea of doing different things didn't bother me, though there were times, obviously, when it could create crisis. I would have a paper due next week on Sophocles, but ten days later I was supposed to send a piece down to New York because there was a concert. And then there'd be just practical problems; those have pursued me all my life. But we all have that. Again, I think John is an exception, and, in his way, Morty too. They are people who have simply decided to make their work the absolute center of their lives, somehow reducing these distractions. For them, there's one life. In my case, it was not so much distractions as a lot of things going on at once. I was just trying to juggle it as best I could.

DUCKWORTH: Did your music change when you left John and had more perspective on what was going on?

WOLFF: I don't think so, no. As I say, John's effect on my life has been tremendous. I never had an identity crisis about my music. It changed, but in the way things change, rather than because I was near or far away or whatever. And I was still writing pieces for David Tudor. John would organize a concert and say, "Christian, what have you got that's new?," so musically I was still living in New York.

DUCKWORTH: Did you participate in any musical activities as a student at Harvard?

WOLFF: As a full-time college student I didn't have that much time. Harvard had a music club, and I made little inroads at first. As an undergraduate I brought David and John up for a concert.

DUCKWORTH: How did you arrange that?

WOLFF: I don't know how that happened. But it did—I doubt there was any money involved. Harvard's a funny place. The music department, I thought, was really out of it. That was one of the things that made it perfectly clear that there was no point in my spending any time over there.

DUCKWORTH: I'm still curious about your choice of a major. Did you grow up with the classics?

WOLFF: I grew up reading. Remember, this was a world before television. For one's diversion, you read. And my father's life was books; he was a publisher. It took a while, because I was into sports so much as a kid, but at fourteen something suddenly clicked. I just got into it with a vengeance. And I read everything in sight that I could get my hands on. The one thing I knew for sure, however, was that I wasn't going to get into publishing. I'd seen my parents work. They didn't just put in time at the office, they were working *all* the time—weekends, nights, you name it. So I thought, "No way can I do that and do anything else."

DUCKWORTH: But you saw John working all the time, didn't you?

WOLFF: Well, yes and no. John seemed to have a very nice structure to his life when I was going down there every day. He would work in the morning, and then he'd take a lunch break, and then we'd talk for an hour or so. Then, he'd go work again for maybe another three hours, and then he'd knock off. Then he'd go uptown. He'd go meet friends, and go out and have supper. I don't think he did much unless there was a crisis, or he had something with a deadline to get done. He did a lot of other things. He went to talk to the artists, went to the galleries, and so forth. And the thing is, well, you know, you can't write music twelve hours a day.

DUCKWORTH: Was there a definite point where you turned to chance and started giving the performers more freedom, or did that happen gradually?

WOLFF: The way I got into that was more or less accidental. When I graduated from college, I had a scholarship for a year in Europe, and at the end of that I went to Darmstadt. And this kid came up to me and said he was going to be in Cambridge and he'd like to come see me. That was Frederic Rzewski, who was then, I think, a second- or third-year undergraduate. And we hit it off. That's when the activity really got going at Harvard, because there was a third person up there, David Behrman, who was also an undergraduate. David, somehow, had managed to get himself elected president of the undergraduate music club, which meant that he had access to Paine Hall, the smaller concert hall. So essentially, if we could just get anything together, we had a place to do it, no money or nothing. It was really a matter of just getting players, or doing it ourselves. So, we were planning a concert. I had nothing new and it was clear that I wasn't going to have time to write a new piece, especially with these complex techniques that I had worked out. It was going to be too slow. So I worked out a scheme whereby Frederic and I could, essentially . . . well, not exactly improvise, but we'd talked about it and worked this thing out. It was a piece for two pianos.

DUCKWORTH: Are you talking about *Duo for Pianists II?*

WOLFF: Not yet, but it was the prototype for both *Duos I* and *II.* I scrapped that particular thing that we did, but then I realized that I really had something that was interesting. It used the earlier notion of rhythmic structures, but in a quite different way where the rhythmic structures now gave you spaces to work in. Rather than being through-composed, so to speak, the structure simply gave various spaces to the performer to do something. And the something—and again I was interested in a wide range—could go from something totally undefined, to some rather precise determinations. For example, you'd have to play, say, three pitches from a given source which consisted of twelve or so pitches. Two of them would have to be mezzo piano, one fortissimo, one would have to be plucked, or whatever. Now, how you did that and how you distributed it was left open, but you really had to prepare a little bit. You had to have some focus on what you were going to do. In practice, what I tended to do was to think of at least three or four ways of using that material, and then wait and see, using whichever one seemed right at the time, with possible on-the-spot modifications. So it was improvisatory, but within a very focused kind of structural framework. Anyway, we did that and liked the process and results a lot. So I pursued it and, as I say, just generated a new technique of composing.

DUCKWORTH: Did that become a second style, or a second period, of your work?

WOLFF: Exactly. A complete change. But in a way, it was actually a third style. The first style is the few notes, right, the minimal style. The second style is when things opened up. That was very much under the European influence, with a lot of notes, very complex, and the interest in these complicated structures. Then the sudden discovery that all this incredibly complex, intricate stuff wasn't really necessary. You could get much more directly to the point by opening up the score to the performer, and allowing those intricacies, which happen anyway all the time in the playing, to happen more spontaneously. This wasn't of course, just improvisation. Since I really am a composer rather than a performer, I had something to do (let me put it that way) as a composer, and to think about. But on the other hand, it gave the piece a certain character and identity and helped the players, because it's very hard to improvise from zero. That's the hardest of all. It's almost impossible. And then the other thing that was important is that these piano pieces were for two people. What we discovered right away, of course, was that your free choices weren't exactly that free. They involved dialogical choices, they were in response to what the other person was doing. So that immediately brought to my awareness this notion of interconnection and interplay between people. It's what happens all the time in chamber music. My music is basically chamber music. In a string quartet, the players tune in to each other. They have to; that's what it's all about. What I did was to take that dimension of music making and make *that* precisely the focus of how I would put the music together, rather than harmonic structures, counterpoint, or all that other stuff. That became secondary to this process of actually making music by virtue of tuning into and responding to other players.

DUCKWORTH: That brings up an interesting question, though. How different do you think various realizations of a piece can be and still maintain an identity as the same piece?

WOLFF: That's something that we all got interested in, the question of a piece's identity. And there are various answers. John's music, at least at that time, had nothing whatever to do with improvisation. That was one of the major confusions that people made, and that, clearly, was dead wrong. We're getting now to the period of the *Variations* sequence, which really pushed the notion of what constituted a piece of music, because nothing was said about anything except you had to make yourself something out of these lines and dots and things that were on plastic sheets. And that seemed to be about as far away from a musical identity as possible. But what always struck me as so mysterious was that what people did with those things almost all the time would come out sounding like John's work. I couldn't tell *Variations I* from *Variations II* perhaps, but I knew that it was Cage, and if I thought a little more I could probably figure out that it was a *Variations* that was being done. There's this mysterious thing that in those days people would try some of John's chance techniques, but their music wouldn't come out sounding like John's.

DUCKWORTH: John knows the right questions to ask.

WOLFF: Right! That always delighted me, because what was so shocking intellectually to everybody was this notion of randomness, that you gave up control. And yet it was clear that control operates at many different levels or angles, and that there was just as much control in John's work as there might be in Stockhausen's or Boulez's. It was just a question of where you applied it and how you focused it.

DUCKWORTH: So is it the control that's holding the various performances of your pieces together?

WOLFF: To a certain extent. But what really holds them together is not one thing, but all kinds of things. The fact that it's two pianos. The fact that it lasts so long or is indefinite in duration. Now it's true that if you don't know the music, I could probably play you two versions of the same piece and you'd say, "Well, those are two different pieces." In other words, one of the things about this kind of indeterminate music is that the indeterminacy of it is not evident, you might say, until—I want to qualify that, but let me just go on for a minute—it's not evident until you've heard say, three, four, five, or six versions. Then you begin to see that you're working with the same structure, that you're just getting different takes on the same scaffolding, as it were. What I want to qualify, though, is that I'm also convinced that the music has a character because of this indeterminacy that it would not otherwise have. Opening it up that way does, in fact, change the music quite drastically. This is harder to verbalize, I think, but I would say the music has more life. It comes alive much more easily when it has that indeterminate quality about it. And that's what I liked about it. The thing that we were beginning to feel pretty soon about this hyperorganized, European/Darmstadt music was that it could be just as dead as a doornail. Theoretically it was very exciting and interesting, but somehow it was like machinery. It just didn't swing. Whereas if you introduced these other dimensions, whether it was in the compositional process as John did, or in the performing situation as I did and, in different ways, as Earle did, then you got something much more interesting.

DUCKWORTH: Is *Duo for Pianists II* the best example of that style?

WOLFF: In a way it is, yes, because that took the thing a step further. In *Duo I* the structure is fixed, and the timings are absolute. When you're playing it you should really use a stopwatch and know exactly where you are. Whereas in the second *Duo*, I got this other notion. That's where I introduced the idea of cues. The time is let loose. You still have these time frames, sequences that you're to observe as a performer, but they are no longer coordinated with the other performers. And there was a kind of inspiration for this: Stockhausen's piano piece—is it IX or XI, I can never remember? It's the one on the big piece of paper with all the separate sections, and the continuity is determined by wherever your eye next lands, which struck me as absurd because that is not indeterminate, as David Tudor once proved by making a two-minute version of the piece that normally lasted twenty, and making Stockhausen absolutely furious. Anyway, I was really interested in a situation where it was *not* in the player's control as to what happened next. But instead of doing it visually, I did it acoustically, aurally. What determines the next sequence you go to—the continuity—is the last thing you hear that constitutes a cue before the end of the sequence you are playing. The cue could be a high, loud sound; a low, plucked sound; or no sound at all for so much time. And whichever of those things you last caught just before you finished cues your next section. The other thing that happens there is that all the sequences are repeatable. (Almost everything; occasionally I put in something you could only do once.) So a kind of kaleidoscopic quality is built into the structure. That is to say, you realize that you have heard something before, but it's not quite the same, right? And hardly ever in the same relation to what the other player is doing. You have that time sequence and those new conditions, but the general conditions are the same and, therefore, you can begin to hear that you're getting another take on the same structural unit.

DUCKWORTH: During that period, how did you handle the criticism that giving performers that kind of freedom abnegated responsibility?

WOLFF: Oh, I never worried much about it, for several reasons. One is that my experiences of the pieces was that they had a very distinct identity. The quality could be good or bad, and that was my fault as composer. That was just sort of empirical, if you will. I, of course, tried to write as well as I could. The other thing was—and here you could talk about responsibility—that I felt the responsibility was equally in the hands of the performers. Now, that's not abnegating, that's sharing, okay? Whenever you play a piece of music, whatever it is, you take on a tremendous responsibility as a performer, you know. You can destroy the piece. You can destroy Bach just as easily as you can destroy Cage. I once said that I really assumed, sort of optimistically, that the players had good will. But in those days that could be open to question, because sometimes people very perversely would undertake to do these pieces and then do them miserably.

DUCKWORTH: Why do you suppose that happened?

WOLFF: It's simply the assumption that the audience wouldn't know any better. Now they do, generally. It depends on what kind of an audience you're dealing with, obviously. But again, it's a question of focus or angle. Whether you played an E-flat or E-natural wasn't that critical. That wasn't where the music was at, so to speak. It is in Mozart. But in this music it's the process, and the intensity, and the focus, and the surprises. It doesn't matter if you miss a note. So the question of responsibility becomes one of getting at what this music is trying to do and making it live. I guess I did begin to feel that for a piece to really come alive the performer had to be engaged in it in a way that would be different from the usual way that performers are engaged in pieces. Not as just a kind of enlightened reproductive machine, to put it perhaps a little strongly, but as a creative participator who not only made choices and musical decisions, but who responded to what somebody else was doing, and did it intelligently and musically.

DUCKWORTH: Where's the point where your music took on an overtly political character?

WOLFF: It was a piano piece I wrote for Frederic Rzewski. I pushed these indeterminate pieces until I finally ended up writing little prose pieces, just practical instructions. And I did one of those pieces in 1969 which is a song on the text "You blew it," which was addressed to President Nixon. I didn't explain it to anybody, so it's not overt, but that was the first time. It was at the end of a radio broadcast of some outrageous piece of news, and that was my response, and it became the text.

DUCKWORTH: What was the name of that piece?

WOLFF: "You Blew It." It's part of a set of pieces called *Prose Compositions*.

DUCKWORTH: Was that the piece for Frederic?

WOLFF: No. The first explicit one was the piano piece I wrote for Frederic. Frederic was going to do a recital and I thought to make him a piece in which he could use his voice as well as play, because I'd heard him do *Coming Together*. He had a solo version of that where he did both the piano and the voice; it was just heartbreakingly powerful. And thinking of that, I thought I'd like to do something where he could do that too. So the text came from a book about a Chinese village. We were, at that time, very much taken with Maoism and various Maoist ideas, and this was a book about what had happened to a Chinese village before and after the Maoist Revolution. I found it very powerful, and extracted texts which were illustrative of how people's lives changed. Frederic had the option of speaking or singing or chanting the text. He also had to play bass drum and high hat with his feet; I associated those with the Chinese New Year. Not only was that piece explicitly political, but musically it was a drastic change. It was called *Accompaniments*.

DUCKWORTH: What makes music political in your mind?

WOLFF: For me to make explicitly political music, almost 99 percent of the time, requires the use of text in some way, if only in the title of the piece.

DUCKWORTH: Other than the use of texts, did writing political music actually change the type of music you were writing?

WOLFF: It involved major musical changes. My music before had been very sparse. It was very much affected by Webern. But because of the political mood of the times and my own response to it, I felt it was rather frivolous writing music like that. Not that I felt the music was bad or anything, but it just didn't seem to have

Christian Wolff, Royalton, VT, 1992. Photo Credit: Rebecca Beguin

anything to do with what was going on. I really felt an explicit need to make a music that people would respond to in a more direct way, music that didn't require so specialized an atmosphere for its appreciation. So I had these endless strong chords and this text which might offend or irritate you, but it was something concrete you could latch on to. Generally, I was trying to make the music more extroverted. I really was making an effort to talk to people rather than just to have the music talk to itself or the performers.

DUCKWORTH: Why did that suddenly seem necessary?

WOLFF: Well, partly because I thought I had come to the end of a line with the earlier work. By then, I'd written a lot of music and some people knew of me as a composer. The world in which I moved mostly knew that, but I was embarrassed to ask them to come to a concert of my work. I thought, "There's no way they're going to get into this stuff. Forget it." But I suddenly felt, "This is ridiculous. These are people whom I admire and respect, yet I'm doing work that means nothing to them. Something's wrong here." In general, I think it happened everywhere that people began to feel that they needed to make a music that was, to put it simply, more accessible, that could really reach a more general kind of audience than the very specialized one it produced.

DUCKWORTH: Had you always been political, or did this represent a new direction for you?

WOLFF: Yes and no. I grew up in the fifties, which was politically the most sodden time, so I was quite apolitical in some sense. On the other hand, the reason I'm in this country is because of the Second World War and my father's connection to Jewish people, so I did have a very direct experience of how the larger world out there affected one's existence. But in this country, you know, everything seemed fine, no problems. McCarthy was rumbling in the background and we all thought it was terrible, but the notion of going out and demonstrating didn't cross anybody's mind. I became a little bit more involved in the sixties during the civil rights movement. My sympathies were strong and I actually did a little practical work as well. And when it looked as though I was going to be drafted, I decided that I had to be a conscientious objector because I couldn't accept regular military service. That's a personal thing, but it's obviously also a political stand. Then the Vietnam War was like a summons. That really woke me up.

DUCKWORTH: Do you think your political music holds up as music today?

WOLFF: Yes, but I'm not sure it holds up as politics.

DUCKWORTH: Are you still writing political music?

WOLFF: Well, yes, but what *is* political music? I've become more relaxed about it. There was a time when this was really a source of anxiety and discussion. And as I say, my first way of dealing with it was rather extreme. I said if you didn't have a text then there was no point, no political context. On the other hand, you may not have a text. My general feeling now is that you have your politics, you have your views, and you should act on them, but it doesn't seem absolutely necessary that you do that through your music. To put it in a practical way, if you have strong political convictions about something, the thing to do that's most effective, presumably, is to go out there and agitate for it. Whether you write your congressman, start a demonstration, or join a political party, you do political work. That seems to me the way to deal with political problems. The other aspects of your life, like your musical work, might or might not be explicitly connected to that. I do believe, though, what people talked about in the sixties and seventies, you know: the personal is the political. Of course, the musical is the political, too; everything that you do has a political meaning. And I think one ought to be aware of that, certainly at least in a negative sense. You should really take care not to do things that are politically bad. In other words, you do have to be on one side or the other. You can't pretend that what you do is neutral. And to that extent I've certainly tried to maintain a political awareness in everything I do. But that doesn't mean I'm going to write agitational songs all the time. It's also a question of what you can do well. I'm not a good songwriter particularly. There are certain other things I think I can do much better. You can do as much damage by writing bad political music as not writing any political music at all. So that's another way of looking at it.

DUCKWORTH: Is *Changing the System* one of your best political pieces in your mind?

WOLFF: Yes. That's an interesting one, because it combines the two worlds. In *Accompaniments* I really tried to change the style, though there were still some indeterminate elements. The whole question of how indeterminacy relates to politics is one that was raised, the argument being that the indeterminate element in the music made it incapable of carrying a message. (One can argue around it, saying that the openness itself was a political message.) But *Changing the System* combines the two. It has a text, you see, but musically it's much closer to the earlier works, say, than the *Accompaniments* piece was. In a way, the politics were there in the text. They were, however, also in the way the material of the piece was given to the performers, because it is a piece that can be deeply and complexly collaborative. And finally, and perhaps the most essential thing, is the sound that it produced. The piece has basically two parts or two kinds of material that you can overlay eventually. The first part is purely instrumental; it's basically chords and melodic material collaboratively played out. In the second half, there's a text. And the text is shared, you see; collaborative again. The text, almost syllable by syllable, is shared by four people like a quartet, so that you're hearing not one voice, but four voices, or multiples of four voices—at least two sets of four. But you can multiply quartets indefinitely; it's been done, I think, by as many as forty-eight players. And the accompaniment of that text is unspecified percussion. You're simply told to choose four objects which will give you an increasing range of resonance. The tendency is for people to choose junk—stones and metal—in other words, strong sounds. And that percussion material—all chords, collaboratively cued—has a revolutionary feel about it. It can have a kind of feeling of suppressed violence, or better, a focused determination, that gives that music, in conjunction with the text, a sound which is strong. I like that.

DUCKWORTH: Let me ask you about the way you work. Do you compose every day now?

WOLFF: No, hardly ever. I work from piece to piece, and I just have to make space for whatever I'm doing.

DUCKWORTH: Does your teaching at Dartmouth conflict with your work as a composer?

WOLFF: Absolutely, yes. I've more or less come to terms with the fact that there are times that I can be working on the music and there are times that I can't be working on it. It's almost reached the point where if I have more time than I know what to do with—well, that hardly ever happens—that I may be at a loss about what to do because I don't have these other constraints, as it were. What I'm saying, I guess, is that I'm not sure that I would write more music if I had more time. Partly it's a supply-and-demand situation. I don't write into the blue. I hardly ever write unless I have a commission or somebody has asked me to do something. And the amount I write seems to fit, more or less, the need out there, as far as I can make out. So I don't feel as though if I wrote a lot more, there would be a great demand for it. It seems to be just about nicely calibrated at the moment, for better or worse.

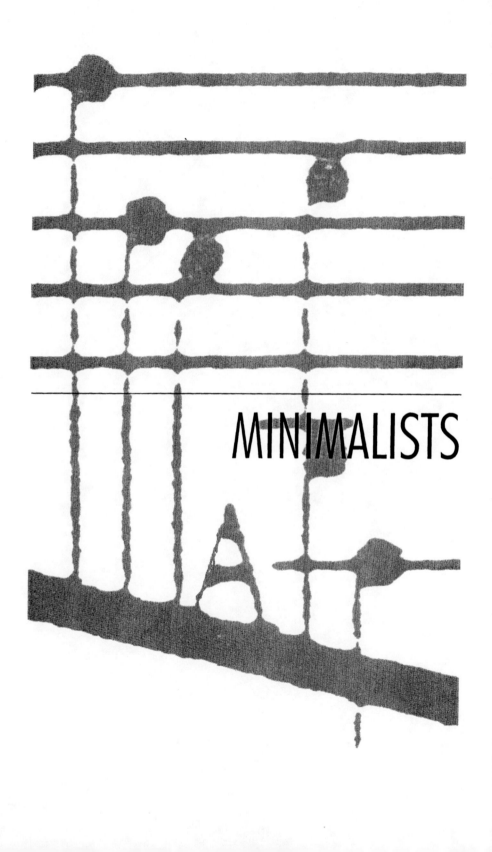

MINIMALISTS

LA MONTE YOUNG

Born Bern, Idaho, 1935

MARIAN ZAZEELA

Born New York, 1940

L A   M O N T E   Y O U N G   A N D   M A R I A N   Z A Z E E L A
have spent every night of their lives together since the day they officially got together: June 22, 1962. And except for a brief period in the early
eighties, when they had a second living space a few blocks away, they
have lived in the same downtown loft on Church Street since 1963, regularly sharing it, since the early seventies, with their teacher, north
Indian classical singer Pandit Pran Nath. In his typically colorful way,
Young recently described their life together as "two turtles, living in a
dream house."

If it sounds as if things move slowly in their lives, the same is dou-
bly true in their art. Even when playing microtonal blues, Young can
take hours to get to the next chord change. And Zazeela's light shows,
normally in a magenta hue, appear not to move at all, except for the
shadows, which are never the same. When I told Ben Johnston I
planned to interview La Monte and Marian, he said, "You'd do well to
remember that they function as close to a single entity as any two people you're ever likely to meet." Certainly, in conversation, they do talk
at the same time, always completing each other's sentences. But the
most compelling thing about their relationship, to my mind, is how
slowly things move in their presence. This is true even in sleep, where
they are on a twenty-seven-hour cycle that, depending on the day, can
have them awake or asleep at any hour of the day or night.

209

Born a Mormon, in a log cabin, in a town of 149 people in Idaho, La Monte Young remembers the vast sense of time and distance he felt as a child. He also remembers the wind blowing through the logs of the cabin, the sound of insects, and the slow-moving clouds, all of which would later have an effect on his music. When he was three, his aunt, who sang at rodeos, taught him to play guitar. When he was seven, his father, a sheepherder, taught him saxophone, beating him when he played wrong notes. Young says he didn't hear any classical music until sometime in high school, after his family had moved permanently to Los Angeles. As he recalls, his "first big taste of modern music" was the Bartók *Concerto for Orchestra*, heard on a class trip to the Los Angeles Philharmonic.

In high school, Young practiced a series of long-tone exercises on saxophone that he eventually came to regard as the beginning of his interest in sound vibrations "on a higher level." He identifies the summer of 1957, when he was in his early twenties, as a turning point, saying he spent the entire summer on a bed in his grandmother's house in L.A., meditating and listening to sounds. Young describes this time as the only point in his life where he ever questioned his direction in music. Later, he said his work with long tones was what led him to work with tunings, since a sustained tone allows the harmonics to be heard, which quickly leads to the area of just intonation.

In 1953, Young began classes at L.A. City College, beating out Eric Dolphy for a chair in the dance band. During the mid-fifties, jazz and experimental music coexisted in his mind, but by the time of his arrival at Berkeley, in 1958, to begin a graduate degree, he had devoted himself to composition. At Berkeley, Young studied with Seymour Shifrin, in a class that included both Pauline Oliveros and Terry Riley. His most important work from this period is his *Trio for Strings*, an hour-long, serial piece from 1958 that is built entirely of long tones and silences. It is probably this work, more than any other, that solidifies Young's reputation as the "Father of Minimalism."

In 1959, Young attended the summer course in new music at Darmstadt, Germany. He went to study with Stockhausen, but came away highly influenced by the music and philosophy of John Cage and the piano recitals given by David Tudor. That next year, showing the influences of both Cage and Japanese haiku, Young wrote his radically different *Compositions 1960*, a group of poetry-like prose in-

La Monte Young's UCLA ID card, Spring 1957, taken about the time he was writing *for Brass*. Copyright © La Monte Young 1990

structions, one of which directs the performer to "Draw a straight line and follow it." Also in 1960, Young moved to New York to study electronic music with Richard Maxfield, and by the end of the year, had organized what may have been the first loft concert series in New York at Yoko Ono's loft on Chambers Street.

Marian Zazeela grew up in a completely different world. Born in New York, she majored in art at the High School of Music and Art, before going to Bennington College in Vermont to major in painting, studying with Paul Feeley, Eugene Goossens, and Tony Smith, among others. Her first New York exhibition, a two-artist show at the 92nd Street YM-YWHA in 1960, was awarded to her by the art department of the college. Her large canvases of this period, with names like *Blue Train* and *Woodcut 1960*, are composed of freely drawn calligraphic strokes suspended in static, contrasting color fields, and show the influence of two trips to Tangiers. Zazeela now says she thinks of these works as seeds, leading directly to her two major lightworks: *Ornamental Lightyears Tracery*, an ongoing series of short-term performances throughout the seventies, and *The Magenta Lights*, the environment designed specifically for performances of Young's *The Well-Tuned Piano*.

In New York after college, Zazeela first moved among a circle of writers, once designing a stage set for Amiri Baraka (then known as LeRoi Jones). During the early sixties, she was also a super-model for Jack Smith, appearing not only as the primary subject for his legendary book of nude photographs, *The Beautiful Book*, but also in the featured still cameo of his banned movie, *Flaming Creatures* (along with Young, who, because of her, had a minor role). She would have been the star of the movie—the part was written for her—but she had recently met Young and found his world suddenly consuming all of hers.

At first, Zazeela's work with Young consisted of performing drone parts as a member of his group, The Theatre of Eternal Music, which at one time included John Cale, Tony Conrad, and Angus MacLise. But in 1964, she also began creating a visual presentation as well, first with light boxes glowing with calligraphic patterns, later, with photographs of these patterns projected onto the performers. By 1965, her calligraphic light projections were incorporating, as she says, the element of time into the work. And by 1968, these lightworks had become environments, creating what she called "three-dimensional colored shadows." Since the 1960s, Zazeela and Young have moved slowly away from the idea of concert-hall performances, creating, instead, these environments in which Young's five- and six-hour pieces gradually unfold, bathed in lights Zazeela once described as the "soft reflected light of dusk, suspended in time."

Although Young and Zazeela have worked together on a number of projects, their two most significant, continuing collaborations are *The Well-Tuned Piano* and *Dream House*. *The Well-Tuned Piano*, currently approaching seven hours in length, is a work for justly tuned piano, begun by Young in 1964, in which events unfold at a glacial pace, with chords and intervals of the microtonal scale appearing slowly, in a prescribed order, over a span of hours. It is also a piece in which new material is developed each time it is played, which is why it gets longer with each performance. Beginning with the 1974 premiere in Rome, Zazeela's lightwork *The Magenta Lights* has always been the environment in which Young performs *The Well-Tuned Piano*. He says he will never perform it any other way.

Dream House, on the other hand, is a much longer sound and light environment designed to exist over a period of weeks, months, or even

Portrait of Marian Zazeela. Photographed at The Living Theatre, New York City, Winter 1960–61. Photo Credit: Charles Rotmil. Copyright © Marian Zazeela 1990

years. Originally begun as a harmonically complex set of drones in their loft in the early sixties, *Dream House* evolved, first, into a series of short-term performance/installations in which Young's *Map of 49's Dream The Two Systems of Eleven Sets of Galactic Intervals Ornamental Lightyears Tracery* was performed, then, into a permanent installation on Harrison Street in New York, supported by the Dia Art Foundation. Unfortunately, after running for six years, economic problems within the foundation forced its closing in 1985.

In 1990, Zazeela's exhibition of lightworks at the Donguy Gallery in Paris was purchased by the French cultural ministry for permanent installation in France. That same year, Young formed The Forever Bad Blues Band, consisting of microtonal keyboard, guitar, and bass guitar, plus drums. Two years later, the band toured Europe, performing a two-hour version of Young's *Dorian Blues* in just intonation, in a light and shadow environment created by Zazeela.

I met La Monte and Marian in the late afternoon at their loft on Church Street. I think it was the morning for them. The loft is a large, open space, but crowded with plants, light sculptures, tamburas, electronic equipment, and the archives of their work. It probably looks a lot like it did in the sixties, although neater now, because of the proper storage needed for all the accumulated stuff. They sat behind a large two-person desk, constantly checking dates and facts as they spoke. And we both taped each other as we talked; La Monte and Marian like to keep a record of everything. But there was plenty of tape, and lots of time, so I decided to start at the beginning.

DUCKWORTH: Everybody always makes a big point out of the fact that you were born in a log cabin. But to me, it seems that being born a Mormon is more significant.

YOUNG: Well, you're right. It did have a vague influence on my overall outlook on life and some of the philosophies involved in my work. But the log cabin was significant, too. There were 149 people in the town when I was born. And there was this sense of space and time; being able to sit out there on the porch and look out across that incredible distance and see the clouds and the hills way far off there. And being born in the country, in the simplicity of a log cabin . . . we had no water inside . . . coal stove. And the winters in that part of Idaho are just notorious. My father told me that once they had a blizzard on the Fourth of July. I told this to my mother's father, Grandpa Grandy, and he said, "Oh hell, that's nothing. I remember one year when it snowed every month of the year!" He said, "The reason I left Bear Lake County is I got tired of wading through snow up to my armpits. Then you come home and take your pants off and they just stand there." So the log cabin had a very special effect on the most important years of my life—this very simple, spacious, open-ended-in-time type of setting. But being born a Mormon was also extremely significant because they have this concept of Eternal Life, and there's no doubt but what that had something to do with my interest in the concept of extended time structures.

DUCKWORTH: You know, I think of you as a highly disciplined composer, and I thought maybe that came from the Mormon background, too.

ZAZEELA: That he got from his father. His father was a real disciplinarian.

DUCKWORTH: Did he really beat you when you played wrong notes?

YOUNG: Oh, yes. Yes. He would really knock me around.

DUCKWORTH: How old were you?

YOUNG: I started saxophone lessons with him when I was about seven.

ZAZEELA: What about the story of the fence posts? That really shows your father's discipline and influence on you.

YOUNG: A very good story. I was born in Idaho. Then, just before the first grade, we went to Los Angeles for about four years. Then we went to Utah where we lived another four years. And while we lived on the shore of Utah Lake, my father managed my Uncle Thornton's celery farm. And down on the border of the lake in the middle of winter one day, Dad had to put up a fence. I remember the great pains he took to run these poles straight. We were just freezing! Literally! The wind was coming off of that lake, you know. It was impossible. I couldn't imagine what we were doing out there, as I look back on it. But he taught me the importance of, if you're going to do a job at all you should do it right. He would line up every pole, and dig the holes carefully, and string the wire perfectly, all in weather that was just unbearably cold. It was terrible. You couldn't stand it. He was a real perfectionist, my father. And a disciplinarian. And I think I assimilated that very early in that underlying desire that every child has to please the parents. Also, you have to understand that my father is Swiss. My grandmother on his side was full Swiss, he's half-Swiss, and I'm one-quarter Swiss, so there is that inherited approach to meticulous, fine-craftsmanship type of work.

DUCKWORTH: What types of work did your father do?

YOUNG: When I was born, my father was a sheepherder. He often had to leave my mom and me at the cabin, and go live in a tepee up in the Bern foothills. Later, he got a job working for my mother's father, Grandpa Grandy, in Montpelier. Grandpa Grandy managed the Conoco plant, and my father was in charge of distributing gas to all the service stations in the area. Then around 1939 or so, my dad hitchhiked to L.A. to get work.

DUCKWORTH: You know, one thing that seems like a contradiction to me is that on the one hand you're talking about this very austere early childhood, and on the other, you're studying saxophone. It's difficult for me to put those two together in my mind. What was the general musical climate of the family like?

YOUNG: They started me singing cowboy songs when I was very young. My Aunt Norma used to sing at rodeos and in school—operettas and so on—and she taught me to play the guitar. I learned "A-ridin' old Paint, and a-leadin' old Dan." My dad taught me "The Red River Valley."

DUCKWORTH: Were you a good guitar player?

YOUNG: I can't say I was good, because it was really a challenge for me at that age. In fact, it was terribly frustrating for me that I couldn't excel at it. I was very serious about trying to learn. But to be able to play and sing at the age of three . . . I don't recall that I was satisfied with it. I know they had me on stage tap dancing and singing when I was four and a half or five in a little theater in town there.

DUCKWORTH: Why did they do that?

YOUNG: I don't know. Mormons like to start the kids young . . . giving speeches in church.

ZAZEELA: The Mormons have a very insular community. They try to do everything within it. In a small, isolated community like that all the extracurricular activities were at the church. And from a very early age they have to get up in church and bear testimony, where they tell everybody in the congregation about their faith.

YOUNG: And in addition to bearing your testimony, you're taught to get up and give little speeches (they're small at the beginning), or to play saxophone solos in church, or to sing in the church choir and all of this kind of stuff.

DUCKWORTH: Did you ever reach a point where you consciously rebelled against it?

YOUNG: Well, yes, when I was in high school. I began to feel that the church's approach was alright but limiting. I met poets, philosophers, and musicians in high school who began introducing me to other ways of thinking. My most immediate problem with the church was that they felt that they were the only true church. And this became my problem with organized religion in general. Whereas I felt that Joseph Smith, for instance, really did have his visions, and really did see the Angel, and that it was all absolutely true—and to this day I have no reason to doubt it—I also feel that all the other visionaries in the world who had their visions also really had them, and that their churches are also true. My feeling is that the Divinity has so many aspects that no one person can conceivably comprehend all of them: that over time, various prophets have been able to see certain aspects of the Divinity very brilliantly. This has been such a powerful manifestation, and such an extraordinary experience for the prophet, that, in the course of conveying it to his followers, it's been extraordinarily convincing. They have right away felt the truth and the power of this strand of information. Sooner or later, however, the followers have decided that this is the *only* truth. This is what Pandit Pran Nath means when someone says to him, "So, you sing religious music," and he'll say, "No. Religions are the beginnings of many of the world's problems. This is *spiritual* music."

DUCKWORTH: How did all this affect your early music?

YOUNG: When I was young and first developing my long tones in 1956, '57, '58, I spent an entire summer—I think around '57—mainly staying in a bedroom in my grandmother's house. I would just lie flat on my back, go off into a meditational state, and think about the meaning of my life—why was I here, and what was I trying to do. Out of that gradually came these long sustained tones.

DUCKWORTH: Were the long tones a philosophical or an instinctive development?

YOUNG: I felt very inspired about them. I felt I was supposed to be doing them. And I had a philosophical attitude about them which was that . . . I felt that rhythm. You know how frequency is rhythm? Well, I felt that my interest in pitch was an interest in vibration on a higher level. Most people, you know, are very involved with rhythmic elements in their music. But I was just interested in these long sustained tones and the pitch relationships between them. I felt that the rhythms, as we find them in normal music, tended to lead one back to a more earthy and earthly kind of existence and behavior, whereas the long sustained tones tended to lead me—and I felt it would other people—toward a more spiritual path. They were a higher form of vibration.

DUCKWORTH: Is it true that hearing the wind blowing through the logs of the cabin was really one of the first sounds you remember?

YOUNG: Yes, I remember that. I lived in the cabin about the first three years of my life, so it's probably the second winter that I was remembering. Not only do I remember the wind, I vividly remember the bottle that they gave me milk out of. It was a brown bottle like a beer bottle. And I remember the grasshoppers. The *1960 Composition* is based on an experience I had when I still lived in the cabin. I walked from my house over to, I guess, Aunt Emma's house, and all these grasshoppers were all over the place. I have vivid memories.

ZAZEELA: I think the thing that is really extraordinary is to look at La Monte's family background. His parents were only sixteen and seventeen when they married, and he was born within the first year. They were just kids. The Mormon Church, at the present time, does a tremendous amount of education of their flock, but at that time, it wasn't very much. His parents had a miniscule amount of education about how to bring up children. They just sort of did it as, I guess, people do, but without much thought. They themselves just had high-school educations, and were totally unsophisticated. And still are to this day. They're very sweet . . . .

YOUNG: They're basically hillbillies . . . .

ZAZEELA: I love them very much, but they really are. They have very little intellectual curiosity beyond the church. And it's just impossible to have imagined that La Monte's kind of spectacularly unique and individual vision could have come out of that circumstance.

YOUNG: Because all my brothers and sisters are quite normal people.

DUCKWORTH: Are they musical people?

YOUNG: None of them went into the arts professionally or seriously.

DUCKWORTH: Do any of them play or sing for self-entertainment?

YOUNG: A little bit.

ZAZEELA: La Monte tried to get his brother to play trumpet.

YOUNG: I really wanted to have another Charlie Parker/Dizzy Gillespie combination in the family. I was playing saxophone and I wanted my brother to play trumpet, but he didn't follow through. It wasn't his interest.

ZAZEELA: One sister, Tyra, did a lot of dancing . . . .

YOUNG: And LaJuana did dancing, too.

ZAZEELA: Right. But in a certain way, the girls—there were four sisters and one brother—the girls were sheltered and very much discouraged from attempting to have individual careers or lives.

YOUNG: Well, you know, the thing in the Mormon way of life is you're supposed to raise a family. Until this day, my parents still ask us if we're not going to have children. Well, now it's too late, but it's the main goal in a Mormon family; there's no goal in front of that. But I really felt that my work was my children. It's been all I can do to present my work—to keep it going, and to try to earn a living from it. And having had a tough, impoverished childhood, I just felt that I could not be a good father. Just think, you know, suddenly you're going on tour. What are you going to do with the kids then? Particularly since we work together.

DUCKWORTH: When did you decide you were different from the other children in the family?

YOUNG: I didn't realize that I was different, probably, until high school at the earliest, because there was a lot of misunderstanding of me as a child. I was a strong achiever in music and also in visual art. When I was a kid it was very uncertain which way I would go. I used to love to draw and paint in grade school. It wasn't until we got to Utah, where all we did was work on the farm, and the only aspect of an art existence was to be able to play a saxophone solo in church, that the drawing and the painting dropped away. By the time I got back to civilization in Los Angeles in high school, I was heavily into music, and I became a music major at John Marshall High School.

DUCKWORTH: I'm still confused about where the saxophone came from. Was there a tradition of saxophone playing in your family?

YOUNG: My Uncle Thornton, whose farm my dad was managing, had been my father's saxophone teacher. He had had a swing band in L.A. in earlier days. He gave me a lot of his dance-band scores and other solos, and he gave me coaching on saxophone. So in addition to my dad's lessons, I got coaching from my Uncle Thornton.

DUCKWORTH: That seems like such a contradiction though. How can a Mormon have a swing band?

YOUNG: Well, you know, the Youngs are very . . . what would you say . . .

ZAZEELA: A little wild.

YOUNG: They're wild! Grandpa Young, my dad's father, was a terror. He rode very bad horses; he would break them for a living.

ZAZEELA: He was known to do a lot of things that Mormons are not supposed to do. La Monte's grandmother divorced him, actually. She was a very strict Mormon . . .

YOUNG: . . . because she was the Swiss side . . .

DUCKWORTH: You must have been really misunderstood.

YOUNG: Oh, totally.

DUCKWORTH: When did you first discover that you had an extremely exceptional ear?

YOUNG: Different manifestations of it were coming along. I guess other people thought I had an exceptional ear long before I did. Some people thought I had a good ear by high school, because I was already beginning to improvise jazz. But I didn't begin to think so until . . . depending on what that means. What do you think it means, to have a good ear?

DUCKWORTH: I think, in general, it means fine pitch discrimination.

YOUNG: Well, I think I most clearly became aware of the idea that I had fine pitch discrimination when I was working with my group,

The Theatre of Eternal Music, around 1963, '64, '65, and '66. I was long into music before I thought that I had an exceptionally special ear for fine pitch relationships.

DUCKWORTH: What's another definition of a fine ear? Were you thinking of something else?

YOUNG: Well, no, I wasn't; that's what I think of, too. But I had a very good ear for improvisation. I was well aware of that by sometime in the mid-fifties. And I was always trying to develop my ear. My approach was that my ear wasn't good enough—that I had to develop it—so I was always working on trying to improve my ability to hear.

DUCKWORTH: What kind of work did you do to improve?

YOUNG: Well, anytime I heard music I would analyze it as I listened. Of course, I couldn't analyze everything I heard, nobody can, but I would analyze as much as I could. I always listen analytically now. There's never a time I'm listening without trying to formulate as much as I can about what I'm hearing—to analyze exactly what intervals I'm hearing.

DUCKWORTH: Does that increase the enjoyment of it?

YOUNG: For me it does. I don't disassociate the enjoyment from the analysis. There are, of course, a lot of times when you're hearing much more than you can analyze. But I tend to always be trying to analyze some part of it. I think that's how I began to develop my ear. As I recall my first experiences in taking dictation, I thought I wasn't so good.

DUCKWORTH: Did you make mistakes?

YOUNG: Yes, I made some mistakes in high school, and then even later, a little bit, at L.A. City College. So I really took seriously that I had to improve, and I just started very strongly, consciously, thinking analytically all the time about everything I was hearing. And when I played jazz, I was always thinking about solos and analyzing those in my head. Gradually, my hearing improved. But I think the really strong area of my hearing is an area which is not even measured in school, which is this fine sense of pitch perception.

DUCKWORTH: It's difficult for me to understand how someone with your sense of hearing could make a pitch mistake.

YOUNG: It was possible back at the beginning. You have to remember that I came out of a very unsophisticated background and that, while I had played the saxophone, that was the extent of my musical training. I had never had any other kind of musical training at all. And I found that other kids had been going to conservatories and so forth, and they had all kinds of backgrounds that put them in a better position. Also, I didn't hear classical music until some time in high school. I had never heard it.

DUCKWORTH: Was the John Marshall High School in Los Angeles a real revelation for you as far as music was concerned?

YOUNG: Yes, absolutely. It was a high school that had a tradition of jazz, and it particularly had a tradition of jazz saxophone players, so that as soon as I got there, kids were saying, "Hey, have you heard this new Charlie Parker record?" and "Listen to this Miles Davis record!" and "Oh, what about Lester Young?" and "Here's a new Stan Getz album." I was just literally eating this stuff up.

DUCKWORTH: Did you consider yourself a musician by that point? Did you know that's what you were going to be?

YOUNG: Oh yes. I had already decided I was either going to be a musician or a visual artist in grade school. I knew that that's what I was going to do. That's all I cared about and that's what I really wanted to do.

DUCKWORTH: Let me ask you one more question about your childhood. When did you first become interested in constant-frequency sounds? I'm thinking about telephone poles, motors, and insects.

YOUNG: I was very interested in listening to them as a child. The telephone poles date back to around the age of three and four, because the Conoco plant where my dad worked in Montpelier was right next to a power station. Not a generating station, but probably a step-down station for the town of Montpelier. Also in that same period, maybe slightly predating it, I remember standing by a single telephone pole and listening to it humming. The same with the crickets. I remember going out at night with my dad to do the chores and listening to the crickets outside. Then later, I worked in a machine shop after school in high school, and there I used to operate a lathe. I would whistle and sing tones over this lathe. I didn't realize that I was singing over drones then, but I was.

DUCKWORTH: Were those natural drones musical in your mind, or were they just interesting?

YOUNG: Well, as a child, I don't think I thought of the power plants and the crickets as music. Later, when I was older—by the sixties, let's say—I made tapes of Marian and me singing with crickets, and by then I was very much thinking about them as drone-based music. The lathes, I guess, I would just sort of find the key of it, and sing in that key. I'm not sure at what point I crystalized on the idea of sustained tones as music. It's definitely true that I heard this Ali Akbar Khan recording that had a tambura on it in 1957. I heard it on the radio, and I literally jumped in my car and ran down to this place called Music City to buy it. I was so fascinated by it. My grand-mother got upset when I would listen to it; she called it "opium music." She was very concerned about what it was doing to me. And I was hearing the *gagaku* orchestra at the same time. It's very possible that hearing Eastern music with drones helped me crystal-lize these childhood experiences into a new musical language.

DUCKWORTH: How early did your interest in other cultures begin?

YOUNG: I was definitely reading haiku before the 1960 compositions, which are very much like haiku, in and of themselves. I bought my first Ali Akbar Khan record probably in 1957. And I was attending UCLA in '57 where I was listening to the *gagaku* orchestra—we had a student *gagaku* orchestra there, and we may have had a gamelan orchestra, too. I was an ethnomusicology minor, so that half the time I was listening to music from other parts of the world.

DUCKWORTH: What attracted you to the Los Angeles City College?

YOUNG: Well, at John Marshall, people literally set me up to make the City College dance band. Everybody talked about it. I absolutely lived for being able to make the L.A. City College dance band my first semester out of high school. And I did. And I had to beat Eric Dolphy out of a chair to do it. Actually, I'm surprised I beat him out, because he was definitely a more experienced, older player than I was. But I played extremely well at that point, and I got the chair.

DUCKWORTH: Were you one of those people who practiced eight hours a day?

YOUNG: Not eight, but I did practice quite a lot. Oh, I could practice eight, but I was extremely poor. To buy my first saxophone, I had to work after school, so there wasn't that much time to practice. But I did practice; I loved to practice.

DUCKWORTH: Was it all jazz, or were you studying classical music by
that time?

YOUNG: Well, I played in the orchestra and the band. And around the
tenth or eleventh grade, I began to study saxophone and clarinet
with William Green at the L.A. Conservatory. You could say my classical studies of the instrument began then.

DUCKWORTH: You also had your own jazz group, didn't you?

YOUNG: Yes I did. I had that group around 1955 and '56, and maybe in
'54. It was a group in which I played alto saxophone, Billy Higgins
played drums, Hal Hollingshead played bass, and Dennis Budimer
and Tiger Echols played guitar. Buddy Mattlock also played guitar
with us sometimes. Dennis Budimer became a Hollywood studio gui-
tarist; he made an album with Ravi Shankar at one point.

DUCKWORTH: Didn't Don Cherry play in that group?

YOUNG: Oh, yes. Don Cherry played with us frequently.

DUCKWORTH: What was the style of music that your group played?

YOUNG: My style was a combination of Charlie Parker and Lee
Konitz, but with my own approach to it. The group was basically
playing some combination of cool jazz and bebop. It was a combination of Lennie Tristano, Lee Konitz, Warne Marsh, Miles Davis,
and Charlie Parker. It was an awareness of all of that. Don, at that
time, was playing just like Miles Davis.

DUCKWORTH: Where was the point when jazz and experimental
music coexisted in your mind?

YOUNG: I would say at L.A. City College. At John Marshall High
School, I really liked harmony; I always got As in harmony. My
teacher was Robert Sorensen, and he had apparently studied with
Schoenberg at UCLA. I remember in one class he played the
Schoenberg *Six Little Piano Pieces*, and I liked those. Then he got
the whole class tickets to go down to hear the L.A. Philharmonic
play the Bartók *Concerto for Orchestra*, and that just knocked me
out. That was, I think, my first big taste of modern music. I just
thought that was fantastic! I must have been about a junior or a
senior in high school at that point. But it wasn't until L.A. City
College that I started to really compose. Leonard Stein, who had
been Schoenberg's assistant, began exposing me to Debussy,

Stravinsky, Schoenberg, and Webern. And Webern really inspired me. But actually, Bartók inspired me before I discovered Webern. About a year before, in 1955, I wrote a quartet in the style of Bartók, *Variations for String Quartet*, which is one of the first compositions that I consider a composition. So I was very inspired by Bartók and then even more inspired by Webern as is evidenced in my *Five Small Pieces for String Quartet*. By the time I got to Berkeley, in September 1958, I had left jazz.

DUCKWORTH: Had you consciously decided to leave it?

YOUNG: Yes. I felt I really wanted to go into composition, because I felt that jazz was very circumscribed . . . the kind of swinging beat that had to be involved. My main criticism in my solos was that I didn't swing enough. That's because I was interested in these very unusual rhythmic approaches. The whole structure of jazz is very limiting, and I wanted to go beyond that. You have to remember that by '57 I became interested in long sustained tones, and there was no place for that in jazz. If I was having trouble selling my saxophone solos as jazz, there was no way to sell these long sustained tones. So in '56, when I was writing *Five Small Pieces for String Quartet*, that's where jazz and contemporary music coexisted.

DUCKWORTH: Didn't you start playing the saxophone again when you came to New York?

YOUNG: I came to New York in 1960. And Larry Rivers heard me play violin at a concert in a piece of Richard Maxfield's. I had invented my own way of playing violin and making these really raucous, individualized sounds. So Larry Rivers heard me playing this way. And somebody told me that he had a saxophone and that I should talk to him, because he might loan it to me. So I asked him about the possibility, and he said he'd like to hear me play. So I went to his loft and he played piano for me, and I played. He was very impressed, and said I could take the saxophone. In the same meeting, he said something that really, I think, was an inspiration. We were talking about money and how to earn it, and at the end he said, "And don't be afraid to go out and earn yourself a thousand dollars." And I think I really took it to heart that I had to get paid for doing my work, because from then on—I may have already started in that direction—I really tried very hard to get paid, and to get paid as well as possible, for doing my own serious work. So then I started to play jazz again. Tenor a little bit, and also some jazz piano during that period, too. So I was playing jazz a little bit after I came to New York in 1960, but by '61 I think I had bought the sopranino saxophone. And once I switched to sopranino I stopped playing jazz and began to play my own music, which at that point was partly inspired by Indian music. I was working on different modal scales, and gradually evolving into my own style.

DUCKWORTH: Before we leave California, I'd like to talk a little bit about your *Trio for Strings*. Do you agree with everybody else's opinion that that's *the* major work of yours from that period?

YOUNG: Yes. In fact, I, without doubt, think that that's my most important early work. In my opinion, it's the first work, to my knowledge, in the history of music that is completely made of long sustained tones. And it's the work where my vision, I think, is most clearly crystallized for the first time. *for Brass* is quite strongly in that direction as is *for Guitar*, but *Trio for Strings* is just totally pure and radically different.

ZAZEELA: Did you know it's a serial piece?

DUCKWORTH: No, I didn't. I assumed, though, that most of those early works were serial to some extent.

YOUNG: Here, too, it's showing the transition between my work in serial music and my own direction.

ZAZEELA: It's almost hard to hear the piece accurately outside of a performance, on a tape for instance, because there may be falterings of the bow. They're such long bow-strokes. It's possible that it's such an idealized piece that it almost can't be properly played. You have to listen to it with the sense of what it's meant to be, and ignore, sometimes, little imperfections.

YOUNG: I think, over time, as players get the concept and as it becomes a part of the literature, they'll develop the technique to play it. Right this minute, it's really hard for players. Even players who want to play it well have trouble getting those intervals to just stand there, because it's not what strings are made to do. I was very young and very idealistic and very innocent, and I didn't realize that this was just about impossible for a string player to play. But I'm sure when another ten years go by, and kids are coming up and starting in junior high school to worry about how to play the piece, that by the time they get on stage, they'll have figured out ways to make it much better.

DUCKWORTH: Do you remember how you got the initial idea for the *Trio*?

YOUNG: Yes, I'll tell you what was happening. Remember I said that there was one summer where I just spent a lot of very quiet time at my grandmother's lying flat on my back meditating, and other times sitting out on her porch listening to the sound of the train yards across the river? In those train yards, there would be signals coming and going—switching signals from the trains—and they would float across the valley.

ZAZEELA: Don't you also think some of them were the sounds of the metal on the tracks? That's what I thought I was hearing when I was there.

YOUNG: Well, they're definitely in *for Brass*; there's no doubt about that. And there are these pulses that show up in *for Brass* and in *Trio for Strings*. I wrote *for Brass* at the piano, but I wrote *Trio for Strings* at the organ. I knew I needed to work at an organ because I hadn't been able to know what the sustained tones in *for Brass* were exactly going to sound like from the piano. So I got permission to work on the big organ at UCLA.

DUCKWORTH: Did you work on the piece in real time?

YOUNG: Oh, yes. I sat there and held the intervals. That's why it's so precisely notated as to duration, and with those tempo markings. I was counting, and thinking, and feeling each one of those tempos. And remember, I was coming out of the Webern period of precise notation, and Stockhausen and Boulez were actively writing very special rhythmic things. So I was interested in the feeling of tempi going on, and what it would sound like to come in on the upbeat of a triplet, and then this long sustained thing, and whether it would end on the first, second, third, fourth, or fifth part of a quintuplet. All of that was very interesting to me. Since then, many people have proposed, "Why don't you just time it with a stopwatch?" I considered it, but I think you lose something that way. In *The Four Dreams of China* there's no notation at all as to the duration of notes. They're all, mainly, long sustained notes. But they're improvised, so that's a different kind of timelessness. In the *Trio for Strings* I was working with that sense of tempo and rhythm, and that's how I like it to be performed.

ZAZEELA: When he started writing it, it was even going to be longer.

YOUNG: Oh, yes. The original notation of the first three notes was much, much longer than what I ended up using. (See, this just shows how I do have a practical commercial bent to me. [*Laughs.*]) I started calculating how long the piece would really be, and it was very, very long. So the version that I ended up with—the foreshortened version—is only an hour long. Because at the age I was then, there's no way I could have commanded an hour's time on a program. So that was already a danger. But I considered it a major work and decided I would wait for my time, when it could be played.

DUCKWORTH: Did you realize how radical that work was when you were writing it?

YOUNG: Yes, I knew it was radical, but I was very inspired to do it. I thought it was really important.

DUCKWORTH: What inspired you?

YOUNG: First of all, there was a *feeling* involved in these long spaces of time that really meant a lot to me. There was some deep feeling that came out of it. Then, there was this idea that I mentioned earlier that these sustained tones dealt with frequency—rhythms on a much higher level—and that it led toward a more spiritual mode of existence or understanding, and that it led one to even understand vibration on a higher level.

DUCKWORTH: Am I correct in assuming that you trace your interest in expanded musical time back to childhood experiences?

YOUNG: Yes, I think so. Seems like I was always very dreamy. I liked to daydream. I was accused of it a lot in school. And I remember vividly these sound experiences of childhood—the wind, the telephone poles, and the crickets. I remember in junior high school the sounds over Utah Lake. These sounds somehow *meant* something to me, and later led toward the creation of this approach— toward extended time duration structures in sound.

DUCKWORTH: You know, one of the things that I think is most interesting about your work is what it does to the listener's sense of time. Do you think about that when you compose, or are you just writing sounds that you want to hear, in lengths of time that you want to hear them?

YOUNG: I very much want listeners to hear my music and I very much want to communicate with them, but I never write for a specific effect in a specific listener. I want the listener to find the level of the music that I'm writing. I think that it's important, in fact, not to write for an assumed level of listeners, because right away you begin to limit yourself to whatever level you think that is. So what I try to do when I create is to open myself up to this flow of information that can be transmitted *through* me—to allow myself to be a pure transmitter—and to try to manifest materially this information in as pure a form as possible as it comes to me, whether I'm performing and improvising as in *The Well-Tuned Piano*, or whether I'm composing in a more notational method.

DUCKWORTH: How long after the *Trio for Strings* was written did it take before you got a performance of it?

YOUNG: Not too long afterward. When I got to Berkeley, Seymour Shifrin, whose composition class I was in, was pretty concerned about whether I knew what it sounded like, so he arranged to have it played at his house. He had these little evenings of the graduate composition seminar. We would go there and listen to recordings and different things. So he arranged for a live performance by some very good players. We heard it, and there was a great deal of discussion afterwards. He pretty much told me that I couldn't write that way in his class, or he wouldn't be able to give me a grade. So I wrote *Study I* for piano to prove to him that I could write music that was understandable on more conventional terms. So I was unable to write the kind of music I wanted to in his class, but it was nonetheless an interesting class because I was very eager to understand traditional approaches to composition. After all, I had excelled at counterpoint, and I was interested to know about the Schenker long lines and ideas that were important to people like Sessions and others. Andrew Imbrie was also at Berkeley, and I had some analysis classes with him that I liked a lot.

DUCKWORTH: It's still a little surprising you got the *Trio for Strings* performed, though; it is an hour long. Shifrin must have taken you very seriously as a composer.

YOUNG: Oh, he took me very seriously, because I practically took over the class. You know, that class had me, Terry Riley, Pauline Oliveros, David Del Tredici, Doug Leedy, Loren Rush, Charles MacDermod, and Jules Langert in it. I occupied a lot of the time in the class, and I had a lot to say about other people's compositions as well as my own. I was able to really speak about my music, to describe the things that I was looking for in composition, and to talk about the feeling of the music and relate it to the technical analysis of the work. I think that it was quite surprising for Shifrin and the other students to find somebody who had that kind of ability.

DUCKWORTH: Have you always been certain about the direction of your work, or have there been periods of doubt?

YOUNG: No doubt! I've always been very strong and very convinced about what I'm doing. The only period of questioning in my life was when I was doing all the meditating in 1957 or '58. I wondered then if I should be doing music at all. And this had to do with several things. One thing was that I wasn't sure whether maybe I was more talented in writing words than music. Another thing I was wondering about had something to do with the truth of music. I was very moved by the feelings, and I was wondering if these feelings were true. And I think the other thing I was thinking about at that time was whether it was possible to write really serious music and survive, although that question became a much stronger question later. I think I was still innocent enough, probably, at that point to think that you could do serious work and that it would be understood and accepted. But I soon found out that that was totally wrong. I learned gradually, over the years, that in order to succeed, a great deal of it is PR. You could be the most talented, most creative individual in the world and totally disappear—never be known—unless you had some way to present your work to the public in a way that they could get a handle on it and realize that it was important.

DUCKWORTH: How should serious work be presented to the public?

YOUNG: Actually, it seems to me, people don't know what to think. You have to help. You have to make work available to them in such a way that you give them keys that unlock doors. Keys that lead them to other levels of the work, so that they start out on a level that is comprehensible to them—a level that invites them in. I think that *The Well-Tuned Piano* is my most successful work in every regard, but also in *this* regard, because it is a work that, without doubt, shows a wide range of my skill as a composer. In particular, it shows my ability to interweave thematic and motivic material over wide expanses of time. And it has information happening on many different levels—the thematic, the motivic, the rhythmic, the frequency, the tuning, the harmonics, the "clouds." And yet, it has material that serves as a key to unlock doors for audience members who come with different levels of evolution in terms of understanding music. So that it helps them without ever compromising in any way. In no way do I make tunes for the workers to whistle. I have no interest in it. I've never taken any interest in writing down to some particular audience level. But as a result of experience with audiences over the years, I have assimilated an approach which has manifested itself in *The Well-Tuned Piano*, which provides this invitational setting without in any way compromising the artistic integrity of the whole of the work. I didn't realize that's what I was doing as I was putting it together, but ultimately that's what I did.

DUCKWORTH: When did you first begin to realize the need for this kind of approach?

YOUNG: I was first writing these radical pieces back in the late fifties and the early sixties. Take *2 sounds*: it's really a very radical piece, and very noisy, and created riots when it was first performed, and I realized right away that I knew how to upset an audience. I could create a riot, or I could write a piece like the *Trio for Strings* that nobody had the foggiest idea what it was about. As time went on, I began to think, "Well, you did that and nothing happened. You didn't communicate enough with them to help them up to the next level so that they understood the piece." So I realized it wasn't sufficient to just be very creative, and have very pure ideas, and to create them, because they could end up just existing in a vacuum. And so in *The Tortoise, His Dreams and Journeys*, and particularly, then, in *Map of 49's Dream The Two Systems of Eleven Sets of Galactic Intervals Ornamental Lightyears Tracery*, I began to develop an approach that opened these doors for people to a work that had all of the profundity and the depth of many different levels of informational activity without compromising the artistic integrity of the work and yet, at the same time, making it potentially available to a wider audience. And that technique got more developed in *The Well-Tuned Piano*.

DUCKWORTH: Can we talk a little bit about when you went to Darmstadt in 1959? What made you decide to go?

YOUNG: Well, I was extremely interested in serial music at the time. Dennis Johnson and I were going to go together; we both were deep into analysis of Webern, Stockhausen, and Boulez. So we both applied and got student scholarships where we would get our room and board. We had to get ourselves there. But Dennis was very interested in astronomy. And on the trip from Los Angeles to New York he traveled with his head out the window studying the stars, and got pneumonia. So he had to stay in New York in Richard Maxfield's apartment, and I went on to Darmstadt alone. At the time, I thought Stockhausen was the greatest composer. When I heard *Gesang der Jünglinge*, I just thought it was the best new piece I'd heard. And I very much wanted to go there and be in his class.

DUCKWORTH: What was the biggest revelation you had there?

YOUNG: The biggest revelation was hearing David Tudor play those various scores that had been written for him, such as the Bussotti piano pieces. And the other thing was—not hearing Cage's music performed live, because the only Cage I heard was the recording of the *Concert for Piano and Orchestra* from the Town Hall Twenty-five-Year Retrospective Concert—but having access to more of his lectures. Stockhausen was talking about Cage all the time, and I realized what an influence he was having on Stockhausen. So, the thing that really influenced me was Cage and Tudor, although I enjoyed Stockhausen's class. But to this day people remember me standing up in Stockhausen's class and talking about my music.

DUCKWORTH: Did your opinion of Stockhausen change any after you had taken his class?

YOUNG: I still respected him and liked him. But something funny happened in the class. I wrote a piano piece that was all based around the number 7; it was a very abstract piece in that sense. In any case, there was supposed to be a student recital, and David Tudor was supposed to play it. But the piece got lost the day before the concert, and it wasn't found until the day after the concert. And I was always suspicious of foul play—that Stockhausen had somehow prevented it from being played because it was not short, and it had long silences in it, and long tones, as well as some very fast passages. And I just got a little paranoid that he didn't want to allot the time to it. But as you may or may not know, he's been one of my strongest supporters in Europe. Due to him, many people from Europe became aware of my music. He came to my studio here in the early sixties and took back tapes, which he played. Jon Hassell first learned of me through Stockhausen's class. And Kurt Schwertsik said that when I sent *Poem for Chairs, Tables, Benches, Etc.* to Stockhausen, he was real excited and told everybody about it.

DUCKWORTH: The reason I'm curious about Darmstadt is that it seems that immediately after you came back your work made a radical change in the direction of Cage, which I assume would be away from Stockhausen.

YOUNG: It would, except that Stockhausen was so influenced by Cage, and was so much talking about Cage, that it was more he supported that approach and, if anything, pushed me in that direction.

DUCKWORTH: Did your piece *Vision* come directly out of your Darmstadt experiences?

YOUNG: Yes, *Vision* was directly out of Darmstadt. It's absolutely, you could say, my assimilation of Darmstadt.

DUCKWORTH: It only has eleven sounds in it, though. How is that an assimilation of Darmstadt?

YOUNG: Well, that's "La Monte Young"; the whole approach to the time framework is "La Monte Young." Eleven sounds in thirteen minutes, and they each have their independent entry and exit, and they're laid out in a contrapuntal texture. It's very much the same type of time structure as the *Trio for Strings*. But the sound *sources*, the radical way to play stringed instruments, the various glissandi, and the idea of picking the sounds and the durations out of a hat and tying them together randomly—that's where Cage comes in, so that it's a combination of the two approaches at that point. *Poem for Chairs, Tables, Benches, Etc.* gets more in my direction because of the static nature of all of these more similar sounds.

DUCKWORTH: I've read, I believe, that you've acknowledged Cage's influence on your work to a tremendous degree. Is it Cage's influence that led to the *Compositions 1960*?

YOUNG: The *Compositions 1960* are after *Vision* and *Poem for Chairs, Tables, Benches, Etc.* and very definitely still show Cage's philosophical approach, although they're getting to be more "La Monte Young" again in that they're focusing on one thing very strongly. It's, I think, reaching back to haiku. The thing I was reading during that summer was the *Tao*, and that was what I was thinking about. I think that Lao-tzu had a strong influence on me at the time I was writing the *Trio for Strings*. I was reaching back to haiku with the *Compositions 1960*. You see, what differentiates my event pieces—those 1960 conceptual pieces—from others that were written, such as George Brecht's and Dick Higgins's, is that mine were crystallized down into this haiku-like essence—focusing on one event—whereas, if you look at the George Brecht *Motor Vehicle Sundown* event, that's got a lot of different things going on at once. That's more Cagean. It was after Brecht saw my word pieces that he also began to pare down his word pieces so that compositions that had more going on, or were taking a lot longer to describe, were getting reduced to events where you turned on a light, lit a match, or did something that was more singular in focus.

DUCKWORTH:　From today's perspective, which one of your event pieces from 1960 do you consider the most radical?

YOUNG:　I would probably speak in terms of two or three of them, and I would also probably speak of a development. See, I was interested in the conceptual aspect of this. And I thought that conceptually "This piece is whirlpools out in the middle of the ocean." was very strong. "Draw a straight line and follow it." was also strong. The line on a card was my answer to Cage's graphic notations. And the butterfly piece is very beautiful. *Piano Piece for David Tudor #3* (1960), "Most of them were very old grasshoppers.," is radical because it's just a poem, and you have to play that. I don't think anybody had done that before, whereas people such as Bussotti *had* made pictures to be performed. But then, in the following year I did the *Compositions 1961*, and I think that became the most radical because of the fact that on January 6th I wrote my entire output for the year. I wrote it in the form of a piece that I had written last year—each composition came on a certain date—and I composed many of them before they were actually dated. I performed many of them before they were dated, too. So conceptually I felt that that was pretty strong, and quite radical.

DUCKWORTH:　What strikes me about the *Compositions 1960* is how radically different they are from the pre–Darmstadt compositions. Were you going through any kind of aesthetic change, or did you see them as coming logically out of your previous work?

YOUNG:　I think there was some aesthetic change because of Cage's influence. Also, I was in a social situation at Berkeley that was very stifling and very academic. Those pieces should be seen in a social context. They're especially meaningful when performed in a traditional concert setting, more so than if they're performed in a gallery/happening-type setting, because they were composed specifically in response to what was happening to me at Berkeley. You

La Monte Young, Marian Zazeela, *Dream House,* "Map of 49's Dream The Two Systems of Eleven Sets of Galactic Intervals Ornamental Lightyears Tracery." The Theatre of Eternal Music: La Monte Young, voice and frequency generators; Marian Zazeela, voice. Light design: Marian Zazeela. Church Street Studio rehearsal, New York, 1970. Photo Credit: Robert Adler. Copyright © La Monte Young & Marian Zazeela

know: "You can't write this way"; or "You can't do this kind of concert in the auditorium." They wouldn't allow me to perform the butterfly piece in Hertz Hall so, as a result of that, I did the chamber opera version of *Poem.* And that was absolutely wild. I had somebody on stage frying eggs, and a girl in the aisle was sleeping in a sleeping bag, and a game of marbles was going on somewhere, and Phyllis Jones was playing Beethoven at the piano, and my *2 sounds* was being played electronically on speakers, and my entire music appreciation class and Gardner Rust's entire music appreciation class were walking through the audience reading from their music appreciation textbooks, and I was walking through the audience shouting "Green" into a bucket. And Bruce Connor, the artist, had a cricket in his shoe—you know, one of those that clicks—and he was walking through the audience and passing out literature.

DUCKWORTH: Do you think of that as a musical composition, or as theater with incidental music?

YOUNG: Well, I guess it was a type of opera, or a kind of musical theater. Remember, I became interested in theater, and named my group The Theatre of Eternal Music then. I'm very interested in a combining of media into a larger whole.

DUCKWORTH: One piece I'm curious about that you haven't mentioned is *Composition 1960 #2*, the one about building a fire in front of the audience. Was it in California where you bought the cheap violin and burned it?

YOUNG: No, the cheap violin was in New York City at the YMHA in a performance of Richard Maxfield's. Richard didn't know I was going to do it. Nobody knew. I played in a lot of Richard's music at that time, and prided myself on being a really creative performer. And I felt he'd gotten a kind of dull group together that time. So I had really been thinking about what I would do, and I decided that conceptually it would be interesting to perform my piece within his. I didn't have much money, so I bought a violin for about five or six dollars and filled it with matches. I also remember sitting in the reception room with a bunch of elderly ladies, pouring lighter fluid inside of it so that it would be sure to burn. On stage, we all had music stands. I just laid my violin down on the music stand, and as the other people started to play, I lit it. It made quite a flame.

DUCKWORTH: Hadn't you gone to New York the year before specifically to study electronic music with Maxfield?

YOUNG: I had passed through New York on my way to Darmstadt because the Berkeley music department librarian, Ken Wollitz, had introduced me to Maxfield's music just before I left. Ken told me to look him up, which I did. And it turned out Richard was doing electronic music, and I found that very interesting. After I got back to Berkeley I presented a concert of Richard's music at the San Francisco Medical Center and I also included his tapes on other programs I presented in Berkeley. Then Terry Riley and I both won Alfred Hertz Memorial Scholarships. The way the rumor goes, they gave me the traveling scholarship to get rid of me, and they gave Riley the stay-at-home, resident scholarship to separate us. In order to get it, I had to be going to study with somebody, so I listed that I wanted to study in New York with Cage and Maxfield. Cage was not here when I got to New York, so I studied electronic music with Maxfield.

DUCKWORTH: Did he have a significant impact on your thinking as a composer?

YOUNG: Richard's main impact on me was teaching me about tape manipulation—electronic music per se. I felt that he didn't particularly influence me as a composer. I certainly enjoyed talking with him, but we didn't necessarily agree a lot on philosophical approaches. He thought I was pretty crazy. On the other hand, I was a staunch supporter of his work and a main performer of it. I think he was really an important composer. His electronic music is very original.

DUCKWORTH: How did you get involved with Jackson MacLow, Dick Higgins, and all the people who went on to become Fluxus?

YOUNG: Well, I was very prominent as a performer when I hit New York. You know, I organized a loft concert series at Yoko Ono's loft.

ZAZEELA: At the time, she was married to Toshi Ichiyanagi, but separating from him.

YOUNG: And she came to my apartment on Bank Street and suggested that I organize a concert series at her loft.

DUCKWORTH: How long did the series run?

YOUNG: It ran from December of 1960, when I presented Terry Jennings, up to around June '61. It was a short series, but as far as I know, it was the first loft concert series in New York. It paved the way for all of these alternative places such as the Kitchen and Roulette.

DUCKWORTH: Are the people who're represented in your *Anthology* the people who performed on those concerts, for the most part?

YOUNG: Basically. The concert series included Terry Jennings, Simone Forti, Richard Maxfield, Jackson MacLow, Toshi Ichiyanagi, and Joseph Byrd. Yoko had a concert. Henry Flynt was one of the ones that I was strong about. And Robert Morris. He was the last event in my series.

DUCKWORTH: Did you consider yourself a part of the Fluxus movement, or had you moved away from it philosophically by the time it really began?

YOUNG: No, I withdrew from the Fluxus movement, if I ever was a part of it. I felt that I inspired it, but . . . You know, George Maciunas was very socialist and very communal, and I'm not a good group member. I am really an individual. What I was trying to do with my pieces was extremely conceptual and far out. What George and Fluxus tended toward was humor and gags. I mean, George was like the Marx Brothers reincarnated. He was hilarious. And he was a wonderful person who did a great deal for me. When I was starving, he would give me cans of food. But when he made a movement out of it, I just told him that I was withdrawing. I didn't want to be a part of the movement. Later, we made a deal. I used to love to do deals with George.

DUCKWORTH: Give me an example of one of your deals.

YOUNG: George hired me to conduct a concert at Carnegie Recital Hall. And the deal was, I wouldn't play unless I got paid, I wouldn't conduct unless I got paid, and I wouldn't have a piece on the program unless I got paid. So the composition that I wrote for that occasion was *Composition 1965 $50*. The way that was performed was that George would come in from the curtains on one side of the stage, and I would come in from the other side. We would walk to the center of the stage, and he would hand me the envelope with fifty dollars in it. Then we would shake hands and go off, and that was that. Then for conducting, George had found a lot of carpets somewhere on the street, and I needed carpets for this loft. So he traded me several carpets. Did we get anything else in that deal?

ZAZEELA: I don't remember. I think it was mostly carpets. We considered it a carpet deal.

YOUNG: Which deal did I get the typewriter from that I typed *An Anthology* on?

ZAZEELA: That was later.

YOUNG: That was on the refrigerator deal . . . different deal.

ZAZEELA: Can I just interject? You didn't speak about *Composition 1960 #7*, but I think that that . . .

YOUNG: Well, musically, that's a very strong piece. Certainly, when it comes to minimal pieces, there're two pieces from 1960 that stand out as being extraordinarily minimal. One is *1960 #7*, the B and F♯ to be sustained for a long time. The other one is *arabic numeral*

(any integer). any integer is a work which consists of some number of forearm clusters on a piano keyboard or strokes on a gong.
The integer represents the number of strokes. You determine in
advance the number of strokes you're going to do, and then you
do them. These two pieces are extremely minimal, and *any integer*
has the element of repetition that is associated with what I refer to
as mainstream or hard-core minimalism.

DUCKWORTH: Are you pleased with being considered the "Father of
Minimalism"?

YOUNG: I think it's true. I think it would have never started without
me. Terry Riley was the person who began the kind of repetitive
phase-shifting music that is known as minimalism, and there's no
question in my mind or Terry's but that I was a primary influence
on him. And although not all of my music shows that aspect, if you
heard some of my sopranino saxophone playing or the early *Well-
Tuned Piano* from 1964, you can hear a great deal of repetitive
activity—very rhythmic, with a very limited set of tones. I think that
both directly through those kinds of works, and indirectly through
the long sustained tones of the earlier works, that Terry was influenced by my music to the point where he produced these minimal
pieces such as *In C*. And he influenced Steve Reich, who played in
In C, and who came to Terry afterwards and said he wanted to
write like that. Actually, Terry discouraged him. He said, "No, you
should find your own way." But Steve really wanted to write that
way, and he did. And although it's different from Terry, it's clearly
out of Terry. Then, according to Steve, Phil and Steve had a group
together, and Phil began to play the way he does after he was in
that group with Steve.

DUCKWORTH: Everybody seems to have different stories about what
happened.

YOUNG: Well, Phil claims to come out of a vacuum. Nobody ever
existed before Phil Glass according to his book. At least that's what
I understand.

DUCKWORTH: What's your interpretation of all this?

YOUNG: Well, the story I tell is that there's only one concert that I
know of where all four of us appeared together. This was a concert
that was put on by a group at Yale called Pulsa. They were doing a
lot of work with light and . . .

ZAZEELA: A lot of art and technology stuff . . .

YOUNG: This concert was in 19 . . .

ZAZEELA: . . . I think '67 or '68 . . .

YOUNG: . . . and it was all tapes. I played a tape of *Map of 49's Dream*—very sophisticated La Monte Young. Terry Riley probably played some of that two-tape-recorder stuff that he was doing with a saxophone—very clearly Terry Riley. And Steve Reich was sounding like Steve Reich. But Phil Glass played a piece that just sounded like a single line. It was either a violin or a saxophone . . .

ZAZEELA: It was a violin.

YOUNG: . . . and it just went on. It was incredibly dull. There was none of what you would call minimalism going on at all. Now OK, maybe it wasn't a representative work. I don't know. All I know is that's what he played. Later on, I heard him . . .

ZAZEELA: It must have been in the early seventies.

YOUNG: . . . and there he was; he had the new sound. I don't know what happened, but that was my experience. Now, maybe it wasn't a characteristic piece. Maybe he had other pieces hidden away in 1968 that were just full of this minimal stuff. I don't know.

DUCKWORTH: How did you go from those conceptual pieces of 1960 and '61 to The Theatre of Eternal Music?

YOUNG: When I started playing sopranino saxophone, I started putting a group together. Angus MacLise was playing hand drums, and Simone Forti was singing drone in the group. Then after I met Marian, she sang drone. (I met Marian on June 22nd, 1962. Or rather we got together then. I had seen her once or twice before.) The next person that joined the group was Billy Linich (now Billy Name). Later, Tony Conrad joined, and then John Cale. Meanwhile, Terry Jennings would float in and out of the group as he would come to New York. And Dennis Johnson, who I had also known from California, occasionally came to New York and would perform with the group.

DUCKWORTH: Some of your pieces have such wonderful titles. I'm thinking about *The Second Dream of the High-Tension Line Stepdown Transformer*. Where did that title come from? Do your titles just appear to you, or do you give them a lot of thought?

YOUNG: Some of them just appear, but some of them get some work. In *The Well-Tuned Piano*, a lot of the titles just came. But the title for *The Second Dream* may have come a little after the first performance. At the first performance I just probably said it was one of the dreams from *The Four Dreams of China*. Later, I was talking with Tony Conrad, and he made me aware that what is up there on a telephone pole is a high-tension line step-down transformer. So then I decided, "Oh, this could be *The Second Dream of the High-Tension Line Stepdown Transformer*." But that sound that it makes . . . I don't know if you've heard the piece or if you know what pitches it has?

DUCKWORTH: Is that the one that uses C, F, F♯, G?

YOUNG: That's it. And those pitches are something like what you can hear in an electrical hum. You can find the 17th harmonic up there and put it in the range of 12, 16, 17, 18.

DUCKWORTH: That comment brings up an interesting question. We've been talking for a couple of hours and we haven't mentioned microtones once. When did you become aware that you were really interested in microtones?

YOUNG: My inspiration to begin working with microtones came through my interest in harmonics—overtones. I probably became interested in overtones through listening to long sustained tones, because there you have a situation where you can begin to concentrate on them and isolate them. I also became aware of the fact that Indian musicians listened to harmonics in the tambura when they were performing. Then, after I began to work with Tony Conrad, he pointed out to me that with the integers you can define all of the harmonics and all of the intervals in o tonalities of just intonation. Then I just took off and ran wild through the integers, composing in just intonation.

DUCKWORTH: Up until that point, had the music that you had been performing sounded in tune to you?

YOUNG: The interesting thing about the *Trio for Strings*, for instance, is that it excludes all thirds and sixths, which are the most out-of-tune notes in equal temperament. I was excluding them because I felt that they did not express the deep feelings that I had when I heard music that I liked—that I was writing, let's say, or wanted to write, or was seeking to write. When I would hear a major third in music, it seemed to take away from the mood and feeling that was very deep and important to me. I didn't realize at that time that it also happened to be one of the intervals that was the most out-of-tune in equal temperament. The fifths and fourths in equal temperament are very close to being perfectly in tune. Similarly, the major seconds. And the minor seconds, if you compare them to an 18/17ths-type interval or to 17/16ths, are also very close. So we're talking about intervals here that are only around two and four cents off, which is not bad. Not perfect, but not bad at all. I don't know to what degree I thought other music was out of tune before I really completely became interested in just intonation and aware of the possibility of analyzing it with the integers, but I do know that from the very beginnings in the *Trio for Strings*, and even to some degree in *for Brass* (but not as strictly), I began to exclude thirds and sixths. And that has been a characteristic of my music until this time. The kinds of thirds and sixths that appear in *The Well-Tuned Piano* are not 5/4ths, but 9/7ths and 14/9ths. What I established when I worked on *The Two Systems of Eleven Categories* is that I was interested in excluding those intervals which were factorable by five or its multiples, because that's how we generate the major third as we know it in Western music and much Eastern music, too. The major third is represented by the interval 5/4th, and its inversion the sixth by the interval 8/5ths. Also, the 6/5ths kind of minor third is different from the one that I used in *The Well-Tuned Piano*, which is a 7/6ths minor third, and the inversion of it (12/7ths). I think my awareness of music in equal temperament being out of tune really came after I began to work directly with intervals in just intonation.

DUCKWORTH: Did that awareness come all at once?

YOUNG: Seems like it. I had been interested in harmonics from my long sustained tones since, for instance, the performance of *Composition 1960 #7*.

DUCKWORTH: Is *The Tortoise, His Dreams and Journeys* your next important piece after the *Trio for Strings*?

YOUNG: Yes. I think that's the next really big work. But *The Well-Tuned Piano* was also started in 1964.

DUCKWORTH: What was a typical performance of *The Tortoise* like? I'm interested both in the length of time involved, and in how the musical elements went together.

YOUNG: It was the group with Marian, me, Tony Conrad, and John Cale. There were certain harmonic rules and restrictions. I was very interested in only presenting intervals that were multiples of seven, three, two, and one. We were excluding five and its multiples. And I was laying down that harmonic palette.

DUCKWORTH: Were you doing that with the sopranino saxophone?

YOUNG: On the very first tape recording we have, which I later called *Pre-Tortoise Dream Music*, I was playing sopranino saxophone. Later, I switched to voice, and everything after that I'm singing on.

DUCKWORTH: Did everybody then improvise around what you were playing or singing?

YOUNG: We would improvise around that preselected harmonic palette with sustained long tones. It was mainly holding long tones. There was very little melodic activity, although there was some melodic activity in the violin going between the tonic and the seventh partial, and the dominant and the seventh partial. That grew out of my saxophone playing, which you can hear as a kind of a fanfare at the opening of the *Pre-Tortoise Dream Music* on that tape, which in turn grew out of my saxophone playing on a tape called *Early Tuesday Morning Blues*. I developed a style of playing blues in which we would sustain the blues changes in the background for long periods of time on each change. Instead of having a certain number of beats to a bar, we would sustain the I chord indefinitely, and I would improvise over that. Then, we would move to the IV chord and then back to the I chord, and then, of course, the V chord, the IV chord, and back to the I chord. On *Early Tuesday Morning Blues*, we just did it over a straight drone. And I did the whole thing over the IV chord so that I was playing a pattern that on the saxophone looks like C, G, B♭, C—using the lower B♭ and then doing the whole thing up an octave—doing extremely fast combination/permutations just on that one chord for the entire set. That kind of playing was the precursor of the "clouds" in *The Well-Tuned Piano*. And that kind of playing is also the precursor of the kind of rhythmic activity that happens in minimalism.

DUCKWORTH: I've never heard *The Tortoise* live, but the one thing that I remember from everybody's description of it who did hear it was how incredibly loud it was.

YOUNG: Oh, yes. In those days we were playing loud.

DUCKWORTH: Why did it have to be so loud?

YOUNG: Well, you know I wrote in "Lecture 1960" about my interest in getting inside of a sound. I liked to be able to go inside the world of the sound and leave the other physical reality that we normally exist in. Also, when you're working with tuning—if you're tuning by beats—when you amplify the tones the beats are amplified. It's like putting something under a microscope. You can hear the discrepancies in tuning even more. You can have a much finer, more precise degree of intonation because of the fact that you have amplified the frequencies.

ZAZEELA: Also, at louder levels you get the difference tones—the acoustic sum and difference tones.

YOUNG: Oh, that was the other thing. We were very interested in producing difference tones and sum tones, and they just produce much more when you play louder.

DUCKWORTH: Didn't Marian also create a visual environment for that piece? Is that the point where the two of you really started collaborating on an equal basis?

ZAZEELA: Well, I suppose in terms of presentation, that definitely strengthened it. Previously, I was performing in the group, but beginning with the Pocket Theater performances in '64, I started to do a visual presentation. The first things were just a light box that I had designed, which was hung over the performers sort of like a votive image. Then I designed another light box. I started to photograph those designs, and then the idea came up to project them on the performers. I don't think we actually did the projections until probably 1965. I guess the performance in '65 at the Filmmakers' Cinemateque was the first time we actually had projections.

DUCKWORTH: Did you and La Monte decide to do that together? Was it a collaboration?

ZAZEELA: I think we must have, yes.

DUCKWORTH: Was that because you were moving toward a more theatrical kind of music?

ZAZEELA: Well, it certainly became that.

DUCKWORTH: Has your work grown to the point now where you see a performance as an integrated unit of sound and sight—a controlled environment?

YOUNG: In many cases, absolutely. In *Dream House* it was very much that. It was inconceivable to have the music without the slide projections on us. Similarly, with *The Well-Tuned Piano*. I will only perform it in those lights. It's completely inspiring.

DUCKWORTH: What difference does it really make?

YOUNG: I do not like a dull concert-hall situation. I think it's very staid and dry. It's like going to church, you know. I mean, these people sit in rows, and that guy stands up there and does something. So I became interested in total environment and the interworkings of the senses. I find that one thing I'm not particularly interested in, when I'm a performer, is to have people focused on me. I don't mind if they look at me, but in Marian's environments there's such an important, extraordinary visual focus that's real artistic work, as opposed to watching a "personality," or cult figure, or something like that. I don't want to be a "personality," and I don't want to be a cult figure. I'm there transmitting this information into sound. It's true I'm interesting to watch and many people like to do it. And I myself find it interesting to watch me on videotapes. But I think that being able to have a total experience of sound and sight with Marian's light environment is much greater than just watching me.

DUCKWORTH: As I understand it, *The Tortoise, His Dreams and Journeys* is a galaxy-sized piece that has movements that themselves can be four and five hours long. What does the macrostructure of a piece that immense consist of?

YOUNG: The structure of that work is a little bit related to the structure of *The Four Dreams of China*. In *The Second Dream of the High-Tension Line Stepdown Transformer*, I had proposed the idea of a work in which there can be long silences and long sounds. Performances begin out of a silence and end with another silence. Then there's a long silence before the next time a performance is taken up. In *The Tortoise*, we were rehearsing daily. There was silence between the rehearsals, but it was one big long piece because, since there was the element of improvisation on those intervals, it was changing as it went on. It was a long structure that was unfolding in time—developing and growing.

ZAZEELA: Eventually the slide projections also came to have a similar complexity in that all the designs were variations on a single design, which in itself was made up of elements of one design. We also had special costumes made. They were colors that related to the colors in the slide series, and helped reflect the patterns.

DUCKWORTH: What do you think the slide projections did to the perception of the music by the listener?

ZAZEELA: Well, it probably helped them sustain the focus for a period of time. In fact, I hadn't so much thought of it this way, but an old friend of La Monte's, Carolyn See, who is a writer and a teacher, had us come and speak to her class once when we were visiting in California. And she introduced my work as creating a visual environment in which La Monte's work became palatable to people who would never have been able to listen to it. She considered his work very austere and difficult, which it was, although I think, in many ways, *The Tortoise* and *Map of 49's Dream* were lush and resonant, and had a very compellingly sensuous sound also. So, probably, the combination was more encompassing and more absorbing for the listener because more of the senses would be involved and coordinated.

YOUNG: And I think, as I suggested earlier, that it helped prevent the listener's sense of sight from getting involved with just watching performers in a white-light type of situation. After you've once performed in an environment like the one in that photograph of *The Well-Tuned Piano*, who'd want to go back to performing in white light? Once you experience the pleasure of that, there's nothing to the other. It's totally dull. I think that our approach was always to try to do something more creative, more imaginative, and more extraordinary.

ZAZEELA: You know, we had also long since gotten away from a regular concert-hall situation. Once we got into really long durations, to sit in a concert-hall seat for four or five hours is terrible. So basically, we were very early on creating a kind of environment. Performing in galleries and lofts was a type of environment situation. Perhaps we didn't alter it initially, but later on we did start to make a whole space of it.

DUCKWORTH: Do you consider *The Well-Tuned Piano* your most important work?

YOUNG: I think it's my most fully evolved work, if you have to choose one. I think my second most fully evolved work is *The Tortoise, His Dreams and Journeys*, and particularly the *Map of*

49's Dream The Two Systems of Eleven Sets of Galactic Intervals Ornamental Lightyears Tracery section.

DUCKWORTH: What do you mean when you say "evolved"?

YOUNG: That it has had more time to develop, and as a result it has made a statement of greater and more far-reaching complexity. *The Tortoise*, had I kept it up, had the same potential, because the interval structure of *The Tortoise* and *The Well-Tuned Piano* are very similar—almost identical. But *The Well-Tuned Piano* goes off in some directions that *The Tortoise* didn't, and *The Tortoise* went off in some directions that *The Well-Tuned Piano* didn't. A very important, fundamental difference between the two works is that *The Tortoise* begins with a premise of sustained tones, and rhythm grows out of that, whereas the sustained tones in *The Well-Tuned Piano* are created out of rhythm.

DUCKWORTH: Was Kyle Gann correct when he wrote in the *Village Voice* that he thought the basic metaphor for *The Well-Tuned Piano* was rain?

YOUNG: It's not bad. I think that there is a lot of rain imagery in it.

ZAZEELA: Well, there's a lot of water imagery in the titles.

YOUNG: You know, it's interesting when you go back to my sopranino saxophone playing. If you ever heard me play with Angus MacLise, Angus felt that rain was the model for his drumming—the rhythms of rain.

ZAZEELA: Well, actually, someone gave him that idea. His teacher told him to listen to the rain, and he went with that.

YOUNG: Something that really appealed to me when I was young was what Debussy said: "Listen to the words of no man. Listen only to the sound of the winds and the waves of the sea." And one of the main images I think of in some of my works is clouds—this big sense of clouds moving. I've forgotten to mention this in many of my interviews, but clouds were the image that I was thinking about around the time I composed *for Brass*. I was beginning to think of a sense of form that grew out of cloud formations and the way they moved across the sky. I thought that that was really important. This cloud imagery was an important basis for the La Monte Young concept of musical form.

DUCKWORTH: I know *The Well-Tuned Piano* is basically an improvised piece. Is anything actually written down?

YOUNG: What I've done is written down the main themes and the
chordal areas *after* the fact of composing them and improvising
them at the piano. The way I've written them down is I've had my
disciple of *The Well-Tuned Piano*, Sarmad Michael Harrison, notate
them, either while I'm practicing or from tapes. Some are just the
bare skeleton of the theme, but in others he's taken quite a lot of
trouble to notate exact rhythmic relationships.

DUCKWORTH: It's such a long piece. How do you remember it when
you perform it?

YOUNG: When I prepare for performances of *The Well-Tuned Piano*,
among my conditions are to have a month on location before the
first concert. During that month I practice and review material. I
remember it by listening to tapes again. Sometimes I do have to
look at the score. But I know a lot of it. A lot of it is just in my head.

ZAZEELA: It comes back into his fingers, you know . . .

YOUNG: . . . once I sit down at the piano . . .

ZAZEELA: . . . because he doesn't play between performance series.

YOUNG: I make a special point of not practicing it except for when I
have a major concert coming up. Because my relationship with *The
Well-Tuned Piano* is extremely deep—it's like a love affair—and I
can't enjoy just sitting down at the piano and tinkling the keys. I've
got to be headed into the real thing, because it's a very big, deep
experience. I can only get involved with it if it's going to lead to
something. Because, you know, here I am. Basically, I'm thousands
of dollars in debt; I'm trying to earn money; I've got to somehow
keep my work afloat; and I can't just be sitting practicing that work
that I'm in love with hoping that I'll get a chance to play it someday.
Because I know the only way I'm going to get a chance to play it is
if I'm out there making phone calls and talking to people and trying to convince them that this is what they should be doing with
their money. But I'm crazy about the piece. It's what I want to play
more than anything else.

ZAZEELA: Before we did this series at the Thirty-Year Retrospective, we
had been mastering the most recent recording of *The Well-Tuned
Piano*, which La Monte last had played in October 1981. So here it

was the spring of '87. It was like five and a half years, or something, since he had actually played it. And we were daily listening to it and timing it to transcribe the score. We were just immersed in it.

YOUNG: Hundreds and hundreds of hours went into it. Hundreds and hundreds and hundreds.

ZAZEELA: And we thought: "It's so perfect!" Looking back on it, it just seemed incredible. And he felt, "Gosh, how can I possibly play this piece again? I'll never do it as well." But when La Monte first started playing it again, he never played a shorter performance than five hours and one minute. And sure, he didn't play it exactly the same. He always has different emphases in some sections, when the tuning will inspire him to play longer. But very soon he started adding new material, and by the end of the series he had brought in six or seven new themes, and a whole new section actually opened up. I mean, it's like he's a *live* composer, you know. It also has a lot to do with his having the courage of his convictions. When he says, "I let it come down and come through me," he really means it. It's a metaphor, but . . .

YOUNG: There's information that you open yourself up to and it just comes out. You allow yourself to be a transmitter, and to transmit it into a physical manifestation that's perceptible by people.

DUCKWORTH: Is that another way of saying that sound is a spiritual medium?

YOUNG: Well, I think that's certainly an aspect of it. I feel that there are some sorts of inspiration that are possible to tune into that, when made manifest, can be a source of illumination for people to be able to better structure and direct their lives.

DUCKWORTH: Do you think you had that attitude before you began working with Pandit Pran Nath?

YOUNG: Very possibly, because I was getting these major-type ideas and trusting myself as far back as the *Trio for Strings*. And I was composing *The Well-Tuned Piano* in 1964. I was very convinced of what I was doing before I met Pandit Pran Nath. I didn't meet him until 1970. But everything he has taught us has reinforced a good deal of what we were already doing, and, if anything, given me a greater understanding. My ability to say what I say right now, possibly, is reinforced by my studies with him. But I think I was already strictly following my intuition and trying to realize whatever my imagination directed me toward without any compromise whatsoever.

DUCKWORTH: What was the immediate attraction to Pandit Pran Nath?

YOUNG: Well, it was the incredible intonation and these beautiful melodies in the ragas.

DUCKWORTH: Were you both equally attracted?

ZAZEELA: I think so. Probably La Monte was better informed about what he was hearing; he had a much more acute ear than I did. I had been performing drone in La Monte's pieces, but I didn't really develop my own ear extensively until I started studying Indian music. La Monte would assign me a note and I would sing it. Sometimes I was given another note, but I didn't have the mental connection, truthfully, until I studied Indian raga singing. Really, that was my total immersion in ear-training, so I had nothing to unlearn, you know.

YOUNG: It turns out that Marian and I make a very strong team in the study of Indian classical music, because she has very strong tonal memory for melodies and the shape of a raga . . .

ZAZEELA: . . . and I'm good with the words . . .

YOUNG: . . . whereas I am extremely facile with improvisation. So she helps me remember things, and I help her to be perfectly in tune and to learn how to improvise. It's much stronger than either one of us could possibly do it alone because her tonal memory is better than mine. She can remember these compositions better than I can. In the early days of the studies, she was sometimes sensing the true structure of the raga a little faster than I was, because I was coming to it with so many preconceptions. She has a good ability to imitate, whereas I'm an originator.

ZAZEELA: Right. And I think I get the feeling. Before I ever could analyze the notes of a raga, I would recognize them by the feeling—the sound feeling—and I would know that I'd heard it before. I could sometimes associate it with the words.

YOUNG: It's hard for me to imitate. I'm a *real* originator. I mean, I had to *learn* how to imitate in my studies with Pandit Pran Nath, because it's all learned through imitation.

DUCKWORTH: Do you still consider yourselves his students?

ZAZEELA: Most certainly.

DUCKWORTH: What do you consider the most fundamental contribution that Pandit Pran Nath has made to your work?

YOUNG: I really consider Pandit Pran Nath the greatest living musician of our time. He has an extraordinary sense of intonation and
an ability to differentiate and delineate the subtle intricacies of the
structure of raga. Raga is a vast science—so vast that possibly no
one individual can really comprehend the scope of the entire subject. And it's something different from what we have in Western
music in that you can have several ragas that use the same modal
scale. Let's say it's the Dorian scale. Within those ragas, the way you
go from the first degree to the second degree of the scale can be
entirely different—the kind of sliding that you do, the kind of orna-
mentation that is characteristic of that degree of the scale, the
notes that characteristically move from one to another in that particular scale, the microtonal inflections in that particular modal
scale. There are a number of elements that differentiate one raga
from another. And when you have two or more ragas that have the
same modal scale, it becomes incredibly complex to be able to
clearly delineate one from the other. This is something that we really don't have in Western music, you know. You just have your C-
major scale, your three forms of your relative minor, and then people talk a little bit about the modes, but they're really from
antiquity and nobody does much with them except a few minimalist composers. But in India, there are hundreds of ragas. And these
kinds of classifications of melodic movement are really outside the
scope of the training of Western classical musicians. Also, the kinds
of pitch relationships that are involved are extremely subtle. Plus,
there's the concept of the mood that a particular raga evokes. In
fact, one can say that the ragas are actually spirits—like of the
deities—and when one properly articulates the raga, he actually
calls forth this spirit, which we describe as the mood. The spirit of
the raga actually comes forth and pervades the space of the room
and the senses of the individuals who hear it.

DUCKWORTH: How do you make use of all of this information in your
own work?

YOUNG: Well, the science of this vast subject of Indian classical music
is something that I find extremely educational, and it's something
that is inspirational toward my own work in musical composition.

So that, while I'm a student of Pandit Pran Nath in Indian classical music and he's my spiritual teacher, I've also gained rewards in my own musical composition, which he doesn't try to teach me. For instance, as I pointed out in *The Well-Tuned Piano* booklet, he never ever said "boo" to me about *The Well-Tuned Piano*. He never said, "Do this," "Don't do that," or "Do more of the other." It's simply he continued to teach me Indian classical music. But my performance of *The Well-Tuned Piano* was enormously transformed over the years that I studied with him. For instance, I began to compose *The Well-Tuned Piano* in 1964 and fixed it on tape because at that time I didn't feel I could get concert situations to perform it in . . . the conditions I needed to tune the piano. Then I was offered the opportunity for the live world premiere in 1974 in Rome by Fabio Sargentini. I had studied, then, for four years with Pandit Pran Nath. And the version that I performed out of the blue, having only a week or two to rehearse in Rome and never practicing the piece between 1964 and 1974—maybe only once had I laid my fingers on it—just took off. I was already a very strong performer before I studied with Pandit Pran Nath, but he developed my musicianship and my performing even more. It's a remarkable thing to perform with him. He's an incredible performer. He's so relaxed that you learn to be totally relaxed.

DUCKWORTH: Can you describe another kind of change that working with him encouraged?

YOUNG: One thing that he did change was my approach to improvisation. It's really radical. In my 1963–1964 sopranino saxophone improvisations I used to like to just start hard and come in with this block of sound that was static from beginning to end. But in Indian classical music it begins with the *alapa* section, which has a very organic beginning. It's a gradual unfolding of tones. The entire raga unfolds in a very organic and, you could say, developmental type of way. As a result of my immersion in *alapa*, and that approach toward improvisational structure, I began to improvise in that way—that's the way I'm improvising in *The Well-Tuned Piano*—so that everything unfolds out of the very first note. There are some very lyrical sections in the 1964 improvisation, but it doesn't unfold organically as one piece. They come as sections.

DUCKWORTH: I'd like to ask you a few questions about *Dream House*. Is *Dream House* a piece or is it an environment?

YOUNG: Ha! Good question. First, there's the architectural structure, *Dream House*. That's how the idea began. I developed the idea of a place where music would go on continuously. I had just composed *The Four Dreams of China*, which is a very strong, important, pivotal work because it ties up the long tones from the *Trio for Strings* with the idea of group improvisation. And I thought that if you had a *piece* that could be continuous, it would be nice to have a *place* where the piece could be performed at a greater frequency. And as I put my group together, I more and more wanted a place where the music could happen. Then, after Marian began to integrate the lights into the work, we did our first so-called *Dream House* performance at Gallery Heiner Friedrich in Munich in 1969. That was with Marian and me singing with sine waves, and a light environment.

DUCKWORTH: What piece were you performing in that 1969 version?

YOUNG: We were, I think, already into *Map of 49's Dream*.

ZAZEELA: Yes, we were. It was two voices, sine wave drones, and sine waves.

YOUNG: So I began calling the performance *Dream House* when it took on these following characteristics: it took place in a sound and light environment, and it took place over an extended period of time. (The earlier *Tortoise* performances were always just one-night stands.) Then, we began to call Harrison Street a *Dream House*, even though we weren't performing *Map of 49's Dream* in it. *Map of 49's Dream* had become the subject matter of all of the model *Dream Houses* that we had been doing as one-week and two-week performances. We even did a ninety-day *Dream House* at *Documenta 5* in Kassel, where the group performed every day for a week, but then the tones ran for ninety days.

ZAZEELA: *Dream House* was, for a long time, associated with the *Tortoise* piece, but then I think we recognized its larger implications . . .

YOUNG: . . . or re-recognized them . . .

ZAZEELA: . . . and we felt that since, now, we really had what could be a "Dream House" at 6 Harrison Street, that we'd better call it *Dream House* no matter what we were performing in it.

DUCKWORTH: Wasn't it the Dia Art Foundation's original intention to set up a permanent *Dream House*?

YOUNG: Yes. That was the intent.

DUCKWORTH: Was that the Harrison Street house?

YOUNG: That was Harrison Street, right.

DUCKWORTH: Were you shocked when that all came apart and you were forced out of the house by the board of directors?

YOUNG: Oh, it was worse than shocked. We were demolished. The problem was that we had worked on the project as if it would be permanent. We'd been given to understand it would. We even had the word "permanent" in our contract. What I mean is, we had a given budget for a year. We could do more or less whatever we wanted, but that was the budget; that's all there was. So we started out by completely redoing the heating in the building, because it made noise during concerts and because we wanted to have fine temperature and humidity control to keep things in tune.

ZAZEELA: Actually, at first we couldn't present concerts there during the heating season.

YOUNG: So we spent an enormous amount of the budget on redoing the heating system. Then the roof leaked; we had to totally repatch the roof. And we had to redo the windows in the building because we were losing money on the heating bills. Then, we ran wires through the entire building, head to toe, so that you could hear music on any floor—you could pipe out music to any floor, and you could record from any floor. And we set up an archive in the building.

DUCKWORTH: Didn't you also live there?

YOUNG: We did live in a part of the space so that we could work on the project full-time, although we kept our residence here at our Church Street studio. (We have been in this place since 1963.) But the directors of the Foundation wanted us to be able to be at Harrison Street so that we could be full-time immersed in the project. The original idea of the *Dream House* was that, not just us, but all the musicians would live there, and would have speakers in their rooms so that they could listen to the development of the piece that would be going on in the main floor. The original idea was to have musicians playing continuously. Then I began to realize over time—long before I had Harrison Street—that it was very costly to keep musicians, even as a regular band, let alone playing twenty-four hours a day, day after day. I began to determine that it would take about eighty musicians, and to pay these people full time. . . .

DUCKWORTH: Well, you need some disciples.

YOUNG: Yes. But even disciples need to live, you know. So you trade that off with the fact that it's hard to have eighty disciples in your own lifetime . . . two or three . . . and if you're Jesus, maybe twelve. So, suddenly, I began to realize that electronics was a good thing. You could have these sine waves. It's true they took some upkeep. It was expensive having technicians around all the time. But it was nothing compared to keeping eighty musicians. And it lacked the spontaneity of eighty live folks—the variety of timbres and so forth—but in exchange you got reliability, solidarity. No unions were formed to fight against you; they kept quiet most of the time and just played their tones. And you could be very creative with them and really compose and express your creative ideas. So what it boiled down to was that I used live musicians as much as I could afford to and really began to develop the concept of a sound environment as something that could keep a *Dream House* running. So, we had the *Dream House* as the original concept of a place. Then we had *Dream House*, which was the title for the short-term places (model *Dream Houses*) where we would be on location for a week to ninety days and do *Dream House* performances of *Map of 49's Dream* in a light setting with Marian's slides projected on the performers, and when we weren't performing, the sound and light environment was running. And then we got to Harrison Street, which really was like the original concept of a *Dream House*—a place where it could happen—but it didn't have the eighty to ninety musicians organically improvising all the time, which is what I had originally thought it could or would or should have. But you have to be flexible and let these ideas develop. It was a miracle I ever had a place like Harrison Street in this lifetime.

DUCKWORTH: What did you ever say to those people to get them to invest that kind of money in the first place?

YOUNG: I don't know. You know what the miracle is? That I never had to convince Heiner Friedrich. He was totally interested in my music from the first. He used to come and sit here in my studio when I was running tones—these long sound environments. He would sit here for hours and hours and listen. He loved it. He's a very unusual person. 'Til this day, he comes to almost every concert we give. I can't say that for any other patron that I've ever known, *ever*—period. Most of them don't even want to be bothered. He's truly interested in what we're doing. He thinks it's important and he wants to try to help us.

DUCKWORTH: How did the Harrison Street *Dream House* project really get started?

YOUNG: Well, what happened was, Heiner had the idea of a Foundation to fund these large projects that were totally noncommercial and that nobody else could possibly finance. And after he married Philippa DeMenil, there was money to begin the project.

ZAZEELA: He basically inspired her to . . .

YOUNG: . . . fund the project . . .

ZAZEELA: . . . let him guide her into how to use her money for this, which he also thought was a very good cause.

YOUNG: They started out by putting us on commission to plan—to design what the space should be like, and look for buildings. They started us out designing space in the Mercer Street—155 Mercer Street—building. We were having an awful time fitting it all into the one floor, but we were trying. And one of the acousticians, after a meeting, said to Heiner, "Well, you know, it's very rare that we work on spaces this small."

ZAZEELA: And Heiner was sort of put in shock by this comment, you know. Here he thought he was doing some wonderful thing, and this guy comes along and says it's too small for him to even think about. So Heiner rethought the thing and decided that it wasn't right for us to be in that building. He told us they would find us another building, and we thought, "Oh, we're being dumped," you know. So, that year we went to India, actually. And while we were in India, we called Heiner to say "hello" and he said he thought he'd found a space for us, and we were just, you know, gaga-eyed about it. We came back, and they showed us this Harrison Street building. At that time they were planning on buying the ground floor and one or two other floors, and we said, "Gee, is there any way you can get the whole building. Because otherwise, we'll always have problems with neighbors." And they saw the wisdom in that, and somehow pulled the money together.

La Monte Young and Marian Zazeela at "FLUXLUX" (Robert Watts memorial), Martin's Creek, PA, 1988. Photo Credit: Sabine Matthes

YOUNG: So we redid the heating system, the roof, the windows, and the doors, carpeted the hallways, wired the whole building, and as a result, didn't have as much money to spend on concerts or producing records or books or things that are about immediate return. You know, I'm extreme and I'm fanatical, but I'm not crazy. If I had known that it was not going to be permanent, why would I bother spending money on that building? I would just do things that would bring immediate return and get our work out into the world.

ZAZEELA: Even as it was, we changed our tune from how we were working on the first building. We decided not to renovate, but just to go along and fix things up as we needed, test out the building and see what it was really good for before we made any major, permanent changes.

YOUNG: And develop one floor at a time, which we did, which was very successful. But then, when the end of the line came, and they were running out of money . . .

ZAZEELA: See, they intended to endow the different projects, but they neglected to do so. And as a result, when there were reversals in the stock that was basically funding the Foundation . . .

YOUNG: . . . because it was all based on oil . . .

ZAZEELA: . . . and they thought the stock would come back up, so they took out bank loans pledging some other part of Philippa's trust. But when the stock didn't turn around, they were suddenly in a position of having to . . .

YOUNG: . . . borrow more . . .

ZAZEELA: . . . and have the debt service on these huge loans that they had taken out. It just wasn't working out; something was not quite well thought through. And then her family got nervous and basically stepped in and . . .

YOUNG: . . . one of the artists threatened to sue . . .

ZAZEELA: . . . because his project was being cut back and . . .

YOUNG: . . . he threatened to sue not only . . .

ZAZEELA: . . . the Foundation, but Heiner and Philippa personally, as well as their whole family. So then they got very alarmed. Because each of the children was supposed to have their fortune and not come back to Mama, you know. There was concern that something untoward was going to happen that would possibly blot out the whole family's fortune.

YOUNG: So then, Heiner got all the blame. And the new board . . .

ZAZEELA: . . . forced Heiner off the board.

YOUNG: The new board that came in was like a hatchet team. They just totally destroyed the artists and their projects. We had somebody to buy the building who would have paid . . .

ZAZEELA: . . . around 3.4 million . . .

YOUNG: . . . for the building. And would have kept our main work in the main floor, and let us stay on the fifth floor. But the Foundation—the new board—wouldn't accept it, because they had found somebody to buy the building for 4.25 million. So they destroyed an entire work of art just for a few extra bucks.

DUCKWORTH: Did you have any warning that this was coming?

YOUNG: No, very little. We only had a few months warning.

ZAZEELA: It was looking very bad at the end of '84. But even as late as November '84, Heiner said the last thing they would ever do was sell Harrison Street. But what he didn't realize was that he was about to be forced off the board. And once he was forced off, they didn't care anything about us.

YOUNG: And we were out of Harrison Street by May '85. That's how fast it went. The new board actually made us move so fast they jeopardized our work. They were literally forcing us out. And they were threatening to shut off the gas and electricity if we didn't leave. They threatened to come and take all my tapes. It was terrible. It was really awful.

ZAZEELA: We had to get truckers in the middle of the night and haul the tapes out in cardboard cartons. Here we had taken care of them to an extreme measure all these years, and then all of a sudden, on a cold night, we had to just put them out in the elements.

YOUNG: We were up all night long smuggling our own tapes out of the building.

ZAZEELA: We had to divide them up. We were able to find two places. One was a sub-basement; a friend had a building. And the other was Gramavision, who let us store some in their recording studio.

YOUNG: The new board was like a mop-up team. They were treating us like terrorists . . . just coming in and wiping us out. And it was awful. It was literally awful. I have never been treated that way in my life.

ZAZEELA: It was like . . . As wonderfully as we had been treated, it was like completely reversed. So that was pretty hard to take.

YOUNG: And I'll never forget it.

ZAZEELA: We lost, really, a whole year in reacting. I mean, we had lawyers trying to see what they could do, and we . . .

YOUNG: . . . went terrifically in debt trying to establish our legal position, and . . .

ZAZEELA: . . . make a last ditch effort to save it. But we just didn't have the clout or the money.

DUCKWORTH: Do you think at this point you're still feeling the effects of it psychologically, or is it now in the past?

YOUNG: We've recognized we've lost it now. At that point it was terrible to think of losing it. It was our major sound and light environment. To wire a whole building—six floors, you know. We really had something there. It was a real entity.

ZAZEELA: And we had a good team working. We had people that . . .

YOUNG: Employees that we had developed over the years, who knew our work inside and out. And we lost all of them.

DUCKWORTH: What did that experience do to the direction that your work took? How did you change your direction?

YOUNG: Well, a lot of people like to say, "Oh, this is the best thing that ever happened to you. You were too insular. You were in your *Dream House* there and nobody even knew you existed. Now you've gone out into the world and people see that you are really there. It's been much better ever since." But I think that that's really a very incomplete view of the situation. Because the thing is, there was so much jealousy when we had the space that people didn't want to realize that we were being very public. We were presenting concerts all the time, and had a sound and light environment open to the public day after day, five days a week, year after year. But it is true that we had to continue to try to do our work. I don't think that we did much that we wouldn't have done anyway if we hadn't had the place.

ZAZEELA: We were already working on putting out *The Well-Tuned Piano*.

YOUNG: It's not that I suddenly put out the record because I lost Harrison Street.

ZAZEELA: It's just that it happened a little too soon. I think that if it had gone on a couple more years . . .

YOUNG: It did make us desperate for methods of earning money with our work.

DUCKWORTH: Are you hopeful of finding another permanent place?

YOUNG: Oh, I really want to have a permanent space to work out of. To produce the kind of things that I want to do, my work really needs a space. I can't do fine work in these temporary setups. You just spend an enormous amount of time and energy setting it up and taking it down and moving it around. And that same energy can be going into creative work. And—okay, it's true—if you only have one of them in one place, the people do have to go to it. But a lot of people did go to it. And if you can get two of them in two places, that's already an improvement. I mean, in my lifetime, there'll probably never be one in every city, but if you could get one in each of the major cultural centers, it would be a big achievement. We used to talk about, "Let's have the second *Dream House* in Houston." And you'd have them all wired together, you know, so that you could have sounds going on in one, and video signals that could be transmitting back and forth, and La Monte Young could be doing a live performance of *The Well-Tuned Piano* in one, and it could be broadcast live in the other one. Or you could have groups of musicians interplaying, and other kinds of intercommunicated lines of information. That excites me. I've been a musician all my life. I don't get any thrill out of doing one-night stands and putting all of that energy into setting it up and taking it down.

DUCKWORTH: What type of work interests you the most these days?

YOUNG: I want to do pure creative work that expands the horizons of art. Most of the projects that I'm really interested in require time and space. And I've found that I do my best performing, for instance, in one of these setups where I can really create an environment that takes place in time and space. A place where I can practice with the acoustics, you know. You practice *The Well-Tuned Piano* in one space and you get certain "clouds" that ring in the air. But you go to another space and find that some of them are a little bit dead because of the acoustic properties. You have to find out which "clouds" really resonate in which space. The other side of this coin is that these kinds of projects and this approach towards creating work that expands the horizons of art—work that I really believe in and that I think is important—is that it's very difficult to earn a living. What most places want is a one-night stand. Most budgets are set up for a one-night stand. It's hard to convince people that there's anything better. And why should they rebuild their whole program just for one fanatic composer who has a different vision? On the other hand, my productions are no bigger than plays or operas, or other types of theatrical productions. But to me, the trade-off has been worth it to occasionally produce works like *The Well-Tuned Piano, The Tortoise, His Dreams and Journeys, Dream House, The Four Dreams of China*—works that couldn't have really developed as well under more ordinary circumstances. And it has been not only worth it to me in terms of the commercial disadvantage, but also in terms of the inspiration that they have provided me toward creating new works.

DUCKWORTH: But it's really a balance, isn't it?

YOUNG: Well, what I find to be one of the really interesting considerations for me today is the fine balance between doing pure creative
work and earning a living and public relevance. The problem, you
see, is that most of the work I want to create now can't be presented. Say somebody wants to commission a new string quartet. I'll
want to write a piece that has four hours' worth of material; they'll
want a piece that lasts ten minutes that they can stick on a variety
show. What's the use? I'd write another one of these little short dit-
ties but it wouldn't please me. Or, I'd write the piece I want and
they'd play it once, put it in a drawer, and never play it again.

DUCKWORTH: Is there no longer any middle ground for you?

YOUNG: Well, what's the use of having a middle ground? We can say I
did a middle ground on the *Trio for Strings*, but then I was very
young, and just didn't have the experience I have now. Now I have
enough experience to know that I should do what I believe in and
not try to make it fit into this plaster mold that everybody calls a
performance format. And I'm not *inspired* to write short pieces.
For instance, what I really want to work on right now is more parts
of *The Well-Tuned Piano*. Yet, when somebody calls me to do a concert, they say, "We want a world premiere." I say, "Fine. I'll do *The
Well-Tuned Piano*; it's got some whole new parts." "Oh, no. You've
done that; we've heard it."

DUCKWORTH: And what does that say to you?

YOUNG: It says that the idea of a composer creating a long complex
work in which themes are inextricably interwoven over long periods of time, with new material developing and evolving, has no
interest to anybody except me, apparently. But to me, it's just really
exciting. And it's a much more profound thing than a little
foursquare piece that takes fifteen or thirty minutes, or even two
hours, and there it is. It's fixed; that's it; that's its life span; and
that's all it's going to do. It's not going to evolve, change, or develop. My skills as a composer begin to really shine when I demonstrate what I can do in this kind of a large framework. But there's
no crying social need for it right at this moment. There's nobody
standing out there saying, "I've got to have a piece like that or I'm
going to die tomorrow." So, it's just me pushing the idea, and saying, "Let me do it. Let me do it." But a lot of people say, "Well, gosh.

I've got this concert today and that concert tomorrow and another one next week, and they're all coming in for four thousand apiece, and they seem to be doing okay, so what do I need you for?"

ZAZEELA: Most presenting organizations and facilities are set up to have, over a season, a tremendous variety. I guess they feel that their membership or their constituency requires that. We feel that what we have to offer is more like an exhibition. It has to be seen more as an exhibition, where it's brought in, and it's open to the public continuously, the way an exhibition is at the Met or something. And it's punctuated by these special performances—if it's *The Well-Tuned Piano*—maybe once a week. We have had opportunities to present it in museums, and I think it's worked well. But it's hard to convince . . . I mean, generally, museum curators are not looking for a music event. It's funny, now that there is currently more interest in performance art. They seem to be looking for things that are more technologically sophisticated, in a certain way, than this is. I think it's a strange genre that we created. I mean, things don't have continuous appeal. They have their ups and downs.

YOUNG: Well, I think our work really is new and it really is different. It's the handicap of creating that kind of work that isn't just part of a convention or an institution. It's work that is completely creative and new in scope. We would like to push in the direction that's even more creative and even more imaginative, but who's going to present it? So then you run into the problem of becoming an "armchair composer," and just creating these totally theoretical works that exist on paper. I think one of the strong things about my position has been that I perform, and in that way make my work into a physical manifestation. And I will continue to try to get situations that support that. But it's very interesting that there's very little support for true imagination. It's not what's wanted. What's wanted is something like BAM, where they just have this entertainment show . . . forced collaborations . . . glitz. And, you know, the average will always be like that. And what was unique about Heiner's vision was that he didn't want that. He wanted to support a few works that he believed in, in a large way. And he was very strongly criticized for that. Everybody said, "Why don't you take the money and spread it around?" But then you would just be right back to square one, where this composer gets a thousand, that one gets a thousand, somebody gets five thousand, and they all do a little bit of work that's very good, but there's probably nothing extraordinary about it. That's business as usual, right at this moment.

DUCKWORTH: There's one final thing I'd like to ask you about, but I don't know whether or not you want to get into it. It's about your hearing, and your need to wear a hearing aid now. Are you willing to talk about that?

YOUNG: Sure. Apparently, my hearing loss is inherited. I tried to convince the hearing doctor that it was an occupational hazard and I had ruined my hearing by listening to loud sounds. But he just would not buy it. He said my hearing graph is a typical congenital hearing-loss chart. And I started thinking about it, and three of my four grandparents have hearing problems. My mother is terribly hard of hearing in both ears. My dad had to have an ear operation. Both my mother's father and mother were terribly hard of hearing in the last years. And my father's mother's side of the family, the Swiss side, were noted for having members of the family who just couldn't hear anything. They always spoke in loud voices to each other.

DUCKWORTH: When did you first notice the problem?

YOUNG: It first became dramatic in 1974, when we went to Rome to do *The Well-Tuned Piano*. We went to some large dinners and I noticed that some people sitting near me could hear things at the other end of the table that I couldn't hear. And I think I had a glimpse of the problem in the very early sixties. I took a bus ride with the poet Robert Kelly, and I noticed that I just couldn't hear half of what he was saying, even though he was sitting right next to me. My problem is, I only had my hearing tested once, in grade school, and I have no copy of that test, so I don't know where I started. And I didn't have my hearing tested again until sometime around 1979 or '80. So that's when I first started keeping track of it. And although it didn't change much for a couple of years, I think it's gotten worse now. Maybe partly because I've become so accustomed to using a hearing aid that when I'm without it I'm just very aware of how much I can't hear.

DUCKWORTH: Is the problem continuing to get worse, or is it pretty stable right now?

YOUNG: It seems like it may be getting worse.

ZAZEELA: I think it's getting worse. I mean, from my point of view, when I try to communicate with La Monte sometimes, you know, I really . . .

YOUNG: It's not uncommon for hereditary hearing loss to get worse. It doesn't have to, but apparently it frequently does.

DUCKWORTH: That must concern you.

YOUNG: It does. I don't know what to do about it though. There's apparently nothing that can be done, except amplification, until they learn how to regenerate nerve cells—which I understand they're working on—but it probably won't happen in my lifetime. I just have to do as much as I can while I can still hear. I'm okay when I'm doing solo performance. But it's already hard when I'm in group performance with Pandit Pran Nath and Marian, even though we have monitors and special devices that help me. I guess I'll just stay on the cutting edge of technology to try to keep up with it. But I have a pretty positive outlook; I don't let it depress me. I mean, it really concerns me, but the other side of the coin is it's very peaceful when you take off the hearing aid. It's really nice, you know. There's a lot of noise going on out there.

TERRY RILEY

Born Colfax, California, 1935

I DIDN'T REALLY KNOW Terry Riley's music until that day in 1968 when I drove over a hundred miles to buy a copy of his new record, *In C*. I had read a lot about it, and couldn't wait to hear it. But like many people first learning about Riley, I wasn't prepared for what I heard. *In C* was different. It didn't sound like either twelve-tone music, or chance, or anything in between. For starters, it was in "C"; in the late sixties, no one could remember the last experimental composer who had used a key signature, much less written anything in C major. Beyond that, *In C* had no melody; or it was nothing but melody, depending on how you heard it. Either way, the whole piece consisted of but fifty-three short motives, constantly repeated, over a fast pulse played high in the piano. Furthermore, it seemed to last forever; the recorded version took both sides of the record, and live performances sometimes went on all night.

More than any other single piece, *In C*, written in San Francisco in 1964, gave voice to the minimalist movement in America. In some ways, it became its anthem. But Riley never thought of himself as a minimalist. To him, music related more to shamanism and magic, and he was an "illusionist," creating "magic in sound."

The only thing Terry Riley says he always knew for certain when he was growing up was that he was going to be a musician. When he began college in 1955 at San Francisco State, he planned to be a concert pianist, but after graduation, he went to Berkeley for a degree in composition. There, he met fellow student La Monte Young, now a lifelong friend, whom Riley is quick to credit as a major influence on his music.

Riley spent most of 1962 and 1963 in Paris, playing piano and saxophone on club gigs, and working at the ORTF studios with, at one point, Chet Baker, but he was back in California by 1964. By 1965, however, he was in New York, trading the Volkswagen bus he used to get there for a loft on Grand Street, within walking distance of Young and Zazeela.

Terry Riley, Munich, Germany, 1992. Photo Credit: Sabine Matthes

A fan of Indian classical music since the early sixties, Riley didn't begin studying it seriously until 1970, when he met Pandit Pran Nath. At Pran Nath's request, Riley became his disciple, studying raga singing with him in India in 1970, along with Young and Zazeela. Through his work with Indian classical music, Riley came to believe that just intonation heightens the experience of music by making it more in tune. As he says, a perfectly in tune, resonant vibration "has a very powerful effect." As a result, Riley had his keyboards retuned, and all of his works from 1970 on, such as *Persian Surgery Dervishes* and *Shri Camel*, use just intonation, along with raga-related scales and rhythmic cycles, as a basis for keyboard improvisation. This idea of creating music directly in the act of playing is a basic feature of Riley's music throughout the seventies.

In 1980, at the insistence of the Kronos Quartet, Riley returned to writing notated music, completing for them such works as *Sunrise of the Planetary Dream Collector* in 1981 and the evening-length *Salome Dances for Peace* in 1986. And throughout all of this time, he has presided over a steady stream of performances of the "anthem" of minimalism, including a gala twenty-fifth-anniversary concert in San Francisco, and a performance in Shanghai, on Chinese instruments. The record catalogs currently list four different versions of *In C* available on CD.

I met Terry at 9:30 A.M. at La Monte and Marian's loft. He was staying with them on one of his infrequent trips east from California, where he has lived since the seventies. Even though it was early in the morning, there was already too much activity in the apartment for an interview, so we walked to a coffee shop in Little Italy. There, in an alcove along the back wall, surrounded by mirrors, we began our conversation. I think I put him at ease by saying I would try to keep questions about *In C* to a minimum.

DUCKWORTH: I imagine you're pretty tired of talking about *In C* by now.

RILEY: Yes.

DUCKWORTH: Has it lost its meaning for you by this point?

RILEY: No, it's very meaningful. It's the piece that opened the door to the world for me, so I respect it. It's like a revered mountain sitting out there.

DUCKWORTH: Do you think it became too famous?

RILEY: No, it probably didn't become famous enough. I think that too famous would have meant that it had spoiled something, and I don't think it ever spoiled anything. It was just a reference point for a lot of musicians. But it became famous enough to alert a lot of musicians to this new style that it was introducing.

DUCKWORTH: Did its popularity in any way hold you back, or send you in directions that you didn't want to go as a composer?

RILEY: No, no. As I watched other painters and musicians developing their own styles, I was looking for a way to make a series of pieces that would be a signature for me. And I think I did that during the sixties, and even a little bit into the seventies. But after a while, it became apparent to me that I really wanted to feel totally free of any restrictions of style and to just use everything I knew about music, to make music that I liked.

DUCKWORTH: One thing I'm curious about is what you were interested in right before writing *In C*. What generated that piece?

RILEY: I think you really have to look at the sixties, and what was going on then. I was never concerned with minimalism, but I was very concerned with psychedelia and the psychedelic movement of the sixties as an opening toward consciousness. For my generation that was a first look towards the East, that is, peyote, mescaline, and the psychedelic drugs which were opening up people's attention towards higher consciousness. So I think what I was experiencing in music at that time was another world. Besides just the ordinary music that was going on, music was also able to transport us suddenly out of one reality into another. Transport us so that we would almost be having visions as we were playing. So that's what I was thinking about before I wrote *In C*. I believe music, shamanism, and magic are all connected, and when it's used that way it creates the most beautiful use of music.

DUCKWORTH: Was *In C* a "drug" piece?

RILEY: Well, no, not specifically. But the drug experience leads towards some kind of *satori*, some kind of enlightening, and that was what I was after. And for a lot of people, the drug experience was the only way that they had of getting into that world. No, I don't think drugs are the answer and I don't advocate that. What I'm saying is that during the sixties that was the way a lot of us entered into a search for higher consciousness.

DUCKWORTH: Do you think that drugs still have a legitimate place in music, discounting the sixties?

RILEY: I think the function of drugs is to remove certain filters that we
    have in our brain to make our lives more ordinary. These filters filter
    out the extra perceptions of angels and all the other things that
    would make our lives a little bit wild. If we could see everything
    around us that really exists, we might not be able to take it. That's
    why people crack up when they take LSD. The person that takes a
    drug shouldn't be dependent on it, but should take it once and see
    that there's another reality, and work towards that. You can't take a
    drug again and again and improve yourself towards that reality, I
    feel. Once you've done it, once that reality is in your mind, then I
    think the drug has served its purpose. Our problem with drugs now
    in our society is people become dependent on them because this
    reality is too brutal for them. They can't accept it, so the drug takes
    them to the other place. But since they're not ready for it psychical-
    ly or spiritually, that other place is too fragile, and their physical
    body can't take it. There's a balance between all of your psychic
    needs, your spiritual needs, and this corporal body that has to be
    maintained while you're alive. And even though you've got this spir-
    itual body inside you, you've got to take care of the physical one
    too. Great mystics, you know, can't even eat because they're so
    much into their spiritual selves. They don't take care of their needs,
    and their disciples or their friends have to do it. But if you're a drug
    addict, you might not have any friends to take care of you. So you
    end up on the street and you die. A person has to recognize that he
    has a responsibility as a human being. And if he's been awakened,
    then it's just work. It's just trying to remember, and to have
    patience, and to know that, eventually, through many, many births,
    you will probably arrive at the state that that drug brought you to.

DUCKWORTH: When you wrote *In C*, did you think you were writing
    a minimalist piece?

RILEY: No. The word didn't even enter my mind during that period. I
    was thinking of some kind of mystical experience. Magic through
    music.

DUCKWORTH: Did you ever think you were a minimalist?

RILEY: No.

DUCKWORTH: What was your term?

RILEY: I felt like a transcendentalist, an illusionist, or a magician.
    Something that has to do with magic. I feel it's my field to try to

create magic in sound. Magic in the sense of transcendence of this ordinary life into another realm. An awakening, you know. To use music to try to awaken ourselves.

DUCKWORTH: Did you realize immediately how radical a work *In C* was?

RILEY: Yes, I knew it was very radical. When I would show the piece to other people I would notice quite a degree of shock in their faces when they looked at it. The musical climate at the time was one of very heavy intellectual activity, for the most part. It was influenced by Europe, by the music of Stockhausen and Boulez, which, at that time, was dominating most of modern music. And John Cage, who was also influencing them. At that time I had already been in community with La Monte Young and working with him, so *In C* had a big relationship to his work, and was a big bow in his direction in terms of musical structure and static form. But it's radical in itself, because it was a radical departure even from La Monte's work. I think because of these repeated motives going on simultaneously, you had these whole vibratory fields out there moving ahead. I don't think any of that concept had gotten into music before, and that's why I think *In C* was so influential on other musicians.

DUCKWORTH: Is there any significance to the fact that you used fifty-three motives? Did that number just happen, or is there some numerological reason?

RILEY: You know, there's a significance to everything, but I didn't plan to have fifty-three. That's just where it ended up.

DUCKWORTH: When was *In C* premiered?

RILEY: It was premiered in San Francisco on November 4th, 1964.

DUCKWORTH: What was the first performance like? Was it a big event?

RILEY: It was a big *underground* event. The audience was made up of the San Francisco poets, theater people, dancers, and avant-garde musicians, so for San Francisco it drew together the underground community of the time. And it received recognition in the San Francisco papers as being a landmark, revolutionary piece. Right at the time, Alfred Frankenstein wrote a great review of it.

DUCKWORTH: Did you begin feeling famous immediately?

RILEY: No, not really, but I felt very good that it was successful. I remember Frankenstein's headline for the first concert was "Music

Like None Other On Earth," and I felt very satisfied that that message had come through and that it was recognized even in the press as being a new thing. But I responded by dropping out and going to Mexico for three months.

DUCKWORTH: Am I correct in assuming that your early background in music was about half classical and half jazz?

RILEY: Yes, it's true. I started out more as a self-taught musician. I began singing when I was very little. My mother said I was singing songs when I was one year old. Even before I could talk, I was singing songs off the radio. And I was always trying to copy what I heard, by ear, and play it at the piano. I took violin lessons first; that was when I was about six or seven. Then the war broke out and we had to move. My father joined the Marine Corps, so my music education got discontinued for a few years because of World War II. During the war my mother got me a piano and I started piano lessons. One of my cousins played really well by ear, so I would listen to him and try to play what he played. He would make up copies of classical pieces like Tchaikovsky's Piano Concerto. You know, he'd start out with the theme and then improvise on it. I thought that was really neat, so I tried to do that kind of stuff too.

DUCKWORTH: Were either of your parents musical?

RILEY: I'd say they were musical, but not musicians. They were music lovers, but they didn't play music themselves.

DUCKWORTH: Did they encourage you?

RILEY: Yes, they did.

DUCKWORTH: When did you decide you were going to be a musician?

RILEY: I think I knew that from the beginning. I think I never wanted to do anything as badly as music. But the time that it really started to become apparent that I was going to be a musician was late in high school.

DUCKWORTH: When you first went to college, what kind of musician were you planning to be?

RILEY: A concert pianist.

DUCKWORTH: Were you that good?

RILEY: I was good, and I had a very nice touch, I thought, and I was really able to get a lot of feeling out of the pieces I played. I studied with a really magnificent teacher, Adolf Baller, who was in San Francisco. Duane Hampton, who was my teacher before him, was also a student of Baller's. Both of them were magnificent pianists and very good teachers so I got some excellent training. But one thing that happened, that I think drives a lot of musicians away from playing classical music, was that I would not be able to play a piece perfectly all the way through. And I would get disturbed because I couldn't do that. I'd get nervous and it'd get even worse, because I knew people were sitting there in the front row with their scores watching me play. So then I'd get rattled and really go haywire during concerts. I thought, "I want to do music, but this is not right because I'm not fitting into this. Even though I can play them well at home I don't play them well in concerts." So about that time I decided I'd be a composer. I'd write what I wanted to write, and then if I made a mistake it was okay because it was my music.

DUCKWORTH: Were you still in high school then?

RILEY: No, that was in the beginning of college.

DUCKWORTH: When did you begin to study the saxophone?

RILEY: Oh, much later, after I moved to New York. It was around 1965 before I got a saxophone.

DUCKWORTH: When did you first begin to pay serious attention to contemporary music?

RILEY: I lived in Redding, a very provincial area of northern California. And up there, even among classical musicians, of which there were hardly any, modern music meant Debussy and Ravel. That would be about as modern as anything would get. But when I moved to San Francisco and started going to San Francisco State—I was about nineteen or twenty, I guess—I got into a composers' workshop. And there were people in the workshop like Pauline Oliveros and Loren Rush. And these people were all much more knowledgeable about music, and they were writing in very interesting styles, so I was a little bit blown away when I got into this class.

DUCKWORTH: Was La Monte in that class too?

RILEY: La Monte was later. I met him in Berkeley in my graduate studies, in 1959, I believe. He was going to Berkeley, and I came over to the composition class. Loren Rush, who was also in the class, and a friend of mine, had invited me over. At that time, I was working. My wife had had a baby and I had to drop out of school for a year or two to work and support us. But I was going to go to school the next year, so I went over to observe the composition class with Loren, and La Monte was in it. And that was the beginning of that. That was a big moment for me.

DUCKWORTH: Was La Monte the star of that class, the way he tells it, or is there another side to that story?

RILEY: Oh, La Monte was definitely the focal point of the class. He was so radical. I had never come across anyone like that in my life before.

DUCKWORTH: When did you move to New York?

RILEY: I came to New York in 1965. After the *In C* performances, I went to Mexico on a bus for three months. I was actually looking for something, but I didn't know what. I guess after *In C*, I was a little bit wondering what the next step was to be, you know. And I guess what I really wanted to do was go back and live in Morocco, because I was interested in Eastern music and, at that time, Moroccan music attracted me the most. I had lived there in the early sixties. In 1961, I went to Morocco and was really impressed with Arabic music. So we went to Mexico. My point was to get to Vera Cruz, put our Volkswagen bus on a boat and have it shipped to Tangier, and live in Morocco on the bus. We drove all the way down to Vera Cruz, but couldn't get a boat; nobody would put our bus on the boat. So we drove all the way up to New York. We were going to try to do the same thing from New York, right? But I started hanging out with La Monte again and renewing old acquaintances. And Walter De Maria, who was a sculptor, had a friend who was leaving his apartment. This guy had a fantastic loft on Grand Street. And he said, "Do you want to trade the loft for the bus?" So I did, and that began my four-year stay in New York.

DUCKWORTH: You mentioned earlier that you began playing the saxophone around 1965. How did that enter into all this?

RILEY: I'd been playing flute and recorder for three or four years when I was traveling around Europe in the early sixties. I wanted an instrument, so I just took a recorder with me for something to play, because I didn't have a keyboard. And I really got into blowing instruments, you know. And I was very impressed with La Monte's saxophone playing in the Theatre of Eternal Music. And of course John Coltrane was then the biggest thing in jazz, in terms of sound.

He had this music as a transportation vehicle, carrying people away with this sound. So I got very interested in the saxophone. Also, the reediness of the saxophone sound matches these Middle Eastern double-reed instruments and Indian double-reed instruments. So it seemed like I had to do a piece for that. I had already written a piece for Sonny Lewis, who was a saxophone player who was playing with me in a jazz group in Europe during the sixties. It involved tape delay, and I'd just recorded it with him. Then I decided I really wanted to expand that piece and the only way I was going to do it was to learn to play saxophone myself. So Jon Gibson took me down to Manny's and we bought a soprano. He picked the horn out for me. And I began to teach myself. In a couple of days Jon came down and showed me a few scales, and from there on I just taught myself to play enough to make this piece, which became *Poppy Nogood and the Phantom Band*. It's really the only piece I ever made on saxophone.

DUCKWORTH: What about *Dorian Reeds*?

RILEY: Well, that was the first version of *Poppy Nogood and the Phantom Band*.

DUCKWORTH: You're giving the impression that you were just sort of roaming around, leading a rather nomadic life. Is that accurate?

RILEY: Yes. I was traveling back and forth across the country. I guess in those days I was a beatnik, and then I turned into a hippie.

DUCKWORTH: Did you have any long-range goals, or were you just taking it a day at a time?

RILEY: I was very romantic, you know. I don't think I had long-range goals. I was very rootless.

DUCKWORTH: But weren't you married and with a child?

RILEY: Yes, we had a child and she was traveling with us. I enjoyed being in the company of poets and storytellers and other travelers. That was the life of the times. It was very exciting. Compared to the fifties, which was so dishwater dull, I thought things were really happening. And I was hoping the world would always stay like that!

DUCKWORTH: How were you supporting yourself?

RILEY: Well, my wife had a teaching credential, so wherever we would go she could always substitute or teach. When we were in New

York, she taught up in Harlem at Headstart. She taught the whole four years we were in New York and supported us until my Columbia Record started making a little bit of money for us.

DUCKWORTH: How did you get to Paris? Was it just more of the nomadic life?

RILEY: Yes. We went to Paris in the early sixties. I worked there as a pianist for floor shows with circus acts. I was the accompanist. I also had a jazz band and we played for dances in the officers' clubs. We traveled all over France. I worked for an agent and he sent us from one military base to another. There were actually some other interesting composers who were also doing this. At that time I was in touch with some of the Fluxus people, so, on the side, we were doing Happenings.

DUCKWORTH: Who are you thinking about?

RILEY: Well, there was Jed Curtis, and George Maciunas was in Wiesbaden. And Nam June Paik. And when I worked in the eastern part of France, I'd jump over and catch a few Fluxus concerts, and perform with Emmett Williams and those people. So there were many interesting worlds going on there simultaneously.

DUCKWORTH: How did you get from those experiences to working at ORTF?

RILEY: Well, Ken Dewey, who had been in experimental theater and doing Happenings, came to Europe. He came to Paris with some of the people from the Living Theatre, and some Italian actors, to put together a production for the Theatre of Nations of his play called *The Gift*. He had my number, and he looked me up and asked me if I'd do the music for it. At the same time, Chet Baker had just gotten out of jail in Lucca and turned up in Paris. So Ken got Chet Baker to be in the musical group, and I was kind of like the musical director and composer for it. So I worked at ORTF with this engineer there, and we developed a tape-loop system which was to become endlessly fascinating for me in the sixties.

DUCKWORTH: Is that also where the idea of repetitive figures over a constant pulse came from?

RILEY: No, this was more of a long loop that interacted in many different ways. It didn't have anything to do with pulse. It was much more dreamlike.

DUCKWORTH: How long were you in Europe?

RILEY: I was in Europe in 1962 and '63, two years.

DUCKWORTH: When you came back, had your attitudes about music changed? Were you a different musician from the one who left?

RILEY: Oh, I'm sure, yes. My interest then was to have some good tape recorders and work with tape loops and tape-loop feedback. The electronics were opening up new ideas in music for me. But I had no money to obtain a tape recorder. So I always used my skills as a pianist playing in bars to try to finance that part of my career.

DUCKWORTH: Did *In C* grow naturally out of this background of tape loops and bars, or was it a radical shift?

RILEY: Watching Chet Baker play live, and using this tape process, I thought, "Well, let's try to do it all live, and give the feeling of electronic music with live instruments." I had this pipe dream of doing something for the Monterey Jazz Festival, so I was trying to write this jazz piece that would be all tape loops. I'd work on it from time to time, but it wasn't really coming out, wasn't formulating. Something was wrong with it. I couldn't tell why it wasn't working, but I kept writing and writing and writing. At that time I was playing piano every night in San Francisco at the Gold Street Saloon. So one night I was riding to work on the bus, and *In C* just popped into my mind. The whole idea. I heard it. It was one of those things. I didn't want to go to work that night. And as soon as I got off work I came home and wrote it all down.

DUCKWORTH: All at once?

RILEY: Yes, almost all of it. I had to revise a couple of the patterns, but it pretty much came as a package, you know. It was quite exciting; a this-is-the-answer experience. Because I *heard* it. Before, I was trying to calculate it. But when *In C* came, I heard these patterns of the beginning just unravel. About the first ten patterns just unraveled, and I thought, "Boy, what a great idea!"

DUCKWORTH: How long was it before you actually heard it with live instruments?

RILEY: Not too long. Have you ever read any of John Lilly? He believes there's a coincidence control center, run by aliens who are directing all of our lives here on Earth. Anyway, I felt that this was

really what was happening, because as soon as I got this idea, I got
a call from Morton Subotnick at the San Francisco Tape [Music]
Center asking me if I'd like to do a one-man show up there. I
wouldn't have been ready to do it before, but just at that time I'd
gotten the idea for *In C* and I also had created a couple of pieces
on tape recorder, so that set it up for this November 4th concert.

DUCKWORTH: Did those first few performances go all night long the
way later ones did?

RILEY: No, not the first two concerts. That was in New York when
they started doing the all-night concerts. The first one I did was in
Philadelphia. This friend, Jim McWilliams, was an art teacher there.
He came to me one day and said, "Would you like to do an all-night
concert?" I hadn't thought of doing one before; it was his idea. He
wanted to make an installation with people lying in hammocks and
sleeping bags. They could bring their families, and some food and
coffee, and then sit there or sleep during the night while I played.
So that was the first all-night concert.

DUCKWORTH: Becoming a Creative Associate at SUNY-Buffalo seems
like such a drastic change from everything you've been describing.
Were you becoming more serious at that point and beginning to
settle down?

RILEY: Well, I needed to have work, and that was a grant that was
going to insure me another three or four months of survival. Also, I
knew people there, like Stuart Dempster, who would be interesting
to work with. So I thought it was a good move.

DUCKWORTH: Did you find it easy to fit into the academic scene?

RILEY: Fortunately, there weren't any real academic demands. I didn't
have to teach. I didn't have to do anything but live in Buffalo and
compose. I even kept my New York loft; I was down there half the
time. And it was during that time when we did the Columbia
recording of *In C* with that group, so that worked out very well.

DUCKWORTH: I'm curious, do you like that recording? Does it say
what you want it to, musically?

RILEY: It's just one kind of statement of how the piece can go. I think
it was very successful for when it was done. There have been so
many different performances of *In C* that I can't say I like it better
than others.

DUCKWORTH: Do you have a favorite?

RILEY: You know, it's hard to get excited by it after a while, because you know it too well. But the one that really surprised me was the twenty-fifth anniversary one we did in San Francisco. I'd just come back from China where we did the Shanghai version. I had wanted to do the Shanghai version because I wanted to hear a real Oriental version of it, although I don't think it's that Oriental sounding, as it turns out, because the Chinese musicians are quite Western influenced, you know. I thought, "I'd really like people to be able to slide in the notes and to give a kind of Oriental inflection to the notes of *In C*." And the San Francisco performance has all that, because the Kronos Quartet was involved, and you can hear them sliding on their strings. And the reed section was excellent; they were doing the same thing. We also had a trap drummer, so it's quite an astounding sound. And it also has an epic quality, because there were thirty-four musicians. When I heard the tape, I was really impressed. Even with orchestras, it had never had the epic quality it does with this performance.

DUCKWORTH: When did you first become interested in Indian classical music?

RILEY: I guess I first went to hear Ravi Shankar and Ali Akbar Khan sometime in the early sixties but I didn't get interested in it then as a study. I just thought it was fantastic. I thought it was a great way to make music. I'd always been interested in improvised music, and here was an improvised music that had such precision that it was a classical music too. That idea, I thought, was quite a stunning one: to be able to develop improvisation to the degree that it sounded like it was all composed.

DUCKWORTH: When did you actually begin to study it?

RILEY: Well, I was kind of studying it just by listening to it, for a few years after that. And La Monte, of course, when I'd get together with him, would play me tapes of things he found interesting. And I was listening to Jon Higgins, who was an American Carnatic singer. He was very gifted and really performed with a true south Indian feeling. He would explain a lot about the structure during his concerts, too, which was very helpful for me to see how he was doing certain things. But I still hadn't begun to study it. But all the time I was becoming more and more aware that there were techniques in this music that I should be aware of, and learning to apply them to my own music.

DUCKWORTH: When did you finally say to yourself, "This music is too important to be ignored"?

RILEY: When I met Pandit Pran Nath. La Monte had helped bring him to America in January 1970, so he was teaching in New York and giving concerts then. And La Monte was in constant contact with him, and had actually become his disciple. I'd been talking to La Monte and Pandit Pran Nath on the phone, and they wanted to come out to California and do some concerts. I was living in San Francisco at that time, so La Monte asked me if I would help arrange some concerts. So I did, and we all met in Los Angeles and gave some concerts there. Then they all came and stayed with me for a while in San Francisco, and we did a concert at Mills College. And while we were in San Francisco, Pandit Pran Nath asked me to become his disciple, too.

DUCKWORTH: Out of the blue?

RILEY: Yes, just out of the blue. And, of course, I was honored, because I was very moved by his singing, but I didn't understand much about what he was doing. It was very mysterious to me how he could create the effect he did with his voice. But I thought, "Well, this is something I have to learn."

DUCKWORTH: Why do you think he asked you to be a disciple?

RILEY: I think there's a deep spiritual connection between people. I mean, we all meet for reasons of spiritual connection, in a way. You and I are sitting here; there's some reason. So I think he asked me because he recognized me as some . . . I believe in the transmigration of souls. I think every time we take birth we get together in other forms. And he recognized that he had to help me along more in this particular lifetime. He didn't *ask* me to become his disciple, he said, "You *must* become my disciple." He's a very special human being. And the power of his music really attracted me. That that one man with his voice, even singing alone, could create the deep effect in music of a whole orchestra just blew me away. I couldn't believe that that was possible until I ran into him.

DUCKWORTH: When you first became his disciple, did you drop everything else you were doing and devote yourself?

(L. to r.) Terry Riley, La Monte Young, Pandit Pran Nath, and Marian Zazeela. Concert at the Rothko Chapel, Houston, TX. Photo Credit: David Crossley. © David Crossley, 1981

RILEY: Yes, I dropped everything and went to India right away. I spent six months there with him, living in his house.

DUCKWORTH: You and La Monte went together, didn't you?

RILEY: La Monte came over after I'd been there about three months. From then on we've all been together, more or less, whenever we can.

DUCKWORTH: This is something of an aside, but why do you suppose that among the four major minimalist composers, Steve and Phil have had such disagreements, while you and La Monte have remained such steadfast friends?

RILEY: Well, I don't know the basis of the disagreements between Steve and Phil; I can't speak to that. But I do know that La Monte and I have been friends since 1958 or '59, and that's never ceased. There probably have been periods when we felt a little bit like rivals because new-music musicians have egos, and if someone gets more attention than another, that ego can get trampled on a little bit. But the thing is that La Monte and I have felt such a close brotherhood, just like any other brothers have, that if any feelings come up they're talked about and resolved. Also, I always feel that La Monte is my elder brother, even though I'm older than him. He taught me a lot when I was younger, when I was in college. He was a much more experienced musician than I was when I met him, and he opened a lot of doors to a lot of worlds for me. I always feel like I owe him a big debt that way. Even though I became sort of famous before him, he's always been very kind and generous with me.

DUCKWORTH: What's your definition of the minimalist hierarchy? Who influenced whom in that group?

RILEY: People say minimalism started with Erik Satie, and it may have started with Gesualdo; I don't know who it started with. But in this group of people, which is Steve Reich, Philip Glass, La Monte Young, and me, obviously it was La Monte who was the first one. The *Trio for Strings* is the landmark minimalist piece.

DUCKWORTH: Other than being first, what do you think is the significance of that piece?

RILEY: What La Monte introduced was this concept of not having to press ahead to create interest. He would wait for the music to take its own course. You start a long tone, that tone has its own life until it extinguishes, and then the next one starts. So it was this kind of Oriental patience that he introduced into the music which created a static form. Even his piano playing and his saxophone playing, even if it was fast, always dealt with repeating the same notes over and over again. So the form is always standing like some kind of a mountain—like La Monte, the mountain—and not creating a real varied form. I think that without that there could have been no *In C*, because *In C* is a static piece in that same tradition. Even though it uses fields with repetitious patterns, it couldn't have existed without this other concept being born first. So then, Steve Reich played in the first performance of *In C*. Before that, he was studying with Berio and his music, I think, reflected more of an interest in European music. So obviously, after *In C* he changed his style, and started using repetition and developing his style of phases and pulses. Then after that, Phil Glass played with Steve, and of course Steve was his teacher. Now, I don't know why they have this problem with each other, but that's my honest impression of what happened, as far as the history of things. You know, there's room in the world for everybody's ideas. But you have to give credit where credit's due. You always have to acknowledge your teachers. Otherwise you won't go anywhere in the world. It's part of the respect of a tradition. It's great to be a student; a student is one of the highest forms. Once you're a teacher, then you're in a very hard role. It's very difficult; it's laden with great responsibilities.

DUCKWORTH: Can you describe what's so personally important to you about just intonation? Why is being in perfect tune so fundamentally important?

RILEY: Well, the effect of music is heightened by being in tune. Resonant vibration that is perfectly in tune has a very powerful effect. If it's out of tune, the analogy would be like looking at an image that is out of focus. That can be interesting too, but when you bring it into focus you suddenly see details that you hadn't seen before. What happens when a note is correctly tuned is that it has a detail and a landscape that is very vibrant.

DUCKWORTH: Is there a spiritual side to intonation as well?

RILEY: Yes, I think there is. You know, the idea of yoga is union, union with God. And tuning means atonement, or trying to make two things one, right? So, just intonation has a lot to do with achieving the correct proportional balances of notes in order to create one. And when you sing into a perfectly tuned tambura, you sing one note, which is as satisfying as any other musical experience. So I think that's the spiritual significance.

DUCKWORTH: What are the major insights that working with Pandit Pran Nath has given you? How has he changed you?

RILEY: It's vast. He showed us everything about the way he has lived, which has been in a very disciplined manner and yet with great love and freedom. And he has very freely shared with us this vast body of work that he collected over his lifetime—his knowledge of raga. He just poured it in. It's like having a whole body of work of a culture culminating in one person. In Western music you have libraries. But in Eastern music it's all embodied by the performer because he has to learn it through a lifetime of study with his teacher. There's nothing else like this system of melodies and melodic subtleties that exist in raga. And he showed us how each one works, what the intricacies are, and what the differences between them are, so we can keep each one separate, and keep the effects of each one separate. And he taught us how to improvise . . . what improvisation is, according to his methods.

DUCKWORTH: Don't you have any concern about taking a thousand-year tradition from another culture and bringing parts of it into the West and using it? Is there any fear that you're skimming the surface, or doing it a disservice?

RILEY: No, because I'm not. The actual tradition of raga I'm keeping as my own practice. The purest form of music that I've ever heard is raga. I wouldn't try to create anything different if I were singing a concert of raga, for instance. I would try to sing it exactly as I've been taught to sing it. But the other work, the work that is outside of raga, that's definitely a different category in my mind. I don't feel like that's doing a disservice to raga, because it's not raga.

DUCKWORTH: Do you think that Western music that's influenced by the East is inherently better than the Eastern music that's been influenced by the West? I'm thinking of the Ravi Shankar concertos for sitar and orchestra, for instance, which I think most of us would say didn't do what they set out to do.

RILEY: In a nutshell I'd say that's true, but it doesn't mean that there can't be. The raga is a very pure form. If you interject any other kind of music into it, you've spoiled it. If you try to make chord changes, for instance, you've diluted it, and the effect is that it's going to be weak. I think that's the problem that pieces like the Shankar concerto run into. And maybe some of my pieces too, where there's too much raga. When you experiment, that's one of the things that can happen. Western music benefits from experimentation a lot more, because Western music is deficient melodically and rhythmically, for the most part. It doesn't take the extra step; it doesn't go the extra mile. But it's very good harmonically. If you take a music like jazz, or any late modern work, or even the early works of Debussy and Ravel, they're very sophisticated harmonically. But the melody suffers a lot, and even a lot of the rhythmic stuff suffers too, because the harmonic structure dominates it.

DUCKWORTH: Do you see any actual points of contact between jazz and Indian classical music?

RILEY: Oh, yes. They're the two forms I feel most attracted to at the moment. Jazz is very, very young compared to Indian music. But if jazz is allowed to continue as a tradition, who knows where we'll be in two or three hundred years. Jazz is only a word, in a sense, anyway. It defines the African music that developed in America. For me, what jazz means, essentially, is blues; blues is the root of jazz. But all of blues is like one raga. When you're playing blues, it's like you're playing a very legitimate raga. You have to create the effect of blues. When people talk about blues—the sadness and everything that's been said of this particular twelve-bar cycle—the music has to express that, has to touch somebody with that feeling of sadness. Now, there might be one raga that would do that. That's why jazz is a short tradition, because it's blues. But there are already other forms developing. I'm thinking of special rhythmic changes, which is another close relative of blues, which could be considered, maybe, another raga. So I'm not going to try to predict where it will go. But I think as long as there are improvising musicians around, there will be a form like jazz to attract them, because it's something to improvise on.

DUCKWORTH: Does Western European art music seem pretty distant to you at this point?

RILEY: Western European art music is in a state of, if not confusion, at least of great variety and multitude of directions right now. So it's hard to know what the field could be. It could mean anything from John Cage to Aaron Copland, you know.

DUCKWORTH: Do any composers appeal to you? Are you particularly interested in anyone?

RILEY: Generally, I hear particular pieces that I'd say sound interesting, but I don't know if I could even bring one to mind right now. And I'm almost hesitant to do so. But I'd say, in general, I'm more attracted to music that is classical but that has improvisation in it. And that would exclude some of my own music. But the improvisation has to go on in my compositional process.

DUCKWORTH: Is Bach still your favorite composer?

RILEY: Bach, for me, is like an avatar. He's like a person who is so close to a god that you could consider him some kind of god that touched down on Earth. He didn't have the limitations that most of us mortals do in creating music. It was flowing to him faster than he could get it down.

DUCKWORTH: I know you live on a pretty isolated ranch a few hours outside of San Francisco. What's a normal day for you like?

RILEY: Well, I rise early, usually at 5:30. And the first thing I like to do, after having a cup of tea, is to say early morning prayers and then do Indian classical music. I sit with a tambura and sing for as many hours as I can. A good day will be four or five hours of singing in the morning. On a day that has other activities in it, I may only get an hour or two in. Then, I use the afternoon to do things that don't take a lot of creative energy. In the early afternoon, I like to write letters; I like either writing or practicing in late afternoon; and then after dinner, more writing and practicing.

DUCKWORTH: Do you compose every day?

RILEY: Not every day, no. When I'm working on a piece I usually compose every day, but then after I've finished it, I might go back and extend my raga practice or my piano practice. I also spend a lot of time playing jazz standards at the piano. All the standard repertoire from the thirties, forties, and fifties. I like to play jazz piano, so I'll try to improvise on those tunes. It hones up my improvising abilities.

DUCKWORTH: Is composing an extension of improvising for you, rather than the more deliberate approach of sitting down with a pencil and plotting a piece out?

RILEY: Mainly yes, although sometimes I'll start out by improvising, but as the piece starts taking shape I'll start writing and filling it in from there. It's quite a varied process with me. Sometimes I even put on a tambura tape and write while the tape's going on. *The Gift*, for instance, which I wrote for the Kronos Quartet, was written over a tambura tape. At least the first part of it was.

DUCKWORTH: What differences do you think that approach made?

RILEY: Well, I just heard melodies. The tambura suggests every kind of melody because of its tuning.

DUCKWORTH: Am I correct in thinking that after *In C* you quit notating your music, and that it was the Kronos Quartet's continuing to ask you for pieces that got you back into notation?

RILEY: That's true, yes.

DUCKWORTH: How did you feel coming back to notation after a decade or more of not writing things down?

RILEY: It was really a good thing to do in my case, because by writing things down I tended to start developing them in a more varied way than I was doing before. It kind of freed me up, because once I saw something on paper, I'd say, "Oh, if that's like that . . . ." You know, your eyes will tell you to do something that maybe your ears wouldn't. So there was a kind of mental process which started happening for me that I hadn't worked with since I was a student. I had put it away in my mind as a thing to do.

DUCKWORTH: After such a long time, do you still remember all the transpositions for the orchestra?

RILEY: Well, the computer does.

DUCKWORTH: Are we living in a good time for music?

RILEY: Oh, yes. Definitely.

DUCKWORTH: How about spiritually?

RILEY: I think that it's a crisis time for the world. There's a very big responsibility put on mankind right now, because we see ourselves multiplying in such numbers that we're causing trouble for every other thing on the planet. But I think that periods of crisis are always good spiritual times, because it's when you're facing your darkest hours that you have to look deepest at yourself and your relationship to other humans and other animals and to all of nature.

DUCKWORTH: Are you basically a positive or a negative person?

RILEY: I guess I'm basically accepting. I feel like whatever happens, it's part of the cycle of rebirth and life and death. If it's meant that this particular phase of our existence is at an end, it's probably not anything more than one part of a very long cycle going on over millennia and millennia. So I'm accepting. I think that it's what's meant to be; it's what's happening. You know, our awareness of ourselves and our daily lives is governed by our understanding. We think that our jobs and our families are the real important thing, but if we could step into other universes and look at the whole picture, we might see that it's just part of what's going on. I do believe that our consciousness, our awareness, our recognition of ourselves always exists.

DUCKWORTH: Do you pay attention to the critics? Do they have anything to say to you of any value, or are they just doing a job?

RILEY: Yes, I do. I listen to them. Of course, it's easier to criticize than to do it. And it depends on who the critic is; a lot of critics write without much awareness of the kind of work that the person they're criticizing is doing. I've had some things written that just astounded me, that they could make these statements about past works that were so false. I guess they get you confused with other people. So it's as fallible as the person doing it. But I think a musician can listen to the critic. Critics can be teachers. You shouldn't feel that because you've done this work that you know everything about it. You're just one viewpoint on it. And it's just something that came through you, it's not something you own. The less ego you have towards that work you've created, the better it is, from my viewpoint. All you're responsible for is protecting it until you get it into a form where it's being performed. Then it's out there like everything else is. If you have ego towards it, that's only going to create pain for you. That doesn't mean that I'm beyond that. But I do recognize that the less attached I am to it once it's out, the freer I'll be to do my next work.

DUCKWORTH: Do you think you've found a pattern for your life now that's going to extend throughout the rest of it? Are you on track?

RILEY: I hope so, yes. I don't know what drives me to do what I do, but I accept it. And if it doesn't work out, I'll change directions. Being a Cancer, I know that I'm controlled by the moon, so I'm very changeable. Yet I'm hoping within all that changeability in my nature, that there's some kind of overall thread in my life. And I think that even if I didn't want there to be, there would be. I mean, we all have that. And we only have the capacity to do what we understand, right? So whatever work we do is going to be defined by that capacity of understanding. That's why I feel freer now than I ever did in my life to do almost anything. If I want to play blues in a concert, I'm going to play blues; I'll try to express everything I know in music through blues then.

DUCKWORTH: Are you the best interpreter of your music?

RILEY: When I'm not playing it, it's not necessarily my music; I always feel it has a lot more to do with the performer. The performer should *own* the music he's playing, in the sense that he feels free to shape it.

DUCKWORTH: Are you saying that when the Kronos Quartet plays *Salome* that it's their piece rather than yours?

RILEY: Well, I gave a prescription of what notes to play and a direction for it, but music is either alive or dead, and the life in that music has to come from the performer. Without that, the notes are dead and they're not going to affect anybody. So *Salome* could be a million different things, using the same notes. I formulated it, let's say that, but I can't own it; it's too abstract. We credit all these people like Bach with the great works, but those works came through them. It was like a gift to them. It came from a higher source.

DUCKWORTH: Is the composer a conduit?

RILEY: Yes, he's an antenna. And the longer he keeps open, the more works that will come to him. If he feels ownership, he's going to close off the receiving end.

DUCKWORTH: What are the ways you've found to keep the channel open?

RILEY: Well, the daily discipline of the work, that's one way. And by not worrying too much about it, that's another thing. Not stewing too much over the work, because that's ego-connection. The worry about it means, "Is this going to make me look bad? Is it going to make me look good?" So you let it come through without that judgment. I always try when I'm writing to be very accepting of the ideas that come and not try to decide right at that moment what a particular idea means. Then, when I get them all collected, either mentally or on paper or whatever, I'll start improvising on them. And then you often will see that there was a pattern in your thinking that drew all of these ideas into this one period of time.

STEVE REICH

Born New York, 1936

STEVE REICH SAYS his music comes "from loving jazz, Bach, and Stravinsky," but A. M. Jones also had a big impact. He wrote *Studies in African Music*, the book that Reich says showed him "a brand new musical technique," one that, ultimately, opened the door on a new way to compose. Reich learned about the book at a composers' conference in California in 1962. At the time, he was a graduate student at Mills College, having already completed degrees in philosophy from Cornell and composition from Juilliard. Reich's teacher at Mills was Luciano Berio, and the class had gone to the conference for reasons more avant-garde in nature. But Reich, who was originally a percussionist, obtained the book and became fascinated by the rhythmic subtleties of African music as demystified by Jones. And in a mix that included elements of jazz (particularly John Coltrane's modal period, experienced firsthand), Reich began incorporating African ideas about rhythm and structure into his own personal brand of Western music, creating large canonic forms that gradually and perceptively unfold over long spans of time. Using these forms inside a steady rhythm, but with almost no harmonic movement, Reich created "process" pieces, some of which have become monuments of early minimalism.

While still at Mills, Reich experimented with electronic music. By 1963, the year he graduated, he had begun making tape loops from short spoken phrases that he had culled from other audiotapes. He would begin by starting the two loops exactly together, then allow them to go slowly out of sync with each other, thus creating, through what he labeled a "phase-shifting process," a continual stream of new musical material, a result of the gradually changing relationship of the two loops. This is how he wrote both *It's Gonna Rain* and *Come Out*, his two most significant early works. Reich says he wrote *It's Gonna*

Steve Reich, New York, 1971. Photo Credit: Richard Landry

Rain while still under the influence of Terry Riley's *In C*. (He had played in its premiere performance in San Francisco the year before.)

Reich moved to New York in 1965. By the following year, he had transferred his musical ideas from electronics to live performers, creating

Piano Phase, for two pianists, and *Violin Phase*, for four violins (or solo violin and tape). The following year, he wrote *Pendulum Music*, for four microphones feeding back as they swing and slowly come to rest, over four upturned loudspeakers. The connecting thread in all of Reich's music from this period is a gradual phase-shifting process of some type that allows a relatively small amount of musical material to be cycled through all its possible permutations, in a slow and orderly way, that is perceptible to the listener. Reich says that even when you can hear the process, there's still a lot of mystery involved.

In 1970, Reich studied African drumming, first in New York, then in Ghana. He says he saw what he learned as validating what he was doing as a composer. The next year, he wrote *Drumming*, a ninety-minute work in four sections for tuned drums, marimbas, glockenspiels, and voices. His most ambitious work to date, it was given three consecutive premieres in New York in late 1971, at the Museum of Modern Art, Town Hall, and the Brooklyn Academy of Music. Not only did *Drumming* start the expansion of Reich's ensemble (from four or five people to eighteen, five years later), it also signaled the beginning of a renewed interest in harmony and orchestration on his part, resulting in such landmark minimalist pieces from the seventies as *Music for Mallet Instruments, Voices, and Organ* and *Music for Eighteen Musicians*. It is somewhere around this time that Reich says "minimalist" stopped being a suitable term for his work.

In the early eighties, Reich, who up until then had worked exclusively with his own ensemble, began writing pieces for other groups. First came *Tehillim*, for four sopranos and orchestra, premiered in 1982 by the New York Philharmonic and conducted by Zubin Mehta. Others include *The Desert Music*, for chorus and orchestra, from 1984; and *Different Trains*, a 1988 work commissioned by Betty Freeman for the Kronos String Quartet, in which Reich incorporates a tape collage of spoken voices and the whistles of trains. In the early nineties, Reich collaborated with his wife, video artist Beryl Korot, on *The Cave*, an evening-length, multiscreen, theatrical event. Called by some a new form of opera, *The Cave* uses Arab, Israeli, and American spoken material, the speech melodies of which Reich cycles back into the music.

I met Steve at his apartment on lower Broadway, close to Chambers Street. We talked in his studio, a small room filled to overflowing with multiple marimbas, a piano, and his tapes and scores. While the room itself was small, the conversation went everywhere. Reich is savvy, educated, and articulate; he knows what he wants to say. And what I really wanted to hear about was how it all began.

DUCKWORTH: How do you define minimalism?

REICH: I don't. I steer away from that whole thing. Minimalism is not a word that I made up. I believe it was first used by Michael Nyman in about 1971. (He is an English composer and writer who wrote a book called *Experimental Music*.) Terms like impressionism— which is a nice parallel because it was taken from painting to apply to music—are useful in that they denote a group of composers. If you say minimalism, I know you're talking about me, Phil Glass, Terry Riley, La Monte Young, and maybe John Adams. But as a descriptive term, I'd say it becomes more pejorative than descriptive starting about 1973 with *Music for Mallet Instruments, Voices, and Organ*. As my pieces extend orchestration and harmony, that term becomes less descriptive, until by the time you get to *Tehillim* and *The Desert Music*, it's only called minimalism because I wrote it. But the larger issue is this: that kind of classification has traditionally not been the province of composers, even when they wanted it to be. Schoenberg was famous for loathing the word "atonal." He said there was no such thing and wanted to have his music called "pantonal." And nobody could give a tinker's damn what he wanted—the words *twelve-tone* and *atonal* have stuck to this day. And I think that that decision is correctly the province of journalists and music historians. I understand the reason for having it, but I don't get involved. My job is composing the next piece and not putting myself in some kind of theoretical box.

DUCKWORTH: Are you sorry the term stuck? Is it useful, or has it boxed you in?

REICH: I leave it for you to judge. Nobody seems to accuse me of writing the same piece over and over again.

DUCKWORTH: Do you find that people are disappointed when you don't write the same piece again and again?

REICH: I'm sure there are some who wish I'd write *Drumming* or *Music for Eighteen Musicians* for the rest of my life, but I'm just not that kind of composer; I move on.

DUCKWORTH: The first piece of yours I remember hearing was the early tape piece *It's Gonna Rain*. Do you remember what was going on in your mind as you were writing it?

REICH: There were a number of things. I became aware of African music via a composers' conference that was held in 1962 in Ojai,

California, when I was still a student of [Luciano] Berio's at Mills College. The class went down to Ojai, and among the various dignitaries was Gunther Schuller, who was writing his history of early jazz. In talking to us, he mentioned that he had wanted to find out what black Americans had done musically before they came to America, and in doing so he had discovered a book. The book was *Studies in African Music* by A. M. Jones. I went back to the Berkeley Library and got it out. And although I had heard African music before—I'd heard records, I knew that it swung, I knew you made it with drums, I knew it was very rhythmic—I hadn't the faintest idea of *how* it was made; *how* it was put together. Seeing this book was quite a revelation for me in terms of seeing a brand new musical technique laid out on paper.

DUCKWORTH: What did you see?

REICH: It can be summarized as repeating patterns, more or less in what we would call 12/8 time, superimposed so that their downbeats don't come together.

DUCKWORTH: Were you also interested in jazz at this point?

REICH: I had a lot of interest in John Coltrane's music, because he was alive and playing in San Francisco. When I wasn't at Mills College during the day, I was going to the Jazz Workshop at night listening to him. I had been interested in jazz since I was fourteen, but Coltrane's music was particularly interesting, because he was working with one or two chords. That was the modal period, when there was a lot of music happening based on very little harmony. It became clear to me that what Coltrane was showing was, that against a drone or a held tonality, you could play basically any note, and noises as well.

DUCKWORTH: Didn't you also conclude your formal education about this same time?

REICH: I got my M.A. in 1963. And instead of applying for jobs teaching harmony and theory, I decided that I really was not cut out for academic life. I opted to take a job driving a cab in San Francisco, which I proceeded to bug with a microphone. I surreptitiously recorded conversations and noises, and made them into a tape collage called *Livelihood*. (I later bulk erased it, which is another story.)

DUCKWORTH: Why didn't you want to go the teaching route?

REICH: I became convinced that I didn't want to get involved with teaching music, because the energies that I needed to compose were the very energies that were depleted by teaching. This is something that I had observed in teachers of mine. And that led to forming an ensemble.

DUCKWORTH: Had you had any previous experience with ensembles?

REICH: I actually had, believe it or not, an improvising group in 1963 in San Francisco. Members of that group included Jon Gibson, the reed player now with Phil Glass; Tom Constanten, who played with the Grateful Dead; and Phil Lesh, who plays bass with the Grateful Dead, but was occasionally a trumpet player in my group. What this group did, basically, was play what I called *pitch charts*, which were pieces influenced by Berio.

DUCKWORTH: What were these pieces like?

REICH: Everybody played the same note—free timbre, free attack, free rhythm. Then everybody played two or three notes, basically building up to the full twelve notes. The way we moved from one group to the other was that one player would play a kind of audible cue. That idea was taken from African music. The effect of these pieces was to hear the same chord atomized and revoiced in an improvisational way. Ultimately, I felt it was kind of vapid and didn't really have enough musical content.

DUCKWORTH: What were some of your other early pieces like?

REICH: I did a piece which was influenced, I would say, on the one hand by Bill Evans and on the other hand by Morton Feldman . . . and on another hand by Stockhausen's ripoff of Feldman called *Refrain*, which is long, very beautiful chords hit on mallet instruments or struck on the keyboard. I made a multiple piano piece, performed at the San Francisco Tape Music Center, called *Music for Three or More Pianos or Piano and Tape*. Basically, it was a series of chords which formed an harmonic progression. It could have been chords for a jazz tune in a sense . . . a little darker, a little bit more à la Schoenberg of Opus 11 or Opus 19. The rule was you could play the chord for any duration, you could arpeggiate the chord, you could play parts of the chord, you could make little sub-melodies out of the chord, but when one of the voices, live or on tape, moved on to the next chord, you moved with it. So you always played over the same notes. I didn't know Morty Feldman's

Pieces for Four Pianos, which is a kind of phase piece, but later I saw the resemblance.

DUCKWORTH: Did you have any composer friends at this point?

REICH: I became friendly with Terry Riley in 1964 and helped him prepare the first performance of *In C*. I gave him a lot of my players to play in the first performance; I played in it; and I also suggested to him in the course of rehearsals that he put a pulse in to keep everybody together: a drummer, basically, who ended up playing high Cs on the piano. While that was important, perhaps, I certainly learned a tremendous amount from putting the piece together, and I think it had a very strong influence on me.

DUCKWORTH: Didn't you start experimenting with tape loops about this same period?

REICH: Tape loops were something I was fooling around with since about 1963. I was interested in real sounds, what was called *musique concrète* in those days, but I wasn't really interested in the pieces that had been done. I thought that they were boring, partly because the composers had tried to mask the real sounds. I was interested in using understandable sounds, so that the documentary aspect would be a part of the piece. And I think that *It's Gonna Rain* is an example of that, as is *Come Out*. *It's Gonna Rain* is a setting of a text about the end of the world. I recorded this incredible black preacher, whose name was Brother Walter. And I must say, I think *It's Gonna Rain* is a good *setting* of the Flood, though not a setting in any conventional way. I would describe *It's Gonna Rain* as a piece of vocal music, albeit obviously from an experimental standpoint and very much from the sixties.

DUCKWORTH: How did you get the initial idea for *It's Gonna Rain*?

REICH: It was when I was fooling around with tape loops of the preacher's voice, and still under the influence of *In C*. I was trying to make a certain relationship: I wanted to get "rain" on top of "it's," so that the net effect would be "rain, rain, rain, rain" coming out of one contrapuntal voice, while the other voice would be going "it's gonna, it's gonna, it's gonna." In the process of doing this, I put headphones on and noticed that the two tape recorders were almost exactly in sync. The effect of this aurally was that I heard the sound jockeying back and forth in my head between my left and right ear, as one machine or the other drifted ahead.

Instead of immediately correcting that, I let it go . . . took my hands off of it for a bit. What happened was that one of the machines was going slightly faster, and the sound went over to the left side of my head, crawled down my leg, went across the floor, and then started to reverberate, because the left channel was moving ahead of the right channel. I let it go further, and it finally got to precisely the relationship I wanted to get to. But what I realized was that instead of making a particular canonic relationship, which was a momentary part of an overall composition, I had discovered a process which was a series of rhythmically flexible canons at the unison . . . beginning and ending in rhythmic unison. This immediately struck me. It was an accidental discovery, but a lot of people could have heard that same phenomenon and said, "Line the machines up." It impressed me that I'd hit something that was more significant than what I was trying to do in the first place. Suddenly, I got the idea for making a tape piece that would be much more of a process.

DUCKWORTH: How was the first performance received?

REICH: I didn't play the second half of it, so it wasn't perceived, obviously, for what it really was. I was feeling very disturbed at that stage in my life. The latter part of *It's Gonna Rain* seemed so paranoid and depressing that I suppressed it. But it's the second half which really sticks it to you technically and musically. After coming back to New York, and feeling somewhat less pressured, I listened to the second half and realized it was obviously part of the piece. Curiously enough, whenever I find people who like the piece, they have a similar attitude: it's very disturbing but they really like it. You know, it's a heavy trip—bad vibes—but there's substance in there that gets to you.

DUCKWORTH: How did you choose the material for *Come Out*?

REICH: *Come Out* is a refinement of *It's Gonna Rain*. The material was selected from ten hours of tape. I was asked to be the tape editor for a benefit for the Harlem Six group. I said, "Okay, but one thing: if I hit some material, allow me to make a piece out of it." So in the course of going through all this material, that little phrase, *come out to show them*, was chosen. I was combing through this stuff trying to find the juiciest phrase I could get, because I realized that that's where it was at: to get raw speech material that really had musical content, and then go from there. The radical step had been taken; now it was time to do some fine tuning. *Come Out* may not have the raw energy of *It's Gonna Rain*, but it has more refinement and musical focus.

DUCKWORTH: I don't want to put words in your mouth, but it seems to me that since those pieces were written you've come to the conclusion that tape music is a dead end.

REICH: Well, that's what I began to feel in 1967, and that led to a dilemma.

DUCKWORTH: What was the dilemma?

REICH: On one hand the phase-shifting process with tape loops struck me as extremely musical, but on the other the process seemed to me not only indigenous to tape, but *only* for tape! I didn't think it could transfer to live music, and therefore it was a gimmick. That was my attitude toward electronic music, and it has remained that ever since. I don't teach, but insofar as I occasionally visit student composers on university campuses who bring me some electronic idea, I say to them: "How would you do that with instruments?"; or, "What does that suggest in terms of instrumental music?" I think those are very good questions to ask. And I kept asking myself that. The answer was, at first, it can't be done. Therefore, what was this?

DUCKWORTH: How did you finally transfer the idea from tape to live performance?

REICH: After several months in 1966–67, I finally sat down at the piano and made a tape loop of myself playing a repeating pattern. Later it became one of the patterns of *Piano Phase*. And I played it back and just started to play against the loop myself. I found, to my pleasant surprise, I could do it. I could control it. And what's more, it was a very interesting way of performing because it wasn't improvising and yet it wasn't really reading either. That seemed very exciting indeed. The next step, which happened in late '66 or early '67, was that Arthur Murphy (who was the first member of my ensemble and a friend from Juilliard), and I went out to Farleigh-Dickinson College to do a concert. It was the first concert I was ever asked to do. So we went out there, and it was a very exciting evening, because, you know—look Ma, no tape—we could do it after all. Very rapidly in 1967 I produced *Piano Phase, Violin Phase,* and *My Name Is.*

DUCKWORTH: Before you left San Francisco in 1965, were you getting many performances of your music?

REICH: Well, various things happened. I did some theatrical music for the San Francisco Mime Troupe. Then there was another concert this improvisation group I had been working with presented, also at the mime troupe's theater. Then there was actually a one-man concert of my works which was done at the San Francisco Tape Music Center in January 1965. What happened between January and August of '65 I don't remember too clearly except that it was not a very happy time in my life and I was making plans for getting out of there and going back to New York . . . .

DUCKWORTH: Did you come back to New York with a reputation, or were you more or less unknown in the community?

REICH: I was totally unknown. Charlotte Moorman wanted me to do something in her Avant-Garde Music Festival. I let a tape be played, but it got lost in the confusion of her festival. And I learned then that it's better to keep silent until you have an opportunity to present your music in the right circumstances. What happened was that in 1967 I gave three evenings at the Park Place Gallery which were pivotal. That *did* make an impression. Basically, the program was a four electric-piano version of *Piano Phase*, played by myself, Art Murphy, James Tenney, and Phil Corner; Jon Gibson played *Reed Phase* against tape; Arthur Murphy and I played an improvisation; and then the two tape pieces, *It's Gonna Rain* and *Come Out*. Everybody downtown ended up coming. Rauschenberg was there, and all the dancers were there . . . it was an important series of concerts.

DUCKWORTH: How had you arranged the concerts?

REICH: I arranged them through a number of friends in the visual arts. The Park Place Gallery in 1967 was the hub of minimal art. Everybody hung out there. I was not very much in touch with composers of the type that would be doing new music, because on the one hand there were people up at Columbia-Princeton who I felt totally out of touch with and unsympathetic towards, and on the other hand there was the John Cage group who I felt totally out of sympathy with. So there was really no place for me. I felt I was sort of forced sociologically—because I lived downtown and felt at ease downtown—to become associated with the Fluxus/Nam June Paik confluence of taste: surrealism and Cage. But I had no use for it, and I still don't. So I waited until something came along. What came along was a group of painters and sculptors who had a gallery that everybody liked to go to, and they invited me to do a concert there. Paula Cooper ran the gallery. It was an attractive and *huge* space on LaGuardia Place near NYU. The first night, not that many people came. But the word spread, and the crowds grew; it was just word of mouth. I learned then that it's better to shut up and wait, and do it right rather than running around trying to get a piece done here and a piece done there. As far as performers were concerned, I felt I had to play my own pieces with my own ensemble. I didn't even know what other performing groups to mail them to. So I was doing what I had done in San Francisco, which was getting in touch with friends. Jon Gibson had come back to New York, Art Murphy was here, and they were the ensemble. James Tenney had taken an interest in what I was doing, and he was someone who was connected with Cage. I got to know Cage at this period of time. I felt the paradox of being thrust sociologically into an area where it was assumed that I would be part of the whole chance mentality, but I really wasn't. More recently I've come to enjoy Cage's *Roaratorio* and my respect for his integrity is enormous. I just never really was close to his ideas about indeterminacy.

DUCKWORTH: Why do you suppose you avoided all that?

REICH: It just wasn't for me. I'm not an opera composer now, though we're living in a very operatic age. I know its "in the air," but I can't be what I'm not. Writing an opera is something you don't do if you're not sure about it, and I'm sure I don't want to do it. So at that period of time, it wasn't any historical consciousness; it was pure intuition . . . automatic pilot. I was someone who had come from loving jazz, Bach, and Stravinsky. That's really why I became a composer. It was that kind of music that brought me to tears, and nothing else. Still is. So all that stuff seemed "interesting," but it wasn't for me.

DUCKWORTH: Did you feel you were going against the current?

REICH: Only when I got back to New York. Then I began to realize that I was somewhat in isolation. I knew what Riley was doing, and I knew what La Monte was doing. They were the people I knew who were doing something like this, but we didn't get on personally at that time. When Phil came along, I befriended him and gave him the ensemble to use because it was nice to have somebody to talk to.

DUCKWORTH: How did you and Phil Glass meet?

REICH: After the last night of the concert at the Park Place Gallery, who should come up but my old friend Phil Glass, who I hadn't seen since we were students at Juilliard together. He said, "I'd like to show you some things I'm working on, because they're sympathetic with the kind of thing that you're doing." He had already done some film music with Ravi Shankar, which undoubtedly had meant something to him. And he showed me a string quartet that he had been working on. The string quartet was beginning to get tonal. There was a hint of repetition, but there was no system to it; it hadn't really gelled. So I would say between 1967 and early 1968, basically what I did was to give him musical ideas and lend him my ensemble. If you look at his early concert programs, you'll see that his early ensemble was myself, himself, Jon Gibson, Arthur Murphy, James Tenney, and Dickie Landry, who he recruited. By early 1968, he had done a piece called *One Plus One*. And *One Plus One* was to Phil what *It's Gonna Rain* was to me. It was his first original musical insight—the additive process. After that, he wrote a piece which he dedicated to me, but later took the dedication away. It was called *Two Pages for Steve Reich*, but is now *Two Pages*, subtitled *Music in Unison*. Basically, what happened between Phil and me was very much the kind of thing that had happened to me with Riley, which is that a lot of things are floating around in your mind and somebody comes along who really sets things straight. The difference is that, for whatever reasons, he has been unwilling to admit that. And that has been the source of some grief between us, for sure. I don't quite understand, with all the success that he's had, why that remains something that he's very uptight about. But those things happened; they are documented in programs, reviews, and scores. It's not conjecture.

DUCKWORTH: You know, what seems strange is that just as you appear to be drifting away from working with tape and electronics, all of a sudden the phase-shifting pulse gate appears out of nowhere.

REICH: No, it didn't appear out of nowhere. The idea of phase shifting obviously made a huge impression on me, and it got carried over into the live pieces. I had the idea that instead of doing it in contrapuntal fashion it could be done as a monophony—a single line of music. And the way it would happen is if every note in a repeating melody was thought of as a little point, all of which could be lined up either in a pulsing chord or moved out of sync into a melody. A light bulb went on with that. And once that light bulb went on, there was no stopping it.

DUCKWORTH: But it went off pretty fast, too.

REICH: It went off as soon as I finished. But I had to finish. I had to slog through everything in great detail. I went out to Bell Labs and wired up I can't tell you how many circuits. I'd never even built a Heathkit before, and suddenly I was wiring state-of-the-art Fairchild integrated circuits.

DUCKWORTH: Did the phase-shifting pulse gate actually work the way you wanted it to?

REICH: Eventually I looked at it all as a kind of technological detour. It took a performance at the New School and at the Whitney, and I began to think, "This thing is stiff; this thing is unmusical; this whole thing is a waste of time." And off it went to the basement. It's still in the basement today.

DUCKWORTH: Are you one of those people who thinks that a lot of the technology is a waste of time because it subsumes you?

REICH: Oh, totally. There are some people that are really dedicated to it, and they get off on it. But I must say that I learned a great deal from that experience. I think it was my final lesson. This one really cracked me over the skull but good, and I think I learned my lesson.

DUCKWORTH: So you turned to writing *Four Organs*?

REICH: Yes. *Four Organs* was very much taking the technical insight from the box, as I refer to it, and turning it into music. *Four Organs* is pivotal because, to put it crudely, I'd been working with short notes and I started working with long notes. The whole phase-shifting process seemed to me oriented to quarter notes, eighth notes, and sixteenth notes. It didn't seem like it would be very interesting to have a phase piece in slow motion. (Actually, I think it probably could have been.) So *Four Organs* was a similarly maniacal, single-minded investigation of one technique—only this time it was gradual augmentation. I must say that I look on *Four Organs*, and most of the phase pieces up to but not including *Drumming*, as études in the best sense of that word. I don't think that they're going to have a tremendously wide currency in the future, but I think that they'll have some place because they teach technique. If the technique has any value, then at least this is an étude for mastering it. Therefore, *Piano Phase* is very useful. Anybody who can play *Piano Phase* on two marimbas can breeze through *Drumming*. It's duck soup after that. *Four Organs* is very different. It's a very radical slant on augmentation, and also, perhaps, a humorous comment on the V-I cadence.

DUCKWORTH: *Four Organs* was so different from your earlier music. How was the first performance received?

REICH: It was done at the Guggenheim Museum as part of a series of concerts that Phil and I and members of the Sonic Arts Group (David Behrman, Gordon Mumma, and Alvin Lucier) talked some curator into presenting. This concert was a media breakthrough. It was a very small concert numerically, because the Guggenheim has a small auditorium, but Alan Rich came and wrote a full page about me in *New York* magazine. In any event, when *Four Organs* was done, the public reaction was rapt attention, because the people had come to hear me, and they were the two hundred people who knew my music in New York.

DUCKWORTH: But did they know what to expect?

REICH: They knew sort of what to expect. They knew it wasn't going to be a great deal of fast changing. The program there was *Piano Phase, Phase Patterns*, and *Four Organs*. Alan Rich not only wrote a full page about it, he perceived it very accurately. He said it had every tone in it, but the third degree was missing. He also noticed the point at which it took on an extra beat and began to grow.

DUCKWORTH: Was the second New York performance as controversial as some of the reviews make it seem?

REICH: In 1971 *Four Organs* was played by the Boston Symphony with Michael Tilson Thomas playing and conducting, along with me and two members of the Boston Symphony, and members of the percussion section shaking maracas. In Boston, it received polite applause and polite boos—and that was that. But Michael decided that he would bring it to Carnegie Hall on the BSO subscription series in 1973. And that concert proved to be quite an event. On this particular concert he had programmed, besides me, the Liszt *Hexameron*, which is a very odd piece for six pianos. I think Liszt had had Chopin and himself and various other virtuosi of the day playing the various quasicadenza sections. So when they performed it in Carnegie Hall, they had various pianists of the day impersonating the virtuosi of the nineteenth century. Now the kind of listener who's going to get off on that, and who's coming to the BSO subscription series . . . the last thing in the world that person is going to want to hear is my *Four Organs* . . . but there it was. I didn't think about that at all at the time. I was so preoccupied, so innocent, thinking about wires and rehearsals, that I didn't think about the program and the audience. But when we started to play the piece, we got about five minutes in and there was noise from the audience. And that noise just continued to grow and grow until we got lost. Michael Tilson Thomas had to yell out bar numbers so that we knew where the hell we were. When it was over I went backstage and said, "Did we get together at the end?" "Forget about that," he said, "this has been a historical event."

DUCKWORTH: How were you supporting yourself during that period of time?

REICH: I was a social worker for NYU. I used to go ring doorbells and say, "Do you have any children between the ages of seven and eighteen?" If they did, I would try to make an appointment for somebody else to come back and ask them some questions. I was making between twenty-five and thirty-five dollars a week. Now don't ask me how I survived. But this was 1965. I was paying sixty-five dollars a month rent. I mean, man, it was another world. Basically, I operated entirely on intuition and did what I wanted to do. I just didn't think about making a living.

DUCKWORTH: Did the concerts at the Whitney and at the galleries come about because you really hustled for them?

REICH: No, they weren't hustled after. They happened because I was friendly with artists who came to rehearsals and who were interested in what I was doing. As I said, I was living in the art world, as opposed to the world of composers, at that time. I was involved with painters, sculptors, and filmmakers because they liked and understood what I was doing.

DUCKWORTH: What about the trip to Africa and your interest in the gamelan? You've said before that that interest developed over a long period of time, but what was the trigger that really got you to Africa?

REICH: As I mentioned, I discovered the Jones book in '62. And I was aware of the fact that what I had done had similarities to African music. But bear in mind that before I went to Africa I'd done *Piano Phase*, all of the tape pieces, *Violin Phase, Phase Patterns* (which is *Drumming* on the keyboard), *Four Organs*, polyrhythmic pieces in 12/8, everything. All the new information came from the Jones book. But what happened was that in 1970 I was still thinking about this and about non–Western civilization generally, and beginning to appreciate its importance. Undoubtedly it grew out of an interest in jazz and an interest in American black people. *It's Gonna Rain* and *Come Out* are both black voices; that wasn't accidental. And *Come Out* was used as part of a civil-rights benefit. The interest in African music was very much a feeling (particularly with Coltrane in his late music) that American black culture was simply a European overlay on an African culture. So what was African culture? Since I was so interested in jazz, where were the roots of this stuff really coming from? I never would have become as interested in African music if I hadn't been an American and raised on jazz. But the trigger was that in 1969 or '70 I found out that there was an African drummer at Columbia University. So I went up one night to Columbia, and sat in on the African music drumming class. And suddenly I was talking about going to Africa. I got a tiny little travel grant of seven hundred dollars from the I.E.E., borrowed the rest from the bank, flew to Ghana, studied there for five weeks, and got malaria. Consequently, when it came time to study Balinese music later, I didn't go to Indonesia; I went to Seattle and Berkeley.

DUCKWORTH: What did you learn on your trip to Africa?

REICH: The trip to Africa was very instructive, not really for new information (as I've said over and over again), but as *confirmation* and *encouragement*. Being in Africa was kind of saying, "Yes, acoustical instruments are more interesting than electronic ones; and yes, an entire civilization can survive on predominantly percussive music; and yes, there's tremendous variety within this." I came back to work on *Drumming*. But what it was really doing was getting me back to when I was fourteen years old, saying, "I can really be me." Africa was a big green light.

DUCKWORTH: How do you respond to the criticism that you were really skimming the surface off of another art form?

REICH: Well, I'm as guilty as Picasso was when he looked at African sculpture. You've got to remember that I had already "skimmed the surface" off that art form, if that's what I did, long before I went there. The African content of *Piano Phase* or *Violin Phase*, because they're in 12/8, is as great as *Drumming*. There's no musical technique new in *Drumming* that hadn't been there before I went, except the very opening of the piece, which is a rhythmic construction completely out of my own head, and has nothing to do with Africa. It simply uses the drums. And the drums weren't coming from Africa. As a matter of fact, they come precisely from a concert at Juilliard . . . a percussion concert. There was a guy who played bongos mounted on stands with sticks. I always remembered the incredible sound he got out of them. The sound and volume was unbelievable. I had always thought of bongos as being played by hand. So when I was ready to do *Drumming* I thought, "Hmm . . . bongos." And that's what happened.

DUCKWORTH: Did *Drumming* go through a lot of transformation and change with the ensemble? Did you put it together over a period of months?

REICH: I put it together over a period of time, but it didn't really change that much. I mean, there were details like resulting patterns that were worked out in rehearsal, but it's not a piece that had tremendous changes due to the working out. What actually happened, though, was that the process of composing *Drumming* was very much tied in with working with my ensemble. What I was doing, and what I did with other pieces, up to *Music for Eighteen Musicians*, was that I would write a little bit and immediately start rehearsals. Rehearsals would rarely result in a change of notes or rhythm, but after *Drumming* they would often result in a change of orchestration. My ensemble became a laboratory for learning orchestration of the sort that I have become involved in. In *Drumming*, there were many conceptual questions, which then suggested orchestration that was then worked out. For instance, at the beginning of the piece I found myself singing along with the drums, so I ended up doing that. (I've since dropped that; I just let the drummer play the resulting patterns.) In the marimba section, when I was composing it, I really heard—because I was in that receptive frame of mind—female voices in the room. They appeared to be an acoustical result of the multiple marimbas. So I contacted Jay Clayton and Joan LaBarbara, who actually helped work out these marimba resulting patterns and sang them later in performance. In the glockenspiel section, I heard whistling, because that's the only vocal thing that you can hear in that tessitura. And eventually it's so high you can't do that; the piccolo has to come in. So the introduction of voices and piccolo in *Drumming*, which are significant because they were pursued later in other pieces, was the acoustical outgrowth of the music itself. I was literally forced to make the selections which the combination of overtones and resulting patterns sounded like. I was merely imitating their sound, and finding the voice or instrument which created that.

DUCKWORTH: Did *Drumming* begin in your mind as a four-part piece?

REICH: No, it didn't.

DUCKWORTH: How did the different timbres emerge?

REICH: I bought the drums and started fooling around with them, which is what I always do. I compose with the instruments—nine out of ten times, the piano. If I can play it, I use it. If I can't play it, I use some kind of electric keyboard equivalent. Out of that, this particular pattern evolved with that basic African 12/8 ambiguity: Are we in three or are we in four? And *Drumming* is constantly going between one and the other. That's why twelve is such a magic number, because its subdivisions are the most ambiguous. But when I got done with the drums I thought about the bells I had brought home from Ghana. I liked them, but didn't want to use them in my music because I didn't want to use any non–Western instrument that I hadn't grown up with. And the marimbas . . . it just seemed like the piece wanted to be longer. I don't know when I got the insight that I would continue the rhythm but the pitches would change. Basically, that's all *Drumming* is—going through the same rhythmic processes in different note combinations and different timbral combinations. Indeed, the transition from one group of instruments to the other is merely a change of timbre, because the notes are identical and the rhythms are identical. When the glockenspiels came along, that was perhaps the biggest surprise. Then it seemed incumbent on me to put it all together.

DUCKWORTH: Why were the glockenspiels a surprise? Did everything develop a step at a time?

REICH: Well, what was happening is that when working with the marimbas I began to realize that I was going to work up higher and higher in the tessitura. I bought three-octave marimbas, and the lowest note is F below middle C. The lowest note in the first drum section of *Drumming* is G♯ below middle C. I was down at the bottom of that instrument. So everything I did was going to go up above there. Now once I got up there I either had to end, or I had to do something else. The tessitura, because it's physical as well—it's literally on the other end of the instrument—seemed to suggest going up above that. So the glockenspiel was the result. It was my bell in contrast to the African bells. Well, that carried the piece up to a range of pitch which is basically at the top of the keyboard where pitch begins to disappear.

DUCKWORTH: Was the amplification that you used a practical consideration to get everything balanced, or did you like the sound that you were getting?

REICH: Both. I like the intensity of it, and I like the projection of acoustical detail all through the hall. You have to hear the detail, so you have to have a microphone. And that has been the way I've been using amplification ever since. You know, there are two ways to use amplification. There's bad orchestration that you patch up with a microphone because you didn't balance things right originally. And there are balances which are impossible unless you amplify. So what I do with amplification is to create balances that are acoustically impossible, and to unify the sound source of the entire ensemble so that it's all coming from the loudspeakers, which is basically why I will amplify the glockenspiels. They don't usually need it. But it takes the piccolo and the glockenspiels and melds them together a little bit more. It makes the mix better. This is my one and only use of electronics. And I'm very committed to that. That's all I ask from electronic music.

DUCKWORTH: As you were writing and rehearsing *Drumming*, did you have the feeling that it was going to be a major piece?

REICH: I began to realize that after I got into the second section. Once I got to the marimbas, I began to see how it was using everything I had learned compositionally up until then. Plus, I was inventing an orchestra. So yes, it became clear to me. And also, other people were reacting. If you'd never heard that sound before, it was pretty striking.

DUCKWORTH: How were you holding the ensemble together? It had grown to a large number of people by this point.

REICH: *Drumming* was where it changed. *Drumming* started out with a quartet or a quintet and ended up with twelve people. Part of *Drumming* was simply finding the additional people. Meeting performers who were in the same neck of the woods as I was: musicians who were interested in non–Western music, particularly percussionists. I met Russ Hartenberger then, who was studying south Indian drumming at Wesleyan, and through Russ, Bob Becker joined the group later. Also, Jim Preiss, who was and still is at the Manhattan School of Music, joined the group. So the whole process of working with my ensemble expanded. Finally, in December 1971, the Museum of Modern Art, followed by Town Hall and the Brooklyn Academy of Music, all presented the premiere performances of *Drumming* one after the other.

DUCKWORTH: In the same season?

REICH: Within a week. Then we went to Europe in 1971, and that, of course, proved to be a major part of my life, because I ended up playing more over there than over here. Now that's evened off, but up to 1980 there was probably more European activity than American.

DUCKWORTH: When did you start supporting yourself as a composer?

REICH: About 1971 or '72. Seventy-one was a pivotal year, because enough concerts began happening to finally make this transition from part-time social worker to performer. I was not making money writing anything; I was making money playing it. So the ensemble, which started with close friends, branched out from there. Finally, there was enough to survive just playing concerts.

DUCKWORTH: When I first heard *Music for Eighteen Musicians*, I was taken with how lush it sounded compared to your previous music. How did it get to that point?

REICH: Well, it got to that point largely through a piece called *Music for Mallet Instruments, Voices, and Organ* in 1973. In that piece what happens is *Drumming* gets married to *Four Organs*. Basically, that piece was the big breakthrough for me, because, so to speak, it put the long tones and the short tones together again. *Four Organs* was this freak piece—an augmentation piece. It had nothing to do with all the other things that I was doing. Finally in the mallet piece I said, "Ah, put these two things together." So that was very important at the time. And *Music for Eighteen Musicians* is merely, in a sense, an outgrowth of that piece with a couple of twists. Of course, the pulse is perhaps the single most important thing in the piece.

DUCKWORTH: You mean the breath pulse with the wind instruments?

REICH: Yes. The breath pulse and the mallet pulse.

DUCKWORTH: What's the difference between the breath pulse and the mallet pulse? Are they two separate concepts?

REICH: Yes. The breath pulse was thought of as a foil and a complete contrast to the mallet time. I thought of it metaphorically as one of the few visual images I ever had with a piece: drummers playing by the seashore, their feet bare and their pants rolled up, drumming with their stands set up right where the water comes in, playing in strict time while the waves wash in and out.

DUCKWORTH: What are the "couple of twists" that distinguish *Music for Eighteen Musicians* from *Music for Mallet Instruments*?

REICH: *Music for Eighteen Musicians* included the idea of changing the harmonic rhythm, so that something that was going on in mallet instruments, woodwinds, or voices would appear to be changing when, in fact, it was merely being reaccented by the changes in harmonic rhythm. This is an outgrowth of *Music for Mallet Instruments*, where the harmonic rhythm, although it augments, always comes in on the second beat. *Music for Eighteen Musicians* is in 12/8, and the reaccentuation—the ambiguity—is played upon by those changes in harmonic rhythm. Now, there's a base that's shifting underneath those ambiguous patterns, highlighting their ambiguity, to create the sensation of longer lines—even though, in fact, they're all one bar long. The breath as a foil for the ongoing metric pulse is undoubtedly very important. And most important of all is that this piece is structured harmonically—the pulse is a series of middle register chords. The reason I stress that is that I've become increasingly clear about this. Everyone talks about rhythm with me; I've talked about rhythm with me. But harmonically speaking, what I've been doing right along has been taking something in the middle register and, when basses finally began appearing in my music, reharmonizing something that continues in the middle register or upper register with a changing bass. Now as we all know from the recent history of Western music, what this goes back to, unambiguously, is Claude Debussy. The reharmonization of the flute motif in *Prelude to the Afternoon of a Faun* is the quintessential statement of that kind of technique. I think it's something which is probably in my head and in the head of lots of American composers from birth, because it's so embedded in jazz, in Gershwin, and in movie music, that we don't even notice it. It's only in the last couple of years, and partly through keeping in touch with William Austin at Cornell, who is a Debussy scholar, that I'm beginning to reassess Debussy myself. You know, if you don't follow Wagner, you go to France. I did and I didn't even know it.

DUCKWORTH: How does this insight effect your music?

REICH: I have now begun to use the idea of harmonic ambiguity in the middle register as a linchpin, allowing you to move from key to key without giving away your hand. I can work in functional harmony, but the functional part of the harmony is the key signature; the bass is coloristic. If I'm in two sharps, don't ask me whether I'm in D major, B minor, or E Dorian. I'll change from section to section. I'm in two sharps—that's functional. But whether it's major, minor, or modal . . . that's coloristic. Now that's the kind of thing that obviously comes out of Debussy. But I've only recently gotten clear about it. That is what is happening in *Music for Eighteen Musicians*, because the pulse was written in the middle register piano and put into the marimbas too. And that's the functional skeleton of the piece. The very first chord is either D major or B minor, and it's harmonized both ways right at the beginning. The pulse has it with the bass clarinets on a B, it comes back, it seems to cadence on a D, it goes back into B, and then it goes to D. The fact of the matter is, what's functional is that series of chords, which stay almost within a constant signature. I think that that piece was a breakthrough to getting clear about the kind of harmony that was implied in *Piano Phase*.

DUCKWORTH: Well, *Music for Eighteen Musicians* certainly has more of a bass line than any of your earlier works.

REICH: To me it was, "How do you use the bass in this kind of a music without using a drone? I don't want to use a drone." I mean, that part of Terry Riley I just completely rejected. That's foolishness to me. So it was a real problem, and then solutions began to appear.

DUCKWORTH: A moment ago you said *Music for Mallet Instruments* was important because it was a marriage between *Four Organs* and *Drumming*. What did you mean by that?

REICH: It may sound ludicrously simple viewed from the outside, but what happened was that in *Music for Mallet Instruments, Voices, and Organ* there was a combination of basically all the pieces that I had written. You see, *Four Organs* had nothing to do with *Drumming, Violin Phase, Piano Phase*, or *Phase Patterns*. All those pieces have no long durations; they are all made up of short notes. There's nothing longer than an eighth note or a sixteenth note in the entire piece. *Four Organs* is not a phase piece; it's a study in augmentation. *Four Organs* stood there like an iceberg. I didn't know how it would ever relate to the rest of my compositional vocabulary. In *Music for Mallet Instruments*, finally, something clicked whereby I saw a way to relate the process of augmentation to the kind of ongoing, fast-moving music I had been writing in eighths and sixteenths. So you get these two processes of building up a canon in the mallet instruments, which when it finally reaches the canonic point turns the key in the latch of augmentation, which allows the voices and organ to get longer and slower. The faster the mallets get, the longer and slower (the more augmented) the voices and organ get, until in the middle you finally get the resulting patterns and everything else I had done to date coming to flower. So at the time, and in retrospect as well, it was a real breakthrough piece. It combined two different, unrelated techniques in a related way within one composition.

DUCKWORTH: What happened in your thinking that caused you to go in that direction?

REICH: Almost all of the compositional breakthroughs happen in one of two ways for me. They happen at an instrument while I'm playing and improvising within the context of what I write, and in the process the "Aha!" phenomenon takes place and I cease improvising and start writing. Or, in the process of writing a piece, while I'm taking a walk, eating a meal, or washing a dish, and running it by in my mind, something that I hadn't thought of suddenly presents itself—usually a rearrangement of preexistent material. As I remember, in *Music for Mallet Instruments* it was something whereby I was playing repeating patterns on the marimba and suddenly began singing long tones over them, and it clicked as to how they could be combined.

DUCKWORTH: What about the arch forms in each section of *Music for Mallet Instruments*?

REICH: Well, I remember thinking, "Ha, another take on the Bartók fourth and fifth quartets," which were works of his that I looked at with a great deal of interest while I was a student at Juilliard. That formal arrangement struck me as a very powerful one. And the arch form, right up to *The Desert Music* and *Sextet*, is an important overall form for me.

DUCKWORTH: Is it fair to say that the way you work is to take one of these powerful, basic forms and explore it for a while?

REICH: Yes.

DUCKWORTH: What attracts you to these forms?

REICH: My experience as a music student was that I dug into a few
works that I felt very attracted to. And that may be a hallmark of my
limitations and my strengths.

DUCKWORTH: How do you get such vitality out of such basic shapes?

REICH: You give them a new slant. As a composer I seem to be able
to stay with a particular bit of material or a particular formal
arrangement and push against it, rearrange it in different ways.
Look, the arch form has been with us a long time in various ways.
It's in Bach's *Cantata No. 4*. Formal invention in Western music can
be reduced to a few forms, and those forms recur. There are an
awful lot of sonatas written, but that is a form I'm not attracted to
because of its lack of formality and, so to speak, its narrative aspect.
I'm much more interested in the earlier contrapuntal forms and the
twentieth-century derivatives of those.

DUCKWORTH: But in 1973 wasn't it radical to be going back to traditional forms, particularly coming from the 1960s where we had to
reinvent the language for every piece?

REICH: First of all, you've got to remember that in the late sixties I
was in a very isolated position. I wasn't at ease with the academic
environment. I didn't enjoy the music of either the very conservative types, who were still trying to preserve Americana, or of the
radical types, who were trying to write like Boulez, Stockhausen,
and Berio. Later on, when I was in San Francisco and was among a
more emancipated type, I also was not at ease because I didn't feel
like imitating John Cage. So there was really nowhere within the
musical establishment at that time that I felt was for me. I was
forced back on my own resources.

DUCKWORTH: What were those resources?

REICH: My resources were a combination of a radical turn of mind—
wherever my musical intuition points, I try to follow it to its ulti-
mate conclusion—and, at the same time, to search for whatever
correspondences I could find to some point in musical history,
Western or non–Western. When you find something new and you
find out how it relates to earlier musical practice . . . that for me is a
great confirmation that in fact you're on solid ground. I began to

realize that basically all the phase pieces were a variation of canonic technique. Then I thought, "Ah, of course this works. Why shouldn't it work? I'm just writing canons at the unison where the subject is short and the rhythmic interval between voices is variable."

DUCKWORTH: Why do you suppose that many of the more conservative musicians don't see any relationship between the kind of music that you write and music history?

REICH: I think that they're looking at music history in a very contemporary and limited sense. If you look at what I'm doing and the music that was in ascendancy when I was emerging, then it's hard to see what the relationship between my music and twelve-tone music, serial, or chance music is. But if you look at my music to see where it fits into Western music, you have to see the diverse areas that originally attracted me: the twentieth century (particularly Stravinsky and Bartók), and Bach and before. Those are your reference points. And, I might add, more recently an understanding that a lot of what I do notewise has to do with Debussy. I have come to what I feel is a very clear awareness now that I am one of the many Americans working in the French rather than the German tradition. Wagner, Mahler, and so on are not composers I can enjoy, analyze, or learn anything from; Beethoven is the last German composer that I can begin to relate to. Whereas Debussy, Ravel, and Satie are an increasing revelation. I'm beginning to understand the relationship between Paris and New York in the twenties and thirties, and Copland's studies over there . . . and Gershwin. I see myself in that sense as a continuation of the French influence in America as opposed to the German one. My love of German music ceases with Bach. I mean, I can enjoy Haydn and, a little bit less, Mozart and, a little bit more, Beethoven, and then it just goes away.

DUCKWORTH: You performed with your ensemble for so many years. How did it feel to give *Tehillim* to the New York Philharmonic?

REICH: Actually, I had a good experience with the Philharmonic vis-à-vis the emotional response from the orchestra. I was girded up like a warrior when I went off to the Philharmonic. I had proofread the parts until my eyeballs were falling out, and I had tried to anticipate any cue that could possibly bother anybody. Unfortunately, what happened at the New York Philharmonic was that, because it was the first concert of the year, a whole day of rehearsal was lost. So

Steve Reich and Beryl Korot filming "The Cave," Hebron, 1989. Photo Credit: Maryse Alberti

there was a Tuesday and a Thursday, but no Wednesday rehearsal. The orchestra almost got lost in the first performance, because they'd never played it through before they were on stage. They did little bits that sounded pretty good, but when they had to get the continuity, catch cues, and move on, it was horrendous. After the first performance, I went up to Mehta's dressing room and spent twenty minutes just going over where he had to throw a big left-hand cue. It got better, but it never got past the hanging-on-for-dear-life stage. But I didn't experience any hostility.

DUCKWORTH: Is *Tehillim* more linear and less cyclic than your earlier work?

REICH: Yes. I did not make a precompositional decision before *Tehillim* that I would write a piece that had no repeats, but the music of *Tehillim* was forced on me by the words. When I was first working on it, I had on the piano the text, which I had transliterated into English after going through the Book of Psalms in Hebrew and in English and choosing those parts of the psalms that I felt I could say with conviction and put them in an order that I thought made sense. In addition to that, I had those little drums, those little tuned tambourines without jingles, which is probably similar to what they had in the biblical period. I found myself just going over the language and a melody would pop into my head, just the way it has been going with composers for thousands of years. So the melodies came out of the words. I felt that in contrast to the earlier tape pieces, which was the last time that I dealt with words as opposed to vocalise, I couldn't just repeat words in the psalms. *Tehillim* has unabashed melody and accompaniment. Basically that is a way of making music I've avoided. I used to make remarks in the seventies about getting rid of the melody and thickening the accompaniment until it became a music in and of itself that contained melodies. That is certainly *not* a description of what's going on in *Tehillim*.

DUCKWORTH: Do you like working with orchestras now?

REICH: I very much enjoy it. It would feel terrible to think that if I didn't play my music nobody else would.

DUCKWORTH: But there was a time when you didn't want anybody but your group to play it.

REICH: That is absolutely correct. I'm very glad I did that too. Because by making it something that was only played by my group, the original performances that people heard were really good ones.

DUCKWORTH: Do you listen to popular music today?

REICH: Not much, no. Occasionally. You hear it whether you want to or not. Occasionally I will listen to a Talking Heads or a Brian Eno record, or something that sounds like a retake of my own music. I don't get very involved in it; I'm not as involved in it as some other composers around.

DUCKWORTH: How do you feel about popular music that imitates your sound?

REICH: Well, I'm pleased. I was a kid who was terribly involved with jazz . . . very impressed with going to hear jazz musicians and trying to play jazz drums. I was never involved with rock and roll, because rock and roll was Fats Domino and Bill Haley, and I preferred Charlie Parker and Miles Davis. But somehow it seems to me there's a certain poetic justice in someone like myself being influenced and affected by Charlie Parker, Miles Davis, and John Coltrane; and then, at a later date, the kinds of people that I might have been in my early teens and twenties, who are now playing rock and roll, are interested in what I am doing. (Not in any kind of a literal sense, but in a broad one.) I had that interest; why shouldn't those who now have that interest have a similar interest in me? I believe that it helps the classical music and the popular music of a period to have some kind of a discourse. Charles Ives, George Gershwin, and Aaron Copland, everything we consider great American music has had either a great or small amount of that in it, because that's a particularly American truth.

DUCKWORTH: Do you think that success has altered your music?

REICH: To the degree that I can answer that I'd have to say no. But let me say two things. First, if music doesn't move people emotionally, it's a failure. I don't want people to find my music "interesting"; I want them to be deeply moved by it. So certainly I care how people react to what I compose and certainly I'm pleased that so many people want to listen to my music. That said, the second thing is that when I'm composing, alone in my studio, I write for myself. I don't believe you can write what you think people want to hear without becoming a hack. So I compose what *I* want to hear, and if I love it, maybe you will too.

PHILIP GLASS

Born Baltimore, 1937

WHILE JOHN CAGE may be the first *name* in new music that most people know, the music of Philip Glass is more likely to be the first *sound* of it they actually hear. Glass's music can be found not only at the opera, where he reigns supreme as America's most success-ful living composer, but at the ballet, on television, in symphony halls, films, jazz clubs, and even the occasional sports stadium. There are times in New York when it seems his music is everywhere; one *Village Voice* headline called 1992–1993 the "Season of Glass." When he was named "Musician of the Year" in 1985 by *Musical America*, joining Igor Stravinsky and Benjamin Britten (the only other composers so honored in the magazine's then twenty-five-year history), the citation began, "Few composers in this century have achieved the sweeping popularity or influenced the musical *sound* of their times as much as Philip Glass." And that was a decade ago. Today, in the post–Cage world of experi-mental music, no one has their music heard by more people.

Philip Glass grew up in Baltimore, taking flute lessons as a child at the Peabody Conservatory. He says he knew he was going to be a musi-cian by the time he was eight. At the age of fifteen, he went to the University of Chicago in a special program for bright kids (Carl Sagan was a year ahead; Susan Sontag was there the year before). Interested by this time in modern music, Glass was first attracted to the Second Viennese School—Schoenberg, Berg, and Webern—but rejected it by the time he left Chicago. After five years studying at Juilliard, and two more as a Ford Foundation composer-in-residence in Pittsburgh, Glass went to France to study with Nadia Boulanger; he says he knew he needed more technique.

In 1965, while still in Paris, Glass worked with Ravi Shankar, helping him prepare his music for Western studio musicians to play for his film *Chappaqua*. At the same time, he also studied with Shankar's associ-ate, tabla player Allah Rakha. This combination of experiences gave

Philip Glass, New York, 1972. Photo Credit: Richard Landry

Glass an in-depth look at the rhythmic subtleties of Indian music, and he came to see how rhythm could be used to shape his own musical ideas, developing, in the process, his particular brand of minimalism based on rhythms with overlapping cycles, something he once described as "like wheels turning inside of wheels." His earliest music in this style was composed for an experimental theater company in Paris, soon to become Mabou Mines.

In 1966, after six months spent in India and North Africa, Glass returned to New York. Forming his own ensemble in 1968, he began giving concerts; both formal ones in downtown art galleries, as well as informal Sunday afternoon ones in his Bleeker Street loft. By the early seventies, his ensemble was touring both Europe and America, playing only the music Glass wrote for them, music that no one else was allowed to play. His most fully realized work from this period is *Music in 12 Parts*. Written between 1971 and 1974, it requires three concerts to perform in its entirety. For its 1990 revival at Lincoln Center, Glass said he hoped the work could be heard, without memory or anticipation, as a *presence*, "freed of dramatic structure, a pure medium in sound."

In 1976, Glass collaborated with Robert Wilson to write *Einstein on the Beach*, the first of his trilogy of "portrait" operas, the others being

Satyagraha, from 1980, and *Akhnaten*, from 1984. *Einstein*, which was a joint commission from the governments of France and Holland, and toured Europe before playing the Metropolitan Opera House in New York, made Glass famous as a minimalist, a style he says he felt had ended two years before. Whether true or not, the period around 1975 does mark a major shift in Glass's musical output. From this point, his attention turns primarily to theater, film, and dance, resulting over the next decade, in addition to more operas, in such film scores as *Mishima* for Paul Schrader, *Koyaanisqatsi* for Godfrey Reggio, and *The Thin Blue Line* for Errol Morris.

Glass's ninth opera, *The Voyage*, written with playwright David Henry Hwang and based on Christopher Columbus, was commissioned by the Metropolitan Opera, where it was premiered in 1992. That same season in New York also saw the premiere of Glass's *Low Symphony*, based on the music of his friends David Bowie and Brian Eno, a revival of *Einstein on the Beach*, and a new theater work at the Joyce Theater. It was, as the *Voice* said, the "Season of Glass."

For all the fame and the demands on his time, Philip Glass maintains a rather strict schedule. He trys to keep mornings free to compose, and limits his contact with the press, the telephone, and interviewers like me to one day a week, a far cry from the first time we met, both leaning against the back wall at a concert in the old Kitchen, just after *Einstein* played the Met. Today, Phil lives in a brownstone on the edge of New York's Lower East Side, sharing the street with the New York chapter of the Hell's Angels and a men's homeless center. It seemed like a long way from Baltimore; I wondered how it had all begun.

DUCKWORTH: Was your family musical?

GLASS: My father had a record store. I began working in the store when I was twelve, so I knew a lot about all kinds of music from a very early age. But I didn't begin seriously playing until I was eight. Actually, I began playing when I was six, but at a certain point musicians become dedicated in what they do, and that happened when I was eight. I later found out that that was considered late. When I was at Juilliard, I discovered that my friends had all begun when they were six.

DUCKWORTH: So you knew when you were eight years old that you were going to be a musician?

GLASS: Yes, I knew. For people for whom that happens, in one way life becomes very easy because you always know what you're going to do. In another way it becomes very complicated. But you never go through that identity or vocational crisis which seems very common to other people. Musicians always seem to know what they are going to do, and who they are.

DUCKWORTH: What influenced you toward music?

GLASS: It's hard to know. Musicians have something like a calling, a religious calling. It's a vocation. I think it happens before we know it's going to happen. At a certain point you realize that's the only thing you can take seriously. It occasionally happens when someone begins late, but it's rare. That isn't to say that we're all Mendelssohns and Schuberts; damn few of us ever get to that point. They seem to be the oddest creatures of all; they seem to be quite rare. It seems, though, that it takes much longer to acquire fluency in the language of music, so we begin at an early age. But when you say, "What makes us do that?," I don't know. You get into very early memories—hearing pieces when you were four or five. Every musician I know can remember the first piece they heard. It may not *really* be their first piece, but they can remember hearing a piece that they will call their first piece.

DUCKWORTH: What was your first piece?

GLASS: Mine was a Schubert trio, the E♭ piano trio. Everyone has one. I'm sure you have one, right?

DUCKWORTH: Yes, Rimsky-Korsakov's *Scheberezade*.

GLASS: It's funny how those pieces can stick with you though. Schubert is funny in my case, because we happen to have the same birthday. In later years I resented that, because I realized that I would never get the birthday concert. The radio stations have those birthday concerts, and it's always going to be Schubert. I've got this other dude who already beat me to it.

DUCKWORTH: How do you think people respond to the memory of hearing that first piece?

GLASS: It's very emotional. They remember where they were sitting; they can remember who they were with. It's a very clear memory, although it can happen very early—four, five, six.

DUCKWORTH: When you started taking flute lessons at the Peabody Conservatory, had you more or less committed yourself to music?

GLASS: It would be a little early to say that. I don't think I realized it until I was twelve or thirteen. But I was acting like a committed person, although I didn't reflect on it at that moment.

DUCKWORTH: What did you see yourself doing?

GLASS: Well, I quickly saw that I wouldn't be a flutist. The literature was far too slim. There are people who can make a big career out of it, but not many. Had I not been ambitious, I would not have noticed that it was a limited repertoire. I would have been happy to play the Telemann, Vivaldi, the few Mozart pieces, and the handful of modern works, which of course I tried. At that time there seemed so few of them . . . I'm talking about the late forties now.

DUCKWORTH: Were you a good flute player?

GLASS: I think I might have been a good flute player. I was certainly good for my age. Since I began early, I had a good physical endowment in terms of my lips, my dexterity, and so forth. I could produce a very good tone. And I had a teacher who understood how to make a good flute sound. But I quit when I was fifteen. It was not the time to stop playing if you were going to be a professional flute player.

DUCKWORTH: Were you interested in modern music then, or mostly classical?

GLASS: By fifteen I was interested in modern music.

DUCKWORTH: Where had you ever heard any of it?

GLASS: I hadn't! I didn't even know what it was! I just knew that I was interested in it.

DUCKWORTH: When you were growing up, did you listen to popular music?

GLASS: Of course I did. That's what was in the store. And I listened to modern music, too. I listened to all kinds of music. I worked in the store, so I heard everything from "Ghostriders in the Sky" to . . . I remember opening the first box of Elvis Presley records. They came to the store in the morning and they disappeared that afternoon. In a funny way, I've been monitoring the history of contemporary pop music since I was twelve, so that makes it since the late

forties. Some of it I liked, some of it I didn't like. I was not encouraged to like only classical music.

My father was a self-educated man. He came into that business
more or less by accident. He loved music and he began to take
home records that didn't sell in the store. He would bring them
home to listen to them, because when he would order he didn't
know Wagner from Shostakovich. He brought home the records
that didn't sell because he wanted to hear what was wrong with
them. Isn't that curious? There was a Shostakovich cello sonata that
someone recorded on 78s. He wanted to know why people
wouldn't buy it, so he would take it home and listen to it. And he'd
listen to it again and again to discover what was wrong with the
music . . . and he ended up loving it. It's very funny! His record collection was very odd. It had no Beethoven symphonies, because
those were the ones you sold. The standard literature wasn't what
we had at home. We had all the odd stuff—American composers
like Foote. There was even an early recording of Gottschalk. He
had Debussy piano music, which didn't sell well in the forties. Then
we switched over to the LPs and there was just a flood of music.

DUCKWORTH: It sounds like you had a good introduction to twentieth-
century music.

GLASS: New music was well served in the early fifties. In those days,
record companies felt a kind of morality about it; they felt that they
had to represent new music. Of course, one hardly runs across that
idea these days. Record companies are run, strictly speaking, by
accountants who don't really care about music. But in those days
there was definitely a missionary quality to it. They felt they were
obliged to play new music, and to produce records of new music,
and if you were a young guy—fourteen, fifteen, sixteen—you could
listen to it. That's the first lot of music that I heard, though I don't
think it made much of an impression on me. It didn't mean anything to me personally until I really began to study it.

DUCKWORTH: Can you identify one or two records, though, from
that early period, as being influential?

GLASS: The important company for me was Dial records, because
they were the ones that recorded Webern and Berg. They were all
78s. I was attracted to the music that we thought was advanced at
the time, which meant of course Schoenberg, Webern, and Berg.
The Symphony, Op. 21 of Webern was recorded very early on Dial

records, as was the Lyric Suite of Berg. Apart from that you had to manage with scores. I learned Charles Ives's music by score. There weren't any recordings in the old days. Now can you imagine a boy of fifteen trying to make sense of *Three Places in New England*? It was impossible.

DUCKWORTH: Were you in Chicago then?

GLASS: Yes.

DUCKWORTH: I'm under the impression that you went to the University of Chicago at the age of fifteen as a math and philosophy major.

GLASS: Well, there were no real majors there. I took elective courses in those fields. At that moment it did not have a very developed music department, though it has that now. When I was there it was basically musicology.

DUCKWORTH: Why did you go there if you thought of yourself as a musician?

GLASS: I was a musician who needed an education. It didn't occur to me at that moment to go to a trade school, which is what I eventually did. By trade school I mean Juilliard or any number of places. But at fifteen I was interested in a general education, and I got that at Chicago. I was in a special program for youngsters like myself. You could go to school there and be very young. There were a number of other people—Susan Sontag was there a year before me; I knew Carl Sagan, he was a year ahead of me. It was all these young, bright kids from all over; I was just taken in with them. But that's when I began to write music.

DUCKWORTH: What was your first music like?

GLASS: The first piece I wrote was a twelve-tone piece because that's what modern music was. It's funny now, isn't it? I was one of the people who began the great rebellion in the mid-sixties. But in the early fifties that was the music I wrote, because that's what modern music was. The only American composer I knew was Charles Ives. I think I did find a William Schuman score at the University of Chicago. I do know that we had plenty of the Second Viennese School there. So that's what I studied. There was no one to study with, so I just studied with myself.

DUCKWORTH: Were you drawn to it?

GLASS: I was, though it's hard for me to remember the feeling of being drawn to it. But I must have been, because that's what I studied. It was at about that time that the Juilliard Quartet recorded the Schoenberg quartets. This was about 1954, and the music was becoming available. The earlier works of Schoenberg, like the *Gurrelieder*, I shied away from. I was more interested in the advanced pieces. Stravinsky's work I didn't really know until I was in music school. I considered the mark of modern music to be the atonal school. I was not alone in thinking that at the time; that was the general perception of contemporary music. The fact is that as we look at twentieth-century music now we see it quite differently. It now seems to me that the mainstream was tonal music, if you think about Shostakovich, Sibelius, Strauss, and Copland. When we look at the major literature from the perspective of the ninth decade in the twentieth-century, it seems that twentieth-century music is tonal music. But there were moments when it didn't appear that way. That's why the perspective of years is crucial.

DUCKWORTH: Were you playing any music in Chicago?

GLASS: Yes, I took my first piano lessons there with a guy named Marcus Raskin. He was a pianist from Juilliard, and that's where I first got the idea of going to Juilliard. Eventually I became good enough to play my own music, but not good enough to play very much else. In other words, I became a kind of composer-pianist. A composer plays his music like no one else plays it. He may not play it as accurately, but he knows what he meant in a different way.

DUCKWORTH: When you decided to go to Juilliard, what were you going to be? Were you a composer by then?

GLASS: Oh, yes. That's what I wanted to do. I went there for a very funny reason. See, I was living in a world where all the composers were dead. Even the living ones were dead.

DUCKWORTH: Like Ives?

GLASS: Yes. All the modern music that I knew was written by dead men. There was no one around. Then I discovered the music of William Schuman. I thought he taught at Juilliard, but actually he was the head of the school. I went to Juilliard with the idea that I was going to study with William Schuman. I finally got to shake his hand when I got my diploma five years later, but that was as close as I got to the guy. But the important part is that he was the first composer who wasn't part of the European tradition. Whatever we may think of his work now is not so important; in the fifties, he was trying to write in a contemporary American symphonic tradition. I don't know what I would think of that work now, but it was interesting at the time. He represented a whole school of music that included Copland and Harris. Juilliard as an institution represented that mainstream. So that when I went there, and by then I was nineteen, I put the twelve-tone music firmly behind me. My twelve-tone period was over by the time I was nineteen, for better or worse. Had I gone to another school, perhaps I would have . . . I never met the people who might have changed that for me. And it didn't really matter. A lot of these things are happenstance. I think that ultimately it didn't really matter, because in the end I gave up all of it and went in a completely different direction.

DUCKWORTH: Why don't you think it matters?

GLASS: In a certain way, until a composer finds his own voice, it doesn't much matter what he does. I think we all tend to sound like the people that we study with. My teachers at Juilliard were Vincent Persichetti and William Bergsma. I was fortunate with both Bergsma and Persichetti to have people with a broad culture, in terms of contemporary music. I could have gone in there with anything and it wouldn't have surprised Vincent. He could have handled a twelve-tone piece, a serial piece, or a tonal piece. Both men were capable of that. I fancied my music after him and I admired him, as we all did. There were some Darmstadt composers at Juilliard at the time who survived on shock effect, but they weren't snubbed. We considered them slightly mad. Don't forget that this was just about the year when Stockhausen came out with that big electronic piece, *Gesang der Jünglinge*. It's important to remember what a powerful effect that piece had. Suddenly the twelve-tone music was going to get updated. Suddenly it went from something that was kind of antiquated and old into something very contemporary again, in the hands of Stockhausen and, a little bit later, Berio and Maderna. There was a very strong Italian school, a very strong German school, and a very strong French school. The American school developed a little bit later. But we're talking now about 1959–1960.

DUCKWORTH: How do you remember your two years as a Ford Foundation composer in Pittsburgh?

GLASS: It was a good period. I wrote over twenty pieces and, as a matter of fact, a lot of them got published. It was all school music, but it was quite playable. And, you know, some of it's still in print. It's nothing special, but to a young composer those are important things. For two years I wrote music that was played almost immediately. After that I went to study with Nadia Boulanger.

DUCKWORTH: What caused you to go to Paris and study with her?

GLASS: Very simply, I became convinced that the technique that I had acquired up to that point—remember I was about twenty-four—was inadequate for what I wanted to do.

DUCKWORTH: How did you know that?

GLASS: I knew it because I knew one or two people who were better than me, frankly. They had a technique that I didn't have. One was a guy named Albert Fine, who's not well known at all, who was a student at Juilliard. He had a phenomenal grasp of the musical language. I quickly found out that he knew more than anyone else knew. Now Vincent knew a lot about composition, but Albert knew something about technique that no one else knew. I found out that he had studied with Nadia Boulanger, so at one point I said, "Well, I guess I'll have to go and study with your teacher." I had always meant to do that. My two years in Pittsburgh were a detour really.

DUCKWORTH: What impressed you about Albert Fine?

GLASS: He just represented in his person a technical understanding of music that no one I knew had, with the exception of someone like Vincent. Persichetti is one of these raw talents—"raw" is not quite fair—a sophisticated talent. But he seemed to have been born with it! He didn't have to acquire it the way the rest of us do. My impression was simply that he was an extraordinarily gifted man for whom things came very easily. But for those of us for whom things come with great difficulty, he can't help very much. I needed a teacher who would be able to work with more common kinds of talent, which mine was as I perceived it.

DUCKWORTH: Can you characterize the way Boulanger taught?

GLASS: Oh, it was very simple. What I did with her—and it amounted to something close to three years—was spend six hours a day doing counterpoint, solfège, and analysis, all day long. When I began studying with her, she decided that I had to start from the very beginning. So I began with first species counterpoint. Now at that time I was twenty-five years old with a master's degree, and the other students were much younger than me. So it takes a certain courage, I would say, to submit to that. You just began early in the morning and worked all day. It was the only way to do it. She set the standards so high, and what she expected of you was so unreasonable, that the only way to get close to it was to work all the time . . . to the point where I almost stopped writing. I had been writing for ten years, so to almost stop was quite a major thing for me to do. And the second year I almost stopped because I simply had no time. There was so much work to do. But at the end of that time I had acquired a very different grasp of music than I had before I came.

DUCKWORTH: Did you have daily contact with her?

GLASS: I saw her three times a week. I saw her once privately; I had a private lesson which was a small class that I went to with four or five other people; and then there was a larger class that she gave. Besides that, I had another teacher, her assistant Mlle Dieudonne, with whom we did other kinds of musicianship having to do mainly with solfège. And as you probably know, solfège for these birds meant reading in seven clefs. There was nothing easy that they couldn't make more difficult without a little imagination! One standard exercise of Boulanger's was that from any note you had to sing all the inversions of all the cadences in every key. It takes about ten or twelve minutes to do, and you go through about thirty or forty formulae. So you become a technician in a certain way. Most Americans don't have that. What you learn in most schools, even a school like Juilliard at that time, are the rules of counterpoint instead of learning counterpoint, and the rules of harmony instead of learning harmony. But that's like reading a book on driving and not knowing how to get into a car. Technique and rules are not the same thing. Technique is a skill, and rules are a formulation based on analysis of past music. She taught technique as an acquirable skill.

DUCKWORTH: What do you think is the most important thing she taught you?

GLASS: Ultimately, all her training, I believe, was directed towards hearing. The great thing that she was involved with was independence of hearing. Now, independence wasn't a political slogan for her; it's being able to hear one voice independently of another, being able to play one voice independently of another. A Boulanger student began the day by playing a Bach chorale—playing three parts and singing the fourth. You did that four times, so that you sang all four parts and played the other three. And that was never done in a piano score. That was done in the open score with four clefs. So the day began with that.

DUCKWORTH: Were you a good student?

GLASS: I wasn't a particularly good student. But she bludgeoned you into . . . The dullest of us acquired some technique, I think. That is, if you did what she told you to do—if you actually did the exercises. If you proceeded intelligently and energetically in the direction that you were set on, you definitely acquired something. There were people that were marvelous at this and other people that weren't so good. To be marvelous at it did not mean that you were going to be the best composer. In fact, very few of the students were actually composers. And she didn't actually look at your music. You could show it to her, but she was more interested in your counterpoint. If you wanted to show her a piece, she would look at it, but her comments were much more careful. She had a great reverence for the creative spirit, even with her students. She would take anyone's work seriously, which was a great thing in a certain way. But you also learned very quickly that you would get more out of her by working with her on technique. A lesson spent on a piece was less valuable than ones done on harmony or counterpoint.

DUCKWORTH: Did you show her much of your music?

GLASS: No.

DUCKWORTH: None at all?

GLASS: Not after the first day. I discovered I had more to learn from her. I had had composition teachers before; I wasn't interested in opinions. Also, during the last year that I was studying with her, I began writing the music that I'm writing now. I'm convinced that she would have thought it was crazy. I was terrified of showing it to her. I was doing repetitive pieces that were basically about rhythmic construction. It had almost no harmony or counterpoint at all, which is what I had been studying with her. It wasn't long after that that I came back to play in Paris. My personal nightmare was that I would come out to do a concert and there would be Mlle Boulanger in the first row. She never was, but I was always afraid she would show up. I was told that she knew my music. Someone asked her and she said that she had heard *Einstein on the Beach*. But she would never make comments about a composer's work.

DUCKWORTH: Do you know why not?

GLASS: I think she was reluctant. As I said, she had such a reverence for the creative urgings and instincts that I think she was not inclined to put a damper on it. Though as a young composer I knew her as a teacher, I was not, on my side, inclined to show it to her. Also, you have to remember that in 1965 this work was in a very fragile state. I had not developed a body of work to support it, or the body of ideas that I knew it would eventually fit into. I was very much in the dark and very much working alone. I was very sensitive to criticisms in those first few years. There were few people that I could show it to. It was years before I really understood what I was doing.

DUCKWORTH: I know you had contact with Ravi Shankar while you were in Paris. Was he your first encounter with non–Western music?

GLASS: Yes, he was. That was also in 1965–66. And I think you have to place that in perspective. Ravi Shankar was not the big star that he became soon after the Beatles discovered him; they went to India in 1968–69. In the early days, you could hear Indian music— traditional music from other countries—in Paris, but not in the big concert halls. Ravi was the closest thing to a big star, but even he didn't have big audiences. The big audiences came with his discovery by American and English pop musicians. Not that it changed his playing. In my opinion, he was as wonderful a player afterwards as before. He was criticized by many people, but I've listened to his concerts over the years, and he's been a consummate artist the whole time.

DUCKWORTH: Did you immediately see connections between his music and your own work?

GLASS: Yes. The thing I learned from Ravi is that the rhythmic structure could become an overall musical structure. In our Western tradition that's simply not the case. Now, it's true that serial music has, in a sense, serialized music structures. But I would hardly call that a structural use of rhythm. There, rhythm is used in the way that timbre and pitch and other aspects are used. In the West, we have an alliance between harmony and melody. That's the basic alliance; rhythm comes along to liven things up. Let's pass over Stravinsky for the moment. That's a whole other subject and one that I didn't understand well at that time in my life. Had I, I might have looked at it differently; I might have come to that realization through a different route. But the non–Western music I knew was Ravi Shankar's music—the music of northern India, and later the music of southern India. There, the tension is between the melody and the rhythm, not between the melody and the harmony. I think that's a fairly accurate analogy to make. The moment that the *tala*, or the rhythmic structure, comes up and meets against the melodic structure at the *sum*—when the beats come together—that's the resolution in Indian music. The complications that that cyclic rhythmic structure can create, and the effects to the melodic development, open up a whole different way of thinking about music. And that's basically what I heard. I knew nothing like that in my own personal experience, or in any Western music that I knew.

DUCKWORTH: Well, you did mention Stravinsky a moment ago.

GLASS: Let me put it this way: with the music of northern India you could hear it immediately; it didn't require an analysis to understand it. To unlock the secrets of Stravinsky took more of an intellectual effort than I was prepared to make at that point in my life.

DUCKWORTH: Did you immediately start working with rhythmic structure?

GLASS: Oh, yes. I began in 1965, when I was still in Paris.

DUCKWORTH: What were those very early pieces like?

GLASS: They were very much like the pieces that you hear now, in a certain way.

DUCKWORTH: Can you describe one of them?

GLASS: One of the very first pieces was for a Beckett play. It was a piece for two saxophones. A guy named Jack Kripl, who still plays with me today, was in Paris on a Fulbright scholarship, and I hired him. I recorded him playing both parts. The first part alternated between two notes in a specific 7/8 rhythmic pattern. The second part was in a different pattern with a different two notes. The result was two overlapping rhythmic cycles that kept creating new rhythmic patterns as you listened to it. Of course, after a while they came together again. If one was in five and one was in seven, every thirty-five times you came back to the beginning. So I began to discover all of those things that make cyclic music of this kind interesting. I discovered there were two kinds of cyclic music: the kind where you combine cycles of an even length, and the kind where one overall cycle can contain all of the other cycles. That's the way it happens in India. What happens in Africa is different. There you can take three or four cycles and they may never, for all practical purposes, come out together. In the end, I became interested in Indian music, because those were the guys I was working with. But I didn't really understand it until 1967 when I began studying with Allah Rakha. However, that didn't prevent me from writing quite a lot of pieces between 1965 and 1967, when I was more or less stumbling along trying to figure this out for myself.

DUCKWORTH: Do you remember how you structured those very first reductive, repetitive works?

GLASS: I did those pieces in parts. There would be a sound recurring because of the overlapping rhythmic patterns. Then there would be a pause, and I would start a new one. Then a pause, and then a new one. I built the pieces out of these smaller sections. They were like a series of non sequiturs. And yet, what they had in common was that the overall structural thinking was the same. It formed the basis of this music for me. It was an imaginative beginning, considering I hardly knew what I was doing.

DUCKWORTH: How did your music at this point relate to Boulanger's teaching?

GLASS: It seemed at that moment that none of it was useful. Here I was, studying six-part counterpoint, and I wasn't writing counterpoint at all. The first appearance would be that I had taken my work with Boulanger and simply thrown it aside. I did not begin with what I learned from her; I began completely differently. Maybe in the end that was the best thing that could have happened. Had I tried to apply what she knew to my music, I would have ended up as a somewhat academic composer. What I did was something totally different that, in my experience, had no model. When I came back to New York, I discovered there were other composers working that way, which was a great relief I must say.

DUCKWORTH: Did you think that you were doing something . . .

GLASS: Totally original? Yes.

DUCKWORTH: . . . significant? Something you felt was important?

GLASS: Yes. I knew it was; that was a great help. I knew it was important, at least to me. And I saw right away that it was potentially an
alternate way of working. At that point, the dominant music of the
time was serial music. Living in Paris I could hardly not be aware of
that. And I was not at all interested in continuing in that tradition. I
considered it a very old way of looking at things. I was aware of the
fact that the people who had created the school were of the age of
my grandfather. It never occurred to me that they could be my contemporaries; it seemed obvious to me that they weren't! But it
wasn't obvious to anyone else. At the time that's what people did.
It's a very European idea though, isn't it? Ancestor worship. You get
more of this in Europe than in America. We don't go in much for
ancestor worship over here.

DUCKWORTH: We don't have many of them to worship before Ives.

GLASS: We don't, really. But Ives is such a humdinger. There was so
much in his music that it seemed to offer so many possibilities. The
closest thing to an American composer to me was John Cage,
because I knew his work. But the thing that troubled me with Cage
was that there seemed no way to follow him. That hardly prevented
several generations, thousands of people, from following him. But
it seemed to me that there was no way for *me* to follow him. On
the other hand, he presented an aesthetic that was interesting, and
a way of thinking about music that was extremely helpful. His ideas
had to do with other ideas that were all connected to creative art in
a general way—Duchamp, and Jasper Johns, and Rauschenberg,
and Merce Cunningham—which led me eventually to work in the
theater. My work in the theater had much more to do with Cage
and Cunningham than with any of the musicians I knew.

DUCKWORTH: How were those early Paris works received? Did you
get support for your music?

GLASS: I was lucky in that I was working with a theater company. It
was the Mabou Mines, the group that I worked with for the next
twenty years. So the music had a context. I wrote pieces for them.
One was that piece for the Beckett play. Another was a concert
piece for two of the actresses, one of whom I had married by that
time. A third was a chamber orchestra piece, and a fourth piece was
a string quartet. There may have been a few others.

DUCKWORTH: Do those pieces still exist? Are they available?

GLASS: The only one that I can lay my hands on is the string quartet. I don't know where those other pieces are. There may be a tape of the Beckett piece around. I'm more careless than most people about manuscripts. Now it doesn't matter; they're more or less taken care of for me. But I've lost a lot of pieces along the way. I don't pay much attention to them.

DUCKWORTH: What was your experience writing for the theater?

GLASS: The theater has always been a haven for progressive music. You can get away with murder in the theater because, first of all, the music critics don't go there. Then, too, the dramatic needs of a work can often justify experiments that you could never get away with in a concert hall. I don't doubt that it's for that reason that some of the great innovations occurred in the opera houses. You have only to think of Monteverdi, Mozart, and Wagner to prove the point. Or Alban Berg, for that matter, though I don't consider his operas that important, to tell the truth.

DUCKWORTH: Were you getting performances outside the theater?

GLASS: No. The rest of the Paris music world refused to play my music. Their reaction was simply, "This is madness; we shouldn't do it; you shouldn't write it." And that was the end of it; no one would play it. That's why I came back to New York in 1967. I couldn't find anyone but Jack Kripl and another guy, Daniel Lipton, to play the music. The French wouldn't play it; it made people very angry. It's hard to realize now, but twenty years ago people got angry, and they would lecture me and scold me for writing it. All through the first ten years, when I got into concert halls, people would throw things at us. People would start fights. That happened for years! People would get up and start violent confrontations during the concerts. It doesn't happen so much anymore. Now people get angry in the newspaper. But I don't read it anyway; it doesn't matter. So I went back to New York and I started my ensemble. I began working with people I had been to music school with.

DUCKWORTH: What was the musical environment like when you returned to New York?

GLASS: I didn't listen all that much to what other people were doing, though there were a lot of interesting composers at the time. There must have been a dozen composers who were writing in innovative ways. The thing that I find rather distressing is that in retrospect people always talk about the same three composers. But, in fact, it really wasn't like that. If you were in New York in 1967–68, it wasn't clear at all who the three important composers were. The way people look at that history is very skewed now. What was really going on was that there was a generation of composers who were in open revolt against the academic music world.

DUCKWORTH: Why do you think some of you became more well known than others?

GLASS: Some of us got singled out more than the others, and some of us got more famous than the others. To an extent, those are accidents of fate. But those are also a result of personal effort and ambition on the part of those people. I wanted to play for thousands of people; I was always interested in a larger audience. I saw that possibility from a very early age and I unswervingly set myself that goal. And as a result, I have a larger audience. It's very simple! When you write operas, clearly you are thinking about thousands of people and not hundreds.

DUCKWORTH: When you first began your ensemble, what were the problems?

GLASS: There was a core of players with whom I began playing in 1968, and in 1969 we did the first ensemble concert. It gelled very quickly. The difficulty was keeping the group together. Now, this is something that any composer will tell you: keeping the ensemble together is the hardest thing to do.

DUCKWORTH: How were you able to manage it?

GLASS: I made some shrewd and smart decisions at that time that made it possible. For one thing, I did not take a teaching job, which I never wanted to do. I had other work and I supported the ensemble by my jobs. After the first concert, I began paying people. Now, that was very hard to do; it usually meant that I never got paid myself. Also, I decided that I would let no one else play the music but the ensemble, because I felt that if I had a monopoly on the music, that as the music became known there would be more work for the ensemble. So for the next eleven years, the only people who played my music was the ensemble.

I set a goal for myself of twenty concerts a year—not at all an arbitrary number. If you do twenty concerts a year, you can then qualify as an employer who can take out unemployment insurance for his employees. What I could then offer my players was twenty weeks when I would pay them, and twenty-six weeks when they could get the money down at the unemployment office. The beautiful part of this was that I didn't need grants. I didn't need the approval of any other composer at all. By 1975 I was doing twenty concerts a year. I had discovered a way of living not only independently of the academic world, but also independently of the foundation world.

DUCKWORTH: Why did you want to be independent of foundation support?

GLASS: None of the new-music foundations would support my music. I applied eleven years for a Guggenheim and never got one. I never got money from the Martha Baird Rockefeller Foundation, the Mellon Foundation, or the Koussevitzky Foundation. List them. All the new-music people—zip! From the New York State Council on the Arts, the amounts I got were so small that I finally gave up applying; it wasn't worth the time. In retrospect, though, I think they were right. After all, they were there to help people who couldn't help themselves. In a way they forced me to survive on my own.

DUCKWORTH: How did you support yourself when the ensemble was first starting out?

GLASS: I did it in a variety of ways. I worked day jobs. These included furniture moving, plumbing, long-distance moving, and taxi driving. I always chose work of a temporary nature. The pattern of my life for many years was to tour with the ensemble for three weeks, then work for three or four months, usually paying off the deficits of the tour. That cycle went on for ten or eleven years. As a matter of fact, I worked day jobs until 1978, when I was forty-one. Then a Rockefeller grant plus a commission from the Netherlands Opera allowed me to concentrate on writing music.

DUCKWORTH: How do you feel, now that you can look back on it, about the built-in conflicts of a cycle like that?

GLASS: It's important to remember that it's common in New York for artists to go through "rites of passage" working like this. The garage I drove for was full of painters, writers, and other musicians. Some made it, and some are still there.

DUCKWORTH: By 1979, you were a successful opera composer. Why did you continue to keep the group together after that?

GLASS: By that point the group had been together over ten years, and they had become the best performers of the music. So I had a more important reason for keeping the ensemble together than my initial one. At first, they were the only people who *would* play it; then they became the best people who *could* play it. At this point we still do fifty concerts a year, which is a lot. It keeps me on the road twelve weeks a year; I only have forty weeks at home. But I'm not the only person of my generation who became a composer/performer. We really came back to the idea that the composer *is* the performer, and that's very, very valuable. For one thing, we became real people again to audiences. We learned to talk to people again. As a group we lost our exclusivity, the kind that had been built up through years of academic life. I personally knew that I didn't want to spend my life writing music for a handful of people. I just didn't think it was worth my time. Now, that's a very different way of looking at things.

DUCKWORTH: Do you have any idea why that change happened in your generation?

GLASS: My generation grew up in the late sixties. We all went through the cultural crises of the sixties. It was civil rights, pop music, and drugs; all over the Western world, many things changed. We saw our friends working in the field of popular music, living in a very connected way with their culture, and many of us wanted to have the same connection in our work. We wanted to be part of that world, too. It didn't mean writing popular music; that wasn't possible for people like myself. I have no training in it, and I have no inclination to do it. But it did mean that we saw the role of the artist in a much more traditional way—the artist being part of the culture that he lives in. We saw that happening to our friends, and we asked why they were having all the fun! It was something very simple like that.

DUCKWORTH: So it was a social and cultural phenomenon rather than a musical one?

GLASS: Very much so. It was easier for some people; some of us had more skills than others. For me to do it, I actually had to form an ensemble. I alone could not have done it. I was not an accomplished enough keyboard player. I did it through chamber music.

DUCKWORTH: When the ensemble first started, how did you actually put your pieces together with it? Did you begin with a finished score?

GLASS: Yes, I always did. I am out of the tradition of notated concert music. I handed out the parts, and we played them. I rarely made changes. Now, there could be a lot of changes later on, when we got involved with synthesizers. But in terms of the composition as such, my apprenticeship with Boulanger really served me well. I knew better than anyone what it sounded like. I rarely had to make changes of *that* kind.

DUCKWORTH: Do you keep up with synthesizer technology today?

GLASS: I don't read the technical magazines, but Kurt Munkacsi and Michael Riesman read them all the time. They have made available to me a world of technology that has kept the ensemble current with my work in a certain way. You can't expect a full-time composer to do that; you know how much time it takes.

DUCKWORTH: When did you actually begin making a living as a composer?

GLASS: At a certain point the ensemble, the operas, and various things became economically reasonable, though I was forty-one before I made a living at it. I was really helped by one major grant I got from the Rockefeller Foundation when Howard Klein was the head there. He gave three three-year grants to three artists: Bob Wilson, Sam Shepard, and me. That pushed me into the world of the self-supporting composer. I was just teetering on the edge of that when Howard gave me the grant. As usual, I used the money in a different way than most people would have. I used it to start my publishing company. I used half the money to copy music, to copyright it, and to make it available on tapes. I figured that if I could get the publishing company working, then I wouldn't have to work again. And it turned out to be true. In fact, you can make a living *and* you can do the music that you want; it takes a combination of a lot of different skills. Don't forget I began working in a record store when I was a kid. The first thing I knew about music was that you sold it; in other words, people paid for it.

DUCKWORTH: The new *Grove's Dictionary of American Music* calls you America's "most popular serious composer." How do you account for your popularity?

Philip Glass at his home studio, New York, 1988. Photo Credit: Paula Court

GLASS: There are a number of reasons. For one thing, I'm out there
    playing it all the time. Also, I tend to pick projects that get heard a
    lot; *Koyaanisqatsi* is a film that millions of people saw. I'm a great
    advocate of my own music. And don't forget the music: I make it
    available in a lot of ways. I would rather write an opera than a string
    quartet, because I'm interested in the theater. In the end, it hap-
    pens that more people will hear the opera, though, in fact, I actual-
    ly like to write string quartets. I've written three string quartets in
    the last few years. But I'm attracted to large-scale pieces, which is
    fortunate because that's one of the reasons why it's popular. I was
    talking to someone recently about this and I said very simply, "If
    you can write a piece for two hundred people or two thousand,
    why not write it for two thousand? I think it can be just as good."

DUCKWORTH: How do you feel about the extent of your popularity
    today? Do you have any worries about it?

GLASS: None at all. But you must realize there are different kinds. We
    have to be realistic about this. I can play for two thousand people; I
    don't play for twenty thousand. Every time Paul Simon plays a

concert, he does the stadiums. I don't play at stadiums; I play in concert halls. The people you could really compare me to, in terms of popularity, are, say, Wynton Marsalis or the Canadian Brass. We're not talking Bruce Springsteen; that's just silly. On the other hand, we're so unused to thinking even in terms of thousands, that the moment someone gets over a thousand we say, "Oh my God, it's popular!" And it's true. It's far greater than what would fit into Carnegie Recital Hall. But I'm a whole decimal point away from mass culture, and a decimal point in this business is all the difference there is. In my opinion, I will never play for more than two or three thousand people. That size audience isn't there. However, three thousand people is a good audience. In fact, my ensemble can do that regularly in major cities.

DUCKWORTH: What about your opera audiences?

GLASS: With the theater works, it's quite different. There you're talking about ten or twelve performances in a two-thousand seat house. But theater is different. It plays by different rules. I think it's silly to talk about mass audiences when all we're talking about is a couple thousand people. My most popular record has sold 200,000. If I were really a pop artist, I would have lost my contract with such few sales. I can be number one on the classical charts. But don't forget that's the classical charts; the numbers are very, very different. People who worry about my popularity truly don't understand what mass culture is. So I think we have to think about what we mean when we say culture. I am not uncomfortable with popularity; it doesn't bother me. I know that it makes some writers uncomfortable. But I enjoy selling out twelve performances of *Einstein on the Beach*.

DUCKWORTH: Do you think your music is misunderstood?

GLASS: No. I think it is by a handful of people, but in general, the people who go to my performances understand the music. Will Donal Henahan understand it? Who cares? I don't write for those people anyway. I discovered an interesting thing a couple of years ago. I discovered that the reviews did not affect my ticket sales and my record sales.

DUCKWORTH: What do you think the function of the critic is today?

GLASS: The critic does have a function in our society. He can be that middleman between the public that thinks Jackson Pollock was an idiot, and the artist who was pursuing his own vision. That person can be a valuable person. I think the function of criticism is a serious function. You have only to read the good criticism to realize that. I read George Bernard Shaw to learn about singing; his remarks about vocal writing are something that any composer can take to heart. So it's not a question of being above criticism. It's just like anything else, there are good composers and not so good composers; there are people who can make an omelette, and people who can't. Some critics have helped me; very few have actually hurt me. A critic can help a composer or an artist by supporting him, but they rarely destroy a career.

DUCKWORTH: So you don't pay attention to reviews at all?

GLASS: I don't read them at all. You know the old saying: "The good ones are never good enough, and the bad ones just make you angry."

DUCKWORTH: Do you compose every day now, or are you too busy?

GLASS: Yes, I have very good habits. I guess I learned them from Boulanger. I usually get up at six and work until noon, except the days when I'm on the road. The afternoons I spend at the studio. I spend every Tuesday afternoon talking to people; I have one day a week for that. I listen to music on the radio and I go out. I'll go to hear new work if I can, once or twice a week. Maybe not that much, actually.

DUCKWORTH: Do you work at the piano or away from it?

GLASS: I work both ways. The thing about operas is that you can't play them on the piano anyway. I write the operas as full orchestra scores and then I write piano reductions. I have someone else do that; I never do the reductions myself. Some people do the piano score and then orchestrate; you can do it either way. Since I was not originally a pianist, it's easier for me to work directly on the orchestration.

DUCKWORTH: What's the hardest thing about writing operas?

GLASS: The hardest thing for me to do is to hear the score in the way that the time really passes. I like to play the pieces in real time, but I can take a fourteen-minute scene and I'll read through it in eight minutes. You know, I can't get the time right. So in order to feel the time unfolding at the proper rate, I have to play it live. I also find that I enjoy playing it. But then again, I rarely can play all the parts. So I'll play some of the important parts, but there are many parts I can't play.

DUCKWORTH: Are you comfortable being known as a minimalist?

GLASS: Well, I haven't written any minimal music in twelve years. The difficulty is that the word doesn't describe the music that people are going to hear. I don't think "minimalism" adequately describes it. I think it describes a very reductive, quasirepetitive style of the late sixties. But by 1975 or '76, everyone had begun to do something a little bit different. Actually, the last holdouts are the Europeans. There are still minimalists in Europe, but not in America. So I think the term doesn't describe the music well. And if it doesn't prepare you at all for what you're going to hear, it's not a useful description.

DUCKWORTH: Is there a term you like better?

GLASS: Not particularly. Fortunately, it's not needed so much anymore. Usually people will say it's my music, or they will say, "Did you hear *Koyaanisqatsi*?" The style is easily described in terms of the music itself. It is concert music. I don't use bass drums or guitars. And it's in the tradition of notated music. It's basically chamber music that's amplified. I think that the diversity of contemporary music stands on its own in a certain way. I just did a solo concert—something I rarely do. No one in the audience seemed to think it needed any particular description.

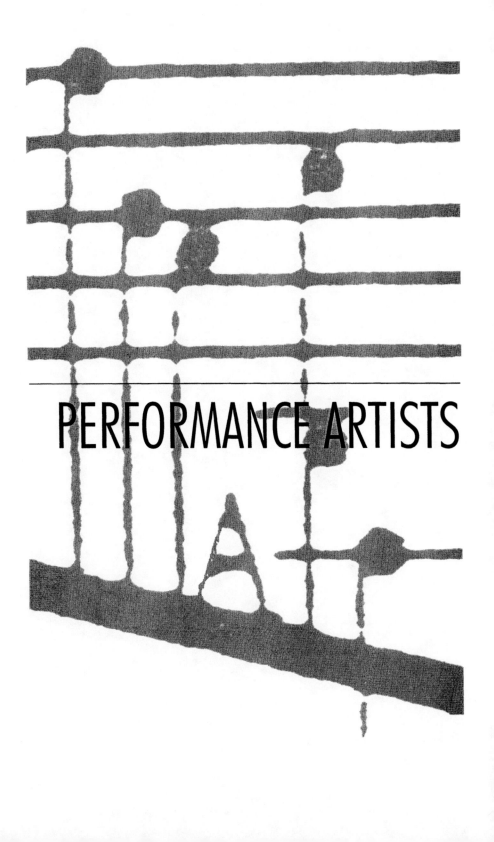

PERFORMANCE ARTISTS

CHAPTER 12

MEREDITH MONK

Born New York, 1942

Until the term "performance artist" came into general use in the mid-seventies, everyone had difficulty categorizing Meredith Monk. Did she sing, dance, or make films? Was she in music or theater? Nobody knew. Even as a performance artist, she occasionally defies description, writing huge music-theater pieces on the edge of opera, or small, intimate, wordless songs, about the universal feelings beyond words. She, of course, has no trouble labeling herself: "I am a composer," she says, adding that no matter what the medium, she always thinks in musical terms.

Monk grew up in an artistic family, at least on her mother's side. Her grandparents, who were from Russia and Germany, were both professional classical musicians. And her mother, a professional radio singer, sang many of the well-known commercials of the thirties and forties. Monk herself grew up in New York and Connecticut, in a family in which musical talent, as she says, was "taken for granted, in a way."

Meredith Monk went to Sarah Lawrence College, graduating in 1964. For a major, she chose a combined performing-arts program that allowed her to sing, compose, dance, and participate in theater nearly every day. Out of this experience, she says, came an insight into the possibility of a single form that would unite all her interests. Her first success beyond college was *16 Millimeter Earrings*, presented in New York in 1966. A theatrical collage involving music, movement, props, and film, it represented, for Monk, a "breakthrough." Three years later, her major large-scale music-theater cantata, *Juice*—a performance piece actively incorporating the environment of the location—was performed in three "installments" over a six-week period: at the Guggenheim Museum; the Minor Latham Playhouse at Columbia; and in an intimate downtown loft, giving, as Monk says, a zoom-lens effect to similar material.

From the mid-sixties to the mid-seventies, Monk worked primarily in a solo format, experimenting and forming a musical vocabulary. She describes it now as a deep investigation into the possibilities of her own voice as a solo instrument. In 1978, she established her own vocal ensemble, saying it was through her 1976 work, *Quarry*, which used a chorus, that she became interested in working with other singers. Her first major work for this group was *Dolmen Music*, from 1979. Monk considers all her large music-theater pieces to be operas. Works in this category, in addition to *Quarry*, include *Vessel: An Opera Epic* from 1971, *Education of the Girlchild* from 1972–1973, and *The Games*, a work from 1983 that deals rather darkly with survivors of a nuclear holocaust. While some critics consider these pieces operas, others argue that they belong more to the theater. In the early nineties, Monk wrote a work that everyone agrees is an opera: *Atlas*. A triple commission by the Houston Grand Opera, the Walker Arts Center, and the American Music Theater Festival, *Atlas* was premiered in Houston in early 1991, toured Europe later in the year, and returned to New York in the spring for a performance at the Brooklyn Academy of Music. Perhaps Monk has found another answer in her continuing search for uniquely integrated forms.

Meredith and I met on a cold January afternoon at her loft in downtown New York, a few blocks below Canal. A full floor in one of the smaller industrial spaces, it was sparsely furnished, a no-nonsense place in which to live and do some work. But on closer examination, there were personal touches, a few jade turtles, a vase, some lucky charms. Meredith herself seemed perfectly at home there, and the longer I stayed the more at home I felt, too. Finally, we settled at a table in the back by the kitchen. I decided to start with definitions.

DUCKWORTH: I've noticed that your reviewers don't seem to know what to call you these days. You're alternately a singer, a composer, a choreographer, and a theater person. The question it brings to my mind is: What do you call yourself?

MONK: I call myself a composer. Even if I'm working with musical theater or with images, I think of that as a kind of musical composition. I'm always thinking in musical terms, even with the images.

DUCKWORTH: Are you comfortable with the term "performance artist"?

MONK: That, in a sense, covers more of the musical-theater branch of my work. But I always say that it's nice that that term was invented,

Meredith Monk performing "The Games," Brooklyn Academy of Music, New York, 1984. Photo Credit: Paula Court

because now I can tell a cab driver in a few words what I do, whereas I used to have to go through hours and hours of explanation.

DUCKWORTH: Did you always have an idea in your mind about the kind of work you wanted to do?

MONK: When I was at Sarah Lawrence, I was taking a combined performing-arts program. I was singing every day, doing musical composition, and doing vocal chamber music. I was also in the dance department, taking dance classes and dance composition, and I was taking a few theater courses. I did have a glimpse of making pieces that combined music, theater, and dance in one form. So I started working in that way, on a small scale, when I was in school.

DUCKWORTH: Did you come from a musical family?

MONK: Yes, and I always wanted to be a musician. My mother was a singer on the radio, and sometimes she did commercials. She was the original Muriel Cigar girl, and she sang "DUZ Does Everything." This was before they had tape, you know, so she was coming in every day and singing Royal Pudding, Bluebonnet Margarine, things like that. She was also in that variety-show format where she would sing a ballad or sing the song of the week. I'm thinking of the *Prudential Hour* or *The Big Show*, from the thirties, forties, and fifties. I grew up in radio studios and radio control rooms when I was a child.

DUCKWORTH: I understand your mother's stage name was Audrey Marsh. Did that name have any particular significance?

MONK: I actually don't know how she got that name. She just recently told me how she ended up singing rather than acting, because she started out as an actress. When she was sixteen, she was on the road and she used to sing at parties. And people would say, "Oh, you have such a great voice." Then a friend of hers went to one of those music publishers that had a man who would play the piano and rehearse people so that they could sing the songs of the publisher correctly. So her friend went to work with one of these guys who was smoking a cigar, and was really bored and chomping away. And since she was there she said, "Well, would you try one with me?," and she started singing. And by the time she finished singing the song the guy said, "I've got to get the head of the publishing house to hear you. Where do you come from?" And she went, "I live uptown." You know, she was completely green. So the publisher came down, she sang, and they signed her immediately. Then they took her across town to CBS and they signed her there. It's sort of like a Cinderella story, but she never told me that all these years.

DUCKWORTH: Was she a model for you when you were young? Did you see yourself doing something similar?

MONK: In some ways it was hard to be around, because it was hard to see how dependent a person is, in that commercial world, on other people. She was very successful for a certain time. But in the commercial world things come and go pretty quickly, and I think that as I watched that happening to her, I realized that I wanted to have a little bit more control over my own life. And I always had some kind of instinct about wanting to create. Even as a kid, I always enjoyed making things.

DUCKWORTH: Didn't you have other relatives who were classical musicians?

MONK: Yes, my grandfather was a concert bass-baritone who came from Russia, and his wife was a concert pianist. And my mother always had a very fine classical voice. That was the thing about her; she was extremely versatile. She could do crooning kinds of things and she also had what they called the "legit" kind of sound for ballads.

DUCKWORTH: Was your father musical?

MONK: My father's family is not really musical. His sister was an actress, but they were a carpenter family; they came from Poland. But my mother's whole family are musicians. Her brother has a piano store. That just was part of their background, as it was mine, and kind of taken for granted, in a way.

DUCKWORTH: Were you precocious? Did they immediately recognize talent in you?

MONK: I don't know if they recognized it or they decided I was going to have it, I'm not sure. But I was singing back melodies very early, and I was reading music at three or four.

DUCKWORTH: Were you dancing, too?

MONK: I was doing Dalcroze eurhythmics, which is a movement discipline. It's a combination of music and movement—a rhythmic way of teaching music. A lot of conductors take it so that they're more flexible in their bodies. For me it was a perfect way of getting moving because I was not very coordinated as a child. I had a very good sense of rhythm, and music was always very natural for me, so it was a smart thing of my mother to send me to those classes. I remember loving those classes because it really was a combination of the body and music. Because I started so early with putting those two things together, I think that I've always kept them together. That sense of the body in the singing . . . it's something that I still believe in very strongly; there's no separation.

DUCKWORTH: When did you actually decide to be a musician?

MONK: I think that throughout my whole childhood music was second nature to me. I don't think that I made a particular decision. I wanted to be an opera singer when I was about ten. I wanted to sing the tenor parts, though; I was really disappointed that I couldn't do that. And there was a certain period of time that I was concentrating more on movement, because I think that it was hard to have a mother who was such a prodigious singer. I'm sure there was a very competitive kind of thing in the house and it was hard for me to get my territory, so I withdrew a little bit. At Sarah Lawrence I was studying and I was singing lieder, but I knew that that was not right for me. I wanted to really make my own way. So when I did start making my *own* vocal music, I had a very strong sense of coming home. I had found something that was really right for me. I had that sense that it was really natural for me and that it was almost like my blood said to do it.

DUCKWORTH: Had your work with movement not been as rewarding as you had wanted it to be?

MONK: Movement was always very hard for me. In a way, I had to find my own ways of doing it because it was so difficult. That was a good discipline to build up, and it has continued in my work in one way or another. I think that all of us have to figure out some way to build strength and endurance in our minds to keep going year after year. I think I learned a lot about discipline because I was fighting a lot in dance to find my own way because it was very hard for me. I always had a natural instrument with voice. I had a wide range and singing was always something that was very easy for me. So after having struggled a lot and then coming back to singing, I think that I got the appreciation that because I had an instrument to work with, I could use that discipline to stretch it and to find things.

DUCKWORTH: Do you remember when you first discovered twentieth-century music?

MONK: You know, I remember hearing *The Rite of Spring* when I was about twelve. I was up in camp and I remember just being so blown away and so moved by it. I just couldn't believe it. It was amazing.

DUCKWORTH: Once you discovered it, did you listen to it a lot?

MONK: At Sarah Lawrence, I would go to the music library and take huge piles of things and listen to everything. One of my teachers was Ruth Lloyd, the wife of Norman Lloyd, who was the dean at Oberlin and head of the Rockefeller Foundation for a while. She was a fantastic pianist. And one of the assignments that she gave in a music history class was to listen to a kyrie eleison that different composers had written, all the way from Palestrina through Stravinsky. So you were hearing how each of these composers throughout music history had set that same text. And I remember it was as if the whole world opened for me. So I would go to the library and take these huge piles of records. I thought I would listen to every record while I was there at Sarah Lawrence. And I remember the first time I ever heard Henry Cowell . . . those piano pieces. I was about nineteen, and I just could not believe these pieces, you know. Then I looked at the back of the album and they were written in 1919. I mean, it was so long ago, but it was so radical. They're just stunning. I feel like he's such an important person.

DUCKWORTH: When you started really listening to twentieth-century music, which composers made the biggest impression on you?

MONK: Well, Henry Cowell was one person, Stravinsky and Bartók; I loved the *Mikrokosmos*. Those three really made a big difference to me at that time.

DUCKWORTH: Did you listen to popular music in high school and college?

MONK: Oh yes, sure.

DUCKWORTH: Who did you listen to?

MONK: Well, after I left college, the Beatles were really important to me, because I felt that a lot of what they were doing was very close to what we were doing in the arts. There wasn't so much of a separation then between the arts and what was going on in the popular music world at that time. In high school, I was listening to people like the Everly Brothers and Little Richard. I even remember pre–rock and roll, like Georgia Gibbs, but that was when I was really small. And I remember when rock and roll came in. I remember "Rock Around the Clock" on the radio. And Elvis . . . I remember "Heartbreak Hotel." I thought that was just a totally beautiful song in those days. And it was an interesting time for me to grow up, because while that was a rite of passage for me, it was also, because rock and roll was coming in, a change of world.

DUCKWORTH: Did the idea of being a composer first occur to you during college?

MONK: I went to college with the intention of keeping up my music, my dancing, and my theater. I didn't know what was going to happen at the end of that time; I just knew that I was keeping up the interest that I had. And it was during college that I started making pieces, and getting a glimpse of a composite form where all these things could be unified.

DUCKWORTH: Did you get performances of your work at Sarah Lawrence?

MONK: Oh, yes.

DUCKWORTH: And encouragement?

MONK: I got a lot of encouragement. I had a wonderful teacher, Bessie Shöenberg, who was a real inspiration. Sarah Lawrence is very geared to the individual person. Usually, they trust that you can take the responsibility for your own education—that you have the discipline to do that. And I think that people who have trouble at that school don't know what they want. But I was very willful and intense. And Bessie Shöenberg knew, with certain people, when she had to pull in the reins and when she could let them out. And I think with me, she knew she could let out the reins. She knew I needed to have space to explore and that I would come out with something. So she was incredibly encouraging. And I felt that by the time I left Sarah Lawrence I was an experienced performer, because I did do a lot of performing there. So I had that twenty-one-year-old, arrogant sense of confidence, which you learn very soon to diminish a little bit.

DUCKWORTH: I'd like to talk about two of your earlier works. Am I correct in thinking that *16 Millimeter Earrings* was a very important early piece for you?

MONK: I think it was a real breakthrough piece because, at last, I was able to find a form. It was really a kind of composite musical-theater piece that included film, images, and a very complex sound score that I did for four tape recorders. The sound was cumulative material that would turn into a loop at a certain time, until finally, there were three loops going on at the same time. Then that went down and something else came in. It was really like a complicated sound environment that I had done. That was the first piece that I really did a lot of singing in, too, and the first piece in which I did film. It had a sense of unity, even though there were a lot of means within one piece. It was woven together in a way that involved a kind of multiperceptual experience for the audience, and required a performer to have a multidimensional performing style that utilized all their resources in as full a way as possible. So that was really the beginning of that branch of my work.

DUCKWORTH: Is that piece in any way autobiographical? I think I remember once seeing it referred to as an "autobiographical collage."

MONK: I don't think that that's what I was thinking about. If I look at a film of that piece now, to me it looks like a young woman's rite of passage into adulthood. That's the sense of it, a real archetypal rite of passage. It was a piece in which I was using, in a sense, myself as material. I was very objective about it, though, so it wasn't really autobiographical. It was more that my hair was material, and my singing with a guitar was material. It was personal in a way that I let myself use myself—anything that I had—as material. But then it was made into a piece of poetry, because it was extremely objectified. It wasn't like some of the work that's being done now, where people are writing monologues about their lives.

DUCKWORTH: The other early work of yours I'm curious about is *Juice*. What kind of piece was that?

MONK: *Juice* was a piece that had three different performance locations. At that time, I was exploring the idea of doing performance pieces that transcended the usual situation of coming to the theater at 8:30, getting your ticket, and then going out for coffee afterwards. I was very interested in thinking about stretching that, so that it was a different ritual. So *Juice* took place in three different locations over a month-and-a-half period of time. The audience got one ticket that let them come to all three installments—I called them installments.

DUCKWORTH: Where was the first installment held?

MONK: The first one was done at the Guggenheim Museum. It had a chorus of eighty-five people singing, a score for violin, and solo singers or movers. The audience was sitting down at the bottom of the museum on the floor, while the piece took place on the ramps, with a 360-degree field of vision. And in a sense, it also used the building as the material, because I was thinking a lot about architecture in those days. There was even a section where those eighty-five people ran down the ramps against the spiral, making it look like the building was spinning. And you heard the sound of those footsteps, so it had a sense of making the building come alive. That was the feeling of that piece. Also, you could say it had a kind of supernatural feeling, almost like a cathedral. It had a very spiritual quality to it, because of those big choral things . . . people singing perfect intervals. And it had that real ritualistic kind of quality. You'd be sitting down at the bottom, and you'd see arms coming over the side of the ramp, and you'd hear a sound. They'd sing one note when they were out of sight, and they'd sing another note as they came to the ramp. And you were getting this happening from all different sides. Also, against that wave kind of movement of sound and chorus, there were solo characters—four people painted red from head to toe (I was one of them). Our journey was to go up the ramp little by little. And at each level there would be a musical interlude that we would do. So there was that movement. Then, there were other solo figures. My sister did a Jew's harp solo, another woman sang a song, and my mother and two of her cohorts from the commercial singing world sang one of my pieces.

DUCKWORTH: Was all of this happening simultaneously?

MONK: No. It was very woven together.

DUCKWORTH: So it didn't resemble a happening?

MONK: No, no. It was very, very structured—very cleanly structured—so that the audience's attention would go to a certain part of the building and then to another part, together. There was also another thing that was happening simultaneously with those other activities. That was three women who were in different period costumes, stacked up on one ramp, and the next ramp, and the next ramp, and they were just slowly rotating. So that became, in a sense, a kind of visual drone for the other things that happened. That was going on simultaneously because it was very slow movement that they were doing. So that was the first installment.

DUCKWORTH: Let's see, that was 1969. You had only been out of college five years. How did you convince the people at the Guggenheim to put on a production like that?

MONK: I had done work. I mean, I had done *16 Millimeter Earrings*, and I had done a solo concert over at what later became the Fillmore East. So I had an audience. And I had also done the Billy Rose Theatre (which was a big "scandal" in 1969), where they had these four—what they called—avant-garde artists doing pieces up at a Broadway house. The other three were Yvonne Raider, Twyla Tharp, and Don Redlick. So there was a kind of notorious thing involved there, even though that experience had made me miserable. And I don't know if this always happens, but sometimes, when you *really* know what you want, I don't know whether I would have done anything, but I was really going to get that building. It was like life and death for me at that time. So, basically, I went in and talked to this guy Robin Green. And there were many, many obstacles that he had to getting it done, but we both worked on it and it worked out.

DUCKWORTH: Where did the other two parts of *Juice* take place?

MONK: The second part took place at the Minor Latham Playhouse at Columbia. The whole idea of *Juice* was like a kind of zoom lens in, so that things became much more compressed as the three installments went on. There were less people in it and you were more intimate with those people. And some of the same material that had happened in the installment before was used in a variation, so you'd have that kind of sense of memory. That was something that I was very interested in: could you have a piece, where you also had the resonance of the past, as well as what you were seeing in the present, be part of it? So there were these different juxtapositions of images. For example (this is a very simple one): at the Guggenheim, I had somebody on horseback riding outside the museum; then in front of the Minor Latham, I had somebody riding a hobby horse; and then in the loft section, which was the last section, there was a tiny figurine of a horse in the room that the audience sat in. So, you know, there was like a scale change. Another example occurred with the four red people. In the Guggenheim, they were only one part of a huge pagent, but in the Minor Latham, they were the four main characters, so you got closer to those four red people. The quality of the music in the Minor Latham piece was also more raw and funky, you could say. We were wearing these big red boots, and as part of the sound score there was the sound of the boots on the floor—rhythmic stamping and stuff like that, almost a percussion track. So everything was pulled in and compressed. Unlike the Guggenheim, which had a sense of expanse—a big choral and airy kind of quality—the Minor Latham had a much more earthy kind of quality.

DUCKWORTH: You mentioned the loft section. What was the third installment like?

MONK: The third part of *Juice* was done a week after the Minor Latham. That was a closeup videotape of those four people in red; you just saw their faces on the screen. It was like a kind of installation, with all the props and costumes from the other two installments. So there were eighty-five white costumes, eighty-five pairs of red combat boots, the four red costumes, eighty-five Jew's harps, and various and sundry other things. In the Minor Latham Playhouse there was a little room in the back of the stage, and in the loft, that became a room that the audience sat in and watched the videotape. And the irony to that piece was that while you got closer to those four red people, there were no actual human beings in that installment of the piece; it was an installation. So I think that I was very interested in scale, and very interested in performer/ audience relationships—you know, if they got close to an image, that would be one thing; if they were far away from an image, that would be something else. What angle they saw things, where sound was coming from in relationship to the audience, all the different things that could be done with that idea of flexible space and sound.

DUCKWORTH: That all sounds pretty ambitious. Where did the idea for a piece like that come from?

MONK: I was thinking about environment a lot at that time. I had done some other large-scale pieces in 1969 at the Smithsonian and a few other places, and I think that *Juice* was a culmination of that kind of thinking—the idea of using large-scale: large numbers of people doing a ritual in a large building, and using the building as the environment.

DUCKWORTH: What was the critical response like?

MONK: Oh, *Juice* was very well received. It was a big piece that I had been working on for a long time—maybe two years—and it was very well received.

DUCKWORTH: There are obviously some exceptions, but, in general, is it accurate to say that between the mid-sixties and the mid-seventies your primary interest turned to solo vocal work?

MONK: Yes. In a sense, I was using my own instrument to experiment with. I was just forming my vocabulary and I wasn't ready to explain to somebody what I was doing, enough to work with a group.

DUCKWORTH: How would you describe your own voice and what you can do with it?

MONK: I'm working with as many possibilities of coloration as possible (even within a short piece), and trying to stretch my range, and trying to use different kinds of resonances to get sound that has some kind of centralized emotional quality to it.

DUCKWORTH: Do you really have a four-octave range?

MONK: No, I have about three. On a good day, I have about E♭ below middle C to E♭ above high C. I can scream higher, but that's about my working range.

DUCKWORTH: You're known for having a wide variety of "voices" that
you can draw on. How did you develop that?

MONK: What happened to me was that I started working alone, and I
didn't really have any references except that I wanted to make my
voice as flexible as my hand could be. And I wanted to find a vocabulary that was built on my own instrument, the way that a choreographer finds movement built on their own instrument. I basically
was working with my own instrument, and seeing what it could do,
and finding character or different kinds of vocal textures and things
like that. I did my first concert of straight music in 1970 at the
Whitney. It was called "A Raw Recital." And a number of people
came back afterwards and said, "Have you ever heard Balkan
music?" And I said, "No, I never have. What is Balkan music? Where
is Balkan?" And they'd say, "Well, you use glottal break a lot in what
you're doing, and they use that in their music. You should listen to
it. Go to the Nonesuch *Explorer Series*." And I would listen to it
and go, "Oh, that's just gorgeous. It's fantastic." And what I started
realizing was that when you're working with the vocal instrument,
you come upon certain things that are archetypal human sounds
that transcend culture. It's kind of like either it's in a culture—you
can learn it from hearing another music—or you can learn it in
your own voice. It's a little like ontogeny and phylageny; the course
of development in an individual is contained in the history of a
group and vice versa. There are universal vocal sounds that you just
come upon as you're working on expanding your own vocal
palette. At the same time, each person's vocal apparatus is totally
unique, so there are certain things, for example, that members of
the ensemble do that I can't quite figure out, and there are certain
things that I do that they can't quite get exactly. Those are the
things that have much more to do with the personal vocal apparatus. At the same time, we all share a common, cross-cultural huge
palette of archetypal sounds that people in the world that sing have
in common. And that's a wonderful combination of things, and it's
kept me captivated all these years.

DUCKWORTH: Do you have what you would call a classically trained
voice?

MONK: Yes, I do. And I still train classically.

DUCKWORTH: Do you practice every day?

MONK: I try to, because I have to really build myself up if I'm singing night after night. And I find that the classical technique, for maintenance, seems like the most basic way of getting the whole breathing and vocal apparatus going.

DUCKWORTH: Were there any voices that influenced you, that you patterned yourself on?

MONK: Well, one of the very early influences was Janis Joplin, around '68. I had done a lot of work for maybe four or five years, and I was in a kind of transitional period. I had gotten a little bit conceptual with what I was doing and I realized that that was not a good direction for me. And there was something about Janis Joplin—that kind of gut, primal quality of hers (juicy, I could say)—that really made me want to start working again. And I realized why: she did not have any preconceived sense of beauty. That's what I liked; it was her own kind of beauty. She was a really excellent musician. I mean, her phrasing is amazing.

DUCKWORTH: The two people who come to my mind in connection with your voice are Laura Nyro and Joni Mitchell.

MONK: Really? That's amazing. I like both of them as singers very much, but I would never think of myself as in that tradition at all.

DUCKWORTH: I don't mean that tradition; I mean the voice quality.

MONK: Well, I love both of them. I think Laura Nyro is a wonderful singer. I wasn't aware of Joni Mitchell until maybe after I had been working a few years, but I used to love her. Thank you very much. That's a real compliment.

DUCKWORTH: How do you find all the different voices that you use? Is it trial and error?

MONK: In a way, yes. It's very instinctive. In each song, I'm looking for *the* voice, you know. And I'm very much interested that each song have a very particular kind of character. I don't mean "character" in a literal sense necessarily, but that it, in a way, creates a world in itself. So I'm always trying to find new ones. I don't want to hear a voice that I've done before. I want to try to find another one.

DUCKWORTH: Does it get harder or easier?

MONK: I think that it gets harder, because you have a lot of baggage that you're carrying with you, and you don't want to just do your same habits.

DUCKWORTH: So much of your singing is wordless. For what you're trying to do, do words get in the way?

MONK: In a way they do. I've always thought of the voice as a language itself. So if I hear English at the same time as I hear the voice, I think of that as two languages. If I do use language—something like the words "scared" and "running scared" in *Scared Song*—it's as much a sound texture as it is a text. That's why those are the only words in the whole song. Usually, if I do use text, it will be very simple, and it will be there as much for the sound of it as for the meaning. I also think that music, itself, is such an evocative medium. It's very openhearted. And I don't like the idea that people have to work through the screen of language. For example, if you see *La Comédie Francaise* and you don't know French that well, you have to wade through language. Language, in a way, is a screen in front of the emotion and the action. I like the idea of a direct communication that bypasses that step so that you're really dealing with a very primary and direct emotion; I think music can do that. Also, I think of the voice as an instrument and instrumentals usually don't have words. So it gives me a little more freedom.

DUCKWORTH: Do you think of your songs as having any ethnic characteristics? I'm thinking particularly of the recording of *Key*, which, the first time I heard it, I thought of as ethnic music for a nonexistent country.

MONK: Or folk music from another planet.

DUCKWORTH: Is that a conscious direction that your work takes?

MONK: I think, in those days, I was really thinking more of just working with what my own instrument could do. I was trying not to rule out anything, and that included sounds that you might associate with ethnic or folk music.

DUCKWORTH: I hear a lot of pain in your early vocal pieces. Am I just reading that in, or do you think it's there too?

MONK: I haven't listened to *Key* in a long time; I'd like to hear it again. But I think that as it has gone along, the music has become much more refined. And I also think that I wanted to have that edgy, raw energy in those days. I'd back off a lot from, you know, "beauty." But as you get older, you realize that expression has a much wider possibility, and warmth and beauty are fine.

DUCKWORTH: You've recently been giving solo concerts again; I'm thinking of the Town Hall concert in late 1988 in particular. With all of your success with your ensemble, why do you feel the need to do solo concerts at this point in your career?

MONK: I felt that for my growth right now I needed to go back to myself, and the simplest form that I could have, which was unaccompanied voice. That's a cyclical thing that I seem to need to do every few years—to get back to my own instrument and vocabulary as a base and find out more about that. Then when I work with other people, I have some new resources. But I was shaking in my boots, I'm gonna tell you. Once I got out there I wasn't, but I had to really fight a lot of resistance in myself to do that. I felt vulnerable, let's put it that way.

DUCKWORTH: When you start a new piece, how do you begin?

MONK: Sometimes I sit at the piano. Sometimes I have a vocal line or a vocal texture in my head. Sometimes I just sit and something happens. It depends. There's not a rule for it.

DUCKWORTH: Do you try to compose every day?

MONK: I try to, in some way or another. I always feel better when I'm not in New York—somewhere like the MacDowell Colony—where I can really have a regular work period every day. And just to have the luxury of that kind of time, with no telephone calls and everything else you have to deal with, is incredible. It's a little harder in New York to be that regular with things like what time of day I'll work, or something like that, but I try to work as regularly as possible.

DUCKWORTH: Do you know where your ideas come from? What generates a song?

MONK: Different things for different songs. Sometimes it will be a technical problem that I want to try. I'm thinking, for example, about a part of *Dolmen Music* where I was really interested in seeing whether you could do a whole piece about vibrato. Other pieces come from sitting at the piano. I might find a base for something, keyboardwise, and then I find a voice that has the right character for what I'm doing with keyboard. Or sometimes, I'll just be here in the studio walking around, trying different kinds of vocal things, letting myself free-associate. I try not to make any kind of judgment about it; whatever my voice wants to do I just let it do.

DUCKWORTH: In general, when you get an idea, does it come to you fully formed, or is it a seed that needs to be nurtured?

Meredith Monk performing "Do You Be," New York, 1987. Photo Credit: Paula Court

MONK: Mostly, it's a seed that has to grow.

DUCKWORTH: In the late sixties and early seventies, did you consider yourself part of the downtown avant-garde movement that was flourishing in lower Manhattan?

MONK: I was part of the community, in a sense. There were a lot of people from very different backgrounds working in different media at that time.

DUCKWORTH: Who did you feel closest to?

MONK: People like Peter Schumann, the founder of the Bread and Puppet Theater, and some of the visual artists. I wasn't aware of Steve Reich and Phil Glass until around 1970, but when I heard their music I appreciated it very much. And La Monte Young. I'll always remember La Monte because I went to one of his pieces in the mid-sixties, and they were playing a drone that you could hear throughout the whole building. You had to sign a piece of paper that they did not take responsibility for your state of mind after you had been in there for a while. I thought that was incredible. I remember that I went there feeling kind of headachy, and left, after about three hours of listening to a drone, feeling much better.

DUCKWORTH: That sense of a downtown community seems to have dissipated in the eighties. Has it been replaced by anything?

MONK: I think that people have gone in their own directions. And in a sense, you can say that there's a little bit more feeling of isolation, ironically so, because there are more people working now. But that might also be part of it. There are so many people working and everybody is having such a hard time surviving, that it's more like pockets of activity today.

DUCKWORTH: When you're in New York, what's a normal day like for you?

MONK: I'll get up. I eat my breakfast. Sometimes I sit. (I've been doing a meditation practice for a few years.) Then I'll use the morning to do my vocal exercises, my piano practice, and also some physical exercises. Then I'll spend the afternoon on creative work, like doing the compositions. That would be an ideal day for me.

DUCKWORTH: When you first started, how did you support yourself?

MONK: I modeled for painters and I taught classes for children in music and dance.

DUCKWORTH: When were you able to give up that kind of work?

MONK: Let's see, I think around the early seventies. In the early seventies I taught my own workshops in my own studio, so I didn't go out and teach children's classes anymore. People came to my studio. Maybe the mid-seventies was when I started doing a little bit more touring.

DUCKWORTH: How much touring do you do now?

MONK: It depends on the year. I would say about three or four months out of the year.

DUCKWORTH: And out of that are you able to support yourself for the rest of the year?

MONK: With a lot of safety pins and Scotch tape, because I have a whole company of people, and I have a foundation, so there are all kinds of things that we do. That's one way of earning money. And in some ways it makes things difficult because you're carrying a big organization on your back. On the other hand, it makes everything that we do possible. If I didn't have that, I would be sitting at the typewriter hours a day, doing a lot of business things. I mean, I participate in my business, but I don't have to do every single letter that goes out about booking and things like that. That takes a lot of time and energy.

DUCKWORTH: I hadn't thought about this before, but it's really just your generation that went that route, isn't it? The composers before and after have not generally established their own foundations.

MONK: What are they doing?

DUCKWORTH: They're doing club dates.

MONK: Well, we do that also. We do everything to try to survive.

DUCKWORTH: Yes, but they don't have a foundation. Apparently, they haven't felt they needed or wanted it, or something.

MONK: Well, I can understand it. I remember at a certain point, around 1980, I felt that I could go in one direction or another. I thought perhaps I should go out and be a soloist, try to do things from a more commercial standpoint. I mean, no grants, no organization; just go out there and put your body on the line, which I do anyway. But I think what changed my mind at that time was that I do like to work with other people and it's very hard to do that without an organization.

DUCKWORTH: Was there a specific point where you decided that you needed to expand your work to include an ensemble, rather than just continuing to do solo work?

MONK: In 1976, when I did *Quarry*—because I needed a chorus of about twenty-eight people—I met a lot of wonderful young people who were good singers. And I did big choral pieces for them that were pretty complex. I decided then that it would be really interesting to work with other singers, in such a way that each of the parts would be as complicated as what I did. Instead of me being a soloist and them a backup group, I was really interested in making music that had four or five very complex parts. So my first ensemble was Andrea Goodman, Monica Solem, Susan Kampe, and me. I worked on a piece called *Tablet* with them, which I had done as a solo in 1974, but I really orchestrated that piece and made it more complicated.

DUCKWORTH: Why didn't your first ensemble have any men in it?

MONK: I guess it was natural for me to start with women's voices first, because I knew more about them . . . you know, the range and everything. I felt more confident in making complicated parts for female voices. Then in 1978, I started meeting people like Robert Een and Paul Langland, and started thinking about doing *Dolmen Music*, which I knew instinctively needed both men's and women's voices. Then, through Rhys Chatham I met Julius Eastman. I needed a bass, so I called him up and he became the bass in *Dolmen Music*. Since he was a composer himself, he was a very supportive colleague in the process of working on *Dolmen Music*, as were the other members of the ensemble.

DUCKWORTH: Do you think of your ensemble works as operas?

MONK: I have always called my big musical-theater pieces operas. I called *Education of the Girlchild*, *Vessel*, and *Quarry* operas. I think of *The Games* as a kind of opera or musical-theater piece. So "opera" is something that I have called my work for a long time, because I think of it as a composite form that includes music, theater, and dance. It's a theatrical form that has music as a primary element, but all those other elements of drama and movement are in it. So to me, "opera" is a wonderful word because it means overall work of some kind; that's why I've used that term.

DUCKWORTH: Do you think you're working in traditional genres, or are you branching out and discovering new ones?

MONK: I would like to think that I'm discovering new ones because that always gives me a lot of delight. Also, I always feel that what I try to do in my work is to offer to an audience new ways of seeing or hearing things that they might take for granted. So that when you leave, you might go out in the street and experience it in a new way because you've opened up certain kinds of perceptions or feelings in the concert. Each piece is a different balance of elements; I like to think that I'm starting from scratch each time. In some ways, that makes it very hard because I don't have anything that I can take for granted myself. So it's a mystery to me, when I start, what it's going to be. It also makes, my process slower than some people who already know what they're doing before they start. But I like the risk of that and it keeps me interested.

DUCKWORTH: How frequently do you rehearse with your ensemble?

MONK: It depends. If we're working on a new piece, we'll work every day. Over the year we have a certain number of tours and we'll always rehearse before that.

DUCKWORTH: Do you ever bring ideas from myths and legends into your ensemble work, or are you really starting from zero everytime you develop a piece?

MONK: In a sense I'm starting from zero, but I like the idea of making music that has a mythic quality or dimension. I don't think of a particular myth, but I like the way that myth itself is a way of translating the world that we live in into a different dimension that everybody can participate in.

DUCKWORTH: You know, one thing that interests me is that a fair amount of your work deals with some of the most fundamental problems of the twentieth century. I'm thinking in particular about *The Games*, which deals with survivors of a nuclear holocaust. What kind of a contribution do you think an individual artist is capable of making to a problem that's so universal, so large?

MONK: I think that anything that we can do to make people more aware is important. I do a lot of thinking about what an artist can do in the society. Sometimes, if I see homeless people out on the street, I think, "Maybe I should be working in a shelter for the homeless; maybe that's a more useful way to spend a life." I wonder sometimes about the validity of a person who's forced to deal with their own survival going to a piece of art; I don't know, exactly, how essential that would be. But I do think that it's very important that we artists keep working, because what we do is not covered by anything else. There are certain things that technology does very well—certain kinds of information that comes across on technology—and it feeds certain parts of human beings. But I think that the heart and soul are not covered that much, and that art can do that. Art can be an affirmation of human life, and an alternative to certain kinds of behavior. After doing *The Games*, I did *Specimen Days* and *Turtle Dreams Cabaret*. All of those pieces have to do with a certain kind of apocalyptic vision. In a certain sense, they state the problem of the society. And yes, it's good that people are made aware of it. But I think that the next step has to do much more with offering a behavioral alternative as a sort of microcosm of what could be possible. John Cage always used to say that what art can provide is a behavioral alternative in nonmanipulative situations. I think that's what I really enjoy about doing the music with the ensemble (and doing the music alone as well), because it's such a direct communication to the audience, and with the ensemble . . . just to see people working together, the way that the ensemble does, with so much caring and energy. In a sense, each person has such a sense of individuality, and a lot of self-respect. But the way that the energy is shared is, I think, very nice to watch—to see people not having to dominate in one way or another. I think that there is something that's very useful in that for human beings.

DUCKWORTH: Do you think that your current work has taken that next step? Are you offering the alternative?

MONK: Yes, that's what I'm trying to do now—these last few years—after I had finished my apocalyptic-message period. And I don't know what else we can do at this point. It seems like that is about as much as you can hope to do, and hope that people will be moved somehow. That it will go into their own lives as a richer kind of feeling life for themselves.

DUCKWORTH: Are you basically optimistic or pessimistic?

MONK: Right now I don't feel one way or the other, because I do see a lot of trouble. But I think that, in a sense, you just have to realize that good and bad are part of basic goodness. It's more like trying, with your own life, to have some sense of genuineness. I think that's about as much as you can do. Sometimes I get very depressed, you know, if I start watching television and seeing about chemical warfare and realizing that the world can be affected so deeply by utter craziness and insanity—behavior that indicates to me something is really wrong. I know that all of that is out there, but I think that all of us have a certain sense of impotence if we think that there's nothing that we can do. So we just try to do it in the best way that we can.

DUCKWORTH: Are you a superstitious person?

MONK: Slightly, yes. I carry turquoise with me when I fly.

DUCKWORTH: Are there any questions that you think I should have asked you, but didn't?

MONK: Oh gosh. I think that I'd just like to mention that I have been very lucky that I've had really great people to work with, and that they have, over the years, contributed a lot to my music. The members of the ensemble are very creative people, and the way that we work has a real give-and-take kind of quality to it. I have a group that I can work with physically. I mean, I can work with a voice the way that a choreographer works with bodies and dance. I can have people try something and I can hear it. Then I can revise it, hear it, and then revise it again. That's an incredible thing that a lot of people don't have. And I really feel very, very fortunate.

DUCKWORTH: If you knew that only one of your pieces was going to survive into the twenty-first century, which one would you want it to be?

MONK: Well, they're all children in different ways. But I would say probably, as a whole, the piece that I listen to and go, "Who composed that?," is *Dolmen Music*. I really feel like I don't know where that piece came from. It has such a mysterious power. But it definitely wanted to exist. I feel privileged to have been able to help bring it to life. When I listen to it, it has a certain kind of objectivity that I think that the twenty-first-century people might like.

LAURIE ANDERSON

Born Chicago, 1947

THE TWO STORIES I've always liked the most about Laurie Anderson are the one about the time she hitchhiked to the North Pole, and the one about her teaching, unprepared, at one of the New York colleges, by making up stories to go with the slides. Stories, it seems, are what's interesting to Anderson. She says that even as a child, she preferred the spoken records to the music. And instead of listening to rock in college, she liked the talk shows on the radio. From all of those stories, she developed stories of her own, stories that often tell us something about everyday life, at the end of the twentieth century.

Laurie Anderson grew up with three sisters and four brothers in a small town, fifty miles from Chicago. Her mother dressed them all in uniforms. She began classical violin at age seven and in her teens played in the Chicago Youth Symphony. She also took advanced art classes at the Art Institute in Chicago, and says that she always split her time equally between music and art. But at sixteen she suddenly put her violin away, indicating there were other things she wanted to learn.

After high school, Anderson went to Mills College in California to major in biology. She stayed only one year, however, before transferring to Barnard in New York for art history. After graduation in 1969, and a year spent at the School of Visual Arts studying with Carl Andre and Sol LeWitt, Anderson went to Columbia, completing an M.F.A. in sculpture in 1972. During the early seventies, she briefly supported herself by writing art criticism for such magazines as *Artnews* and *Artforum*.

In 1972, Anderson began creating/installing/performing a series of works with titles like *Story Pillows, Juke Box,* and *Stereo Decoy.* These performance pieces, as they were called, continued through most of the seventies, and include the one in which Anderson, frozen in ice skates in a block of ice, plays her violin until the ice melts. Almost from the start, these works included music; and the violin, which Anderson had taken up again, became a prop, complete by 1975, with a magnetic-tape

Laurie Anderson, video image from "O Superman," 1982. Photo Credit: Paula Court

bow in which the horsehair had been replaced with prerecorded audio tape. Anderson says that in the early seventies she thought of herself as an artist, not a musician, but that by 1975, she thinks she left art and became a performance artist.

Anderson's first major success as a performance artist was *Americans on the Move*, a commission from Holly Solomon that premiered at Carnegie Recital Hall in 1979. This work was the first version, and then Part I, of *United States*, Anderson's seven-hour, four-part multimedia event about transportation, politics, money, and love. It was premiered in its entirety in 1983 at the Brooklyn Academy of Music, and was followed the next year by a five-record set and a companion book. This extraordinary amount of attention was all a result of Anderson's unexpected success, and subsequent signing to Warner Brothers, following the climb up the British pop charts of a self-produced single from *United States* titled "O Superman."

During the mid-eighties, Anderson turned her attention to film and television. In addition to writing and directing *Home of the Brave*, her feature-length film for Warner Brothers, she also wrote the sound track to Jonathan Demme's *Swimming to Cambodia* and, in 1987, cohosted the PBS series *Alive from Off Center*, assisted by her video "clone." In the nineties, her work has taken on a more decidedly political bent, with stories that discuss Jesse Helms and Robert Mapplethorpe, or question the issue of rap censorship and the law. These stories also discuss feelings of aloneness and disconnection; Anderson always seems to know what people are talking about.

Laurie usually has several projects going, and often she needs to be in two places at once, which is why I found myself riding with her in a taxi on our way to the Museum of Modern Art on the afternoon we were supposed to talk. Fortunately, it was early afternoon. Eventually, we rode back downtown, to a restaurant a few blocks below Canal, close to the river, just below her home. Midafternoon by now, the restaurant was almost empty, and we settled into a booth, with only the waiter and the Muzak to distract us.

DUCKWORTH: I understand you started out as a violinist. Did you think you were going to be a musician when you were in high school, or were you just playing violin?

ANDERSON: There was a point, a little bit before high school, when I really did want to play the violin, and I had some fantasies about doing it professionally. I practiced a lot and went to music camp. But I was always equally divided between that and painting. But then, I changed my mind about what I wanted to be fifteen times before I was twenty—a doctor, a chemist, all kinds of things.

DUCKWORTH: Was anybody in your family musical?

ANDERSON: My mother played the violin. All the kids were more or less forced to play an instrument. And some of them had absolutely no musical talent whatsoever. But they banged away on things anyway, because my parents thought it would be nice to have an orchestra.

DUCKWORTH: Did they also encourage you to do art?

ANDERSON: They did encourage that, but we had a lot of freedom. I had four brothers and three sisters. We were all able to do pretty much what we wanted, although we did have to wear the same clothes all the time—a uniform. It was run a little bit like a camp.

DUCKWORTH: Did you grow up with a sense that you were different from other kids because of that?

ANDERSON: I did. But I think every child grows up with the sense that they are different. Maybe that's not true; maybe there are some very social children. But I think that most children, because they can't express things as well as they would like, feel different. I certainly felt different from other kids.

DUCKWORTH: Were you introverted or extroverted?

ANDERSON: I was both. I loved to read, but I had a lot of friends. I was in a lot of gangs.

DUCKWORTH: Did you listen to music?

ANDERSON: Not much, no. We had a big record collection. I would listen to the same record for a few days and then go on to another one. I liked the spoken records more than the music; we had a big collection of those.

DUCKWORTH: Poetry and prose?

ANDERSON: The first one I remember was something called *Letters from Dad*. It was from a soldier to his family. I thought those were really good, because he described what life in wartime was like.

DUCKWORTH: Were the music records mostly classical or popular?

ANDERSON: Classical. But in our collection—the kid's collection—we had whatever we wanted, so there were singing animals and Chubby Checker.

DUCKWORTH: Did you listen to rock?

ANDERSON: I never went through that, no. In college I didn't have a record collection. I just liked to read and look at things.

DUCKWORTH: As you look back on it, how would you characterize your talent? Did you have a lot of talent for the violin?

ANDERSON: It depends on when you are talking about. I was not a child prodigy. I was probably best at around thirteen or fourteen when I practiced six hours a day. I was very serious about it. Then when I was sixteen, I quit totally.

DUCKWORTH: Stopped taking lessons and playing?

ANDERSON: Everything. Absolutely locked up the case and walked away.

DUCKWORTH: Why?

ANDERSON: Because I realized that it was so much like a sport—you can only do one thing like that. And there were too many other things I wanted to learn. I also met a lot of professional musicians at that point and I realized that they had never read books. They never did anything except practice and play in chamber groups. I didn't have anything against that. I thought it was wonderful to be in a string quartet, play in the orchestra, and teach. But I loved books and I loved to paint. So I thought that I would either play the violin all the time or not play it at all. I chose not to play. It's one of the few things in my life that I'm proud of: that I actually had the foresight to know I didn't want to do that.

DUCKWORTH: Do you remember any particular instances that made you question being a professional musician?

ANDERSON: There was a cellist who was a wonderful musician. I remember talking to her once, and there were a couple of words that she seriously mispronounced. I remember thinking, "How could you be such a good musician and so illiterate?" I was quite astounded and I thought, "I don't want to be like that. I want to learn to talk."

DUCKWORTH: Did you assume that your decision to stop practicing was going to take you totally away from music?

ANDERSON: I didn't know. I didn't assume anything.

DUCKWORTH: You just quit?

ANDERSON: Yes, I just quit. It was very freeing.

DUCKWORTH: Were you also making art during this period of time?

ANDERSON: Oh, yes. A typical Saturday of my childhood was going to Chicago to take a lesson or play in the Chicago Youth Symphony and then, in the afternoon, going to the Art Institute and being in painting classes. It was always split right down the middle.

DUCKWORTH: How would you characterize your talent for art as opposed to your talent for music?

ANDERSON: It was the same thing. I've tried not to make any distinction between visual things and aural things. For me they come totally from the same sensibility. When I started playing violin again, it was just as a prop. It looked like a violin action, but it wasn't music; it was a gesture. I still try to mix them up as much as possible. I try to make records that are cinematic, movies that are musical. The thing that they have in common is the sense of time that I'm trying to use. If I had to define my work, it would probably have something to do with time: how I try to stretch it, compress it, turn it into a couple of ice cubes, spread it all over the place, or turn it into air.

DUCKWORTH: When you finished high school you went to Mills College. What attracted you there?

ANDERSON: Distance. That was the farthest place away from Chicago that I could think of.

DUCKWORTH: Did you want to get away from Chicago, or your parents?

ANDERSON: Both. I wanted to have a change of scenery.

DUCKWORTH: What did you major in?

ANDERSON: Biology.

DUCKWORTH: How did that come from music and art?

ANDERSON: It didn't. I just loved finding out minutiae about things. But then I figured out that I liked doing the drawings more than representing the information. I did a lot of things with chlorophyll at Mills—taking it from plants and figuring out things about it—and in connection with that I did these graphs. Soon I realized that I liked doing the graphs more for the color than for what they were supposed to represent. At that point, I realized that I really did love to paint, so I decided to go to New York.

DUCKWORTH: And you stayed at Mills for only one year?

ANDERSON: Yes. I wanted to go to New York and Barnard was there, so that's where I went. It was pretty much like living in New York and going to school on the side, which was ideal for me. I liked that a lot. It was not at all rah-rah; it didn't have that kind of quality.

DUCKWORTH: Did you go to Barnard as an art major?

ANDERSON: Art history. They didn't have an art major. I hadn't bothered to check on that. They thought that *art* was too messy; you should be more theoretical about it.

DUCKWORTH: Didn't that strike you as a dichotomy?

ANDERSON: No. I was glad about that, because the feeling of making art seemed pretty private to me. I did a lot of painting. I had a studio that had nothing to do with school, and I worked there. And I didn't take any art classes. You could take them, but they were so stupid that you didn't want to. But art history was something that fascinated me.

DUCKWORTH: Were you a good student?

ANDERSON: Yes, I was an excellent student. I've always loved books. I was kind of a model student in a bad sense. I would learn everything. Now that I look back on it, I don't think I questioned things enough. But the universities encouraged that. The moment you questioned things, you were tagged as rebellious, when you were just using your mind.

DUCKWORTH: Did you feel a part of the New York art scene at that point?

ANDERSON: Not when I was in college. I was much more interested in learning what was in the Metropolitan's basement, poking around down there, than learning about the contemporary art scene.

DUCKWORTH: Were you thinking about music at all?

ANDERSON: No. In college I didn't have anything to do with music.

DUCKWORTH: Did you listen to it?

ANDERSON: No. I listened to talk shows on the radio.

DUCKWORTH: Did you own a record player or tape recorder?

ANDERSON: No, nothing. It wasn't part of what I was doing at all. I liked the radio and I loved to hear people talking on the radio, but that was it. At Mills, actually, I thought that I might like to do something musical, and I did take my violin, but I never opened up the case.

DUCKWORTH: In 1970, right after you left Barnard, you had an exhibit of sound sculptures at the School of Visual Arts. Where had the sound sculpture idea come from?

ANDERSON: Listening to the radio. The sculptures were voices that were up in boxes on very tall stilts. There were stories that I had written coming from these boxes.

DUCKWORTH: So you thought of yourself as a sculptor at that point?

ANDERSON: Yes.

DUCKWORTH: How did you get from painting to sculpture?

ANDERSON: Probably at the School of Visual Arts. I studied there with
Sol LeWitt and Carl Andre. The sculpture department was much
more interesting than the painting department there. I was very
excited by minimal art and minimal art theory. Actually, I loved the
way people talked about it more than the work itself. I always feel
that I like the words better than anything else . . . books and talking. I liked the catalogs for the work more than I liked seeing the
actual work. I liked the way it was described. And it was very much
by description. The actual events within the sculptures themselves
were very minimal.

DUCKWORTH: How long did you study at Visual Arts?

ANDERSON: A very short time—just a year. It was right after Barnard.
Then I went back to Columbia to study sculpture, which was a dis-
aster. The sculpture department there was not exciting . . . not like
the School of Visual Arts at all. It was about a certain kind of
machismo. The value of a sculpture was determined by how much
it weighed. It had to be welded. It had to be heroic. I thought that
was so stupid. I had absolutely no respect for that, and I was kicked
out of the school four times.

DUCKWORTH: For what?

ANDERSON: For doing things that weren't welded and weighty. I was
working in fiberglass, which is very fragile.

DUCKWORTH: You stuck it out though, didn't you, and got an M.F.A.?

ANDERSON: I did, yes. I liked working in the studio, and I liked the
students. I didn't like any of the teachers.

DUCKWORTH: When you left Columbia in 1972, did you think of
yourself as a sculptor?

ANDERSON: I thought of myself as a sculptor who needed a job. So I
did a lot of jobs—art criticism, teaching at all kinds of places.

DUCKWORTH: Is the story true that you eventually got to the point
with teaching where you would flash slides on the screen and make
up stories about them for the students?

ANDERSON: Yes, I'm afraid so. I would just draw a blank.

DUCKWORTH: Give me an example of a story.

ANDERSON: The stories were really half true, but quite embellished. For example, there was one pyramid with a slot like a mailbox on the outside of it. That slot lined up with a slot over the mummy's eyes so that on his birthday the sun would shine into the slot and right down into his eyes. That was sort of a hypothesis, but I elaborated on it a bit. So I had a lot of theories about light. We talked about light a lot. People would write this down and I would test them on it! That's why I finally got kicked out of that job. Too many people wrote down what I said.

DUCKWORTH: How did you begin writing art criticism for the major art magazines?

ANDERSON: Through a teacher that I had at Barnard, Barbara Novak. It's not true that I didn't have connections to the New York art world in college, because it was through her that we went to artists' studios and met some of the minimal luminaries of the moment. I wrote about them in school. I also met some magazine people through her. Later, I would just show up at their offices and say, "You need a writer?" "Yes, what can you do?" I took a lot of other jobs around that time, too. I did books of drawings, some of them published through Bobbs-Merrill. But I thought of all of those things—writing, and teaching, and books of drawings—as ways to support myself, because I was a sculptor.

DUCKWORTH: Where did music come back in?

ANDERSON: The first time was 1973 when I did a concert for cars.

DUCKWORTH: Was that *Automotive*?

ANDERSON: Yes. It sounded great. WBAI has broadcast it a few times. I sent them a tape after the concert and said, "Here are some nice cars in harmony. If you ever want to play it, you can."

DUCKWORTH: How did you move from sculpture to the performance pieces that you began doing in the mid-seventies?

ANDERSON: I think through film. One of the shows that I did in 1973 had a lot of huge photographs in it. Then I began making Super 8 films. Then the films began to have a life of their own. But I never finished them in time for the downtown New York Super 8 film festivals. So I would go and project the film and then do the soundtrack live. I would project the film, stand in front of it, and talk.

Laurie Anderson in her loft/studio, New York, 1983. Photo Credit: Paula Court

That's how the performances started. They were based in film—in moving photographs—more than in sculpture.

DUCKWORTH: When did you open the violin case again?

ANDERSON: 1974.

DUCKWORTH: What kinds of things did you do with it?

ANDERSON: Anything but play it. I filled it with water and tried to play it. I didn't use it as an actual instrument. It may have been 1976 that I started recording with it. Recently I haven't played the violin very much at all.

DUCKWORTH: Your pieces that I know best from the mid-seventies are *New York Social Life* and *Time to Go (for Diego)*. Are they representative of that period, or are all the pieces from that time dissimilar?

ANDERSON: No, they're all similar. I did a lot of things for jukebox installation in that period that sound amazingly similar.

DUCKWORTH: Were you thinking of yourself as a musician then, or as an artist who made musical sounds?

ANDERSON: As an artist.

DUCKWORTH: I understand you also made an effort to go places without money at that time.

ANDERSON: I've been meaning to do that again.

DUCKWORTH: What encouraged you to begin doing it in the first place?

ANDERSON: The desire to leave.

DUCKWORTH: New York?

ANDERSON: Anywhere. Just to leave.

DUCKWORTH: Did you really hitchhike to the North Pole?

ANDERSON: Yes. The summer I hitchhiked to the North Pole was 1973. I almost got there . . . 200 miles.

DUCKWORTH: How did you become affiliated with the Holly Solomon Gallery?

ANDERSON: Through Joan Simon and about fifteen people that I used to hang out with . . . a mixture of people . . . Tina Gerard, Dickie Landry, and Phil Glass.

DUCKWORTH: But you were an artist and they were musicians?

ANDERSON: No, we were everything. We were sculptors and musicians basically. It was a very tight group for a few years.

DUCKWORTH: I understand Holly Solomon commissioned *Americans on the Move* for her husband's birthday, and you performed it in 1979 at Carnegie Recital Hall. Did she give you any guidelines to follow?

ANDERSON: No. She just said, "How about a party?," and I said, "How about a concert?," and she said, "Fine."

DUCKWORTH: Why did you think of a concert?

ANDERSON: I had been doing little things in bands. I would get a band to do one song or something.

DUCKWORTH: What would you do?

ANDERSON: Country and western songs that I would write. Actually, they were not really country and western songs, but they had sort of country and western lyrics.

DUCKWORTH: How had that started?

ANDERSON: Because I knew a lot of musicians from this group and from the scene in downtown New York, where everyone was all mixed up—dancers, painters, musicians—and sometimes we would work together. So we all did lots of different things. The sculptors would do things with the musicians, and the musicians would do things with the dancers. It was completely mixed up.

DUCKWORTH: Did *Americans on the Move* become something more than you had originally intended for it to be?

ANDERSON: I began to think of it as a series when I realized that it was fun to do that kind of work. And that's the first version of *United States*.

DUCKWORTH: Did you always feel comfortable with that style of performing?

ANDERSON: Yes, I liked it a lot.

DUCKWORTH: Is that the crossover piece? The one where you went from being a sculptor to being a performance artist?

ANDERSON: No. That was much earlier, in 1975.

DUCKWORTH: What was the piece?

ANDERSON: It was called *As If*.

DUCKWORTH: I don't know that work very well. Can you describe it?

ANDERSON: It was a series of stories, and the metaphor was always water—frozen or in liquid form. The stories were very personal, about my own memories. I was working with tape for the first time, and with cheap equipment I would find on Canal Street. So that was the origin of it. The first time I did this, I used a small speaker that I put in my loft and changed the volume and pitch of things. That was the first time I used film, slides, tape, action, and stories. And I realized that that was what I really wanted to do.

DUCKWORTH: And you saw it as significant at the time?

ANDERSON: Yes.

DUCKWORTH: Was there ever a point when you were listening to contemporary musicians seriously?

ANDERSON: I listened to Phil Glass a lot, especially in the mid-seventies. I went to all his stuff, and sat around with the rest of the musicians, dancers, and artists for five-hour rehearsals. Sol LeWitt, the sculptor, said, "I do my best work at Phil's concerts." And I think a lot of people felt that way. It was pretty freeing; you could sit there and daydream.

DUCKWORTH: Do you listen to new music now?

ANDERSON: I listen to cassettes that people give me. I don't have a radio, and I don't have a television either.

DUCKWORTH: How do you work? How do pieces come to you?

ANDERSON: All different ways: I'll want to do something with a voice, or I'll like the sound of the double bass, or I'll want to use a certain kind of rhythm, or I'll hear a word . . . all kinds of things. Always different.

DUCKWORTH: Do you go into a different state of mind when you're working?

ANDERSON: Yes.

DUCKWORTH: Can you take yourself in and out of it consciously?

ANDERSON: Yes.

DUCKWORTH: So you control *it*, as opposed to it telling you when it's going to happen?

ANDERSON: Well, no. It's not automatic. I'm not saying that it's easy or automatic. It's not like pushing a button and then writing a song. But yes, there is a state of mind that means being open to anything and trying to be extremely vulnerable to things. I try to know nothing, to be simple, curious, and open. And I try not to be clever. That's the state of mind. And you can't always get into that. If you are feeling frazzled or preoccupied you won't make it. So I don't try. If I know that I'm feeling like that, I'll scrub the floor instead.

DUCKWORTH: Do you like working under pressure, or would you prefer not to have deadlines and commitments?

ANDERSON: I would prefer not to have deadlines, but I work best under pressure, unfortunately. The videotape *What You Mean We?*, that I did for the PBS series *Alive from Off Center*, was done real fast. I wrote it, shot it, and edited it in five weeks. It's a twenty-minute video, so that's a lot of work.

Laurie Anderson performing "New York Social Life" from "United States, Part III" at the Beacon Theatre, New York, 1984. Photo Credit: Paula Court

DUCKWORTH: For quite some time you have used the latest electronic gadgetry in your work. Are you comfortable with it?

ANDERSON: Yes, I like it a lot. I don't like manuals very much, but I like to find one or two things that it can do, and then try to make it do things that it doesn't necessarily do.

DUCKWORTH: What are some of the limitations of the equipment?

ANDERSON: When you have too much equipment, that's a real limi-
tation. It's a strange sort of paradox. I use old electronics as well.
I like trying to push them into other modes—use them for things
that they were not supposed to be used for. That's satisfying. But
you can get into a trap. I think a lot of musicians are in that
trap—trying to get the latest thing that's going, to fix everything
up. It won't. You have to read the manual, first of all, in order to
understand it. And work with it; it's an instrument. You have to
work with it intimately, not just go off in a studio and plug it in to
fix up your music. You have to try a lot of things with it, experiment with it. You can't force it to do things. It won't work that
way for you.

DUCKWORTH: I've heard a number of people say that they think your
music is becoming more rock oriented. Do you think that's true?

ANDERSON: Some of it, maybe. In *Home of the Brave*, you could
probably say that for only about one and a half of the songs. The
others, I don't think that you could. Certainly "Language Is a Virus,"
which was produced by Nile Rodgers, is definitely that.

DUCKWORTH: How did you begin working with people like Adrian
Belew, William Burroughs, and Peter Gabriel?

ANDERSON: Adrian I met in Chicago when he came to a concert. I
had a koto that I was trying to learn to play and he started to play
it. He could immediately play it; it was amazing. He is a very intuitive, wonderful musician. Peter Gabriel I had met because he had
talked to me about doing video projects. So we did some of those
and I wrote some songs. William Burroughs I met in 1978 at the
Nova convention during a celebration of his work. I was one of the
MCs for that. I respect him a lot; he is very, very funny.

DUCKWORTH: What's a normal day like for you now?

ANDERSON: There is no such thing.

DUCKWORTH: Were you surprised at the success of "O Superman" in
England? Was it totally unexpected?

ANDERSON: Yes.

DUCKWORTH: How did that change things?

ANDERSON: I got some new equipment from Warner Brothers.

DUCKWORTH: The story I've heard is that you got a big advance for signing, and that you spent it all on new equipment. Is that close to the truth?

ANDERSON: No. With records you have to spend the advance on the record. But when you have a hit record you get royalties, so I spent all of that on equipment.

DUCKWORTH: How did your friends react when you signed with Warner Brothers? Did they think you had sold out?

ANDERSON: My friends were happy. People I didn't know, I'm sure, thought I had sold out. But I had a choice at that point, which was to keep doing concerts for fifty people, or to make records. The record had a lot of possibility. I had more flexibility. I really don't feel I have a right to complain about the people in the art world who think I sold out, because I once got support from those same people. But the whole aegis of the avant-garde is to say, "We in the avant-garde know things that you out there don't, and you're not going to find out because we're never going to tell you!" It's a pretty snobbish kind of thing. And it has to be, in a way, to continue to be an environment for people to invent and go beyond what is on the airwaves, which is for twelve-year-olds it's so stupid. Not that twelve-year-olds are stupid, but pop music and popular culture are pretty inane. So the avant-garde has an obligation to be very closed. When you do something outside of that, it's resented. But not on the basis of the work. It doesn't have anything to do with that. It has to do with the system of distribution. I always felt uncomfortable in the art world, in a certain way, as a sculptor, because I was dependent on collectors, writers, and the whole terrible party scene that the New York art world is about. It was very social, very gossipy, and very ingrown.

DUCKWORTH: Do you ever feel any pressure from Warner Brothers, or are you totally free?

ANDERSON: They never come around and listen to things while I'm doing them. They figure there's no bass line anyway, so how can they say, "More bass"?

DUCKWORTH: Do you get any kind of advice from them, or is it really a free situation?

ANDERSON: Yes, it's wonderful. It's much freer than the art world, and I like the economics better. A lot of artists are in a real bind, because they tend to be politically somewhat left, while collectors tend to be politically somewhat right. It's a conflict for them to have to deal with that.

DUCKWORTH: What are the advantages of commercial success?

ANDERSON: Good question! I sometimes wonder about that. You get to meet people that maybe you otherwise couldn't. And you get seats in restaurants. The most distinct one, though, is being able to meet people.

DUCKWORTH: What about the problems of success?

ANDERSON: Sometimes it makes it harder to work. You can get so sure of what is expected of you that you actually start to do that. And that's very stupid. I always try to do something that I don't expect. But it is hard sometimes to be simple.

DUCKWORTH: Does the fear of failure increase?

ANDERSON: I have always had a fear of failure. It doesn't matter what has been successful and what hasn't. I've feared failure since I was five years old.

DUCKWORTH: Do you pay attention to the critics?

ANDERSON: It depends. Some I do, some I don't. I try not to.

DUCKWORTH: Are you comfortable with the term "performance artist"?

ANDERSON: Yes. It's kind of clumsy, but I don't mind it.

DUCKWORTH: How do *you* see yourself?

ANDERSON: Well, I think I'll be doing more films and videotapes in the future—making things that are solid. So probably for the next ten years, I see myself more as a director, and occasionally a performer and composer, than as a performance artist.

DUCKWORTH: Do you intend to keep touring?

ANDERSON: I might do some more, but it's not a direction I want to go in.

DUCKWORTH: How far ahead do you see?

ANDERSON: Tomorrow, at the moment.

DUCKWORTH: Are you surprised by where you are right now?

ANDERSON: Yes.

DUCKWORTH: Where did you intend to be at this point?

ANDERSON: I probably intended to be about here.

DUCKWORTH: Well, then you shouldn't be surprised.

ANDERSON: You would think you wouldn't be surprised, but then suddenly you realize that you are.

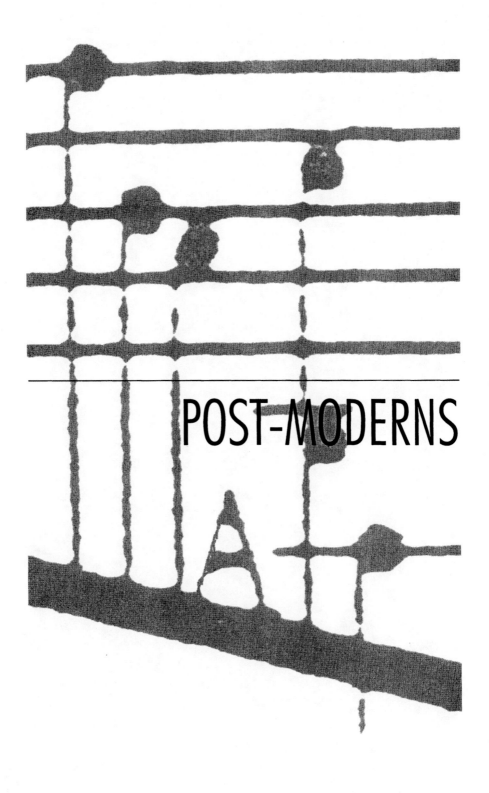

POST-MODERNS

"BLUE" GENE Tyranny

Born San Antonio, 1945

"B LUE" GENE TYRANNY is one of those musicians who, no matter how much you know about them, you only know about half. As a composer, he writes not only concert music, but music for theater, dance, film, and video. By this point, for example, he has written over forty soundtracks, and has a continuing collaboration with film and video artists Kenn Beckman and Kit Fitzgerald. As a keyboard player, he can play everything: boogie-woogie, jazz, rock, classical, and avant-garde, touring, during the sixties and seventies, with just about everybody in the process. In the early eighties, *Alive* magazine said Tyranny was "truly the world's greatest piano player." Later in the decade, Laurie Anderson (who featured Tyranny on her album *Strange Angels*) said that listening to him play was like watching a huge ocean liner set out to sea.

Tyranny enjoys saying that he has lived a decade in each of the four corners of America. He currently lives in New York, but he grew up in San Antonio, Texas, staying there until he was sixteen. And although from a nonmusical family, he studied both piano and composition privately, winning a BMI Composer's Award as a high school student for his *Piano Sonata*. He also studied arranging and conducting through the large music program then available in the San Antonio public schools. So it didn't seem unusual to him that, while still in high school, he and fellow composer Philip Krumm became interested in experimental music, and began giving concerts of music by the people they had met or corresponded with, people like Christian Wolff, Richard Maxfield, and Yoko Ono.

After graduating from high school, Tyranny, whose formal education more or less ended at this point, followed his friend to Michigan, lured by the ONCE Festival, which Krumm described to him in great detail. Within months of his arrival, Tyranny was a regular on the Festival, both as a performer and as a composer. While in Michigan, he also played with Iggy Pop in the Prime Movers Blues Band. Tyranny says he played with a lot of jazz and rock bands throughout the late fifties and sixties, beginning with "Texas kick-ass bands" while still in junior high school. His own music from this time is perhaps best represented by his 1967 piece *Country Boy, Country Dog*, a verbal score of procedures that Tyranny says is one possible realization of his *How to Make Music from the Sounds of Your Daily Life*, which was written the same year. In describing the piece, he rejects the term "collage," offering "assemblage" instead. Various transformations of the material from *CBCD* have continued to appear in Tyranny's music over the past twenty-five years, including *The CBCD Intermediaries*, for tapes and electronic circuits, from 1971, and *The CBCD Variations for Orchestra and Soloist*, from 1980.

During the seventies, Tyranny lived and worked in California, teaching music theory and recording-studio techniques at Mills College, and working in the Center for Contemporary Music, a public-access, not-for-profit facility in Oakland. While in California, Tyranny also began long-term collaborations with composers Robert Ashley and Peter Gordon, composing the harmonies and piano improvisations for Ashley's seven-part opera for television, *Perfect Lives*, and playing keyboards with Gordon's ensemble, the Love of Live Orchestra.

In 1983, Tyranny moved to New York, claiming he was spending a third of each year there or in Europe anyway. Well known by this point, his artistic life included composing, performing (both his own and other people's music), producing, and recording. In 1988, he won recognition from the New York Dance and Performance Awards, better known as the Bessies, as both a composer and a collaborator with his work for the Otrabanda Company. Several years later, his first "audio-storyboard" (opera), *The Driver's Son*, was produced in Philadelphia. And in early 1994, Tyranny's record label, Lovely Music Ltd., which has released a number of his compositions and performances, added *Country Boy, Country Dog* to its list. "Blue" Gene Tyranny, it seems, is still making music from the sounds of his daily life.

For some reason I don't remember, I met "Blue" (which is what everybody calls him) at the apartment in the Village where I was staying that summer. He came in from Brooklyn. We met out front, and it was hot, humid, and six flights up; no elevator. No air conditioner either; we opened the windows. We were tired even before we began. And "Blue" can be very soft-spoken; sometimes the traffic coming up Sixth Avenue drowned out a word or two. But as we sat there and revived, I began thinking about labels.

"Blue" Gene Tyranny, New York, 1982. Photo Credit: Paula Court

DUCKWORTH: Do you object to being called an art/rock composer?

TYRANNY: Yes, actually. I'm not an art/rocker. I've played rock and roll, but I've also played jazz and all sorts of American popular music, as well as avant-garde and electronic music. Besides, all the art/rock people write completely tonal music. And although it has original elements, their music can be played in venues other than avant-garde concerts. While my music, even the tonal stuff, doesn't really fit in that. The jazz, pop, and art/rock people all misunderstand my work. My work is all straight avant-garde. I was too young for the beatniks and too old for the hippies, you know.

DUCKWORTH: Who do you think of as your contemporaries?

TYRANNY: My contemporaries, although they're slightly younger, are the generation of composers who were at Mills College when I was working there. Peter Gordon, for instance, who does exclusively tonal music now and has produced many pop albums, was then doing a lot of electronic work in more expanded forms. And Frankie Mann, Paul De Marinis, and Laetitia (de Compiegne) Sonami.

DUCKWORTH: You've had a strong association with rock music throughout your career. Do you remember what first interested you about rock and roll?

TYRANNY: My idea of rock and roll is very southern. When I was a kid, I listened to, and also played, a lot of New Orleans/Texas music . . . you know, early rhythm and blues. We had a jazz club a couple of blocks away underneath the icehouse on the corner, and I'd sneak in there and hear jazz. You could hear all these people going from California back along the southern route. I also listened to the radio really late at night when the black music came on; this was like early to mid-fifties. And I played in four-piece bands that had the "battle of the bands" at the drive-in theater.

DUCKWORTH: What about pop music? What interested you there?

TYRANNY: Maybe it was just because of where I was living, but in pop music I exclusively liked black, honest, pop music, and always have. It's really the only thing that thrills me: Motown, New Orleans music, Delta Blues, and Gospel-influenced styles.

DUCKWORTH: I'm curious about your early background. What kind of work did your father do?

TYRANNY: I was adopted as a child. My adoptive father was a businessman; he had a dress shop and sold ladies' clothes. And my adoptive mother worked both there and as a saleslady in other shops her whole life.

DUCKWORTH: Was there an interesting musical environment around the house?

TYRANNY: No, not at all. There was no musical environment whatsoever.

DUCKWORTH: When did you know that you were musical?

TYRANNY: I don't know. I just always enjoyed music.

DUCKWORTH: Did you study piano as a kid?

TYRANNY: Fairly late. Actually, I started when I was twelve. I remember that I liked watching Liberace on TV. And I listened to a lot of music on the radio. Finally, I studied with an old German lady in San Antonio named Meta Hertwig. She took me through the standard sonatinas, and all that business.

DUCKWORTH: Were you a good student?

TYRANNY: I guess so. At least, she was very helpful and very enthusiastic. And I think I was good because I really loved it, you know.

DUCKWORTH: Did you talk your family into letting you take lessons, or did they think that was something you should do at that particular age?

TYRANNY: I don't actually remember, but I know the whole musical thing was my impetus. I mean, they never suggested it. There was no music. They really weren't musicians. They liked certain show tunes, and my stepfather liked early country-western, but that was about it.

DUCKWORTH: When did you begin composing?

TYRANNY: Miss Hertwig got me studying with Otto Wick. He was a pupil of Engelbert Humperdinck; the real one. He introduced me to all the basic compositional theory, and took me pretty much through Wagner and up to Debussy.

DUCKWORTH: Did you also continue to study piano after you began composition lessons?

TYRANNY: Yes. Miss Hertwig finally sent me to study with Rodney Hoare. He was a big fan of Schnabel, so he basically pushed Beethoven. But he also introduced me to a lot of new music. Then, when Otto Wick passed away, Rodney Hoare found me a new composition teacher. This was the year before I started high school. His name was Frank Hughes. He was at Trinity University and I studied privately with him. For my first composition lesson, he gave me a Harry Partch record and a recording of Charles Ives's First Sonata. And I took them home and flipped out. I thought, "Oh yeah! Right! God! Give me more!" So he would give me the most modern stuff that he could.

DUCKWORTH: What about high school? Did you have any good musical experiences there?

TYRANNY: Thomas Jefferson High School in San Antonio was a huge preparatory school. We had two orchestras, three enormous choirs, and two huge marching bands. So I got to arrange for orchestra, conduct, and sight-read for two of the choirs thanks to the head of the music department, Mr. Raymond Moses, a man with a wonderfully universal understanding of music. It was just constant, constant music every single day. And I met my first new-music friend, Philip Krumm, there. He was just leaving high school when I was coming in, but we got to be really good friends. And because San Antonio is surrounded by five military bases, we met a lot of New York composers who were drafted and sent to San Antonio before being sent to Korea. (This was after the Korean War.) So we met Philip Corner there, and Christian Wolff. And we got names and addresses, and began corresponding, mostly with New York people, but eventually with people around the States and in Europe.

DUCKWORTH: Who, for example?

TYRANNY: Yoko Ono—before we knew whether she was a man or a woman; we didn't know what the name "Ono" was. Dick Higgins—we did a lot of his early theater/verbal pieces. Richard Maxfield—we did one of the few concerts of his music outside of New York.

DUCKWORTH: I've always thought your background was more rock oriented than you're indicating. I think the first thing I ever knew about you was that you had played keyboards with Iggy Pop and the Stooges.

TYRANNY: Oh, yes, but that's all late. And that's all just fun stuff.

DUCKWORTH: But you must have been pretty good. How much rock did you play in high school?

TYRANNY: In junior high school, I was asked to play with fifties rock bands. My brother played guitar with one of those Texas kick-ass rock bands—few of which were recorded, but they were fabulous. It's a different kind of sound because there were usually two guitars plus a bass guitar, two saxophones, and sometimes two drummers, which is a sound you just don't hear again until the sixties. During the sixties, I played more pop things.

DUCKWORTH: A few moments ago you mentioned giving concerts of experimental music while you were still in high school. Where did you give these concerts?

TYRANNY: Mostly around San Antonio. We did several at the public library. We also did one large festival and then several concerts at the Marion Koogler McNay Art Institute, which is a beautiful place. It was a huge adobe mansion that brought all the very latest in art. I saw my first Rauschenberg and Noguchi there. Anything that was in New York, they would have also. Those were the major spaces, but there were also a lot of smaller art spaces.

DUCKWORTH: Were you writing your own music during high school?

TYRANNY: Yes.

DUCKWORTH: Am I correct in assuming that your early music was either theatrical or graphic in nature? I'm thinking about pieces such as *How Things That Can't Exist May Exist.*

TYRANNY: Those pieces are what we at one time called "process music" or "verbal music." And that collection continues to this day. Those pieces could be realized in many different ways—sometimes as sound, but most often as theater, sometimes what we called "events."

DUCKWORTH: Did they consist of verbal instructions rather than pitches and rhythms?

TYRANNY: Verbal notation, exactly. And the verbal notation would sometimes indicate very specific acts. But often, it was more suggestive or poetic. And it was a completely new form. They were all very different, you know.

DUCKWORTH: What were you using as a model?

TYRANNY: That's hard to say. I don't know where it first came from, but I remember Dick Higgins's pieces, Cage's silent piece, and some of Yoko Ono's early things. Basically, it was just the idea of writing music without notation. And yet it wasn't playing with roles; it was another form. And that form hasn't really been explored as much as I think it could be.

DUCKWORTH: How was music like that accepted in Texas in the early 1960s?

TYRANNY: All sorts of ways. Mostly, people would either really like it, or they'd be slightly mystified but polite. At one Cage concert there was a fistfight. Some of the boys from one of the local bases walked into the wrong space, and started up with "What's this shit?" And then a local artist shouted, "Shut up!" BANG. You know, that kind of thing. But that was rare. It hardly ever happened. They didn't quite know what was going on, and that was just as well. But it was enthusiastic. It was a very fresh kind of feeling.

DUCKWORTH: Did you feel it was "homegrown" music?

TYRANNY: Yes, I did. I'm still to this day not at all interested in the idea of international style.

DUCKWORTH: Did you have aspirations beyond San Antonio at that point? Did you want to take this music somewhere else and present it?

TYRANNY: Yes. Take this music, and take myself, someplace else, too. I mean, there was no support. And it's where I was born; you always want to leave, you know. It's like you get to a certain age and you've just got to go. I was sixteen and I left.

DUCKWORTH: You won a BMI Student Composers Prize about the same time, didn't you? How did that come about?

TYRANNY: I heard about the contest from Dr. Hughes, and wrote this *Piano Sonata* which they liked, so they gave me some money. It was $250, which at that time was considerable. And since I had graduated from high school by then, the thing you were supposed to do was apply to colleges. So I applied to Eastman and to Juilliard. I happened to be in Houston accompanying a student who was doing one of the Richard Strauss French horn concertos, and one of the Juilliard teachers came up to me and complimented me on the accompaniment. He asked how long we had worked on it and I said, "Well, I got the music two days ago." He said, "You're kidding." I said, "No." (I happened to be a good sight reader at that time just because of my enormous experience. I was doing that kind of thing all the time.) And he said, "Have you applied to Juilliard?" I said, "Yes," so he became my champion. I eventually got a thing in the mail that said I was accepted for auditions at Juilliard. It came in the same week as the money from the BMI contest. I don't want to go into too much personal stuff, but there were some real personal reasons why I wanted to leave Texas. And also, Phil Krumm had a year earlier gone to Ann Arbor because an uncle of his was in the English department there and helped him get a scholarship. There he met all the six composers who were at the first ONCE Festival, and he said to me, "Look, you've gotta come up here. There guys are doing what we were doing in Texas, plus they have this organization. They want to do it in a big way." And I said, "That's for me." So I left Texas and I went to Juilliard for one day, took all the exams, and was met with a very hostile board.

DUCKWORTH: Why were they hostile?

TYRANNY: Because in addition to sending them the sonata I wrote, I had also sent them some of my first graph pieces. And there was a huge, political, anti-Cage thing, which I didn't know about. You know, little innocent critter from Texas. So I walked in with my Texas accent: "How you? Fine. How you? Nice to meetcha," and all that sort of shit. And they said, "Do you think you can really play this music? Do you think *anybody* can really play this music?" My champion was there and he was being real nice, but they gave me a really hard time. I just talked to them as much as I could about it, but I was slightly mystified by the hostility. So I went through the normal thing of taking the ear-training tests and the harmony tests, and I thought, "Shit. I don't want to do this all over again; I've had it all." (I had two wonderful private teachers, you know.) So the next day or so I got a card saying I was accepted with a scholarship. It said, "Do you accept it or not?," and I just wrote "Hell no!" on it. (I'm exaggerating here.) And I spent my money, I got on the bus, and I headed to Ann Arbor. So that's how that went.

DUCKWORTH: Before we leave it, tell me a little about the *Piano Sonata*. What style was it in?

TYRANNY: I called it "open composition" or "free composition." It's difficult to describe how that form works. Usually—probably because I'm a pianist—it starts with something that's between a tonal and a tactile idea. The sound has a certain kind of density or "textureness" to it. From that, I just sit down and write. Usually not at a piano. I never write at a piano; I just check it later, if it's a tonal work. It's like musical free association, but it's beyond modulating or hearing harmonies. It's more the movement of the things. And the *Sonata* was like that. The beginning of it was two artificial scales that made these strange harmonies together. And as I remember it now . . . see, it was burned up in a fire in San Antonio. I can't re-create it exactly, but I may write another piece that's a memory of that piece. I can still see pages of it in my mind. I know the first page, and I can see pretty much the first page of each of the four movements.

DUCKWORTH: Was it completely notated, or did it have improvisational elements to it?

TYRANNY: It was totally notated, but it wasn't metrical. It was open metric. I was interested in the improvisational thing, and I still am. Robert Schumann made a remark that articulation is the second and deeper level of music. And that really struck me as a pianist. That dealing with articulation in the time sense, apart from any of the ways of representing it—harmonies, melodies, sounds, whatever. For a human being, that's the really profound level, I think, of music. In the *Sonata*, I left the things open because your sense of timing would be very different each time. And I would often not indicate a specific articulation, but leave that open, too. (That's just as true now when I play jazz or pop.) So that was the basis of the music of the *Piano Sonata*.

DUCKWORTH: When you first arrived in Ann Arbor, were you accepted immediately?

TYRANNY: I was made welcome. I arrived with all my possessions in a paper bag, and I stayed at Gordon and Jackie Mumma's house. I just called them on the phone and said, "Hi, I'm in town." Phil knew I was coming, so I think he told them to expect me.

DUCKWORTH: Had you known Gordon Mumma previously?

TYRANNY: No, I never knew any of them before, but I had sent them a tape of my last two concerts. I did a concert where I played one of Bob Ashley's pieces, which happens in the dark, and Phil Krumm's *Four Pages of Sound*, and, oh God, a bunch of things. So they knew of me and I knew of them, and it was a mutual admiration society.

DUCKWORTH: How old were you when you first got there?

TYRANNY: Sixteen.

DUCKWORTH: And you just took a bus from New York to Ann Arbor?

TYRANNY: Well, you know, I'd never been anywhere, so I had all these mythical pictures about, oh . . . Detroit . . . this cosmopolitan, civilized stuff. But I thought Ann Arbor was very beautiful, because I got there in autumn and it was just gorgeous. And I went, "Ah, God, this is Heaven, or something close to it." And yes, I was made very welcome by everybody. I found a basement to live in eventually, and Mary Ashley found me a job at the University of Michigan in the Institute for Social Research. I began as a coder/clerk-typist, and that turned into statistician, which was very fascinating because I learned a lot of the basic mathematics of statistics, which came in handy for certain conceptual things I did later. I did that for, I think, about six or seven years.

DUCKWORTH: Was your family not helping you financially at that point?

TYRANNY: No, no. They didn't have the money. No, I've been completely supporting myself financially since I was sixteen.

DUCKWORTH: How long had the ONCE Festival been going before you arrived?

TYRANNY: It had been going one year.

DUCKWORTH: Did you begin performing on it immediately?

TYRANNY: Yes, immediately. Actually, I got there in September of '62, and in December I did a ONCE Friends concert. There were several other concerts besides the actual Festival itself, and they were always labeled "ONCE Friends." So we did a ONCE Friends concert in December. Three people played a piece of mine, and I did a series of Ives's songs with the soprano Peggy Ericson. Then there were about eight other pieces by different people. It was a good concert.

DUCKWORTH: I'm still thinking about how young you were at that point. Did you have any sense then of how well you must have played the piano?

TYRANNY: Not in the sense of saying to myself, "Gee, I play the piano well." It's just something . . . I did well at it, and I loved it. I loved making music, and that just made me do it. I think anything you really get attracted to and love doing, you do well.

DUCKWORTH: If you have talent.

TYRANNY: Well, I don't know. Talent. I mean, what's talent, you know?

DUCKWORTH: Anyone who works with students can tell you the difference between talent and no talent.

TYRANNY: Yes, I know. I've heard a lot of bad piano players.

DUCKWORTH: And some of them are dedicated, too.

TYRANNY: Yes, I know. It's true. Talent. It kind of seems like an after-image or secondary . . . almost like an adjective. Yes, I guess I was talented. I mean, everybody's got to be talented at something, you know.

DUCKWORTH: Did you eventually become involved in the actual planning of the ONCE Festival?

TYRANNY: No, I wasn't involved in the planning as such. But I was involved in a lot of ideas, and the gathering of things. There were a bunch of us from Texas: I was sixteen; Phil Krumm was in his early twenties; and a painter, whose name I don't recall, was maybe twenty-one. And Karen Fierce, who was a violinist, was there also. We were known as "Mary's Crew," and we were assigned things. We were like the junior level.

DUCKWORTH: If you had to pick one or two events as the highlights of the ONCE Festival, what comes to mind?

TYRANNY: One that comes immediately to mind was the performance in the VFW in 1965 of Cage's *Variations IV*. It was a revelation. Suddenly, in the middle of it, I got a biological/religious experience, which I've only had two or three times in my life. I suddenly experienced that enormous sense of insideness/outsideness, space and clarity, that I learned later that Buddhist texts talk about. I had never had such freedom from peripheral vision and all the emotional things that go with that. And if there's a reason that music must exist, that's one of the basics—to try to give somebody an experience that they've never had, or to show them that there are these other further possibilities.

DUCKWORTH: Have your other experiences of that type always been in musical environments?

TYRANNY: No, the others haven't.

DUCKWORTH: What else comes to mind from the ONCE Festival? After that one the rest must all pale.

TYRANNY: They sort of pale, but no, there were a lot of good ones. I remember when they did my piece *Diotima* for flutes and electronics in 1964. I stood up and took a bow, and Morton Feldman, who was there, looked at me and turned to somebody and said, "He's the composer? He's just a kid. He wrote that?" So that was pleasant; I remember that one. Another really intense moment was when we did the *Combination Wedding and Funeral* by Bob Ashley in '67 or '68, I can't remember. We did these exchange concerts in New York with the Judson Dancers, and with Rauschenberg, Cage, and Tudor. They would perform at our place and we would perform at theirs. So we did the *Combination Wedding and Funeral* in the Judson Church. I was one of the pallbearer/ushers. And in the middle of it, it did the same kind of take on me. I don't know whether it was because I was so nervous, or had to stand still, or whatever, but my mind was screaming at me, "What am I *doing* here? What am I doing?" But that was just one part of me; the other part was going, "Huh? What? This is great." It was really a schizoid thing. And after the piece was over, all hell broke loose. There was enormous applause, but it was also an extremely disturbed moment. People were banging things to get out. One guy came over and grabbed me by the collar and said, "What does this mean? I've read the Bible six times. You've got to tell me what this means." It really, like, hit a core, you know. And I'm sure I was picking up on that as a performer, because you do, to a certain extent, feel things your audience is feeling. You're all calculating together, or however a person wants to say it . . . vibes, or whatever. That was a very memorable, wonderful performance.

DUCKWORTH: Do you look back on the ONCE Festival as, basically, your education?

TYRANNY: Yes, that in combination with the Texas experience. I never went to college.

DUCKWORTH: Well, where did Iggy Pop fit into all of this?

TYRANNY: Ann Arbor. These guys wanted to get together a blues band. So I said, "Sure, I'll play keyboard with you. We'll play in the bars; we'll make a little money."

DUCKWORTH: When was this?

TYRANNY: This was 1963, I think, or '64. I don't know how I met them, but I met Michael Erlewine and his extended family. And they wanted a keyboard player. And Iggy—well, I first knew him as Jim— was a drummer, a very good drummer. And he was a real spunky kid. Nice, very polite, very quiet. Sweet guy. But he was weird for the time. He had longer hair than usual (slightly longer than Beatle length, which hadn't come into style), and he also dyed it silver, which was unheard of in high school. (He was in his last year of high school.) So he was like in some zone already. We played together for several years in this band called the Prime Movers Blues Band.

DUCKWORTH: Didn't you perform some of your own music with that band?

TYRANNY: I did some theater pieces with them, including a piece called *Home Movie*. I had a 16mm camera, and I made all sorts of multiple exposure things that had certain kinds of movement. Then I interpreted those with a kind of frequency/rhythm score thing. And then, basically, I showed the band real simple ways of doing it. We did a performance at the Ann Arbor Film Festival in 1963 or '64. We also did a couple of other things like that, but main- ly we played fraternity gigs where you spill a little beer on the floor so if a guy grabs the microphone he gets a slight shock. You know how it is . . . fraternity boys . . . they'll kill you to impress their dates. Or we'd live on ham sandwiches for a month, or something like . . . Oh, God, the memories . . . .

DUCKWORTH: This is slightly off the subject, but how did he get the name Iggy Pop?

TYRANNY: He got his name because he was in a high school band called the Iguanas. So we called him "Iggy," you know, because he was the new boy, and the new boy gets a name, right? And he hated it; then he got to like it; and then he really liked it. So that's how I first knew him. When I eventually went to California, he called me up from Los Angeles—in '73 I think it was—and said, "Would you play piano with us; we have this short six-month tour."

DUCKWORTH: Did you enjoy getting back into that side of music?

TYRANNY: No. Well, I enjoyed performing, but the rest of it was total shit. Oh, God! I had my nice quiet place in Berkeley. Why the hell did I leave it?

DUCKWORTH: What happened?

TYRANNY: I went down to Los Angeles, and we were put up on Mulholland Drive in front of Errol Flynn's old house. David Bowie was living in part of the house (it was his first tour), and we were at the other end. And Ig, unfortunately, was into a lot of drugs, so there were unbelievable amounts of Quaaludes, which I had to take because I was so nervous about everything. That was a mistake, because I couldn't handle it. And we would rehearse, but they had the weirdest schedule. We would start rehearsing at like two in the morning and finish at sunrise. That fucked up my whole body. Then there would be nothing. It would be just more lying around, you know. And I had no car, no way to get around. I'd have to depend on taxis or somebody to give me a ride. And all these weirdos would show up, you know, all these creeps. I remember one time after one of Bowie's "Spider" concerts, somehow the rumor got around that there was going to be a party at our place. So I was watching TV with two of the Stooges. It was the middle of the night. Suddenly all these cars . . . it was like *Night of the Living Dead*. I mean, it was frightening. People started banging on the doors and the windows, yelling "Let us in!" And we were screaming, "There's no fucking party! Go away!" It was actually terrifying.

DUCKWORTH: When you stopped rehearsing and finally did the tour, what was that like?

TYRANNY: Typical rock and roll band. All the money the star wants, but let's put the four band members all in the same room to sleep. Just treated like utter shit, you know. It's horrible. It's more hierarchical than the academy or the corporation, which are both bad enough. Then Iggy got the bright idea of sending me out onstage first. He said, "Hey, 'Blue,' I want you to go out and play for just a bit and warm up. We'll be out in a minute." Well, I was out there playing five fucking minutes, while people were screaming and throwing things, not in hate, but just, you know, punk. I was out there playing rock licks or some shit, and eventually these guys came on. That wasn't too pleasant.

DUCKWORTH: Did you finally just get tired of it and leave?

TYRANNY: I left, finally, because they were all borrowing money from me, and I had only enough money to get back to San Francisco. And there was no money coming in. Iggy still owes me money from that gig.

DUCKWORTH: That's funny. You never think about those problems with rock bands.

TYRANNY: It's funny, but it's weird. There have been other rock and jazz tours that I've gone on that I've pretty much always regretted, just because of the way that they're handled. Now I don't play with anybody whose music I don't really like. I only play with those people, and with people who also take care of things. Otherwise, it just kills you. That's why all these rock bands are like into drugs, because it's just such a horrible life. The use of the natural hallucinogenic plants, God's gift to educate ourselves about how our mind really works, is fine with me. I don't want to give the impression I'm antidrugs. It's just that when you're not actually playing on the tour, it's really awful, you know.

DUCKWORTH: Let's back up a moment. What made you decide to move to California originally?

TYRANNY: Well, a combination of boredom with Ann Arbor, and also the idea of doing, full time, something that I was really interested in. Bob Ashley had offered me a job as a technician at the Center for Contemporary Music at Mills College.

DUCKWORTH: What were your actual duties at Mills?

TYRANNY: First, I had the technician job at the center. Then, two years later, Darius Milhaud left, and his protégé, who taught a lot of the harmony and counterpoint classes, left also, and they needed someone to do that. There was only one Ph.D., Margaret Lyon, and her attitude was you don't have to have the degree, it's the experience that counts. There were several teachers there older than me who also didn't have degrees or only had a bachelor's degree. And Mills had a new-music tradition going back for many years, largely due to Margaret Lyon, who didn't like the music, necessarily, but believed that that's what a college should support. She had the very classic idea of a college: you are supposed to develop knowledge; you're not suppose to spoon-feed them training for jobs, which is partly the idea now, I'm afraid. So she supported that whole idea, although she only taught Renaissance and Baroque music; that was what she really loved. And we all admired her greatly for that.

DUCKWORTH: Did you actually become a member of the faculty?

TYRANNY: Yes. First I was a Lecturer in Music, and then an Instructor. I taught classic harmony and counterpoint—three different levels of it, lots of students—for three years. And I taught an analysis class for two years, and jazz improvisation and literature for about the same amount of time. I taught in the so-called regular music department, and I sometimes had the technician and recording job, so a lot of times I was working well over forty hours a week. Often fifty hours. It was quite a lot.

DUCKWORTH: Did you find the basic environment at Mills conducive to writing music?

TYRANNY: The whole atmosphere of the center was extremely conducive to imagination. The social thing was incredible. People would constantly give information and support. Just the way the center itself was organized, if you can say it was organized, was conducive to a great deal of creativity.

DUCKWORTH: Did your work with commercial music carry over into the experimental music that you were writing?

TYRANNY: Yes. I learned some things doing commercial music and film music. You learn how to simplify things. You deal with problems in commercial music that you don't necessarily deal with in your own original musical ideas. In film music, for instance, the whole idea of sync and nonsync, and the parameters thereof, is a very important thing to learn. If you do music that's not synced, or you do a scene with many different kinds of musics, you see how the visual field has its own totally different level that moves separately from the music, just as in music you can appreciate that harmony really moves very differently from melody, which moves very differently from rhythm. So you have that kind of freedom, which you can learn from Bessie Smith as well as John Cage, frankly, if you really listen, you know.

DUCKWORTH: In terms of aesthetics, though, did you take ideas from popular music into experimental music?

TYRANNY: Not the way Gershwin did. What I was always trying to
     bring together were the emotions of popular music and the ideas
     or the information of avant-garde music. I was interested in how to
     make that not be separate, because experientially it wasn't. While I
     would be playing in a band, I would have images and ideas that
     would occur just as much as when I was listening or playing some
     so-called avant-garde piece. But the cliché was that pop music was
     emotional and avant-garde music was somehow intellectual or con-
     ceptual. But conceptual, to me, has a certain feeling, you know. Just
     like they say good Zen smells like roasted chestnuts. I don't believe
     in abstraction per se. I think that every structuralization or imaging
     has an emotional component as well as intellectual and social com-
     ponents. And I don't care to emphasize that one is more important
     than the other. But I do think they should be presented in a way
     that the experience is communicative and powerful. That's what
     brings the thing together for me.

DUCKWORTH: Do you still listen to popular music?

TYRANNY: No, not any more. I just sort of hear things randomly, you
     know. I don't even know any of the names of the groups now, but I
     do still recognize some of the tunes or the sound of a singer's
     voice. And I haven't heard anything I'm terribly interested in.

DUCKWORTH: Do you pay any attention to jazz?

TYRANNY: Oh, yes. Well, I pay attention to advanced black music, or
     whatever you want to call it. It's "black classical music," although I
     don't quite like that term. It reminds me of ragtime or something.
     Muhal Richard Abrams, George Lewis, Roscoe Mitchell, the AACM
     composers. That's pretty much it for me. I know there's a lot more
     out there, but those are the people whose music I know the best.

DUCKWORTH: When did you move to New York City?

TYRANNY: September of '83.

DUCKWORTH: What made you decide to move?

TYRANNY: Well, I was no longer working at Mills. Also, I was in New
     York or Europe, I think, about three or four months a year. Plus,
     there's very little support for new music in California, despite all
     the surface things. The California scene is very college-educated
     tastes, so that you have your midstream jazz festival, your sympho-
     ny, and your opera season—all the things you're taught are the

culture, you know. The PBS idea of culture. I'm not trying to be ironic, I'm just saying that's literally what's there. So the wonderful musicians and composers who are still out there, pretty much when they do a concert, have to start from ground zero every single time. Everybody there is working second jobs and doing everything they can. They put out some CDs and they do some concert tours, which is great, but it's very hard.

Also, I had a desire to see if I could possibly live off doing music and nothing else, which I've never been able to do in my life. I've always had to have one or two other jobs. Which is not that unusual, but I just wanted to see if it could happen. So I came here. I met a very good friend, the dancer Timothy Buckley, and we roomed. Also, Bob Ashley had moved here several years before. And there was Performing Artservices. And I knew David Behrman, who had decided to move back. So there were a lot of things that were pulling me here. Unlike the California situation, there was no job waiting for me, so the first two years were very difficult. Now, I can live off what I make, and I have a nice living situation that I'm happy with. And I can actually make music. Right now I do, on the average, at least one commission a month. I've been fortunate lately in getting commissions for my own concert music. And record companies have started to call me. And always dance and theater commissions. Then, usually, at least two or three performances, and in some months several weeks of performance. So it's very, very busy. But it's, nevertheless, very active and interesting, and sometimes just overwhelming. But it's closer to what I want to have my life be.

DUCKWORTH: Do you think your abilities as a performer have overshadowed your work as a composer?

TYRANNY: Yes, for the moment. But what I'm aiming to do is to take care of that problem by putting out a lot more records of my more advanced music. I have a lot; there's a lot in the can ready to go. And also to eventually get some kind of touring group. I've managed to do small concerts of my music with one or two people, or commissions with large groups, but I'd actually like to have a group where I could work on the music and investigate the possibilities, make it interesting, and see how far it could go.

DUCKWORTH: Would you stop performing other people's music?

TYRANNY: I'd stop performing other people's music *all the time*! But I really distinguish between jobs and my own music, although I know the public doesn't see that. They see me as a member of a group.

DUCKWORTH: Well, you were such an integral part of Bob Ashley's *Perfect Lives* from the beginning.

TYRANNY: That's different.

DUCKWORTH: That's almost a collaboration, isn't it?

TYRANNY: It is a collaboration, in fact.

DUCKWORTH: How did you get involved with *Perfect Lives* originally?

TYRANNY: Bob had been writing these paragraphs about a small town in the Midwest. And that appealed to me because I'd written the *Country Boy* works and that sort of thing. So he did all the structural work, the timing work, the verbal work, all the stuff that a composer has to do, and then he asked me, basically, to write music—harmonies and melodies—that would outline that temporal structure and make something for the piano to play off of. The main idea was that there was this character, Buddy the piano player, and that the music would set off, or emphasize, or actually grow to define that character. Not define, exactly, but make that character *appear*, much as an actor discovers a part. So that's what I did. Now, to a lot of people, that's writing the music. But I didn't do that. It was a collaborative musical act. It's Bob's music. It's like if you gave a jazz chart to a musician. They might completely change the harmonies, and God only knows where they'd take it, but they're still writing music based on materials that originated with someone else. That's exactly the same relationship. This weird myth, and I've heard it, has grown up somehow that I wrote the music. And that's just bullshit! The most difficult part of building the music, of course, is the basic temporal and timing aspects. And in *Perfect Lives*, as in all of Bob's operas, the cross-relations and the cyclic thing are just profound. It's so complicated mathematically, and, consequently, geometrically. And it's not any way I think; it's the way Bob thinks. So it's not my piece, of course.

DUCKWORTH: When you think back, who are the two or three composers who influenced you the most?

TYRANNY: Well, obviously John Cage. He influenced everybody. Besides knowing his music, the main thing that influenced me is just the freedom. I mean, you can really make your own music; you can just do it, you know. I know somebody would say Bob Ashley, but that's a difficult one because, you know, we've known each other for almost thirty years now. And sure, we've influenced each other. Things I've said, and his other friends have said, turn up in the operas. *El Aficionado* uses a whole modal system and a way of writing that he borrowed from me—and said so in my company and everybody else's—which is perfectly fine, because he uses it in his own way. Actually, influence isn't the correct word, the correct word is *shared*, that we've shared ideas. Because people are going to eventually do what they want to anyway, even if they think they were influenced by someone. Their piece always has more to do with themselves and never resembles the so-called influence, even if they wanted it to. I've borrowed from Bob his way of notating vocal texts, and made the piece *Remembering* for a voice speaking of internal states at about the same time Bob made *Automatic Writing* and Peter Gordon made his piece about Patty Hearst, in the atmosphere of that time.

But the main thing I want to say is that Bob always offers an idea, story, or concept that has been particularly fascinating him, and in that way encourages people to think and do their best, their most honest, and to really search for what they are trying to realize, and it's as natural as breathing for him to create that kind of positive atmosphere. He's never trying to get someone to behave in a certain way. He has, through his working example, encouraged me to take my musical ideas seriously and to follow through on them, and by studying his music I gained a more practical understanding of the nature of structure, mainly cyclic structure, its real and human meaning, not as an abstract procedure. Otherwise, Bob's only fifteen years older than I am, so it's been a friendship of two people who make music quite differently. I don't want to sound ungrateful or anything like that, but it's just I don't write like Bob at all, really.

DUCKWORTH: What are the ways in which you two are alike?

TYRANNY: Besides a lot of talking and thinking about problems in the positive sense, we share the general idea of conceptual music—conceptual, not abstract—that music can really do a lot more than just lull you to sleep. That, for many reasons, it's really a very profound art and profession. It deals with time, and there are very few time arts. To me, it can also demonstrate the thing you're talking about as you're talking about it. It illustrates and is also the illustration. So it's different than philosophizing or a written page about something. It doesn't have that removal and, therefore, it uniquely teaches another kind of awareness. And there are a lot of other things, you know, but that's why I'm just glued to it. That's it, you know. So we do share, I think, a lot of basic assumptions and root feelings about what it is to be a composer.

DUCKWORTH: Am I correct in assuming that the piece you mentioned a moment ago, *Country Boy, Country Dog*, is your most well-known piece?

TYRANNY: I don't know. Perhaps. But I would say it's my most original piece, and I would say it's the most developed conceptual piece. I was able to follow a very complex intuitive idea for a long time—it's been over twenty years—and develop it. It's a very generative idea. I try to work with ideas that are generative in some fashion, that really go someplace, and that you can give to somebody and they can do something else with it.

DUCKWORTH: Is it a piece that has gone through a series of transformations, or is it one that you keep adding parts to?

TYRANNY: It's a piece in which I actually learned something from the initial intuition and, consequently, it kept being added to, only because the intuition kept unfolding; I'd say that.

DUCKWORTH: How did the piece first begin?

TYRANNY: David Behrman asked me to do a piece for the Odyssey label. So I did the initial tape piece, which was six months of taping daily sounds. I wanted to do something that was very rich, exclusively with natural sounds. I also wanted to do something with sounds that had to do with real life, so it would be possible to examine those sounds in relation to the person.

DUCKWORTH: I understand what you're saying, but I don't have a good conception of what it might sound like. Can you be a little more concrete in describing it?

TYRANNY: Well, there was the idea, first of all, of the sounds of daily life, and of then examining the minutiae of those sounds and deriving sounds from them—rhythm, melody, harmony. Sounds that were hidden within sounds.

DUCKWORTH: So you taped parts of your daily life?

TYRANNY: Yes.

DUCKWORTH: And then analyzed the sounds?

TYRANNY: Exactly.

DUCKWORTH: And from that extracted musical material?

TYRANNY: Musical material which then became large pieces, orchestra and electronic pieces.

DUCKWORTH: Did each little part of it become a large piece?

TYRANNY: Yes. And you can listen to every part either simultaneously or slightly overlapping.

DUCKWORTH: And from that you produced a tape piece?

TYRANNY: That produced a tape piece initially for David Behrman. It was ten minutes long. And the initial idea was about how to make music from your daily life.

DUCKWORTH: Wasn't that your original title for the piece?

TYRANNY: Eventually that became the title. And it had to do with transformation, and with the relativity of inside/outside, of dualistic categories. But it's a procedural score. It's a verbal score that anybody could realize and have quite different contents for their own life. My particular content—in Ann Arbor, Michigan, in 1967— resulted in a piece that's called *Country Boy, Country Dog*. That's because that was one of the lines somebody was saying about another guy that I just happened to record. And it just happened, without any of my manipulation, that these things kept coming up about boys/dogs and inside/outside.

DUCKWORTH: You mean as you taped, those words kept coming up?

TYRANNY: As I taped, exactly. So the organization that grew from that content—the relationship between the seemingly abstract and the actual experiential—was this dualistic thing. It got into the relativity of insideness and outsideness. The inside things were physically recorded in a relatively enclosed space—a house, or a clump of trees. The outside things were recorded in a relatively unenclosed space. That's how the original piece was organized. So you have these complementaries that you're hearing. And sometimes they seem to refer to each other. And often you get, without me planning it, rhythmic and harmonic complementaries that are really amazing.

DUCKWORTH: It sounds as if you were doing a collage piece.

TYRANNY: Initially it was a collage. But the collage was not controlled by meaning or by taste. Rather, it was by the place where the things were recorded, the sequence in which they were recorded, and, only to a certain extent, how they sounded together. I know that's a little "collagey," but I don't care for the idea of collage. I like the idea of assemblage—a lot of things which may or may not have much to do with each other being in relatively the same space. And this is much closer to the idea of assemblage. Also, I was very profoundly affected by Rauschenberg's art. I love his art. And more than any music, this idea was with that piece.

DUCKWORTH: If I understand it correctly, what you've just described is a piece called *How to Make Music from Your Daily Life*. How did that piece transform into *Country Boy, Country Dog*?

TYRANNY: Well, it was a realization of that score. See, the score and the *Country Boy* piece grew at the same time. So the procedural score itself was called *How to Make Music from Your Daily Life*.

DUCKWORTH: And the music that you made from it you called *Country Boy, Country Dog*?

TYRANNY: That particular realization, yes. Now, if I went out and did that procedure again, it would be something else.

DUCKWORTH: How did those early versions turn into the electronic keyboard piece that you played at New Music America/Minneapolis in 1980 that was also called *Country Boy, Country Dog*?

TYRANNY: Well, the entire title of that is *The Country Boy, Country Dog Concert for Improviser and Electronics*. It's one of the large pieces that was made from the electronic analysis of those sounds. See, I had this tape piece, which was natural sounds, that I gave to David Behrman. But the guy at Columbia said, "That's not music. There aren't any tones in it." And David said, "I want to put it out anyway."

DUCKWORTH: Did they?

TYRANNY: No, and that was the end of that. They decided to fold that project. But the piece was done. Then, I took those sounds and began to analyze them, especially after I got to California. Basically, I analyzed all the different components with different kinds of windows, either trigger windows, filter windows, or different kinds of resonant-filter windows. From that I got musical material that was primarily rhythmic, melodic, harmonic, or, in some cases, that would have a lot of cross-modulation happening.

DUCKWORTH: Were you then taking some of that information and improvising on it?

TYRANNY: Yes, exactly. That's exactly what I did. As I remember, I took four sets of the analyses, called the *CBCD Intermediaries*, and mixed them together and put a pulse track with it. The pulse is a scanning track. It changes in three or four ways, but it scans the same information, which is essentially nonpulsed. So that was the orchestra I played against. And the orchestra was tuned with the resonant filters in various modes. The modes had unique characteristics, and they were all played at the same time. And I just played freely at the keyboard. So that's how that piece works.

DUCKWORTH: Do you expect a listener to hear a relationship between these various transformations of that material?

TYRANNY: I do, yes. When you hear the natural sounds with a slight delay, and you hear them triggering the tone, it's really very obvious, you know. It's really simple. I want to make it very obvious, without being crude, that this is a transformation. I'm really talking about something that's very real in consciousness. It's not a question of rightness or wrongness, as far as understanding. The important thing is to understand what the procedure is. Really understanding something is very different from finding something or fixing something.

DUCKWORTH: Is the recording Lovely Music released of *The Intermediary* another variation on this same principle?

TYRANNY: It's similar, yes.

DUCKWORTH: But it's not directly related?

TYRANNY: No, it's really a different idea. It is a transformation, but it doesn't have anything to do with the daily life idea. It's more akin to musical transformation, and sort of the 3D-ness or 4D-ness of time. It deals with the illusion of beforeness, afterness, and nowness. When you're playing, you're not sure where the message is coming from. It's all a complex of things that are making the music while you're, so-called, improvising. For *The Intermediary*, I played spontaneously, using a technique made up of long gestures, with many varied inflections and articulations, that I call *statements*. And the electronics are set up so that they overamplify that relationship between the before, the after, and the now. So you're really in an intermediary state. That's what the title refers to.

DUCKWORTH: Do your pieces have any kind of mystical or religious elements in them?

TYRANNY: If they do, it's only in the way that you have a religious experience. I'm very interested in the original experiences of religious things, or the original experience that gives rise to something. And sure, they're related in that way. But as far as content, not until lately.

DUCKWORTH: Are you superstitious?

TYRANNY: No, if I understand it in the sense you mean it. I won't deny that there are extremely deep feelings of all sorts. But I don't think that has to do with superstition. I think that the symbolic works to a frightening extent in societies, from bigotry of all kinds to the mysticism of the Nazis, to the exploitation of fears for political or advertising manipulation. Your immediate reaction may carry a superstitious bias, say, in what you would do if a man stood up in a crowded restaurant and started wordlessly screaming. I notice that I do have anxiety dreams every once in a while that have to do with the frustration of being misunderstood, or of trying to be understood. In another way, I suppose it could be considered to be a superstition that any words, like notes at a concert, would convey a certain meaning or image to each listener. Especially over great time and distance—like how could I possibly hope to feel what an ancient Egyptian felt upon hearing a certain text, or even feel what someone living in a totalitarian regime might be suffering at this very moment. The most you could say I suppose is that there is a sympathetic reaction which will differ according to the listener's experience and inherent personality. You can wonder whether but never assume that another person felt or feels something similar or very different from what you feel.

I know I'm throwing together the ideas of illusion, superstition, and reaction but these seem to be only sorted out by our experience. But I try not to react superstitiously in terms of having only certain beliefs. I try to be open to things as they are. Of course, there are those silent moments before and after you act and speak when you wonder if you've been dreaming your way through life. In a way, language is like a lucid dream, where everything is real except for one item that is out-of-place or "wrong." That may be a superstitious feeling, but it's also a revelation of some sort: a feeling of leading a double life.

DUCKWORTH: Do you have favorites among your pieces?

TYRANNY: I guess I do, because there are certain ones that I want to work on in preference to others. When I did each piece and, also, what each piece is about, is like a very different kind of experience, you know.

DUCKWORTH: Do you think you succeeded more with some than others?

TYRANNY: Yes. Definitely.

DUCKWORTH: Which ones would you identify as the most successful?

TYRANNY: Well, I think the *How to Make Music* piece, the *Country Boy* piece, is for me the most successful in that I realized my original intentions. If you're going to have musical criticism, the basis of it should be a comparison between the originally stated intentions and what actually happened. That's a legitimate and useful way of making criticism.

DUCKWORTH: Do you compose every day?

TYRANNY: Yes. I think about music every day.

DUCKWORTH: Does that mean you actually sit down and write it every day?

TYRANNY: No. I carry it around in my head, and I write it on scraps of paper, and I plug it into the computer. But I work on musical problems every day.

DUCKWORTH: Are you aware of where your ideas come from? How do you get a musical idea?

TYRANNY: It's pretty much like anybody else. You get notions, images, feelings, or a problem. And I think the thing that happens as a composer, which Bob Ashley pointed out one time in his wonderful way of having exactly the right words, is that the thing that you improve is the technique. The thing you never improve is the initial idea. That's certainly true. And that, somehow, is the core of compositions that you generate yourself.

DUCKWORTH: Is your compositional technique where you want it to be at this point?

TYRANNY: It's always changing. That's the fascination. There's always a new thing. It just suddenly goes, "Oh yeah! Right! Wow! Of course! Yeah, right!" Or sometimes it'll be like, "Oh Christ, it was so simple. Why didn't I see that before?" One is always doing that in one's life, but it also happens in music.

DUCKWORTH: Before we stop I want to ask you where you got the name "Blue" Gene from?

TYRANNY: A lot of people were making conceptual names for themselves in California in the early seventies, especially in new music. So you have your Phil Harmonic, or your Clay Fear. And besides, there have always been nicknames. Nicknames, stage names, whatever. So when Iggy asked me to tour with them, I thought, "I don't want to just do rock and roll on the stage. I think I ought to do one of my pieces unbeknownst to them at the same time." Iggy and the Stooges were all into "glitter rock" at the time, which was $600 high boots. So I did several of *"Blue" Gene Tyranny's Genetic Transformations* that were realized at first onstage as "clothing pieces."

DUCKWORTH: Can you give me an example of one?

TYRANNY: *The Returning Gay POW*, coming back from Vietnam. We're talking about someone going from one set of problems to another. So I went to a military clothing store and bought all this ripped military stuff. I just wore military gear and torn things, like punk wear.

DUCKWORTH: Did anybody know you were doing a performance-art piece in that outfit?

TYRANNY: They must have suspected it, but they couldn't figure it out exactly, you know. Because it wasn't what you did in rock and roll. But they all let me do it; they didn't mind. And the audience went crazy. I remember at the Whiskey à Go-Go in Los Angeles I walked on totally punked out, with LEDs under my hair. This was like 1973, and nobody had ever done or even heard of that. In fact, people kept trying to put out my hair because they thought it was on fire. (I had the battery hidden under my shirt.) Unfortunately, when I sweated I kept feeling little electrical Zzzzzzs behind my ears. And then I had this other idea (which I only partly did), which was for a monster, a kind of swamp thing at the piano, which was, I guess, an ecological statement or something: *The Primeval Concert Pianist* with an inborn instinct for playing the keys. Later, I constructed a reflector jacket with many glass studs, and wore it while sitting in the front row at one of the Ann Arbor Film Festivals, so that whatever movie was showing would be broken up into dots or pixels of light reflected in motion off the walls of the theater.

DUCKWORTH: Were these all *"Blue" Gene Tyranny Transformations?*

TYRANNY: Exactly, exactly. It started as a theater piece.

DUCKWORTH: Where did the name itself come from?

TYRANNY: The name is a complex of things. The Gene Tyranny part is short for genetic tyranny. That came about because I was living in Berkeley at the time that William Shockley, who invented the transistor, was giving his lectures about the genetic inferiority of blacks. Of course, there was a huge movement against that racist nonsense. Then, there's obviously the take on blue jeans, which is sort of a cheap populist trick. But I put it in there anyway. Then, I remembered also that when I was seventeen or eighteen, I read a book on schizophrenia. And in the book they said that schizophrenics will talk about blueness a lot because of the distancing effect. And, of course, in art, and also in real life, as a thing gets farther away, the blueness increases to suggest the distancing effect and being tyrannized by your "blue" emotions. So I thought of "Blue." That's also why it's in quotes; it's a culturally borrowed idea. So all those things were really involved with the stage name, or nickname, "Blue" Gene Tyranny. (My nickname as a child was Buzz.) When I went to L.A., they all thought I was making a joke on the actress Gene Tierney, who I had just totally forgotten about when I was doing the name. Since then I've seen her and thought, "Sure. Why not? I like her acting. What the hell."

DUCKWORTH: Do you plan to continue using the name, or can you see a time when you'll want to return to Bob Sheff?

TYRANNY: I don't know. The name Sheff is my adopted name. I have no idea what my original name was.

GLENN BRANCA

Born Harrisburg, Pennsylvania, 1948

GLENN BRANCA may be one of the most difficult people in experimental music to explain. This is probably because he began, not in music, but in theater, with a 1971 degree in stage direction from Emerson College in Boston. So his earliest work was frequently half-theatrical, half-musical. In fact, his move to New York in 1976 was made solely for theatrical reasons; he didn't even take his guitar. But once in New York, he formed a quasitheatrical rock band, calling it Theoretical Girls. The band moved among the downtown clubs of the early art-rock/no-wave period of the late seventies, playing a loosely rehearsed, high-energy music that audiences found electrifying. Branca says this was the moment when he stopped being a theater person and became a musician.

By 1979, Branca, who had written experimental music for his theater company, the Bastard Theatre, while still in Boston, was writing and conducting ensemble pieces for groups of electric guitars; pieces that he still called rock, and that he performed at a volume some called deafening, others labeled exhilarating. These pieces, however, were already moving beyond rock, crossing the boundaries of both minimalism and the avant-garde. It was while performing this music that Branca first began to focus attention on the high harmonic overtones in his music, overtones that were emphasized by the combination of the extreme volume plus the timbre of the electric guitars. When he discovered that he could control the overtones, he began creating secondary melodies with them that danced and sang inside the seeming wall of sound. He even began experimenting with alternate tuning systems in order to explore this new world he had discovered.

By 1981, Branca was writing large ensemble pieces of high volume, using primarily retuned guitars. He began calling these pieces symphonies, and by 1983, when he premiered *Symphony No. 3*, he said he was writing "music for the first 127 intervals of the harmonic series."

Glenn Branca performing at Great Guildersleeves, New York, 1981. Photo Credit: Paula Court

He also said that he first became interested in the harmonic series through the music of La Monte Young and Harry Partch.

Even in the experimental rock scene of the early eighties, this was difficult music to classify. For the traditional press and others, it was almost impossible. The *New York Times* questioned whether it was serious, classical, rock, "or all three," while the *Village Voice* claimed "Branca is now frighteningly good, one of the best composers alive." John Cage was reported as saying Branca was just frightening. What he actually said was, "Branca had me shaking. . . . My feelings were disturbed." He said this, and a lot more, after hearing Branca's *Indeterminate Activity of Resultant Masses*, a 1981 piece written around the time of his *Symphony No. 1*, which deals with extreme harmonic density, and massive clusters that move and resonate. While Cage was taken aback, Ben Johnston, who was at the concert with Cage, was quoted as saying "it was like looking through a microscope at a world I've never seen."

During the mid- and late eighties, Branca began moving away from using electric guitars toward orchestral and choral mediums, creating, in 1989, both his *Symphony No. 7* for full orchestra, and the choral work *Gates of Heaven*. He also began writing for film and dance, creating some of the music for Peter Greenaway's film *The Belly of an Architect*, in 1986, and the ballet "The World Upside Down." Throughout this time, however, Branca also continued to write symphonies, and has completed his *Symphony No. 10*, as well as an opera.

I met Glenn at his studio in Soho in the middle of the afternoon. It was a long narrow room on the second or third floor. The broken blinds let in wide bars of light. The room was filled with instruments, books, and the notations of his work. Previous to this, we had met only once, in a coffee shop after a performance in Hartford. So we were really talking to each other for the first time. And what interested me the most at that moment was how he had gotten to where he was, by the path he had chosen to take.

DUCKWORTH: Am I correct in assuming that you had no formal musical training?

BRANCA: Yes.

DUCKWORTH: Had you played guitar?

BRANCA: Well, yes. I got a guitar when I was fifteen and I took music lessons for about six months. Actually, I did learn to read music. But I hated it, so I didn't touch the guitar for about a year. I completely forgot everything about reading music.

DUCKWORTH: What style were you studying?

BRANCA: I guess it was classical guitar. That's why I didn't like it; I wanted to play chords. I wanted to play folk music, I suppose.

DUCKWORTH: Who did you listen to when you were in high school?

BRANCA: I listened mainly to Broadway show music, to tell the truth. I was completely obsessed with it, as some kids are. I didn't listen to the radio; I didn't have any idea of what was going on in pop music; and I didn't have any exposure to classical music at all. In my immediate circle it just wasn't happening, so I didn't even know that it existed. It wasn't until I was a senior in high school that I started listening to rock music.

DUCKWORTH: Were your parents musical?

BRANCA: My father was. My father sang opera when he was in high school; he went to music school to study opera. Then the war came. That was the end of his opera career. He came back and never sang again. I heard him sing a couple of times in church. He was truly amazing. He wouldn't even sing around the house, but hearing him sing twice was very important for me. He was unbelievably emotional . . . riveting. He would have the audience absolutely in the palm of his hands. So I learned a lot from that (as a little kid you are very impressionable). And it was kind of scary, because he sang with incredible emotion. His parents were Italian, so I guess it was that Italian tenor thing happening!

DUCKWORTH: But you listened mostly to Broadway show tunes?

BRANCA: Yes. My parents used to take me to New York for our vacation during the summer, and we would see musicals, so I fell in love with them. One of the ones I especially liked was *Anyone Can Whistle* by Stephen Sondheim. I was pleased to have that one in my record collection because it was so obscure; it played for, like, a week on Broadway and then closed. I collected records and listened to them incessantly. At the time, I often listened just to the overtures. That's one reason I liked Stephen Sondheim. He has quite a few instrumental sections in that, and quite a few extended pieces that aren't songs but have development in them . . . interesting formal considerations. I didn't look at it that way at the time; I just thought it was incredibly interesting. I was interested in anything that was different.

DUCKWORTH: Did you listen to the radio when you were in high school?

BRANCA: Basically, the kind of thing that was on the radio when I was in high school was blue-eyed soul. I hated the stuff. It was the only thing anybody wanted to hear. I can listen to the stuff now, but something like the Righteous Brothers . . . I just couldn't stand it! So I couldn't listen to the radio until I started hearing hard rock. Then I got into it. Then I heard the Stones. I was young. I got into the whole image of the thing.

DUCKWORTH: What brought you into it? Who interested you?

BRANCA: It was simply a matter of finally hearing something on the radio that I liked. Specifically, the song was "Just Like Me" by Paul Revere and the Raiders. There were a couple of others. There was a Kinks song that was similar to that—"All Day and All of the Night," I think it was called. It was very hard-rock stuff.

DUCKWORTH: What style did you discover after rock?

BRANCA: I guess the next thing after rock was jazz. I was continually attracted to the fringes. Of course, you can't get to the fringe if you don't know it's there. So I started hearing a little jazz. I did listen to Herbie Hancock when I was real young . . . I remember that. From Herbie Hancock I got to Miles Davis, even though it should have been the other way around. I was heavily involved in that when I was in college. At that point I still didn't know there was anything such as new music that existed. Classical music, to me, was entirely nineteenth-century music—movie soundtracks—no contact with my own reality whatsoever.

DUCKWORTH: When did you finally come across new music?

BRANCA: While I was still in school I worked in a record store. I would ask some of the people who worked there about interesting kinds of music. With classical music, I was interested to see if there was anything there. People were recommending early twentieth-century stuff, so I started listening to Mahler and Scriabin. Then I finally got to Messiaen and Penderecki. Then I really went crazy. That was it for me; I didn't listen to anything else. This was still before I discovered Philip Glass, which was the penultimate discovery. That was basically the progression.

DUCKWORTH: Weren't you also interested in theater in high school?

BRANCA: I started taking acting classes when I was eleven. I fell in love with it entirely, so I never thought about music at all seriously; it was strictly a sideline. The acting was it. When I went to college, I went to study acting. Then, finally getting out of Harrisburg, I discovered there were other things in the world besides acting. So I became interested in directing. Eventually I started to write my own things.

DUCKWORTH: Were you exposed to much contemporary theater in Harrisburg?

BRANCA: There was a semiprofessional theater company in town for a couple years, and they did some amazing work. Almost their entire repertory was serious plays. That's where I saw *Who's Afraid of Virginia Woolf?*, for instance, a few years before the movie came out. I did discover there were things in the world other than Broadway musicals (which I still love), but that was the only thing I knew. But of course it was pretty dry in Boston, too, at least it was fifteen years ago. In the theater, Ionesco and Beckett were about as far as you could go into the avant-garde. We're talking about the early seventies, and that's the avant-garde of the fifties. The idea of Richard Foreman, A Living Theatre, Mabou Mines, or Robert Wilson was completely impossible to get a taste of up there.

DUCKWORTH: Didn't you start a theater group of your own in Boston?

BRANCA: Yes, I had a group called the Bastard Theatre. It was my dream to have my own theater company. I had a loft space, and it was incredible because I could work six months on a production in the actual space where it was going to be performed.

DUCKWORTH: How were you earning a living?

BRANCA: Just here and there; wherever I could get it. When I completely ran out of money, I would go and wash dishes or something like that. Those were the days when you could still get on welfare and unemployment. But the productions would have budgets of forty dollars at that point . . . forty dollars for six months' work.

DUCKWORTH: How long did you keep the Bastard Theatre going?

BRANCA: About two years. We did two major productions and we had a third underway that didn't happen. We got kicked out of two different places because we never had any permits for performance. We never used nudity or anything like that; it was just this legal stuff. The funny thing was that I was completely and totally broke while I was in Boston. But I had this incredible amount of time to work. It has only been recently that I've been able to get to the point where I have the same kind of time I had before I started working more publicly.

DUCKWORTH: How did you begin using music with your theater company?

BRANCA: Well, I was finding myself becoming obsessed with music. The theater was a collaborative thing; I was doing it with another guy who was very interested in music and art but knew virtually nothing about theater. I was also very interested in music theater. So I kind of introduced him to theater, he introduced me to art, and we did this thing together. But the common bond we had was music; both of us wanted to do a music theater, but not in any conventional sense. A lot of the early work we did was just working with music. Working with pure sound mainly: finding junk on the street and trying to get sound out of it. We weren't necessarily interested in garbagey sound, but we had to use elements that were garbagey to get some very pretty sounds.

DUCKWORTH: How long had you been thinking in that direction?

BRANCA: At that point I had been working with stuff like this for about ten years. All the way back to when I was in junior high school and my parents would buy me these little cheap reel-to-reel tape recorders. I would have three or four of these broken things in my bedroom and sometimes I would play with them . . . make little pieces . . . play them all at the same time and then record that and play along with it. At the time I didn't think of that as music, but eventually I found myself continuing to do this kind of work on the side. When I finally got a guitar, I would do feedback pieces and combine that with a tape that I had made of my grandmother's birthday party. Things like that. I don't know why I was doing this, because I didn't know that there was any kind of a discipline established for this kind of work. I couldn't hear it anywhere else, so I had to make it myself. I didn't play it for anybody else (because I knew they wouldn't want to listen to it) until I met this character named John Rehberger. He was interested in my stuff, as well as things like ancient music, Oriental music, instrument building, and jazz. We had everything in common; it was perfect. So I guess I had been doing this for so long that it finally became clear that it was music.

DUCKWORTH: As you became aware of more people in the avant-garde, did that also confirm your belief that what you were doing was musical?

BRANCA: Sure, sure. The first time I heard Cage's *Variations IV*, for instance, I was on my knees. I couldn't believe it. It's an absolute cacophony of radios, ambient sounds, orchestras . . . everything is playing at the same time. I had never heard anything like it. When I heard it, it scared the hell out of me!

DUCKWORTH: By the time you moved to New York, were you thinking of yourself primarily as a musician?

BRANCA: No, I came to New York to do theater. Period.

DUCKWORTH: So music was always just a sideline while you were in Boston?

BRANCA: No, by that time I was going back and forth between music and theater. I had wanted to start some kind of experimental rock band, but it was obvious that such a thing was completely out of the question in Boston. I went to the clubs a lot there. And I knew that the band I visualized on the stage in one of these clubs was never going to get booked, so I didn't even try to do it.

DUCKWORTH: What kind of band did you have in mind?

BRANCA: A quite austere kind of band. A band that was much more theatrical than musical.

DUCKWORTH: When you finally did get a band going in New York, what was it like?

BRANCA: It was an incredibly wild thing. I was into a very antagonistic stage at that point. My work is still considered to be antagonistic, but that was meant to be solely antagonistic—solely meant to throw people off balance, and upset them, and even to piss them off. To go against the grain in every possible way: do everything wrong as much as possible, as often as possible. We were still sort of in the hippie era: "People have got to wake up!" So I was essentially the one who got out the baseball bat. It was something that was in the air.

DUCKWORTH: What made you think that taking a stance like that would be successful?

BRANCA: Because I'm unbelievably optimistic, and because most of what I heard was garbage.

DUCKWORTH: How did the New York band actually get started?

BRANCA: I came to New York specifically to start a theater company, and I actually didn't bring a guitar with me on purpose. I didn't think about music at all for eight to ten months. I was just writing theater pieces. What eventually happened was I met a strange character named Jeffrey Lohn. He had studied as a concert pianist, but became a conceptual artist. When we met he was in his theater phase. Obsessed with it. Of course, I was also obsessed with it, and our sensibilities were definitely compatible. He had this great loft, so we decided to set up a theater in the loft. I would work with him on his pieces; he would work with me on mine. We were going to work together but keep our work separate. But what happened was that at one point I just flipped. I couldn't keep the music thing out of my head anymore. I decided, for no reason whatsoever, that I was going to start a band. I didn't own a guitar; I didn't have enough money to buy a guitar. I figured: "I'll find the money, I'll find the instruments, I'll get it done." So I put up posters looking for musicians. When I told Jeff about it, he immediately said he wanted to do it. And, of course, Jeff is a very talented musician and also a very interesting composer. So all of a sudden it all came together. We borrowed stuff and we got a drummer from another band. A friend of ours who was doing a performance at Franklin Furnace said, "Why don't you come and play after my performance?" This was three weeks after we had decided to do this thing! So in three weeks we got all the music together—we wrote it, we rehearsed it, and we put it on. People absolutely flipped about it. It was just this little node in time—this little freak—that occurred. The whole time, Jeff and I said that for a while we were going to do this band, that we had named Theoretical Girls, but then we would go back and keep working on the theater.

DUCKWORTH: When did that decision change?

BRANCA: There was a point when our audience was so big, and interest in the group was so great, that it was absurd for us to leave. We made a very conscious decision that this group was now our theater group. And then we started really pushing it far. The thing that was bizarre about it was that we didn't care if people came or not. We weren't trying to get an audience; we just wanted to do our work. We were just reaching that point where we weren't kids anymore, but we were still frustrated. We had finally found our audience, so basically we went crazy. I mean, the amount of excitement and inspiration that was going on was amazing. The feedback between the two of us was a very inspirational kind of competition. Both of us were competitive, but not with each other, at first. We fed off of each other and developed some interesting things.

DUCKWORTH: When you think about Theoretical Girls now, was the stronger element theatrical or musical?

BRANCA: It was equal in that band; it was absolutely equal. When I say theatrical, we made a conscious decision . . . . It was unspoken, but we didn't want the band to be stagey in any way. If anything, we were going absolutely in the opposite direction. As it turned out, the band was incredibly stagey! The drama was quite high in the band—very emotional, very physical, very intense. We played these songs, and eventually pieces, as fast and as hard as we could possibly play them. We couldn't stand rehearsing, which I think is part of what was good about the band. We would set up the rehearsals, and we would come to the rehearsals, and we wanted our pieces to work and to be properly rehearsed. But we would just sit and talk on the couches almost the whole time. We would get up the last fifteen minutes, after maybe three hours of sitting around, and struggle through the pain of actually having to play. Some of the songs were never rehearsed more than one or two times before we played them. That's what was good about the band. The electricity in that band was so amazing. Since then I've never felt anything like it. I don't know what the word was, but there was a magic that would happen. No matter how badly we played the song (we didn't really have to play the right chords!), it sounded incredible.

DUCKWORTH: No fear of failure?

BRANCA: We were so excited that the newer, the more dangerous it was, the more excited we were. We thrived on danger; that's what the whole band was about. That's why people liked it. That's why they came. It was always different. We would keep feeding the audience something that was more ridiculous, further out, more extreme, more outrageous, to the point where it seemed like they couldn't possibly swallow this. And the further we went, the bigger the audience got. That's what was ridiculous.

DUCKWORTH: Were these downtown, early morning, New York City audiences that you were playing for?

BRANCA: Yes, they were very early morning, very downtown. This was at a flux in the art-world period. It was also at a time when everyone had finally come to New York, because of all of the excitement about the pop thing, but the bands were gone—they were all on major labels touring the world. You could only see Patti Smith or the Ramones occasionally. There were no bands. We were actually drawing bigger audiences in the downtown scene than Patti Smith or the Ramones ever drew before they were signed.

DUCKWORTH: Where were you playing?

BRANCA: Max's Kansas City and CBGB's at first, and then a club scene started to happen. It started out with two clubs and ten or eleven downtown bands. Three years later, in about 1981, there were more than twenty clubs where so-called "art bands" could play, and easily over 200 bands. Then a year after that, it went right back downhill again.

DUCKWORTH: Did Theoretical Girls ever become widely known outside of New York?

BRANCA: Yes and no. We did do three concerts in Paris, so there will still be some people who might remember us from that. The band existed for about a year and a half. Basically, Jeff and I were having trouble working together. He was already off of the rock thing and onto something else in his head. I still wanted to do a band, so I started this other group called the Static. That was a different idea; that was two girls and me. It was a very strange band. It was much more austere than Theoretical Girls, much further out, and much closer to the band that I was talking about and visualizing in Boston.

DUCKWORTH: When did you, in your mind, stop being a theater person and start being a musician?

BRANCA: In my mind . . . ? Exactly at the moment of Theoretical Girls.

DUCKWORTH: Do you listen to rock anymore?

BRANCA: All the time. That's the only thing that I listen to. I listen to the pop music stations and I think it's become so sophisticated now that it's incredible. As far as modern music is concerned, without a doubt, it is the most sophisticated music that's happening today. Period.

DUCKWORTH: What makes it sophisticated?

BRANCA: Manipulation of actual technique, plus the development of the song form itself. It's something I'm not interested in anymore. I was never particularly good at it in the first place. I've always been interested in long forms . . . very long sometimes. But if you look at what the rock song form was in the late sixties, and then look at it now, it's amazing. Some of the new stuff that's being done with rap music could have been so-called avant-garde music in 1971 and people wouldn't have known the difference! I've been into rock for so many years that I don't even think about it most of the time. You know how it is: "They suck; they're great." You just know what's good and what's not. So that's the level I'm on with rock.

DUCKWORTH: Didn't you tell Cole Gagne in an interview some years ago that you had quit listening to rock?

BRANCA: I did. Now I'm back on it again. The music is better now.

DUCKWORTH: How did you get from rock bands to your first non-rock piece, *Instrumental for Six Guitars*?

BRANCA: I was touring with the Static, but Theoretical Girls wasn't officially disbanded. Theoretical Girls was invited to play on Max's Easter Festival. Jeff took the gig, because I was out of town, and booked himself and Rhys Chatham, who was the music director of the Kitchen at the time and also had a band called Tone Deaf. When I got back from Europe I found out about this, so I called Max's and said, "I'm Theoretical Girls and I'd also like to do a solo on the bill." My solo thing was a piece for six guitars, which was completely outside of the band format. I had wanted to do some things with tunings and some things with more than three or four musicians. Well, this was the opportunity.

DUCKWORTH: That's the first time you've mentioned tunings, although that's one of the things you're best known for today. Where did your interest in various tunings come from?

BRANCA: Before Theoretical Girls, I had already started to do unconventional things with the guitar. I had many ideas in the notebooks that hadn't been done yet, and that was one of them. Some of the other ideas have been long forgotten, but the tuning kind of stuff stayed. What happened with *Instrumental for Six Guitars* was that I didn't really know what six guitars playing this tuning was going to sound like before I heard it in rehearsal. The piece went through four varied sections. All of them sounded good, but the last section sounded stunning! The last section was so amazing that I actually stopped in the middle of the first rehearsal. I couldn't continue. I couldn't stand hearing anymore. I was completely flipped . . . everybody was. So that was the beginning. We knew we blew their minds at Max's Kansas City that night.

DUCKWORTH: What exactly had you heard at the first rehearsal that made you stop?

BRANCA: I didn't have the vaguest idea what I was hearing.

DUCKWORTH: What did you call it?

BRANCA: I first started calling it "field of sound." I had been using a kind of double strumming technique to get a very fluid, continuous sound out of the instrument. This was the kind of sound I had been working with even in the Bastard Theatre—the rich field of changing colors. Subtle changes, where you're not really noticing chord change or key change. The ideal was to figure out a way for sound to change without it being perceptible. That goes through all of my work. I completely succeeded in this piece, except I also succeeded in some other things, too. What I later called "acoustic phenomena" was occurring. You could hear voices and choruses and horns and strings. All of this happening completely separately from anything I had written, conceived, or even knew was there. I became obsessed with that immediately. The Static continued for another couple of months and then I just had to can it and start working with the larger group. Basically what happened was that I called Max's back about getting another gig for the Static and they said, "What about Glenn Branca?" So I did a concert. Instead of booking a second band on the bill, we had *Instrumental for Six Guitars* plus the Static on the same bill. That kind of thing went on for awhile.

DUCKWORTH: Before we go on to something else, can you give me a fuller definition of "sound fields"?

BRANCA: Working with extreme harmonic density; massive cluster groups moving around in a variety of ways. I was also dealing with resonance. I was working *within* the field. I guess you could say it was nonlinear music. That's still an idea I'm working with—I'm trying to get away from—since music isn't nonlinear. But I wanted to create a sense of the music not progressing from left to right so much as from out to in: music spiraling in on itself. That's certainly what it sounded like it was doing, that's for sure. Also, I was trying to figure out how to bring out the things that I wanted to hear more of. So I would keep paring it down and paring it down until it was just that one element that I wanted to hear. It's still indescribable. I started studying acoustics and I discovered quickly that there was no physical explanation to describe what was happening. It certainly had nothing to do with any kind of classical description of any combinational tones.

DUCKWORTH: How do you describe to yourself what you're hearing?

BRANCA: It's kind of an interpenetration of chords that then results in this acoustic phenomena of hearing voices, strings, choirs, brass, and all of that. To simply hear these things is not interesting, because I can go to the Philharmonic and hear that. It was the way that it was superimposing on top of itself to create an incredibly frenetic but, at the same time, seemingly homogenous field. That's what was so amazing about it. It didn't sound cacophonous necessarily. It didn't sound ugly. It had an incredibly beautiful sound.

DUCKWORTH: When you heard it, did you actually hear how to create it simultaneously?

BRANCA: I knew when I was doing it compositionally when a certain thing would happen. So I would take that compositional element and carry it further. For instance, I discovered that it tended to be happening more in very close harmonies, so I made the harmonies even closer. I also noticed that when I was using open strings. Also, it tended to be happening when I was compressing as much sound (which has to do with the close harmonies) on a macro scale into as small a range as possible. It was by accident that I saw that when I changed the dynamics I could get the pot boiling a little harder. So I discovered that intensity was a very important aspect of it.

DUCKWORTH: Are these things that you try out and then tell other players, or do you imagine them first.

BRANCA: It's a combination. The whole creative process includes the performance, the stage rehearsals, and me sitting in my room.

DUCKWORTH: The first piece of yours I think I heard was *Lesson No. 1*. Where did that fit in?

BRANCA: After *Instrumental for Six Guitars* there was a piece called *Spectacular Commodity*, then *Dissonance*, and then *Lesson No. 1*. *Lesson No. 1* was written about seven months after *Instrumental for Six Guitars*.

DUCKWORTH: Did you have a permanent group by that point?

BRANCA: That was the beginning of the permanent group. *Lesson No. 1* was actually premiered for two guitars and drums at Pier 3. Why I did it with only two people I don't know.

DUCKWORTH: Somewhere during those first seven months, did you stop thinking of yourself as a rock musician?

BRANCA: No, I was still calling it rock at the time. That was part of my persona. But it was also the idea that I was trying to push: This is rock. I knew it wasn't, but I . . .

DUCKWORTH: What did the audience think?

BRANCA: The audience that came to see it certainly thought it was. But the critics weren't too happy about it. It wasn't until around *Symphony No. 2* that I started getting people from the serious music world, or at least the classical music world, as opposed to the downtown scene. I remember they had that thing called *New Music, New York* that was the first New Music America festival. I was invited to a discussion group to play one of my tapes. That was my involvement in the festival. Rhys was trying to keep me hidden in the closet and keep the guitar thing to himself. I played about half of a live tape I had done of *Instrumental for Six Guitars*, which wasn't too bad, and the composers (this was at Phill Niblock's Experimental Intermedia) were absolutely shocked. They said, "But this is rock music; this isn't serious music."

DUCKWORTH: But four years later you were one of the featured composers on the New Music America festival in Chicago, weren't you?

BRANCA: Yes, but that was after I had done *Symphony No. 1* and *Symphony No. 2*. So it was calling the things symphonies . . .

DUCKWORTH: . . . that caused you to become known?

BRANCA: Right. Immediately. It was ridiculous.

DUCKWORTH: Your thinking changed too, though, didn't it?

BRANCA: Oh, yes! My thinking was always changing. It never stopped changing.

DUCKWORTH: I've always thought of you as walking a line between classical and pop music. Is that a fair characterization?

BRANCA: I'm changing the position of the line. That doesn't make the line any less narrow and steep, but the position is definitely changing.

DUCKWORTH: Well, the danger, it seems to me, is that you risk alienating the audience on both sides. For instance, when you shift from being a rock musician to being someone who writes *Symphony No. 1*, you've got a lot of downtown rock people who are perhaps going to begin thinking of you differently and turn to somebody else.

BRANCA: It took a while for that to happen, because if you heard *Symphony No. 1* and *Symphony No. 2* there was quite a difference between that and what Elliott Carter was doing. *Symphony No. 1* worked very well. That was a real risk at the time. I wasn't trying to make a change or a transition at that time; I was still trying to say that this was rock. I didn't want to say that this was a rock symphony; that was the last thing in the world I wanted it to be. I was saying, "This is a symphony, but it's also rock." That was the idea that I was pushing and everybody knew it. And it was working.

DUCKWORTH: When you wrote *Symphony No. 1* and *Symphony No. 2*, were they on paper, or were they all in your mind?

BRANCA: They were all on paper.

DUCKWORTH: What did the notation look like?

BRANCA: It was mostly in longhand.

DUCKWORTH: How did you give that prose information to your musicians?

BRANCA: I sat down with each one separately and said, "In the introduction you play . . ." I showed them the finger position; I showed them the strumming technique; I explained how it progressed. I just told them and then they wrote it down in their own language.

DUCKWORTH: When you compose a piece, where does it come from? Do you imagine all of it?

BRANCA: I have a number of different approaches to the way I work: all the way from entirely intuitive—indescribable—an emotional kind of thing, to the driest possible approach—unbearably logical. I think every movement of *Symphony No. 1* was a completely different approach, although they were meant to work together. I'm very much into form (and always was very heavily into it). It's so strange that my music has been called formless so often by so many people . . . from both sides. My music is more formal than just about anybody's has been for quite a while . . . right from the start, including the rock bands.

DUCKWORTH: What's the significance of the form in your music?

BRANCA: I work with different types of form, so there's no one statement I can make about any form that I'm working with at the moment. The kind of form that I would like to get at eventually, as with everything I do, is some perfectly harmonic combination of absolutely everything I could ever conceive. I guess the thing that I don't like about form is the fact that it's not meant to be perceived . . . the idea of seamlessness.

DUCKWORTH: But the forms of classical symphonies were perceived. Everybody could hear the B section, right?

BRANCA: Yes. Everybody hears the lead break in a rock song too, but that's only a very large part of the form. Form gets broken down into some very small parts. I seriously doubt that everybody was recognizing all of the themes, inversions, and key changes. Those are all parts of the form. I'm not trying to attract attention to every single little change. But the purpose of form, originally, was to make it possible for people to write music more easily and more quickly, for one thing, and also to create more dynamic impact. Because form contains impact. Part of the whole thing is that you create a shape that has a certain resolution to it.

DUCKWORTH: Do you think we have an inherent need to experience that?

BRANCA: It's what we want, yes. I think the real impact of it still is emotional. And I'd like to get a little more of the head into it. Let's say people did once listen to music like that. If they did, they certainly don't now. Maybe a few people who go to Carnegie Hall and Lincoln Center listen, but the general audience in this country does not know that the idea of listening like this even exists. So you've got to start there. Plus the fact that one reason why Beethoven was successful is that he worked with such simple musical language. His words were as recognizable as you could possibly imagine. I think that he knew this. This is really what I'm trying to work towards: very clear, simple, obvious, tonal language that is perceivable. It's the opposite of twelve-tone music. I don't know for a fact that this is going to work; I just have this feeling that it's the right way to go. One reason I don't know whether it will work is that I tend to be drawn in that direction myself. That kind of thing interests me. But if there's no dramatic impact, then it's worthless to do it simply for some theoretical reason. So I'm trying to get it to work.

DUCKWORTH: How did you get from song form into the really long pieces like your symphonies?

BRANCA: I didn't. I was writing the really long pieces before I was writing the song form. One of the ideas of the Bastard Theatre was that music was not used as background. Music had an equally important part. The actors actually played instruments. I had a fairly large ensemble that I worked with. And I was working with long forms then—fifteen- to eighteen-minute pieces. I wrote at least five or six of them. And I had certainly made a few long tape pieces.

DUCKWORTH: So it wasn't a progression?

BRANCA: Exactly. If it had been a progression, the song form wouldn't have entered into it.

DUCKWORTH: When did you begin conducting your pieces?

BRANCA: The conducting began with *Instrumental for Six Guitars*, because then, all of a sudden, I had six people with quite a variety of parts. But I was still holding a guitar. It wasn't until *Symphony No. 1* where I had to actually put the guitar down for two of the movements and conduct, because there were too many cues to give while I was playing. That's when I found out what I could do with the conducting. I had already been physically gesturing with the guitar as much as possible, but then I saw that when I didn't have the guitar I could gesture quite a bit more. So the gesturing became a very important part of it, which was somewhat problematic, because what was happening when I was working in my room and what was happening on stage were starting to become very separate. The actual content of the written piece became different from the content of the piece that was performed. That happened to an extreme with *Symphony No. 5*. That became more of a dance piece, to some extent, than a piece of music. The performance had almost nothing to do with what I conceived when I wrote it.

DUCKWORTH: Are your scores like recipes? Do you have all the ingredients and know the sequence, but then use audience feedback and your own feelings on stage to either stretch or pull back?

BRANCA: It depends on the piece. Some pieces are very tightly structured; they have no room for any kind of change, except for the fact that I can change the dynamics, the tempo, and things like that in a normal way. In other pieces, I leave indeterminate space where I can give a cue whenever I want. In some sections, I work a lot with structured improvisation. *Lesson No. 1*, for instance, is a structured improvisation. The macrostructure and the tonal structure are very specific. The strumming technique . . . well, it's structured improvisation. Exactly what note is played at what moment is entirely up to the player. I give them a certain number of notes, I tell them how to play the notes, and I tell them which strings to play at which times and which strumming techniques to use. There are plenty of cues in the piece. But exactly what note is played at what time only comes up a few times in the whole piece. I shouldn't say that. General ideas are given—as far as whether to play an octave or a unison—but the actual, physical note to play is up to the player. It's just that mode of the pentatonic scale.

DUCKWORTH: Once you decided that you were really interested in acoustics, how did you start finding out about it?

BRANCA: I started reading books and asking questions. Everything led to something else. There were times when I thought, "Well, maybe this idea of a combination of resultant tones is what's really happening." I worked with that a little bit, thought about it a little bit, and it finally became very clear that it was not going to be possible to sit down and on paper determine, from some mathematical process, this sound. So all of this led to the harmonic series. Basically, the harmonic series was originally started as another kind of tuning system with *Symphony No. 3*. I knew very little about it, but I decided that it would be an interesting system. When I started to work with it and found out what it was, the form itself became interesting to me and I was hooked, so to speak. So *Symphony No. 3* was basically a demonstration of the ideas that I had discovered in the series—specifically being chord progressions based on the series with no effort to exert any intentional compositional form onto it. Much of that piece was as unintentional as possible. I wanted to hear what the series, so-called, sounded like. I saw potential for compositional forms within the series; the series implied certain kinds of mathematical forms, for instance. Development; an evolutionary kind of developmental form. I actually began this project to try to somehow derive a compositional system based on natural growth itself. That's when I started studying physics and mathematics. I was looking for mathematical descriptions of natural growth. That's when the problems started with my own work, because that slowed everything down to a snail's pace. I was getting immersed in this entirely theoretical area.

DUCKWORTH: I think it's an occupational hazard that people who work with systems, if they're not careful, can leave music completely behind.

BRANCA: That's what started to happen. I dropped everything. I just completely immersed myself. In some ways it was good that I went off the deep end, because then I was able to come back. I saw that I went too far. It was all meant to return to music in the end, but I saw that it didn't return. What had happened was that I had written three symphonies based on the harmonic series, and in none of them did I come anywhere near where I was trying to get. Everytime I made the effort to find the compositional form I came to a dead end. I just couldn't get it out of the thing. I began to realize that I was going to have to start studying music. At that point, that was clearly the answer. That's why, at the moment, I've left the harmonic series and the mathematics behind. I'm now writing music again, which is what I'm good at. I've dropped the very, very symmetrical idea of the harmonic series and I'm working entirely with what makes music move, what makes it talk, what makes it sing.

DUCKWORTH: What have you found so far? What does make music sing?

BRANCA: I think tonality and form are the two most important areas that have to be dealt with in music right now for a whole lot of reasons. I don't think it's something that's going to happen in the near future. I think music is going to go through a few changes. But inevitably this is where it has to go. I know that because I see what the problems are going to be. If we think of tonality as a tool, not as a form in itself—a tool that we can use to create the form—we see it from a totally different point of view. Something I've always known from the very beginning of my music is that when you lose a tonal center entirely, you also lose the concept of dissonance that a tonal center creates. A tonal center is what creates dissonance. So the work that I've done with the harmonic series becomes absolutely invaluable, because I understand the vertical chord relationship as well as you could possibly understand it. Now I've got to get the horizontal down. That's what I'm working on. Music is linear; I've finally reconciled myself to that. There's no way out of it. I was one of those fools who tried to get out of it, but you can't. So now I'm going to write linear music and it's going to work.

DUCKWORTH: At one time you were interested in going in the direction of synthesizers and computers, weren't you?

BRANCA: Well, no, not necessarily. I had ideas about things to do with them. I had designed a few digital instruments and things, but I'm always doing this and that. No, that was never a serious area. The reason I'm interested in the orchestra—the one area of the orchestra that's superior to the synthesizer—is the number of individual voices I can work with. This is the key to my music and always has been. And in some ways it makes sense that the next step I take is to the orchestra, because putting together an ensemble of forty-eight people isn't feasible. It isn't just a matter of how many strings I have, or how many instruments I have. In the end, it's how many people I have: how many separate voices I can deal with entirely individually. That is the key to the harmonic theory that I'm working on. The kind of movement I'm doing, the kind of interpenetration of the chords and stuff, can be done in so much more subtle ways than I've ever done it before.

DUCKWORTH: Who do you think of now as your musical colleagues?

BRANCA: I wouldn't want to name names, for their sake more than mine. It might be unfair to some people. But the two people who came up with me on this thing were Rhys Chatham and Jeffrey Lohn. I feel my closest connection with those two people. I don't feel a personal connection in my music with what they do, but rather a feeling that we all came up together.

DUCKWORTH: What about composers whose work you relate to?

BRANCA: The minimalists I'm absolutely in love with. Now I see places where those ideas can be progressed and developed, but that in no way changes the beauty of what has already been done. My sense is that if both Glass and Reich had died five years ago, they would have written as much great music as anyone could ever hope to write. Then there are the people who are related to the minimalists in a different way, Phill Niblock especially. I think Phill Niblock is probably the most . . . I shouldn't say underrated, but a person who should be quite a bit more well known than he is. Not only has he contributed incredibly to new music with his Experimental Intermedia Foundation, but his own work is, without a doubt, as important as what the minimalists are doing. And he's the only person who is doing it. Anyone who comes close doesn't touch him. I like some of the stuff that Charlemagne Palestine has done, although he hasn't been working for a long time. People who are working with extended forms and fields of sound.

DUCKWORTH: Does criticism of your work affect you seriously, or do you even read it?

BRANCA: It definitely affects me. I can't imagine that it doesn't affect people. But when I say that it affects me, I don't necessarily mean that bad criticism makes me feel bad. Once someone has planted something in your mind it's like the power of suggestion. They put

Glenn Branca, Berlin, 1988. Photo Credit: Sabine Matthes

in a line like "He believes his own press." That idea never even crossed my mind, but all of a sudden I hear myself saying, "Do I believe my own press?" That's when you're dead. Especially with people like the *New York Times*. They are actually trying to manipulate movements; they are trying to create movements; they're trying to push composers in certain directions; they're trying to hold down certain ideas and hold up other ideas. And they're doing this very, very overtly. The creative process is a delicate enough thing as it is. You're sitting in front of your desk saying to yourself, "Will I ever be able to write another thing again in my life? Is any of my work any good?" Everybody thinks these things in some way or another, some more than others. It doesn't help when you have these jerks coming down your back, who haven't the vaguest idea of what you're trying to do. And don't care either! In a strange way they are trying to be composers themselves. They're trying to get somebody else to compose the music they want to hear. It's sick.

DUCKWORTH: Were you surprised when John Cage called the piece you performed at New Music America in Chicago fascist music?

BRANCA: Yes, I was shocked out of my mind! There was a panel discussion the morning after the performance and I decided to go to it. I walked in late and there was Cage attacking my piece as viciously as I could ever imagine anyone ever attacking the work . . . and me personally.

DUCKWORTH: Do you think he misunderstood your work?

BRANCA: Yes and no. I've looked at this from every possible side, and I love to imagine that he is absolutely and totally right. But what am I supposed to do, slit my wrists? So it puts me in a problematic situation. I happen to like Cage's work and I think he's very important.

DUCKWORTH: Do you think that your music has any connection with his music?

BRANCA: I always thought that it had quite a strong connection with his music. On other levels, it has absolutely no connection. His music, it is becoming clear to me, is not about music at all. Not only that, it's antimusic and antiart. And I never realized that, never thought of it that way before. The thing that's great about Cage is that you can read anything into it, because it is *the* most vague, ambiguous work that anyone's ever done. Period. On that level, my work is the antithesis of what he's doing. I can see that he would have a problem with my work, because everything that his generation tried to do—everything they tried to tear down—me and a bunch of other people are trying to build back up again. At least from their point of view.

DUCKWORTH: What do you mean by that? What is your generation trying to build back up?

BRANCA: From their point of view we are just reconstructing the orchestra all over again; reconstructing the tonal system all over again; reconstructing fascistic, despotic, centralized-oriented music. It's antihumanistic music, you might say. Antiholistic. It's appealing to the most base instincts in the human being. Reactionary . . . political on every level. Because you have to realize that their work was very political. What they were doing was very much a part of the sixties, really. Their work still is very political, Cage and a lot of the people he influenced. They don't realize that our approach has been different. Now I can understand why they wouldn't want to see it. Basically, we're saying that (and this was the whole idea from the beginning with the bands) we've got to take the word to the people instead of sitting in our ivory tower. It's not as though we are going to pander to the masses, but we like rock music, too. And we also like Beethoven. What's wrong with Beethoven? It's like saying, "We not only understand what you're doing, Mr. Cage, and we not only agree with it, but we also no longer have to feel defensive about it. We can be strong; we know what we're doing." It's not just a matter of avant-garde music or some new interesting idea about working, it's a whole way of thinking—a whole way of looking at the world. It isn't an approach to art; it's a very political thing that's happening. I've always been very political, but I'm not going to pick up a gun, run for office, or start a religion. My approach is to show by doing, by being. And I think that's the strongest way to do it. That's what Cage did, too. That's what is too bad about the whole thing.

DUCKWORTH: Your music seems to elicit some very powerful reactions, both positive and negative. I'm thinking about Tim Page's review of the 1986 concert at Alice Tully Hall, in which he reduced your work to "sound, fury, and rock-and-roll moves."

BRANCA: Tim Page was one of my very first supporters.

DUCKWORTH: Why did his opinions change so radically?

BRANCA: I don't really know. I do know that the *New York Times* is a very political situation; journalists are vying for position. It basically comes down to the worst reviews get the biggest attention. I'm not saying that's why he wrote it, but that's one thing I really hate about it. I know I'm being used by Tim Page. This isn't the first time that he's written bad things about me and I knew that when he came he had been saving this up. He actively works against me. But I won't get into that; just let it be said that that is the case.

DUCKWORTH: Do you think that what bothers people the most about your music is the extremely high volume level?

BRANCA: No, I know that that's not what bothers people the most. That gives them an easy way out. What bothers them the most is the unsettling nature of the music. It's scary for one thing; it's absolutely scary. And I never realized that. My music was scary back in the days of the Bastard Theatre and I didn't realize it until a friend of mine who heard a tape I was playing (and enjoying) said she couldn't stand to listen to it. Not because she didn't like it, but because it scared her. I know that my music scares people, which is too bad. I don't see it like that, but I've heard the music so much more often. I can see where it could be shocking.

DUCKWORTH: But in order to be effective, your music does have to be loud, doesn't it?

BRANCA: No. It's just that I have to deal with different elements. I had to curtail the complexity I would normally have in a piece, because at high volume it simply becomes mud. First of all, I was working with the idea of great simplicity (some people call it simpleminded-ness). So I saw at high volumes that it was absolutely necessary to keep certain ideas, if you want to have a certain kind of impact. Consonant things have to make a very clear statement of a certain kind of chord; they have to be written as simply as possible. And then I knew that I was writing the pieces for the stage. I never imag-ined them on a record with somebody listening to them in their room. I imagined them at a club packed with hot people who want-ed to "get off." I knew what was going to do that—the most exciting possible music. It was theater, really. I was writing the most densely dissonant stuff I could possibly imagine and every single bit of it sounded absolutely consonant and transparent to me. I guess I've listened to this guitar stuff too long, but it sounded like silk!

DUCKWORTH: Do you think that you have to listen to loud music differently? Must your listeners bring a different kind of ear to your performances?

BRANCA: You have to go to the concert and be ready to have sex with
    the fucking music! That's what loud music is all about. If you don't
    know what it means to be into rock music, if you don't know what
    it means to go to a concert because it's going to be loud, and
    intense, and beating right through your chest, if you don't under-
    stand that you're getting up there to have a physical experience,
    then you're going to have trouble with my music. You do have to
    listen to it differently, but who thinks about that when they go to a
    rock concert, when you're into that? What are they going there for?
    They're going there to have sex, adolescent sex. And we've all got
    plenty of adolescent sex in us.

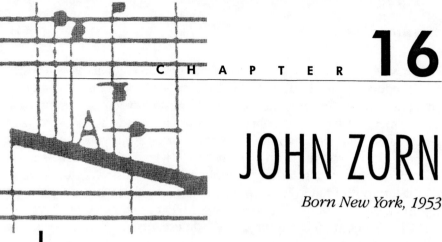

JOHN ZORN

Born New York, 1953

J OHN ZORN ONCE told *Option* magazine: "I'm not afraid of styles; I like them all." He also said that he has an extremely short attention span. Put these two statements together, and you have a good idea how his music sounds. To many people, the most startling thing about Zorn's pieces is how fast they crosscut styles, one moment sounding like jazz; the next, noise; and thirty seconds later like twelve-tone, honky-tonk, Bartók, or perhaps the blues. Zorn's music— whether his own, or his arrangements in tribute to other people—is a crazy-quilt collection of sounds, held together more by form and structure than by content.

Zorn grew up during the 1960s in Queens, watching TV, going to the movies, and buying all the records he could afford. He liked everything. Later, he singled out the cartoon music of Carl Stalling and Scott Bradley, composers for Warner Brothers in the forties, as being particularly influential. Zorn says he first became interested in composing at the age of nine. At fourteen, he began composition lessons at the UN School, working with Leonardo Balada. He says Ives, Partch, and Cage were his early heroes, along with Boulez, Stockhausen, Kagel, and Stravinsky. And Zorn played saxophone, so of course there was Coltrane. After high school, Zorn went to Webster College in St. Louis, but stayed only a year and a half. While there, he studied composition with Kendall Stallings, and learned about jazz through the Black Artists Group (BAG), who were then active in St. Louis, and the Association for the Advancement of Creative Musicians (AACM), active in Chicago. After dropping out of college, Zorn traveled for several years, improvising noisy solo saxophone concerts that often included such unusual instruments as duck and wild game calls.

In the early seventies, Zorn, who was back in New York by this point, began writing in a style he labeled *game theory*. His *game pieces* consist of often elaborate sets of rules that determine when and who

John Zorn performing at the Kitchen, New York, 1980. Photo Credit: Paula Court

plays, but not what the result will sound like. Zorn said his interest at that time was primarily in composing for creative improvisers. The game pieces include titles like *Archery, Pool,* and *Lacrosse,* as well as *Cobra,* his most complex work in this style, which he composed on a blackboard.

Somewhere around the time of *Shuffle Boil* (his tribute work to Thelonious Monk), Zorn began composing in a manner he called *file-card composition.* With this method, he begins by making lists of impressions, ideas, and snippets of sound, some of which are later transferred to file cards as individual events. As in *Spillane* (his tribute to Mickey Spillane, the author of the Mike Hammer detective series from the fifties), for example, these file cards, once they are sorted and arranged in the proper order, become the actual score. Zorn then takes this file-card score, along with the particular musicians he has chosen, into the recording studio, where he slowly builds the piece, section by section. This way of working is true both for his own music and for his arrangements. Although he also produces more conventional looking scores, such as *Cat-o'-Nine-Tales* for the Kronos Quartet, Zorn continues to write in a collaborative manner, even today.

During the mid-eighties, after years of self-producing low-budget records and poorly attended concerts, Zorn suddenly became famous.

It happened around the release, in 1987, of *The Big Gundown*, his tribute album to Italian film composer Ennio Morricone on Nonesuch, but
it was also fueled by the release of *Spillane* the following year; a favorable profile by John Rockwell in the Sunday *New York Times*; and the
success, first in New York, then in Europe and Japan, of Zorn's
rock/jazz/new-music group, Naked City, a super-tight bar band that can
turn stylistic corners on a dime.

During the late eighties, Zorn began spending time in Japan, saying
he enjoyed the culture because it borrowed so heavily from other cultures. Currently, he tries to live half of each year there and the other
half in New York. We met in New York, at eleven one morning at the
apartment he keeps in the East Village. Invited into one of two small
rooms, I was immediately struck by the LP records, tapes, and CDs
stored on shelves around the walls. They were everywhere, thousands
of them, floor to ceiling. The rest of the room was taken up with a television and a bed on the floor. There was no room for a chair, so we sat
on the bed. John reluctantly turned off the television. As we talked, he
began turning first one way and then the other, pulling records from
just the right spot, to illustrate a point.

DUCKWORTH: I understand you have the biggest record collection in
the East Village.

ZORN: Well, see, it's not really true. There are only about 13,000 pieces.

DUCKWORTH: How did your collection develop? Who did you listen
to when you were growing up?

ZORN: I think it really came from the movies, pretty much. I'm a
complete media freak; a TV baby. When I was less than a year old,
my mother used to put me in a laundry basket in front of test patterns to keep me quiet. The first record I actually remember buying
was *The Sorcerer's Apprentice*: I saw *Fantasia*, you know, and I
liked Mickey Mouse running around in that. And I thought the
music was great. I must have been six or seven then, maybe eight.
After that, I got into the monster movies, you know, *The Werewolf*
and *The Hunchback*. And the Phantom of the Opera played the
organ, so I got into organ music; I bought every Bach organ record
I could get my hands on. I've still got them.

DUCKWORTH: Do you ever get rid of any of your records, or do you
just continue to collect them?

ZORN: If something is bad and I don't like it I'll get rid of it, but, believe it or not, there are very few things that I really want to get rid of. Sometimes I'll buy a record and on first listening I'll say, "Well, I just threw seven bucks down the drain," and I'll put it in an "out" pile. But then I'll come back to it a few months later and listen to it again and go, "Well, now wait a minute, there's got to be something here because three people have told me this is an incredible record. I've got to check it out." So I'll listen to it again and again. That's how I got into hard core and thrash. I just went into a store and said to some skinhead who was working there, "Pick out five or six of your favorite hard-core records that never left your turntable for three months." And he picked out five records and I took them home, but I didn't really get it. All the cuts were like a minute and a half. And I thought, "Well, it all sounds the same to me. There's nothing going on." But I went back and back and back. Ultimately, you have to trust somebody, you know. That's how you get into something.

DUCKWORTH: Have you always been able to do that?

ZORN: Yes, always. Like I was into this organ stuff, right, through *The Phantom of the Opera*. Then someone told me, "Oh, you should hear *Second Wind for Organ* by Mauricio Kagel. Wild, crazy record, you know, go check it out." *Improvisation ajoutee* was the name of the piece on that record. I must have been fifteen when I bought it. My parents live in Queens but I went to school in Manhattan. And I used to try to avoid going home as much as I could because my parents were always fighting. After school I'd go to movies and then sleep over at a friend's house. So I took the record over to a friend's house. And I remember his mother walking around while I was listening to it, making incredible faces like, "What? Take this off. This is horrible. You call this music?" I remember that experience really clearly because it was at that time that I thought, "Yes, this is the music for me. This is what I want to be doing." This was really the record that turned me on to modern classical music, to experimental music.

DUCKWORTH: When you think about that piece now, what do you remember most clearly about it?

ZORN: There were four people who changed the stops of the organ while one guy was playing. They're also like knocking and pulling the pipes out, causing problems for the guy, yelling and screaming.

And it created a whole world that I had never been exposed to before. So from that I got into more adventurous stuff. I had listened to people like Stravinsky, Bartók, and Ives before, but this is the record that opened me up to Stockhausen and Cage. Then *2001* came out, and through that I got into Strauss and Ligeti. And the Morricone influence was very strong when I was small. When the first Clint Eastwood film, *Fistful of Dollars* I guess it was, came out, I remember really liking the soundtrack. I think that was 1962.

DUCKWORTH: Were records an escape for you?

ZORN: You know, I don't think psychologically about what went on in my childhood, but I guess in a way it was, because it was a difficult. . . . My parents never supported my music at all.

DUCKWORTH: Was anyone musical in your family?

ZORN: No, no. Not at all.

DUCKWORTH: When did you first realize that you were going to be a composer?

ZORN: I went to a private school in New York called the UN School. My teacher was Leonardo Balada; he's teaching in Pittsburgh now. He was my music teacher from the time I was very small until he left the school, so I was kind of familiar with him for years and years. And he gave me an assignment at one point. . . . When I look back at my grade cards in school, music was about the only good thing I did. I mean, I got consistently good grades in music and the rest of it was like . . . well, we don't want to talk about what the rest of it was like. So he gave me an assignment to write a piece for guitar. And I remember that this was the first piece I ever wrote down. My grandparents had a piano in the basement of their house and I used to fool around on it, like goof around. My uncle used to improvise by ear, play pop songs and stuff. And I remember thinking, "How can this guy do this?" But I couldn't play anything by ear; my ear was really not happening. So I taught myself to read music.

DUCKWORTH: Do you think of yourself as self-taught?

ZORN: For the most part. I mean, I studied with Balada, and I then went to college for a year and a half. I studied with Ken Stallings at Webster College in St. Louis, a small little place.

DUCKWORTH: How did you decide on Webster?

ZORN: It was the only place, basically, that accepted me. And it was the only place that gave me the freedom to do whatever I wanted. I had already done a lot of musical studies up to that point, and I didn't want to slog through requirements that I already had under my belt. So I went to Webster knowing that I would only be there for a short time. I just took classes when I thought I was deficient in something. I didn't go for a diploma. I didn't go for credits. I said, "I know orchestration; I know counterpoint; I'm just going to do composition." So I took composition workshop, and learned other instruments through a brass class and a string class.

DUCKWORTH: Had all of your information about orchestration and counterpoint up to that point come through Balada at the UN School?

ZORN: No. I think, ultimately, maybe self-taught is the best way to say it. I bought a dictionary and I used to buy scores. And every morning before I'd go to school I'd listen to my favorite records like *Wozzeck* or *Three Places in New England*, and follow along with the score. That's basically how I did it. Then, I used to copy the scores over and see how the things would work. Then I started writing my own. And from the beginning, even when I look at some of my older scores, it's very similar to what I'm doing now in terms of the plagiarism involved.

DUCKWORTH: What kind of plagiarism are you talking about?

ZORN: You could call it stealing, you could call it quoting, you could call it a lot of different things. Basically, it's like I'd hear a sound element in a Bartók section and I'd say, "That sounds neat," so I'd take that section out of the score and transcribe it into my own notation. Right? Then, I'd hear an Elliott Carter theme that I thought was neat, so I'd take that out of the score and put it someplace else. And then I'd have my transitions and . . . Do you know what I mean? I'd hear a sound; I'd copy it. That's still pretty much the way I work now. I write music with the TV on or with music playing, and I work things out. If I hear something on the TV, like in a commercial or something, I'll say, "Hm, that's neat," and I'll just stick it in. The same thing with records. In a lot of ways it's got a collage element to it, but it's not so much what you're taking as it is how you transform it into your own world.

DUCKWORTH: Well, Stravinsky said a good composer doesn't borrow, he steals.

ZORN: He steals, yeah. I always took that to heart. I take that seriously.

DUCKWORTH: Was there one special event that happened somewhere along the line that made you decide you were going to be a composer?

ZORN: I don't think so. I don't know if you know Stephen Hartkey. He won a lot of BMI awards as a kid. He's done some orchestra pieces that have been read by the New York Philharmonic, and stuff like that. We went to the same school and he was really a big influence on me in many ways—turning me on to different musics and encouraging me to write. He was always someone I looked up to when I was in junior high and high school. He kind of took me under his wing, turned me on to things, lent me scores, and showed me things he was working on. And he had a very close relationship to Balada that I didn't have. I was more of an outcast.

DUCKWORTH: Why was that?

ZORN: At that time, I couldn't really play any instrument well at all. I didn't pick up the saxophone until I was in college, when I was twenty years old. I fooled around on the piano improvising, but I never had ability on the keyboard to sit down and play a Chopin piece or even Mozart. So my musical abilities were always suspect, from my parents and from my teachers. I'd have to use Berlioz as an example of a composer who made it and wasn't a performer. He could play the clarinet, but not the piano. Eventually, in college, in getting into closer relationships with performers, I began to realize how important it was at this particular time to learn to play an instrument, and get the respect of these performers so that they would then perform my work. I'd run around with my scores and try to convince people to play them, but why would they want to play my shit? I mean, they don't know who I am; I can't play; I'm not going to be in the band with them. This was a time when improvisation and composition were coming together more, and being a performer as well as a composer was really essential. Philip Glass was working in his own ensemble; Reich was working in his. And more than the sound of their musics, the fact that they had an ensemble of their own and they were in the band playing their music, was more of an influence on me than their existence in the classical music world. Harry Partch was another one who did that . . . created their own ensembles and worked with the musicians closely to create a music. This was something that in jazz, blues, or rock traditions was there all along. Maybe it was in the classical world years and years ago, but it disappeared, and the image of the composer as some kind of ivory-tower figure became very popular. And the separation between composer and musician became more rampant. Ultimately, I think, composers do have close relationships with musicians. Maybe they don't play in their own performances all the time, but you get a relationship between the guy who's writing and the guy who's playing, and you write a piece for this person. I think this relationship is an important thing in the development of music.

DUCKWORTH: What gave you the confidence to do what you did? You're saying that you knew when you first went to college you weren't going to finish. And you didn't play well, yet you knew you were going to compose. Where did that confidence come from?

ZORN: I don't know. Even my father looks at me now like a success. I went out there and we had this enormous fight a couple of months ago. It was like this big catharsis kind of stuff. He said, "God, you know, ultimately I have to tell you I respect you. I can't believe you did what you did and came out on top, despite all the obstacles. I'll never know why you stuck to it." And I don't know why either. I'm just a stubborn kind of a guy. I always had a drive that this is what I'm going to do. I was interested in both film and music when I was a kid. When I left high school, I said, "Well, I'm either going to do music or film. One or the other." But because the film industry to me was one where you had to schmooze to get money (you had to get a big budget together to be able to make a film), I knew I was not the kind of person who could kiss someone's ass to be able to get the bread together. Just because money was involved, it made me doubt the authenticity of that as a vehicle for myself. So I went into music. But from the beginning, they were very related to me. I got involved in music because of film, because of the editing involved, the sense of time. There's a lot of film elements in my music.

DUCKWORTH: Is college the place where you first got interested in jazz?

ZORN: Yes, when I went to St. Louis. I never listened to much jazz even though my father had a jazz collection. I remember listening to Henry Mancini because he wrote soundtracks, you know, *Peter Gunn* and *The Pink Panther*. And I remember listening to Louis Armstrong because my father had old 78s of his around. But I never actively went to concerts. Friends of mine would say, "Wow. I went to see Monk at the Vanguard last week. It was incredible. You should go." But I never went, you know. I went to St. Louis, where I got exposed to BAG (Black Arts Group) and the AACM in Chicago. I remember going to a record store and asking, "What's new? What's going on?," and them telling me, "Well, these guys in Chicago are doing this strange stuff. You should check it out." And I remember buying *For Alto* by Anthony Braxton and just getting blown away, in that it had the kind of energy that I was looking for. I was tired of the kind of overly intellectual, very dry approach that a lot of con- temporary classical music was moving towards. I wanted like a real kick-butt kind of thing. There was an emotional aspect to the new romanticism, but even that seemed very sterile to me. I wanted someone who was up there, you know, blowing his guts out, but I also wanted the structural complexity that contemporary classical music had reached.

DUCKWORTH: In your mind, when did experimental music begin going in the wrong direction?

ZORN: In high school, I was into all of that shit; I was soaking in as much information as I could. Maybe it was a dissatisfaction in my own ability to perform that music. Or maybe it was not the music itself so much as the situation that the music was being played in. I went to the rug concerts of Boulez, and I saw premieres of Stockhausen pieces. It was exciting, but at the same time, it was, like, very dry. No one was standing up going "Yeah!" An emotional quality was missing, somehow.

DUCKWORTH: Why did you decide to play the saxophone instead of some other instrument?

ZORN: I wonder if I picked the Braxton record up first and then the saxophone, or whether it was the other way around. I can't really remember the chronology. But I do remember that the first jazz records I listened to were the Jazz Composers' Orchestra, the two- record set with Cecil Taylor and Pharoah Sanders, *Ascension*, and *Free Jazz*. Those were the records that a friend of mine, like an elder, turned me on to in college and said, "Check this out." And I was impressed with, say, Cecil Taylor's *Unit Structures*. It had a real structure to it; it wasn't just a blowing session. I enjoyed the blow- ing session quality of *Ascension*, but at the same time, I really got into Cecil Taylor's work with structure. And then I was attracted to the AACM because it seemed that they were really involved in taking the emotionally charged blowing sessions that Coltrane and Albert Ayler had put together, and putting them in a new kind of context that created more of a compositional atmosphere instead of a strictly improvisational one.

DUCKWORTH: Were you a natural saxophone player? Did it come easily?

ZORN: Yes, I picked the thing up and it was there from the first minute I started playing. Maybe that's why I stuck with it. I remember my composition teacher saying, "You know, you're never going to be a great saxophone player. You're starting so late." And I said, "Well, I don't care if I practice ten hours a day for the rest of my life. I love doing it and I'm going to do it. I don't care what you think." He was trying to tell me, "Don't bother with the saxophone; study the piano." And when I was a teenager and got into the organ, I wanted to study organ but my parents said, "No, no. You can't play the organ; play the piano." Or I wanted to play bass for a while, but they said, "No. We're not going to buy you a big bass. Study the guitar first, and if you like the guitar, then . . . ." Do you know what I'm saying? It was like everything I wanted to do they wouldn't let me do, no matter where I went. So when I got to the saxophone, I said, "No! I'm going to do it." I studied with a teacher, but I was pretty much self-taught on the saxophone. My teacher played bass clarinet with the symphony, but really remembered lovingly his experiences in Juilliard when he would go up to Harlem and sit in with a jazz band on saxophone, and then come home drenched in sweat and drop down on the bed. I remember him describing those things to me, and maybe that kind of romantic notion seeped into my brain. It seemed a lot more interesting than the work he was doing in the symphony. So I said to him, "Look, I can't afford a lot of lessons. I'll come for four times and that's it. Teach me everything you can." And I'll tell you honestly, he gave me enough information in the first half-hour lesson to keep me going for ten years, in terms of exercises and where I should head: "Play with records for your ear . . . these are finger exercises . . . these are breathing exercises . . . these are technique exercises . . . ." In that one half-hour, I had enough to go for the rest of my life as far as I was concerned.

DUCKWORTH: You were talking a moment ago about not being able to play things by ear. How did your ear develop?

ZORN: It's been hard, you know. I never had what traditional musicians would call a musical ear, which is chords and melodies. Now I take things off the record and it goes down pretty quick, but it was a long time in getting to that point. I think I have more of an improviser's intuitive ear, where I can hear something and know how to react to it.

DUCKWORTH: Did you always want to improvise when you started playing saxophone? Was that the goal?

ZORN: I think it was. I mean, ultimately, my first musical experiences were improvisational ones. You know, fooling around on the piano at my grandparents' or my aunt's house. That was just improvising, picking things out and working that way. That was maybe, you know, the purest, when I didn't even know what music was. So my history goes way back in that sense. When I look at my scores from when I was a teenager, a lot of them are completely notated, but a lot of them are influenced by the graphic scores that happened in the sixties, and Cage's different approaches to notation. They're kind of a mishmash of all different things, which is again similar to what I'm doing now where I will just say, "Pianist, do Renaissance kind of shape for ten seconds." And at the same time that's going on, you know, everybody's clapping and whistling. And then the next event would be, "Flute player, play as fast as you can. And bass player, very long notes." So I'd describe shapes. Sometimes I'd get specific with them and sometimes I'd leave them open. And that's exactly what I'm doing now; I'm describing shapes that I want people to do and composing the overall arc of the piece, sometimes being specific and sometimes being loose. When you're loose, you get an improvisational edge to it. Maybe that was something that was lacking in the music that I was attracted to as a kid, but became disillusioned with because of its sterility. It didn't make sense to me that Cage could put a few squiggles on a page and give it to a musician, and they would go and play the piece—be up there, pretty much improvising—and say it was John Cage's piece. That dichotomy created a whole new approach to composition for me because I knew that you had to inspire the musician from the page. That's what a composition does, it inspires a performer to do the best that they can. But a few squiggles on a page was not very inspiring to me. And I couldn't bring myself to hand that stuff out to musicians. So I began to incorporate as many different kinds of ways of approaching notation as I could. And eventually I found my own way that seemed to work.

DUCKWORTH: What made you decide after a year and a half at college that it was time to quit and move on?

ZORN: These are difficult questions. I never thought about this shit. "Why did I become a composer; why did I stick with it; why did I drop out?"

DUCKWORTH: Well, you've made it big, John. You've got to have the big answers.

ZORN: I don't have any answers for those questions. I really don't. I don't know why.

DUCKWORTH: Did you just quit?

ZORN: I just quit. Taking independent study and dropping out was what happened.

DUCKWORTH: Weren't you afraid of quitting? How were you planning to support yourself? Were you making any money?

ZORN: No. There was no money involved at all. I was going to school on scholarship.

DUCKWORTH: So how were you going to eat after you dropped out?

ZORN: Well, I had a little miracle happen, which is really no big deal. When my grandfather and grandmother died, they left me a small pension which was like $1,600 a year. It came in two installments of $800 each six months. My parents were really pissed that they had done this. "How could they leave money not to us, but to our kids?" My brother also got the same thing. He sold all the bonds immediately and spent all the money. But I decided, "Well, $1,600 a year is a little over $100 a month. I could live on that."

DUCKWORTH: When was this?

ZORN: This was 1974 when I dropped out. I think one of the reasons I left school was because I wanted to meet other musicians who were doing similar things to what I was doing. And I wanted to go back to New York to do it. I felt that I had put enough time in studying and it was time to just go out and do. Ultimately, come to think about it, I really was kind of self-taught all the way. And kind of a real wise guy. I never had a good relationship with any of my teachers. Balada and Stallings were very nice to me, but ultimately, you know, I'd look at my other peers at the schools where I went and they'd be closer to the teacher. You know, like going out and having coffee with them, and working very closely. I was always on the outside of all of that. Maybe deliberately. Maybe I did that to myself because I don't want to be told anything. I want to learn about it myself. That's why I have all these records. You know, I'll buy a record and it'll turn me on to another record, and I'll read the back notes and it'll turn me on to something else. I always wanted to do things on my own. And I dropped out, I think, for the same reason.

DUCKWORTH: How did you buy all these records on a $100 a month?

ZORN: Ah, well, maybe you should turn off the machine in order for me to tell you that I used to rip off an incredible amount of records. I used to steal a lot of records when I was a kid. When I left school I went to stay with my brother in Oregon. And I used to practice all the time. I was playing eight to ten hours a day. That's all I would do and I drove him crazy, so he kicked me out of his house. And I went to San Francisco and met some musicians down there. I hung around Oakland and San Francisco for a while and then went back to Oregon where I got my own apartment. I had had my own apartment in San Francisco; I was staying with some people. These were the end of the hippie days where you could find a place to live for twenty to thirty dollars a month. It wasn't much of a problem to share in a house, bake your own bread, you know. I was spending seven dollars a week on food, buying potatoes at five cents a pound, twenty pounds for a dollar. I lived on potatoes and cabbage. And I baked my own bread. And anything I had left over, I'd buy records. Or steal them if I couldn't afford it. All my jazz records were stolen, pretty much.

DUCKWORTH: Did you ever get caught?

ZORN: No, never. And I did some pretty wild things.

DUCKWORTH: What was your technique?

ZORN: Sticking them under my shirt. In the summertime it was tough because I'd go in a T-shirt to steal records. And I'd have to take the records out of the jacket and stick them under my shirt and then walk a certain way. And like I said, I was a real wise guy. I'd go right up to security guards with like five records under my shirt and go, "Do you know what time it is? Oh God, I've got to get going." And then I'd go out the door. So a lot of the records I acquired illegally.

DUCKWORTH: Do you still listen a lot to your records?

ZORN: Yes, all the time. First thing in the morning, last thing at night.

DUCKWORTH: Do you pay attention when you listen, or is it just background?

ZORN: Sometimes I pay attention, sometimes it's background. You know, it comes and goes.

DUCKWORTH: Do you listen to your own music?

ZORN: No. I think the *Spillane* record was the first thing I really enjoyed listening to. I still come back to that record. All the *game pieces* I never listened to; all the improvised records I never listened to. And I never listened to live performances until the Naked City band. It was bad enough having to play the shit without having to listen to it.

DUCKWORTH: What happened to get you back to New York?

ZORN: Well, I did a lot of work on the West Coast meeting musicians in jazz-oriented, improvisation-oriented music. And I started promoting my own concerts. I'd just go into a coffee shop and say, "Hey, can I play here on Friday?" And they'd go, "Well, yeah, why not?" I'd make my own posters and put them around. That was 1974. I kept making my own posters until something like '83 or '84. And it was a really great period. No one would come to gigs, but I just loved the opportunity to be able to play, and to compose and then perform it. I think another one of my dissatisfactions was writing these big scores that never got played. In high school, I maybe did one or two performances my whole time, and even that was not very satisfactory. It was like watching my music get butchered by people. And another reason I think I got involved in performing my own music was that I'd get it done right. So I started paring the stuff down. That's something that I learned in college. Not writing symphonic works that would never get played, but doing a thing for four, five, or six players, then getting the people together, rehearsing them, and doing it. So, starting from where I dropped out I just said, "Okay, I'm going to meet people, write, perform my music, and play wherever I can play." I played on the street for years. And I had met musicians on the West Coast who eventually gravitated to New York, and we began working together. But in 1974, '75, '76, there were maybe two people I could play with, so I booked trio pieces, you know.

DUCKWORTH: Where were you playing then?

ZORN: In my apartment on Lafayette Street across from the Public Theater, at a place I called the Theater of Musical Optics. We used to do weekly concerts.

DUCKWORTH: Were you getting audiences?

ZORN: Two, three, four people.

DUCKWORTH: Did you get reviews?

ZORN: The only review we got was from Tom Johnson, who came and said, "I saw this little poster and I went to check it out and it was just another jam session dedicated to special instrumental effects." It was a miserable review. And we continued to get miserable reviews. But each reviewer then turned around. Tom Johnson reviewed a concert I did at the Kitchen that George Lewis gave to me in 1979 in a very positive way. And Greg Sandow was a very early reviewer of our work. When Tom Johnson left, he was the one who was putting us down. But he turned around like in '83 or '84. Same thing with that guy [John] Rockwell from the *New York Times.*

DUCKWORTH: Do you think your music changed, or did they have a change of attitude?

ZORN: I was doing the same fucking shit. My music now is very different than what it was, say, five or ten years ago. But at that particular time I had been doing the *game pieces*, and that was improvisational stuff. And sure your music grows. But as far as I was concerned, their attitudes had changed. The music connected with them in some way. And it was very nice to read a review where Sandow said, "I was wrong about this guy. This guy's interesting." Same thing with Rockwell, who had walked out of my Kitchen gig. I saw him leaving. They said, "Wow, there's a guy from the *Times.*" I went, "Wow." Then, three minutes into it he was out the door and that was the end of that. But then five years later he comes to a gig at the Kool Jazz Festival and he wrote a really beautiful review of it. Somehow it connected. But it takes time. We played at the Theater of Musical Optics for years.

DUCKWORTH: Who's we?

ZORN: Polly Bradfield, a violinist, and Eugene Chadbourne, a guitar player. This was after I had spent a lot of time with Joe Foster and Philip Johnston, who work in a band called the Microscopic Septet, which was, I would say, closer to the jazz tradition, the beboppy kind of stuff. Eventually I broke away from them and met Chadbourne and Bradfield, Fred Frith, Tom Cora, and Wayne Horvitz. One by one, people would gravitate to New York and somehow get involved in the maelstrom of the downtown improvisers. That was what we were back then; even more so now. We were finding places to play on our own. We were working, you know, on our own music, in our own little clubs, putting our own little posters up, and developing our own audience. And it was a very exciting time. Clubs would come and go within a few months.

DUCKWORTH: Were you making any money by this point?

ZORN: No, nothing. Nothing at all. My apartment was $50 a month. It went up to $75 in 1978 and I couldn't afford to live there anymore, so I moved here. And I paid $50 a month here until about 1986.

DUCKWORTH: What kept you going?

ZORN: I don't know. I think it was all the people I was working with. The excitement of working with someone who respected what you were doing, and thought you were onto something. Meeting someone who not only liked Albert Ayler and the Art Ensemble, but had been listening to John Lee Hooker, ethnic music from Bali, Cage, Stockhausen, and Conway Twitty. I mean, you name it. We were all into all of those kinds of music. Maybe one person was more involved with one than another, but ultimately we all were excited about all of those different genres and saw them in the same way. There was no real difference between Stockhausen and Albert Collins. They were musicians who were working in different genres, but they were on the same level and they should be respected in the same way. And we were able to talk to each other about all this stuff.

Now that I look back on it, it's like the simplest thing in the world. But at that time it was really a challenge. I tried to make each new piece that I wrote like a learning experience, something new, a new way of approaching improvisation or something. Each new piece I tried to make another step, tried to deal with a different parameter. Because what I was taught in school was that each piece deals with a different problem. And in each piece, every note is essential. You can't take one note out without the whole thing falling apart.

DUCKWORTH: That's so different, though, from improvising. How did you put those two concepts together in your mind?

ZORN: I don't know how, but I did. My early compositional efforts in
improvisational structures, like *Lacrosse*, were about making every
note count. That's what that piece was about. What each person
was involved in doing was creating short little events between three
and ten seconds long. Playing something, concentrating completely
on that one little thing, and making sure that every note counted
was the best thing that you could do. And then stopping, pausing,
thinking of another little event to do. And then doing another
event where every note counted. When you get six or seven people
doing this, what you get is a tapestry. Everybody's really concentrating on the little thing that they're doing. At the same time, they're
listening to other people and relating. If each person concentrates
on each little moment and tries to make it the best thing they can
do, you end up with a composition that's the best that all these
people can do. Do you see what I'm saying?

DUCKWORTH: Yes, but perhaps you get individual gestures with no
form, right?

ZORN: I had another way of solving that, which was, to me, very similar to the way Schoenberg dealt with his early atonal pieces. He
used a text, and at the end of the text the piece was over. *Moses and
Aron* was like that; *Erwartung* was certainly like that. The text was
what gave the piece a form. For me, the form was taking all the possible combinations of players involved, and then ordering them in a
certain kind of way. If it was a sextet, using all the duos, all the trios,
all the quartets, all the solos, and so on. When we had finished all
the permutations of players, the piece was over. What I'd do was
first create a concept, which I called statues; these little events. And
then everybody did these events; whatever they wanted.

DUCKWORTH: Where did the term *statues* come from?

ZORN: I called them statues because they were like little solid objects.
I had these little "objects," and then I'd have a form that went on top
of that, which was this permutation of players. And there was the
piece, you know. That's the beginning of the *game theory* things that
I did. But they got much more complicated than that.

DUCKWORTH: Where did the *game theory* idea originate? How did
you get started in that direction?

ZORN: A desire to get something happening that I didn't hear in free
improvisations with people. I'd improvise with someone, and at the

end I'd say to myself, "Well now, why didn't we change right together? Why didn't anything go, like BLAM, into a different shape?" Pretty
much, the *game pieces* came about as a dissatisfaction with improvisation and wanting to get something different happening. And some
of those things were like the statues you know; concentrated events
followed by silences. There were things that I, perhaps, heard in
other pieces that I really liked and wanted to incorporate.

DUCKWORTH: You've been quoted as saying you were interested in
composing music for improvising musicians. Isn't that a dichotomy? How do those two approaches fit together?

ZORN: I don't see it as a dichotomy at all. People like to say improvisation and composition are the opposite ends of the spectrum, but
they're not. They're two ways of making music.

DUCKWORTH: Well, maybe we should back up a step. What's your
definition of composition?

ZORN: Composition is a way of putting music together. And so is
improvisation. There's really no dichotomy.

DUCKWORTH: Do they both come from the same place?

ZORN: The one difference is that one is spontaneous and one is a little more thought out beforehand. But that's not much of a difference because when you improvise you have a concept that you live
with: a way, a style. That's like your composition, in a sense.

DUCKWORTH: But aren't the results different?

ZORN: Pure improvisation is going to be different from pure composition, you know, in terms of a day-to-day approach. Improvisation
has a broader palette that it draws from, but ultimately it's the same
piece over and over. And composition is literally the same piece
over and over, too. But when you mix the two, you get the best of
both worlds or the worst of both worlds, depending on the way
you go about it.

DUCKWORTH: Are the *game theory* pieces your way of mixing the two?

ZORN: They're one way that I use. *Spillane* is another way.
Forbidden Fruit is another way. There are improvisational elements
in all of my music.

DUCKWORTH: Is *Cobra* perhaps the most complicated of your *game
theory* pieces?

ZORN: Yes, that is the peak of my *game pieces*. There's something special about it, because I put together ten years of thinking in that one piece. And it absolutely stands up. I'm getting a lot of calls now from people who want to do *Cobra*, which is a real shock to me.

DUCKWORTH: Is *Cobra* notated in such a way that other people can perform it?

ZORN: It is, but I would rather be there to tell them the details, because there's always a few mistakes on paper.

DUCKWORTH: Was that one of the pieces you wrote on index cards?

ZORN: No, the index cards came later. *Cobra* was written on a black- board. It's just a series of instructions about how to relate and how to structure. It's a series of on/off switches, really: when to play and when not to play. But it's very complex, like a computer.

DUCKWORTH: Am I correct in assuming that, in general, the way those pieces worked was that you told people when to play, and sometimes a style in which to play, but never *what* to play?

ZORN: I never specifically told anyone anything. I set up rules where they could tell each other when to play. It's a pretty democratic process. I really don't have any control over how long the piece is, or what happens in it. I pick the band when I perform it. And when you're picking improvisational players, that pretty much determines what the sound is going to be like. I know what people's languages are, and I get a balance for a band and put it together. Not always in terms of the instruments or, sometimes, not even just in terms of the sounds that they make; there's their personalities, too. It can be like a psychodrama with these *game pieces*, because everybody has control over the whole band. If you free-improvise with a ten-piece group, it's going to be a mess, pretty much. But what I try to do with my pieces is create a context where people can, at any time, say, "Okay, I want to do it with this guy *now*." And then they get a chance to do a duo. And someone else decides they want to do something else, so they make a decision and now it's this.

DUCKWORTH: What are the rules that allow that to happen?

ZORN: It's really like a football game. Someone wrote the rules to football, right? I mean, there's a lot of little details in it, but depend- ing on the two teams that are playing and the weather conditions, it's different all the time.

DUCKWORTH: Did the idea of composing this way come to you gradually, or did it come all at once?

ZORN: It came a step at a time. With early pieces in high school and college, I was dealing with Earle Brown-kind of ideas, *Available Forms*. I moved that into a little more open area in pieces I called *Linear Bubbles*, that dealt with choices, like George Crumb's circle, where you start anywhere in the circle and go around. And from Earle Brown's *Available Forms* things, where I the conductor would actually make a cue—"Do number one, do number four"—towards *games*, where the musicians would cue off of each other. If one player did this long sound, then you have the choice of these four things. If someone else did a very sparse event that means you have these choices. So it was different people controlling each other.

   That built into different, more complicated concepts for improvisers to deal with, in addition to just the structure. Then I pushed the concepts away and stopped talking about short things or long things. That was just one element in a composition that had fifty elements in it. And one of those elements that could be chosen from by any of the players at any time was events—when the downbeat happens. Everybody in the group can do one event. Where they put it is up to them; how long it lasts is up to them; the sound is up to them. But when this downbeat starts, everyone can do one event. When you've done your event, you can't play anymore until someone makes another cue. And then at that downbeat, people who are performing have to stop; people who aren't performing have to come in. Then another downbeat, when only the people who are pointed to can come in. And another downbeat, where whoever's playing loud has to play quiet, and whoever's playing quiet has to play loud. And another downbeat . . . You get the idea.

DUCKWORTH: How do the performers remember all that?

ZORN: It's all on a piece of paper. And it's all on cards that I have, so I work as a prompter. They look at the sheet of possible choices and say, "I want this to happen." So they make a cue to me. "Nose One" means everybody stops except the people I point to. They point to the people. I hold up a sign that says, in that case, "Runner." Everyone knows what "Runner" means because they've gone through it all. So it happens. And then someone else does something else. And then someone else does something else.

DUCKWORTH: That seems very much in the Earle Brown tradition.

ZORN: It is.

DUCKWORTH: Have you ever seen him conduct? How did you learn
about that?

ZORN: I think it's mostly from reading the liner notes on those early
Time recordings of his pieces. I don't think I ever saw him perform,
although I went to a lot of new-music concerts at Columbia,
Cooper Union, and various other spaces as a kid. When I was a kid,
my whole learning process was additive, ending up with the mishmash that I've got now, which draws upon all these different possibilities. It's not like I tried to strip away and only get into one thing.
I added all these different compositional approaches and all these
different kinds of music together. Every time I get into something
new, like hard core, it will be added to my palette. Now I'm writing
pieces that have improvised sections, reggae, rhythm and blues,
jazz, hard core, and classical music, all stuck into one little two-
minute piece. Those are the things I'm working on now for Naked
City. And they're pretty much strictly notated, in the sense of
blocks where I'll describe shapes that I want: sometimes bass lines,
sometimes melodies, sometimes chords. But, you see, it's a mishmash of all different kinds of music and all different approaches to
composing.

DUCKWORTH: How did you become so involved in arranging other
people's music? I'm thinking about *Shuffle Boil*, the Thelonious
Monk-inspired piece.

ZORN: As I studied jazz music, I began wanting to perform Charlie
Parker tunes or Ornette Coleman tunes. That was something I did a
lot of in performance, along with strictly improvised things, and
also my kind of improvised compositions. So Hal Willner was making this Monk record and, God knows why, he asked me to do a
Monk tribute. That was the first time I ever really took seriously
actually putting something together that would pay tribute to
someone who was an incredible influence on me. Monk was one of
my real heroes. But at the same time, I was sick and tired of people
doing Monk like he was a mainstream composer. Here was someone who was avant-garde in the forties and fifties, and then became
a little more mainstream in the sixties and seventies. Now it's like
singing along with Mitch Miller or something. And it's disgusting

because he *is* an avant-garde composer. So my approach to Monk, as my approach to any tribute project I do now, is to treat them the way they saw themselves, the way they were taken when they were in their prime. So I tried to do a tribute piece that drew upon what I got from Monk, which was that incredible sense of timing that he had, the use of space and silence, his love of the blues, his work with different instrumentation. And the piece directly relates to every aspect of what I feel about Monk. There's not one moment on the *Cobra* record, *Archery*, my Kurt Weill tribute, my Monk tribute, or my *Spillane* piece that I can't justify in terms of why it belongs there and why, if you took it out, the whole piece would fall apart. I mean, that was my uptight twelve-tone upbringing, where everything had to have its place. And that transferred itself even into my free improvisations. Everything has to have a reason for being there. And with pieces like the Monk and the Kurt Weill tribute, sometimes my explanations why something is there may be so oblique you don't even understand what I'm talking about.

DUCKWORTH: Can you give me an example of an oblique reference?

ZORN: Kurt Weill was involved in the decadence of Germany, so a section with marching sounds in the back was enough to make this particular improvised section belong in a Kurt Weill tribute. Or the *Spillane* piece. For every single section of that piece I can tell you, specifically, what image I was thinking of and how it related to Spillane and his world. And sometimes they'd be way off the wall, but that doesn't matter. The point is, to me, it holds together.

DUCKWORTH: Was the Monk tribute where all of that started?

ZORN: That was the beginning.

DUCKWORTH: Did you immediately see new possibilities for yourself?

ZORN: Absolutely. That's why I agreed with Yale Evelev to do the Morricone record. I wanted to get back into that studio and have someone pay for it, because I was broke. Up to that time I'd made eight or nine albums, but they were all really low budget. Nobody got paid. I'd foot the recording bill and then put the record out with my own money. And it cost a lot of money, but the musicians would get nothing. They did it because they loved doing it; because they wanted to be on a record, because it was good for them; and because they loved me. This was at a time when everybody was making their own records, and we were all sharing and helping each other. It was a great time. There's always an underground. It comes and goes in waves. The music industry gets involved in the mainstream and becomes very afraid of anything experimental. Then the wave shifts and they start taking chances.

The sixties were an era where all the major labels were taking chances on bozo groups. Anybody who got out of high school and had long hair, round glasses, and wore beads could make a psych record on Columbia. I have an incredible collection of psych records by the most ridiculous bands. Everybody was making records back then. But the seventies were a period where the industry got burned, and they went into the mainstream. The eighties turned around again a little bit, and major labels like Nonesuch/Elektra hired people like me and Wayne Horvitz. We had made our own records all through the seventies. So the eighties were a good period for experimental music in the sense that we got a chance to get some big budgets and do some adventurous things. God knows what's going to happen in the nineties; the wave's probably going to go down again. But all through the seventies, a few people stuck with it. And, you know, I believe in a kind of survival of the fittest, because I'm one of those survivors who, from the beginning, had it hard but stuck with it. People who stick with it are the ones who really have something to say, for the most part.

DUCKWORTH: Let's talk about *Spillane*. Were you always a Mike Hammer fan?

ZORN: Yes, yes. Mickey Spillane was really one of my heroes. Since I was a kid, I loved the hard-boiled detective genre; not the books so much as the films. And the Mike Hammer films really bowled me over as just the most sexist, violent, and dark. It was the peak of the genre to me. When people talk about the big trinity, it's Hammett, Chandler, and Spillane. Some people think Spillane was just a hack writer and he was in it only for the money. But that guy is a genius because he created his own world, in terms of language and imagery. He's one of the great American mavericks. And that's a tradition that I really feel a part of: Ives, Partch, Cage. These are the great individualists; that's what America is about. To me, Elliott Carter does not belong in that rugged-individual, American tradition. His music is American, but it really goes through this European superserious filter. It's almost more European than it is American. Even though I really respect Carter and he is a great American composer, in many ways he's not one of the individualists.

DUCKWORTH: Where did the idea of doing a piece on Spillane come from?

ZORN: Do you know the Godard piece I did? I was approached by a man in France, Jean Richard, who was making a tribute record to Godard. He had already done one to Hitchcock and Satie. I didn't think they were very good records because I'd listen to the music and say to myself, "This has nothing to do with Hitchcock." So Jean Richard wanted to do a Godard record, but I had a feeling that this was going to be the same kind of thing. So I said, "Well, if I'm going to do a Godard tribute, it's really going to be about Godard," because this is someone who is very important to me in terms of his concept of time and sound. His early films—*Alphaville, Pierrot le Fou, Masculine and Feminine, Weekend*—were really seminal influences on me. So I said, "I don't think I'm interested in this. I love Godard, but I have a feeling it's going to end up like these other records and I don't think I want to do it." And he said, "No, this is going to be different. I want you to do something. I'll pay your studio time and give you 800 bucks," or whatever it was. I said, "Fine." That year I got another phone call from a man named David Breskin, who's involved with an organization called the Shifting Foundation in Chicago. This is an organization that picks out people involved in a wide range of creative activity, and gives them grants. It's not a lot of money. They'll lay $3,000 to $5,000 out on you. So I got a call from him and he said, "I think that they'd be really interested in what you're doing. Fill out an application." Now, I never got a grant in my life. And I never believed in getting grants. You do it the hard way, your way; you don't suck up to somebody. And I never liked filling out forms. So I said, "Forget it. They're not going to give me a grant." But he was very persistent, and he said, "You're not going to be wasting your time with this. Just fill it out." So I filled it out. And he said, "Usually we give $3,000 grants." And I said, "Well, if I'm going to do this, I'll go for broke. I'll ask for $6,000." And I'll be damned if they didn't send me the fucking $6,000. When I got the bread and put it in the bank, I thought, "Well, what am I going to do with this now? I don't really need this money. I don't need to buy any equipment." So then the Godard thing came about and I started working on the file cards. I bought all the books I could about Godard; I resaw all of the films. Then I started working the way I had worked on the Monk and the Weill tributes. I made a long list of things that I though Godard was about—the politics, the romanticism, my favorite sections from some of his films. I ended up with maybe seventy different events that I copied onto file cards. Then I scored the piece and took it into a recording studio with the Shifting Foundation money.

DUCKWORTH: Wait a moment. How did you get from the file cards to the score?

ZORN: The file cards are the score.

DUCKWORTH: Is that also true of *Spillane*?

ZORN: Yes.

DUCKWORTH: Then let's talk about how *Spillane* was written, since more people will know it because of the record.

ZORN: Okay. First I'd just write images and ideas: "I heard the scream through the mist of the night." I took the first phrase from my favorite books by him, because he's got great first lines. Or images: "Girls #1: Velda," you know, a portrait of who Velda is. Or *Kiss Me Deadly*; I have synopses of the six major books. "Knife fight": I just picked different things that I thought related to Spillane. And then I kind of orchestrated like this: "Harlem nightclub; blues guitar and backup; Arto vocal; question mark; narration; shoot out." That's all it would say. Later I'd pick the musicians involved: Weinstein, Hofstra, Staley. So it would start out with images, then I'd begin to get a little more specific in terms of orchestration, then I'd order the thing.

DUCKWORTH: Did it turn at that point into notes on a page?

ZORN: Not always. I write every day. I just write things down that I like. Then I may go through my notes, just independent events, and try to find something that sounds like it fits with something else. So I'd go into the studio equipped with these file cards that have been numbered, and we'd start recording the piece from the beginning. We started with the scream. I have everybody there all the time, so it's kind of like an artist's palette. All eight musicians were there ten hours a day, every day, in the studio. It took about seven or eight days.

DUCKWORTH: How were you able to afford that?

ZORN: The Shifting Foundation.

DUCKWORTH: I thought they funded the Godard project.

ZORN: The Godard was first. Then I wrote to Shifting again and said, "Hey, you changed my life with that grant. I'm going to do another piece based on Mickey Spillane."

DUCKWORTH: Why did you pick Spillane?

ZORN: I picked Mickey Spillane because it had elements of jazz, and jazz was very important to me; it had elements of soundtrack, and I always loved movie soundtracks; it had that kind of sleazy rhythm-and-blues edge that I always loved (that's what my sax style is based on, really; I'm basically a rhythm-and-blues bopper); and it's about New York, and I lived in New York all my life. So I had all these things that I knew were just perfect for me. And Shifting said, "Wow, this is interesting. We loved the Godard piece. Here's more money. Do it again." But this was a very difficult period for me because people were going crazy about the Morricone record, but thought my shit was garbage, you know. They didn't want my music at BAM; they came out and said so. They wanted the Morricone project. I wasn't even going to do it. I said, "The first time I play at BAM, I want to do my music, so go screw yourself." But Yale was like, "Really, come on, it's going to be good. This is going to open the door, not just for yourself, but all the other musicians involved. It's going to be a first shot. It's going to be a landmark." So I did it. And maybe I'm not really sorry I did it, but it was a very distasteful experience. Those bastards were really assholes. The same thing happened at Nonesuch. Horwitz was really interested in my music. "Well, the Morricone record is good, but that's Morricone, you know. I don't know about Zorn with those *game pieces*." So I brought him up a tape of *Spillane*, and he called me back the next day and said, "I want to sign you to an exclusive six-record contract for Nonesuch."

DUCKWORTH: Is that what you got initially, a six-record deal?

ZORN: Yes, but that doesn't really mean six records. It's like two records, and then an option for two more, and then two more. And Nonesuch became my home. Nonesuch was a label that I used to buy almost indiscriminately when I was a kid. It had the New American Composers Series; I got turned on to all different kinds of musicians through that. And it had the ethnic series that, again, really turned me around. So Nonesuch was a label that meant a lot to me. It wasn't just some business guy saying, "We want to exploit you." It really meant something to me that they wanted to put my music out.

DUCKWORTH: How do you see *Spillane* relating to the classical experimental tradition? Does it extend the maverick tradition?

ZORN: If you're asking why I feel I'm part of the maverick tradition, it's because I've created my own world. It stands on its own. It's multifaceted. It's like a little prism. You look through it and it goes off in a million different directions. It's a world that comes from my world view: since every genre is the same, all musicians should be equally respected. It doesn't matter whether it's jazz, blues, or classical, they're all the same. There's a very deep element of quotation in my music, which is something that relates to Ives very directly. But it's quotation also in the way that, say, Berg liked to play games with himself—the way that Webern liked to play games with pitches, Berg liked to play games with melodies, and so did Ives. I have a piece, *Cat-o'-Nine-Tails*, which is filled with not just quotation after quotation, but rather tribute after tribute to the people who I think are important to the string-quartet tradition.

DUCKWORTH: Do you hear a collage like that fitting together as you write it, or are you putting it together to see what it sounds like?

ZORN: I put this together as a game, but I can also hear it fitting together. I mean if I can't, I can always put it through the computer and hear it. The point is the game that I'm playing. One section is the pitches from a melody by Ives broken up the way Webern would do it. Then an improv section. Then something I completely wrote out that's mine. Then a section dealing with noise. So the piece is kind of like five different things going on, but intercut from one to the next. And this piece was a breakthrough for me in terms of being able to relate to classical players on their own terms. In other words, improvisers like to improvise and make up what they do. To best take advantage of improvising musicians you don't give them written material. On the other hand, to take advantage of classical musicians at their best, you give them written material, because that's what they do best. But you have to inspire them from the page. I try to put as much extra musical material and information into my music as I can possibly squeeze in. A very important thing all through my musical life is to make sure that the musicians involved are having fun and like what they're doing. If that means I turn it into a game, then I turn it into a game. If it means I have to play compositional games to excite the musicians, or include impro-visational elements if I think those musicians are into it, then I'll do that. Making it fun is the best way to get a good performance.

DUCKWORTH: How do you respond to listeners who say your music is too episodic?

ZORN: Do you mean episodic in the sense that it doesn't develop the way normal music develops?

DUCKWORTH: Yes.

ZORN: Well, that doesn't bother me at all. Their perception of what development is is different from mine. See to me, cartoon music is important because it follows a visual narrative. It's following the images on the screen. Now separate it from those images and you still have music—valid, well-made music. But it does not follow any traditional development that I know of. It's following a visual narra-tive—all of a sudden this, all of a sudden that.

DUCKWORTH: Does all of your music have a visual narrative, whether listeners are aware of it or not?

ZORN: I would say it does, yes, in the sense that I think visually. But I'm not going to impose a visual narrative on someone else. Like I said, I'll create a mode, a prism, and each person will get their own narrative. One person's interpretation of what *Spillane* is about is different from another. But that's okay. The point is that I'm trying to create something that generates thinking patterns that spark ideas, excites the intellect, or excites the heart as well as the mind. I'm just trying to get things going, make some trouble. And if critics say that it's too episodic, great. I'm making some trouble and they can't figure it out. To me it all works perfectly, you know.

DUCKWORTH: Is your attention span really as short as you claim it is, or is that just hype?

ZORN: No, it is very short. I mean, I don't know what this interview has been like, but I usually go off on tangents.

DUCKWORTH: Another criticism I've heard of the whole Lower East Side group is that those guys don't know what has happened in the past. Is there any validity to that?

ZORN: Oh, that's not true. You talk with someone like Wayne Hor-vitz, Elliott Sharp, or Fred Frith. All of those people have an incredible encyclopedic knowledge—more than any other generation—because we were the people who grew up in the sixties when the LP boom completely exploded. We were exposed to more music on a firsthand basis than any other generation of composers. I mean, you had composers who were involved in different things, but nobody had the direct access that we had. And with the next generation, it's even more so. But I think our generation was very privileged because it was in on the first explosion. There was something very exciting about it. There's almost something lethargic about it now; so much is available.

DUCKWORTH: Do you compose every day?

ZORN: I don't work on the keyboard quite every day. It goes in phases. Sometimes I'll work a lot, get a lot of stuff on paper in a period of a week—abstract little moments that I just put in a file. And sometimes I don't do that at all. But I think I'm composing every day, in the sense that for me composition isn't sitting at a piece of paper and working like that. It's not even working on my blackboard, the computer, or the keyboard. It's taking in information and processing it. And everyday I'm taking in new information. That's why I go to Japan half the year, to take in more information. There's a lot there for me that's relevant to what I'm doing. Whereas in Europe, there's a lot there too, but nothing's relevant to me. Japan's a vast, multifaceted culture that also steals . . . leeches upon all other cultures, takes influences and mixes them in their own way. New York is the same way. So composition for me is like with the *game pieces*. Those were a slow process of working month after month after month; but not like sitting at a page and staring at it, and at the end of five hours putting one little squiggle down, which sometimes happens. It wasn't that so much as playing with people, thinking, going to movies, checking things out, talking, hearing different musics, and then getting an idea and putting it up on the blackboard. I mean, you get stimuli from all different places.

Ultimately, I think my talent doesn't come from an abstract point inside me, like a folk musician or someone like that. It's not natural in that sense. It comes from outside stimuli and the way I process it. It's like some people's sense of humor; they can just sit alone and write funny stories. I need to interact with someone to get a joke out. I need something to bounce off of. And the same thing with writing music. I need a stimulus to give me an idea so that I can change it and incorporate it into something else. For example, sometimes going out to eat is part of the compositional process. Sometimes it's actually sitting down and making a list of all those things that are going to end up on file cards. Sometimes it's writing out the file cards. Sometimes it's working here. Sometimes it's in the studio with musicians. Those are all parts of the compositional process. It becomes more like a living. I mean, that sounds like it could be bullshit, but it's more like a living experience, man. It's there all the time.

DUCKWORTH: Are you always thinking about music?

ZORN: Always. It's like when I'm in a car riding down the road, I'm always counting the lines and making polyrhythms out of them. Do you know what I'm saying? When I'm walking down the street, my steps become a rhythm. It's just always there. I grew up on TV; there's always been sound with the image. It's like I live in a movie or something. I see an image and I hear music with it. I was brought up that way. I walk down the street and I hear a soundtrack in my head for the movie that I'm in, which is my life. It's kind of sick.

DUCKWORTH: Do any of your pieces come as flashes of insight, or do they all grow slowly as you put these various images and gestures together?

ZORN: The pieces grow. The process of putting a piece together is just the slow process of developing the information, collecting the material, and compiling it. It's almost like a librarian's job, putting it together. Then I work on permutations of players, making sure that there's nothing repeated, that each section has a different group, a different feel, an instrumentation, sometimes specifically written music. Then the actual working out of it is in the studio with the musicians. It becomes more collaborative. And every step along the way is composition. With *Cat-o'-Nine-Tails*, I worked out that I wanted the piece to deal with collage elements, cartoon elements, noise elements, improvisational elements, and interludes. And I decided that there were going to be twelve of each of them, sixty sections, and they would be ordered in some way. And I knew what the cartoon stuff would be like; that's in my head day and night. It's always there. With the collage elements, I knew I wanted to draw upon the great string-quartet composers. The improv stuff was going to be permutations of the players. And the interludes would be like interludes, slow and melodic kinds of pieces. At that point, basically, the piece was finished; it was in my head. I just had to do the slog work of actually writing it down. Now, which is more important? Which is the real compositional process? Is it in the thinking up of the ideas, processing them in my head, and creating a whole? Or is it in writing it down? I don't know. I don't think it's like, "Blam. Wow. What an idea!" It's more like constantly taking the info in and processing it. Entire pieces of music don't come to me in a dream. I don't think I'm that kind of a composer.

DUCKWORTH: So you're not the overnight sensation that everybody thinks you are? You know. You're unknown, and then suddenly you're on Nonesuch Records all over the country.

ZORN: Oh sure I am. I was completely unknown. There's no doubt about it. But you know, it's not like I was a plumber and then I was a composer. It's more like I spent my life putting music together and then, all of a sudden, Nonesuch said, "Okay, we'll do something with you." And that's marketing bullshit, you know. It's only a matter of time before someone gets dissatisfied with that and drops me, or I become unfashionable. It doesn't really matter to me.

DUCKWORTH: What's the sustaining factor in your work? What *does* matter to you?

ZORN: What matters to me is that each piece, ultimately, will stand up on its own. Fifty, a hundred years from now, it'll still work. That's what I care about. Of course, I want the musicians involved to be happy with it as well. When I finished *Cat-o'-Nine-Tails*, I would have been really upset if the Kronos Quartet didn't like it. But on the other hand, I know this is a great piece and if they don't like it I don't give a fuck. But I want them to enjoy it and to have fun doing it. And the same thing with my next recording projects. You know, I come up with a great idea. I know what it's going to be. Now I just have to go through the process of writing and recording it. When I introduce it to the musicians I want to have involved, I want them to go "Wow!" But then, part of the job of picking the band is picking people who are going to go "Wow!," because you want to have people who are excited about what they're doing. You pick the right person for the right job.

DUCKWORTH: Do you feel you've created a unique place for yourself musically?

ZORN: Yes. I see myself as someone who has created his own world. And that world exists on its own steam, like a well-oiled machine. I found a way of working that can't fail. With the way I work, I can't make a piece that I'm dissatisfied with. It's impossible, because I've got all the time in the world to get it exactly the way I want. I go into the studio and I work on one section until it's perfect; I won't go on to the next section until that one is perfect. It usually takes eight to ten hours to finish three minutes of music. But it's three minutes of what, to me, is perfect music.

DUCKWORTH: Are there any other people in the Lower East Side group who you think are also creating their own worlds?

ZORN: That's hard to say. It's one thing to create music and it's another thing to have a world view, a way of looking at the world that's different from anybody else's. I think Anthony Coleman has that. But it's hard for me to pick anybody else, to tell you the truth. I respect all the musicians that I work with, they're doing great work. But they all relate to other musics.

I don't think of myself as a jazz or rock artist. I think of myself as someone who's using all these different elements to create something else. But if I had to pick one line where I came from, it would be more classical than anything else. I don't think Elliott Sharp would pick classical as where he's coming from. I think he has created an individual approach, but I don't know if he's got a way of looking at the world that's different from anyone else's. I mean, I can name the people who I think are really individuals in this group: Wayne Horvitz, Fred Frith, Elliott Sharp, Christian Marclay, Bill Frisell, and Anthony Coleman. But I think Anthony has a way of looking at the world that nobody else has seen in quite the same way. And to me, he has more of a possibility of creating that world than any of the other players. I don't know, maybe that sounds completely egotistical or something. I love all those people and I wouldn't want to be put on record as putting them down in any way whatsoever, because they've supported me and we've supported each other for fifteen years. But honestly, I'm really pretty rigid when it comes to the concept of someone creating their own world. Everyone has their own kind of style, but that's different than really creating a world that actually comments on the world we're dealing with.

INDEX

AACM. *See* Association for the Advancement of Creative Musicians
African musical influence, 290, 292, 293–94, 304–06, 307
All-night concerts, 278
Anderson, Laurie, 368–85, *369, 377, 381*
  Americans on the Move, 369, 378, 379
  art background, 372–75, 376
  As If, 379
  Automotive, 376
  electronic equipment, 381–82, *382–83*
  Home of the Brave, 369–70, 382
  Juke Box, 368
  New York Social Life, 377
  on Tyranny, 389
  "O Superman," 382–83
  performance pieces, 376–77, 379
  political stories, 370
  Stereo Decoy, 368
  Story Pillows, 368
  Time to Go (for Diego), 377
  United States, 369, 379
  violin playing, 370–72, 377
  Warner Brothers contract, 382–84
  What You Mean We?, 380
  work methods, 380–81
Andre, Carl, 375
Arch form, 312–13
Ashley, Mary, 399
Ashley, Robert, 390, 398, 401, 404, 407, 408, 409–10, 415
Associated Music Publishers, 67

Association for the Advancement of Creative Musicians, 406, 444, 452
Avant-garde music, 28, 97–98, 362, 383, 392, 406
Avant-Garde Music Festival, 299
Avant-garde theater, 422–23
Ayler, Albert, 453

Babbitt, Milton, 52–93, *53, 69,* 153
  All Set, 79
  Aria da Capo, 84
  audience for music, 85–88
  clarinet playing, 56, 70
  complexity of music, 83–85
  Composition for Four Instruments, 75, 88
  Composition for Orchestra, 76
  computer music, 88, 91
  Elizabethan Sextet, 85
  Fabulous Voyage, 52, 79
  Generatrix, 67
  intelligence work, 77–78
  Johnston and, 143
  orchestral music, 85, 86
  Pathescope film score, 52, 80
  Philomel, 54
  popular music interests, 60–61, 70, 79–80
  RCA Mark II synthesizer, 54, 89–92
  study with Roger Sessions, 66–68, 71–76, 98
  twelve-tone works, 75, 76–77, 82–83, 89

Printed in the United States
80936LV00006B/113